VOID

CHILDREN AND YOUTH
Social Problems and Social Policy

CHILDREN AND YOUTH
Social Problems and Social Policy

Advisory Editor

ROBERT H. BREMNER

Editorial Board
Sanford N. Katz
Rachel B. Marks
William M. Schmidt

United States. Children's Bureau

STANDARDS OF CHILD WELFARE

Edited by

[William L. Chenery]

and

[Ella A. Merritt]

ARNO PRESS
A New York Times Company
New York — 1974

HV
741
.U52
1974

Reprint Edition 1974 by Arno Press Inc.

Reprinted from a copy in
The University of Illinois Library

CHILDREN AND YOUTH
Social Problems and Social Policy
ISBN for complete set: 0-405-05940-X
See last pages of this volume for titles.

Manufactured in the United States of America

Library of Congress Cataloging in Publication Data

United States. Children's Bureau.
   Standards of child welfare.

   (Children and youth: social problems and social policy)
   A report of the Children's Bureau conferences, May and June, 1919.
   Reprint of the 1919 ed. issued by the U. S. Children's Bureau, Washington, as Conference series no. 1, Bureau publication no. 60.
   1. Child welfare—United States—Congresses. I. Chenery, William Ludlow, 1884- II. Merritt, Ella Arvilla, 1882- ed. III. Title. IV. Series. V. Series: United States. Children's Bureau. Conference series no. 1. VI. Series: United States. Children's Bureau. Publication no. 60.
HV741.U52 1974   362.7'0973   74-1672
ISBN 0-405-05952-3

U. S. DEPARTMENT OF LABOR
CHILDREN'S BUREAU
JULIA C. LATHROP, Chief

STANDARDS OF CHILD WELFARE

A REPORT OF THE CHILDREN'S BUREAU CONFERENCES MAY AND JUNE, 1919

CONFERENCE SERIES NO. 1
Bureau Publication No. 60

WASHINGTON
1919

CONTENTS

	PAGE
LETTER OF TRANSMITTAL	7
GENERAL SUMMARY ....William L. Chenery	11

SECTION I

THE ECONOMIC AND SOCIAL BASIS FOR CHILD WELFARE STANDARDS 21-77

Social Medicine ....Dr. René Sand................. 23
The Financial Cost of Rearing a Child...William F. Ogburn............ 26
The Economics of Child Welfare........Dr. Royal Meeker............... 31
Family Budgets ....Dean S. P. Breckinridge........ 34
Cost of Living........................Miss Florence Nesbitt.......... 44
The Child's Home......................Mrs. Eva Whiting White......... 46
The Leisure of the Child..............L. H. Weir and Miss Abbie Condit 54
Standards for Children's Play.........Joseph Lee..................... 63
Racial Factors ....Professor Kelly Miller......... 66
Belgian Children in War Time..........Miss L. E. Carter.............. 71

SECTION II

CHILD LABOR.. 79-141

Legislative Prohibition of Employment..............................81-108

General Standards ....Owen R. Lovejoy................ 81
    Discussion 85
Minimum Physical Standards...........Dr. Emma MacKay Appel......... 86
Defective Vision Among Chicago
    Working Children.................Dr. E. V. L. Brown............. 91
Dangerous Occupations ....Dr. D. L. Edsall............... 93
    Discussion 96
British Educational Standards........Sir Cyril Jackson.............. 98
    Discussion 102
American Educational Standards.......Charles E. Chadsey.............105
    Discussion 108

Legislative Regulation of Employment...............................109-131

State Control ....Hon. Albert E. Hill............109
Hours ....Miss Agnes Nestor..............113
Wage Principles ....Professor F. S. Deibler........116
Minimum Wage ....Dr. Jessica B. Peixotto........118
Administrative Standards ....Miss Tracy Copp................125
    Discussion 131

CONTENTS

	PAGE
Vocational Guidance and Placement...............................	132-141
Juvenile Placement in Great Britain....Ronald C. Davison.............	132
Discussion	137

SECTION III

THE HEALTH OF CHILDREN AND MOTHERS........................143-304

Maternity and Infancy...145-193

Standard Requirements for Obstetrical
    Care ....Dr. J. Whitridge Williams.......145
    Discussion 148
The Control of Venereal Infection.......Dr. Philip C. Jeans.............149
    Discussion 155
The Control of Midwifery..............Dr. Charles V. Chapin...........157
    Discussion 163
Essentials for Public Care of Maternity
    and Infancy ....Mrs. Eleanor Barton............167
    Discussion 171
Serbian Experience ....Dr. Radmila Milochevitch
                                   Lazarevitch 173
Urban Problems ....Dr. Henry F. Helmholz..........176
Maternity Centers in New York City....Dr. R. W. Lobenstine...........179
    Discussion 185
Rural Problems ....Miss Elizabeth G. Fox..........186
    Discussion 189

The Preschool Child..194-237

Health Centers for Preschool Children...Dr. Merrill E. Champion........194
The Public Health Nurse...............Dr. C.-E. A. Winslow...........199
    Discussion 205
French Experience ....Dr. Clothilde Mulon.............211
Day Nursery Standards.................Dr. S. Josephine Baker.........219
    Discussion 225
Dental Clinics ....Major Lewis Terman.............234
    Discussion 237

The School Child..238-268

Nutrition Clinics ....Dr. William R. P. Emerson......238
    Discussion 244
Health Examinations and the
    School Nurse.....................Dr. Thomas D. Wood............248
The Nutrition of Adolescence..........Dr. Graham Lusk................256
    Chart. Comparative Estimates of
        Physiological Needs for Food.........................Faces page 261
The Need for Sex Education...........Robert D. Leigh................262

CONTENTS

	PAGE
European Experience	269-304
British Organization....Sir Arthur Newsholme	269
Belgian Organization....Dr. René Sand	289
A Physical Classification of Children....Professor Fabio Frassetto	292
Plate I	299
Plate II	300
Plate III	301
Plate IV	302
The International Red Cross and Child Welfare....Livingston Farrand	303

SECTION IV

CHILDREN IN NEED OF SPECIAL CARE 305-407

The Function of the State 307-338

The Responsibility of the State....Robert W. Kelso.......... 307
State Supervision of Agencies and Institutions....C. V. Williams.......... 313
Discussion 318
Child Welfare Work in Japan....Takayuki Namaye.......... 321

Care of Dependent Children 339-367

The Conclusions of the White House Conference—Ten Years After....Dr. Hastings H. Hart.......... 339
Discussion 344
What Constitutes Sufficient Grounds for the Removal of a Child from His Home....Judge Victor P. Arnold.......... 345
Discussion 350
Standards of Child Placing and Supervision....Edmond J. Butler.......... 353
Discussion 360
Child Caring Work in Rural Communities. Miss H. Ida Curry.......... 363

Care of Juvenile Delinquents 368-390

Standards of Organization in Children's Courts....Judge James Hoge Ricks.......... 368
Discussion 373
Standards of Probation Work....Dr. Louis N. Robinson.......... 376
Discussion 379
Medicopsychological Study of Delinquents....Dr. William Healy and Augusta F. Bronner.......... 382
Discussion 388

CONTENTS

PAGE

Care of Mentally Handicapped Children..................................391-407
   The Place of Mental Hygiene in the Child
      Welfare Movement.................Dr. C. Macfie Campbell..........391
   A State Program for the Care of the Men-
      tally Defective....................Dr. Walter E. Fernald..........399
   Discussion 406

SECTION V

STANDARDIZATION OF CHILD WELFARE LAWS....................409-427
   General Statement......................Rev. William J. Kerby..........411
   The Need for Standardization...........Judge Franklin Chase Hoyt.....413
   The Method of Procedure...............C. C. Carstens..................416
   The Minnesota Child Welfare
      Commission ....W. W. Hodson.................420
   Discussion 427

SECTION VI

STANDARDS 429-444
   Committees 431
   Minimum Standards for Children Entering Employment....................433
   Minimum Standards for the Public Protection of the Health
      of Children and Mothers...436
   Minimum Standards for the Protection of Children in Need of Special Care..440

INDEX..445

LETTER OF TRANSMITTAL

U. S. DEPARTMENT OF LABOR,
CHILDREN'S BUREAU,
Washington, D. C., June 15, 1919.

Sir:

Herewith are submitted the proceedings of a conference on Child Welfare Standards recently held under the auspices of the Children's Bureau as the conclusion of its Children's Year program.

Children's Year, as the second year of the war was called in this connection, grew out of the studies made by the Children's Bureau of child welfare abroad under war conditions. It was seen that, under circumstances of such difficulty as we happily can not conceive, the civilian population of Europe were achieving new laws for the protection of childhood, new ideals for the future development of the race. It was felt that the second year of the war in the United States ought to show a popular sense of responsibility for child welfare in some degree commensurate with our opportunities. Hence a program was stated briefly in the Fifth Annual Report of the Children's Bureau, which was adopted by the Women's Committee of the Council of National Defense and, for the purpose of carrying it forward, an organization of the great bodies of women associated under that committee was effected by a specially created Child Welfare Department, of which Dr. Jessica B. Peixotto was the secretary.

When the President wrote a letter approving Children's Year, he concluded with the following statement:

"I trust that the work may so successfully develop as to set up certain irreducible minimum standards for the health, education, and work of the American child."

So that this conference was a natural part of Children's Year, and by means of a special allotment from the President's fund, and with your approval, it was held. It was felt that the presence at the conference of guests who were engaged in the practical protection of children under war conditions in the allied countries would be an invaluable stimulus to this country.

The following guests from abroad attended the conference at your invitation:

Sir Arthur Newsholme, late Principal Medical Officer of the Local Government Board, England.

Mrs. Eleanor Barton, of the Women's Cooperative Guild, England, an organization of the wives of British wage earners.

Mr. Ronald C. Davison, Director of the Juvenile Labour Exchanges of England.

Sir Cyril Jackson, Board of Education, England.

Dr. Clothilde Mulon, War Department, France, who has done special work in the supervision of industrial creches during the war.

Dr. René Sand, Professor of Social and Industrial Medicine at the University of Brussels, and Adviser on Medical Inspection of the Ministry of Labor.

Miss L. E. Carter, Principal of High School C, Brussels.

Mr. Isador Maus, Director of the Division of Child Protection, Ministry of Justice, Belgium.

Mr. Takayuki Namaye, Department of Interior, Japan, in charge of reformatory and relief work and the protection of children.

Dr. Radmila Milochevitch Lazarevitch, from Serbia, a physician and leader in social service activities.

Dr. Fabio Frassetto, Professor of Anthropology at the University of Bologna, Italy.

Their coming to this country to attend the conference gave signal proof of the new international sense of responsibility for child welfare. The generosity and graciousness with which each individual has assisted the conference is gratefully recognized.

This conference consisted not of a single meeting, but of a series of regional conferences, eight in number, beginning with one in Washington, May 5, 1919. Following the Washington conference, meetings were held in New York, Cleveland, Boston, Chicago, Denver, Minneapolis, San Francisco, and Seattle. In addition, certain of the foreign guests were speakers at various national associations, such as the Southern Sociological Congress, the National Conference of Social Work, the National Women's Trade Union League.

Because of the crowded living conditions in Washington, it was practicable to invite to the Washington conference only a small number of American experts upon the different subjects considered, and the discussions were of an informal round-table character. The attendance at the regional conferences was large and representative.

Naturally somewhat varying views of method and approach are presented by the different authorities whose contributions make up this volume. On the great essentials of a child-welfare policy for the nation there is, however, marked agreement. Public responsibility for the growing generation, confidence in constructive measures, insistence upon greater uniformity in laws, and upon the necessity of enlisting able and devoted citizens to carry on both public and private child-welfare activities, are all steadily emphasized. At the end of the Washington conference the tentative child-welfare standards which appear in this book were agreed upon. They were printed and distributed for discussion by the regional conferences and a committee was named to revise them in the light of criticisms and suggestions which might be received from the later conferences and from other interested citizens and associations.

This committee consists of Dr. Hastings H. Hart, of the Russell Sage Foundation, New York City; Mrs. Ira Couch Wood, of Chicago, Director of the Elizabeth McCormick Memorial Fund; Mr. Owen R. Lovejoy, of the National Child Labor Committee, New York City; Dr. H. L. K. Shaw, of the State Department of Health of New York, Albany; and Mrs. Helen Sumner Woodbury, of Chicago.

The Bureau invited the head of the Public Health Service, Dr. Rupert Blue, and the Commissioner of Education, Dr. P. P. Claxton, to act with it as a Committee of Arrangements.

Miss Grace Abbott was the secretary of the conference, and Mr. William L. Chenery has written the general summary and, assisted by Miss Ella A. Merritt, has prepared this volume of proceedings for publication.

                Respectfully submitted,

                              Julia C. Lathrop,
                                      Chief.

Hon. William B. Wilson,
    Secretary of Labor.

STANDARDS OF CHILD WELFARE

GENERAL SUMMARY

By WILLIAM L. CHENERY

Nothing illuminates more searchingly the character of a State than the methods it utilizes in the upbringing of its young. The progress which any nation makes, or fails to make, is faithfully recorded in the history of the rearing of its children. The conditions under which infants are brought into the world, nourished, trained and inducted into the responsibilities of maturity compose the indisputable realities of every social order. The manner in which its children are nurtured is in truth perhaps the best measure of the civilization of a race.

During many years, furthermore, knowledge has been available that among all modern peoples a large proportion of the children born were dying needlessly, and that other large groups were vainly being wasted by unnecessarily damaging circumstances. A recognition of this has been the inspiration of the large body of ameliorative legislation and private effort characteristic of recent years. The war, moreover, by its manifold testing of the sources of strength revealed suddenly evils for which the very continuance of civilization has demanded remedy.

It was accordingly for many reasons desirable and appropriate to endeavor at this season to state clearly what contemporary civilization has learned concerning the nurture of children. Chief among these is the universal recognition of the appalling price which war exacted of the young, and the consequent equally universal conviction that the society preserved by such sacrifice, in order to assure its own sound future if for no more lofty motive, must rear all its children with a wisdom and a justice which hitherto have nowhere been attained. It is, too, peculiarly fitting at the end of a period during which the best work of men's hands and all the cunning of human science have been devoted to destruction that thought should be turned to restoration, to upbuilding, to the development of a way of life which most effectually will heal the wounds of the past. The memory of the dread season through which the world has struggled is a potent inspiration to all to create a happier future.

The Children's Bureau Conferences reported in this volume represent perhaps the most conspicuous single attempt yet made to state what contemporary civilization has learned concerning the welfare of childhood. The Presidential sanction under which these conferences were summoned called for the statement of "certain irreducible minimum standards for the health, education, and work of the American child." That required common counsel of those in the United States and in other countries who by reason of their experience and of their achievements were qualified to formulate such standards. The undertaking attracted the cooperative effort of public servants, of social service technicians, of labor leaders, of publicists, of physicians, and of scientists in many fields. Actuated by the faith that the scientific method is the most useful of the tools possessed by the modern world, the organizers of the conferences brought together men and women whose sole purpose was to apply to the service of the American child what has been proved to be incontestably true. Nothing doctrinaire nor anything unsupported by the burden of scientific data now available was admitted.

A wide section of the earth was naturally culled for advice. Guests came from Great Britain, Canada, France, Belgium, Italy, Serbia, and Japan to the conferences. A considerable number of Americans distinguished in their various fields were invited to participate. An energetic endeavor was made—within the practical limits of such an experiment—to leave untouched no source of information which might conceivably be of value to the better protection of the children of the United States. A very direct effort was put forth to ascertain what the nations with whom the United States was associated in the Great War had learned concerning the safeguarding of childhood. This was done because it was known that despite the stress of war a splendid advance in the nurture of children had been made in Europe during the years immediately past.

An impressive body of evidence assembled by the Children's Bureau of the Department of Labor, by other divisions of the Government, by officials of other governments, as well as by scientists, private organizations and individuals, has long since abundantly indicated many of the perils surrounding childhood. Information as to existing menaces and activities to reduce and to end known losses have naturally fallen into four classes. The work therefore of the conference was divided along those lines. The first springs of waste are those attendant upon birth and the early months of infancy. Consequently, men and women reputed to know the actual losses now suffered and the most effectual means of eliminating these were brought together. Since, furthermore, the safety of the mother is the key to the well-being of the child, maternity could not be excluded from consideration. The protection of the health of mothers and children thus became an initial topic of discussion. In this, leading American authorities, together with representatives of Great Britain, France, Belgium, Serbia, and Italy took part.

The greatest, as well as the most futile, from the standpoint of contemporary medical and economic science, of human losses is the death of very young children. But fortunately the tragedy of squandered infant life is preventable. England especially during the war has done much to lessen this waste. Sir Arthur Newsholme, late chief medical officer of the Local Government Board, as a delegate from Great Britain, described the measures which are achieving this happy result in England. Mrs. Eleanor Barton, another British representative, set forth the program promoted by working-class women for the purpose of assuring universal public provision for maternity. Mrs. Barton described the work of the Women's Cooperative Guild in the securing of governmental aid for the care and protection of women during childbirth. Dr. René Sand, Professor of Industrial Medicine at the University of Brussels, explained the methods through which Belgium, despite the grim horrors of enemy invasion, reduced the infant death rate to a degree unapproached in that country by the records of peace. Similarly Dr. Clothilde Mulon, of the French War Department, elucidated the devices utilized in Paris to accomplish a like result. Professor Fabio Frassetto, of the University of Bologna, offered the novel hypothesis of the Italian anthropological school looking toward a fundamental reduction of the health disadvantages from which children suffer. Dr. Radmila Lazarevitch described the terrific losses endured by Serbia as a part of the price of war, and Miss L. E. Carter pictured the consequences of war's hunger and terror on the school children of Brussels.

American science was brought into counsel with the contributions from foreign lands. Dr. J. Whitridge Williams, of Johns Hopkins University, proposed certain standard requirements for obstetrical care in order to render as safe as possible both mother and child. Dr. Philip C. Jeans, of St. Louis, suggested general measures to be taken to prevent the blight upon infant life due to venereal infections. Dr. Charles V. Chapin, of Providence, Rhode Island, supported the development of prenatal clinics, maternity wards, and better obstetrical training as a means of further protecting infancy and maternity. Dr. H. F. Helmholz, of Evanston, Illinois, advocated the development of both prenatal and postnatal care of infants in order to lower present morbidity and mortality rates. Dr. R. W. Lobenstine, of New York City, outlined the New York plan for the establishment of maternity centers. Miss Elizabeth G. Fox, of the American Red Cross, proposed the creation of an organization to give to rural mothers competent prenatal, natal, and postnatal care.

In the discussion of the health needs of the child of preschool age Dr. Merrill E. Champion, of the Massachusetts State Department of Health, proposed the establishment of health centers on a scale comparable to the public-school system as a means of preventing unnecessary sickness and death. Dr. C.-E. A. Winslow, of Yale University, described the part which public-health nursing should take in the reduction of the national sum of juvenile disease. Dr. S. Josephine Baker, of the New York City Health Department, and Dr. Clothilde Mulon, of the French War Department, discussed standards essential to the right conduct of day nurseries, while Professor Lewis Terman, of Leland Stanford Junior University, presented the need for dental clinics. Nutrition clinics to discover and to correct the malnutrition from which many public-school children suffer were advocated by Dr. William R. P. Emerson, of Boston. Professor Graham Lusk, of Cornell University, discussed the nutrition of adolescence and as an illustration of the importance of this subject reported upon the consequences of an inadequate food supply among German children during the war. Professor Lusk stated that the amount of food needed by adolescent boys exceeds the requirement of adult men. Dr. Thomas D. Wood, of Columbia University, stated that three-fourths of the 22,000,000 school children in the United States have health defects which are actually or potentially injurious to them as prospective citizens. Dr. Wood advocated a program of regular health inspection and examination in the public schools as a way of avoiding the loss which results from negligence of the health defects of the young. Mr. Robert D. Leigh, of the United States Public Health Service, dealt with the need for sex education in the protection of the health of children.

As a result of discussions at the Washington conference definite standards for the protection of the health of mothers and of their children were formulated and referred to the consideration of the country.

The time at which children should enter the ranks of industry, the training which all should have preliminary to employment, the conditions under which young people should assume the obligations and the burdens of mature citizenship, are elements of the great problem of child labor which all modern nations have found difficult. Throughout the industrial era, however, an increasing body of pertinent data has been accumulated in this field and accordingly it is now possible to found standards on the assured basis of ascertained fact.

To the Children's Bureau Conferences on this subject came leaders of American thought. In these deliberations two British representatives were able to present the particularly useful experience of Great Britain. Mr. R. C. Davison, Chief of the Juvenile Labour Exchanges of Great Britain, reported the progress toward a solution of the great problem which England has made by means of a national control of employment. Sir Cyril Jackson, spokesman of the British Board of Education, was able to describe the meaning of the educational revolution in Great Britain signalized by the passage of the "Fisher" Education Act.

American workers presented the conclusions derived from their observations of the employment of children in industry. Mr. Owen R. Lovejoy of the National Child Labor Committee stated that the needs of the child himself must supplant all other interests in the formulation of standards for the protection of children against premature labor. Dr. Emma McKay Appel, of the Chicago Board of Education, described the minimum physical standards required in Chicago before permits to work are granted children. Dr. E. V. L. Brown, of Chicago, reported on the work being done to correct defective vision among Chicago working children. Dean D. L. Edsall, of the Harvard Medical school, reported his conclusion that it is necessary to study not only the nature of industry but the particular fitness of the individual child for certain types of employment before permitting him to work. Mr. Charles E. Chadsey, of Chicago, urged that continuation schools providing instruction up to the age of 21 years be established.

The Hon. Albert E. Hill, of Nashville, traced the history of child-labor legislation in Tennessee. Miss Agnes Nestor, President of the Women's Trade Union League of Chicago, discussed the question of hours and proposed that minors between sixteen and eighteen years of age be not permitted to work longer than six hours a day. Professor F. S. Deibler, of Northwestern University, suggested that advisory committees composed of school officials, representatives of industry and of labor exchanges with social workers might work out satisfactory scales of wages at which children properly could enter industry. Dr. Jessica B. Peixotto, of the University of California, while advocating school laws rather than labor laws for the protection of children, urged that minors be paid the minimum wage awarded women as soon as their output equals that of the ordinary adult. Miss Tracy Copp, of the Wisconsin Industrial Commission, described the administrative system by means of which children in Wisconsin are passed from school to industry.

In the end minimum standards for the greater protection of American childhood against the charted wrongs of premature labor were drafted, approved, and commended to the consideration of the American people. The convincing weight of testimony was to the effect that the lengthening of the period of actual childhood, and a more intelligent physical and intellectual training for entrance into productive employment, offer this nation the opportunity for an unprecedented increase in national strength.

The protection of health affects all children, and measures to prevent premature employment concern the great majority. But another group, those indicated by the phrase "children in need of special care," present a third well-defined and urgent problem. These are the dependents—the poor, the incurably weak, and the delinquent. For them first effort at reform began. Their plight inspired the beginnings of the child-welfare movement.

Mr. Robert W. Kelso, of the Massachusetts State Board of Charity, discussed the obligation of the state toward the child with special needs. Mr. Kelso stated that the care of such children is a function of the state and that the private agency performing this governmental function must conform to state standards. Mr. C. V. Williams, of the Ohio Board of State Charities, advocated the state supervision of public and private agencies in order to guarantee the maintenance of proper service. Judge Victor P. Arnold, of the Cook County Juvenile Court, outlined the grounds considered by the court sufficient to justify the removal of children from their homes. Mr. Edmond J. Butler, of the Catholic Home Bureau for Dependent Children, New York, proposed certain criteria to be applied to foster homes in which children are placed. He advocated the necessity of continued supervision of children so placed. Miss H. Ida Curry, of the State Charities Aid Association, New York, outlined a plan of child-welfare organization suited to rural districts. Judge James Hoge Ricks, of the Richmond, Virginia, Juvenile Court, discussed the organization of juvenile courts. He argued the advantages offered by the development of these courts along chancery lines. Dr. Louis N. Robinson, Chief Probation Officer of the Municipal Court of Philadelphia, asked for a greater specialization in the work of probation officers, with a larger experimentation in methods of reform. Dr. William Healy of the Judge Baker Foundation, Boston, treated the medicopsychological study of delinquency. Only by the use of such technical methods, Dr. Healy argued, is it possible to avoid the failures of ordinary efforts at juvenile reformation. Dr. C. Macfie Campbell, of the Johns Hopkins Hospital, discussed the place of mental hygiene in the child-welfare movement. He urged a greater consideration of the important problems of health involved in the personality of the child. Dr. Walter E. Fernald, of the Massachusetts School for the Feeble-Minded, set forth the need for the mental examination of backward school children, the establishment of clinics and of training classes, and for other items in a state program for the care of the mentally defective. Dr. Hastings H. Hart, of the Russell Sage Foundation, treated the principles adopted at the "White House Conference" in the light of recent experience. Mr. Takayuki Namaye, of the Japanese Department of Interior, presented graphically the organization of child-welfare work in Japan.

In this territory American experience has been rich. At the close of his last administration a decade ago President Roosevelt summoned the "White House Conference," which formulated standards for the better national treatment of these children so much dependent upon society. The urgency of a progressively better care for them while

GENERAL SUMMARY

stimulated by purely altruistic motives is buttressed by society's need to protect itself against the parasitic and the criminal—drafted largely from delinquent and defective children whose special necessities are ignored by the state. The "White House Conference" standards were reaffirmed at the Children's Bureau Conference, and brought into harmony with the knowledge which has been obtained during the past decade.

Consideration was also given to the place of legislation in crystallizing and making effective standards for child welfare. Mr. C. C. Carstens, of the Massachusetts Society for the Prevention of Cruelty to Children, dealt with the need for standardizing child-welfare laws and discussed the methods applicable. Presiding Justice Franklin Chase Hoyt, of the Children's Court of New York City, stated the necessity for a codification of children's laws from the standpoint of New York experience. Mr. W. W. Hodson, of the Minnesota State Board of Control, described in this connection the work of the Minnesota Child Welfare Commission. At the same time the need for well-organized children's codes coordinating the various phases of the State protection of childhood was emphasized. The Rev. William J. Kerby, secretary of the National Conference of Catholic Charities, drew attention to the need of synthesizing separate lines of legislation into children's codes in order adequately to protect the personality of the child. Practical methods for developing such codes were presented.

Precedent to the selection of any single opportunity for the betterment of the conditions surrounding childhood is, moreover, a consideration of the social and economic situation of the people. For the expression of any standard is merely an amiable generalization unless the material means for its application are available. At the very outset, therefore, conference was had concerning the general basis upon which the structure of progress might be built. Dr. René Sand, of the University of Brussels, in this connection discussed "Social Medicine." Dr. Sand pointed out the facts that "the human saving science has not kept pace with other sciences," and that the utilization of knowledge for the protection of mankind has lagged behind the actual advance of the science. His plea was for a scientific organization of society with a development of social medicine to cover the field which now lies unoccupied between public hygiene, economics, social science and philanthropy. In this way, Dr. Sand argued, the constructive democracy which must be a scientific democracy may be made real.

Professor William F. Ogburn, of Columbia University, presented data showing the actual cost of rearing a child, based upon a study of budgets collected for the Bureau of Labor Statistics of the Department of Labor and for the National War Labor Board. Miss S. P. Breckinridge, of the University of Chicago, treated in detail the gap between the cost of living at any defensible American standard and the incomes obtained by large sections of the population. She recapitulated the evil national consequences as revealed by infant mortality rates and other such indices of social waste which come from this material insufficiency. She urged the establishment of an economic minimum below which, for the sake of the nation, no family should be permitted to fall. Miss Florence Nesbitt, institute instructor in dietetics for the American Red Cross, reported that in places such as Chicago or Cleveland, $1,500 is the minimum cost of the essentials for maintaining an average family of five at what might be called a normal standard. Commissioner Royal Meeker stated that the budgets studied by the United States Bureau of Labor Statistics disclosed the fact that every increase in the size of many families compelled the sacrifice not only of the comforts but of the necessities of life "to meet the most pressing need—the need for food." Professor Kelly Miller, of Howard University, drew attention to the special handicap of the negro child because "the stress of economic pressure falls heaviest upon the black race."

Mrs. Eva Whiting White described the war housing program of the Federal Government as it relates to the present needs of the American child. Mrs. White urged that the development of a sound national housing policy is prerequisite to the attainment of homes fit for the upbringing of children. Mr. Joseph Lee and Mr. L. H. Weir, of the War Camp Community Service, in collaboration with Miss Abbie Condit, of the Playground and Recreation Association of America, presented recreational schemes for organization of the leisure of children.

Because the practicability of progress is determined by the material possessions of the people, the discussion of family budgets, of the cost of child care, and of the allied social factors involved, makes explicit the obligation which must be accepted if modern standards for the nurture of children are really to be put into operation. The logic of the evidence adduced seemed to indicate that a very large ratio of the families of the United States obtain incomes too small to make possible the rearing of children in the manner which scientific and humane considerations, as well as the prosperity of the nation, demand. This conclusion in itself is not wholly novel, but the precise presentation of the actual expenditures necessary to a wholesome upbringing of the young is a distinct gain in social knowledge.

In the following pages appear the principal papers read at the Washington conference, and a few of the more significant contributions made in the regional conferences. Attached are liberal quotations from the discussions which followed the papers. These show the trend of the argument through which the standards were formulated. Finally the three groups of minimum standards appear. These it should be realized are tentative and provisional and in no sense maxima. But they do represent a serious effort to apply to the service of childhood those principles of wholesome care so clearly indicated by science and common experience. No longer can it be said that the knowledge concerning how to safeguard childhood is lacking. The data are available. They bear the imprimatur of sane and forceful thinking. Only the will to achieve is now wanted. With that the United States will be able to create a new era of safer, stronger, happier childhood, an era in which the oncoming generation is better equipped to carry on the work of the republic.

Section I

The Economic and Social Basis for Child Welfare Standards

SOCIAL MEDICINE

By DR. RENE SAND
University of Brussels, Belgium

I should like to say a few words about the general principles on which we ought to lay the foundations for the laws concerning child welfare we all wish to introduce, and about the best way to secure their enforcement. I think you all agree that laws have to be based on science and experience, more than on sentiment or party lines. Yet this has been very rarely the case. Interests and prejudice play an important part, I am afraid, in forming public opinion. There is not much room left for science.

At this moment, however, things look distinctly more hopeful. The war has taught us to question all our methods, and to ask for better efficiency. Now, efficiency means a scientific organization, and cooperation. Those two factors have really won the war. Think what improvements our munition factories, our army, the life of the nation at large, have shown in the last four years. The scientific and the cooperative spirit have made the whole difference and have achieved wonders.

If we try to pervade our peace activities with those elements of success, we strike at two very paradoxical facts. The first is that the human-saving science has not kept pace with the other sciences. We have gathered a few facts only about eugenics, about the physiology of labor, about the factors affecting the growth of children, all things of first-class importance for our prosperity and happiness. But sciences like archaeology (I do not want to attack the archaeologists; I have a number of friends in that branch) loom large in our museums and publications, at least in Europe, although they cannot boast the same usefulness. It seems that instead of doing the urgent job first, mankind has always preferred to begin with the less important task.

That is already bad enough. But here comes the second point: the utilization of science has not kept pace with its advance. Professor Frederick S. Lee has told us so in a recent book, in which he shows what we know about the working of the human machine, and the little use to which that knowledge has been put. You could take other examples; we know perfectly well how to eradicate malaria and yellow fever, yet these diseases still claim many victims. We know that we could prevent half of the deaths which occur every year, and yet we do not prevent them. Thirty per cent of our blind infants would see if only a few drops of an antiseptic solution were put in the eyes of every newborn child.

The reason of all those deficiencies is that there is no program for the scientific organization of mankind, no agency to study such a program, no teaching given on the matter. I think we will never reach the point where we will really govern ourselves and master the world, until we make the universities constructive. It is from these centers that the laws ought to originate, and not from the political associations.

A university is not primarily a place where young men play football and learn Greek or mathematics; neither is it primarily a school for lawyers or physicians, nor a place where an expert studies at leisure, in a comfortable environment, some old Assyrian inscription. These activities are very valuable and necessary. But we must put foremost a higher and more general purpose; the building up of civic and human efficiency. The constructive university will not include many more sciences than it does now, but it will teach them from another viewpoint.

Let us take, for instance, public health. We tell our undergraduates how to prevent tuberculosis by avoidance of contact, a well-balanced diet, a comfortable home, and rest. Very well. But we do not tell them how to provide those things. I would have public health taught in a way that would strike at the root of the question and proclaim, as Surgeon General Gorgas did, that the greatest public-health measure you can introduce is a minimum wage law. I would have hygiene studied not only in the laboratory; I would take the undergraduates to the workingman's home and ask him and his wife about their needs and the reforms they themselves suggest.

In short, I would go a step further than preventive medicine, and teach sociologic medicine. There is a field between sociology, statistics, biology, medicine, hygiene, and philanthropy, which is a kind of no man's land. Some patrols start from the biology border, explore a little stretch, and then come back. The same occurs from all the borders. When two patrols, coming from different borders, meet each other, they sometimes fraternize; more often there is a big scientific fight. I do not mind very much this kind of fighting after having seen the other kind. The worst feature is that the patrols seldom meet, and so every bit of knowledge which one border gains about no man's land is lost for the others. There is no coordination of effort, no planning together, no team work.

I think this could be avoided and a real need be met if we started frankly to organize that field under the auspices of Sociologic Medicine. Sociologic Medicine means the medical end of social questions, or the social end of medical questions, as you prefer to put it. It would have been constituted long ago were it not for the fact that it requires teaching biological, statistical, and social methods to the physicians. Now, biological methods the actual or future physician will accept without too great trouble. There will be more resistance to statistical methods; they need the use of higher mathematics, and fumbling about in terrible books like the Census. But even that, the better type of undergraduate or doctor will finally admit, on account of the scientific stamp that statistics receive from mathematics. When it comes, however, to sociological methods, the average medical man revolts; surveys, inquiries, social case work, all seem too humane to be scientific. And then they mix up with all sorts of social questions, nearly related to political questions. That is a slippery field.

And yet we have got to plough this field, and it will give us the richest crop that science has ever reaped, because then we will no more guess, we will know about the social questions. Marriage, child welfare, education, vocational guidance, labor, poverty, delinquency, all those problems have to be taken up by sociologic medicine. If this new science is comprehensive enough, if it is recognized and developed, I have no doubt results will follow quickly.

A conference like this where public officials, social workers, physicians, sociologists, and teachers meet together is already a step toward the reclamation of this common field. The school of industrial medicine organized recently at Harvard is another very valuable progression in that direction.

We constituted in Belgium in 1913 an association of sociologic medicine which published a bulletin (Bulletin de l'Association Belge de Médecine Sociale Bruxelles) and it was progressing favorably. Sociologic medicine was taught in our universities to doctors who wanted to take the public-health diploma. But war has nipped those activities in the bud. We will have to take them up again, however, as they will not only help toward making better laws, but also assist us toward enforcing them in an easier and more effective way. Constructive democracy means scientific democracy.

THE FINANCIAL COST OF REARING A CHILD

By WILLIAM F. OGBURN
Bureau of Labor Statistics, U. S. Department of Labor

During my past year's work with the National War Labor Board and the United States Bureau of Labor Statistics, I have received many inquiries concerning how much it costs to rear a child. I am in a position now to throw some light on this question from data collected by the Bureau of Labor Statistics in all parts of the country and particularly from the special methods employed in working up these data.

In Philadelphia, for instance, two hundred family schedules were collected from workingmen's families with incomes between $800 and $2,000, showing the expenditures in detail for the year 1918. These data were generalized into a series of equations in such a form as to show, by merely substituting in the equations the size of the family and the total year's expenditure and solving, the average amounts spent for food, for clothing, for rent, for fuel and light, for furniture and furnishings, and for miscellaneous expenses. One such equation is the following: $[X_4] = 45.60 - 0.0103\ X_3 + 3.132\ X_2$, in which X_3 is the total annual expenditure in dollars, X_2 is the size of the family, X_4 is the percentage of the total expenditure spent for food, and [ ] means the average. For instance, if it is desired to know the average expenditure for food of a family of three with a total annual expenditure of $1,000, we substitute in the equation 3 for X_2 and $1,000 for X_3, and solving, we find $[X_4] = 44.7$. This means that on the average 44.7 per cent of the total annual expenditure went for food; and since the total annual expenditure was $1,000, then the amount spent for food was $447. And so from this equation we can find the average amount spent for food by a family of any size and with any income (between $800 and $2,000).

Not only can we find the average amount spent for food for a family of a given size, but by comparing the amount with that spent in a family having one additional member we can ascertain how much is added to the food budget for the extra member of the family. Thus, we can, first, substitute for X_2 in this equation a family of husband and wife (just married and with no children) and learn the amount spent for food; then, secondly, we can substitute for X_2 the same family with a child one year old, and ascertain the total amount spent for food. The difference between the first result and the second result will be the

THE ECONOMIC AND SOCIAL BASIS   27

amount added to the food budget for the child from birth to one year old. We can, thirdly, substitute for X_2 the family with the child two years old and the result will be the amount spent for food for one year by a family of husband and wife and child from one to two years old. By subtracting from this third result (cost of food for husband and wife and child from one to two years old) the first result (cost of food for husband and wife with no children) we can find the amount added to the food budget for a child from one to two years old. As we first figured out the amount added to the food budget for the child from birth to one year old, by adding the amount added to the budget for the child from one year to two years old, we can tell how much is added to the food budget for a child from birth to two years old. And so by repeating this process we can ascertain how much is added to the food budget of a family by rearing a child up to sixteen years of age.

In order to make these successive substitutions, we must have some unit to represent the sizes of families with children of different ages. After considerable research it was thought justifiable to substitute for the size of the family its equivalent in terms of adult male units, using a scale based on relative food requirements measured in calories. There are several such scales. The one already adopted by the Bureau of Labor Statistics was used. According to this scale, a man equals 1.0, a woman equals 0.9, a child from birth to three years inclusive equals 0.15, a child from four to six years inclusive equals 0.4, a child from seven to ten inclusive equals 0.75, a child from 11 to 14 inclusive equals 0.9, a girl over 14 equals 0.9, and a boy over 14 equals 1.0. (A discussion of the representativeness of this scale and also a full discussion of the formation of the equations is found in a forthcoming bulletin of the Bureau of Labor Statistics of the United States Department of Labor.) This scale enables one to express a family with children of any ages in a single number, which may be substituted for X_2 in the equations. We can thus substitute in the equation just discussed the successive sizes of the family until the child is 16 years of age. Thus the size of the family when the boy is from 15 to 16 years old is 2.9 (husband equals 1.0, wife 0.9 and boy 1.0).

In working out these amounts spent for food from the above equation, it is necessary to substitute the size of the total annual expenditure (which is usually about the same as the income) for X_3. We can, of course, choose an income of any size, say $1,500, and find out how much is added to the food bill because of rearing a child up to say 16 years of age. But during these sixteen years, has the income remained the same? If not, how much has it gone up? If the income has gone up, probably more has been spent on food than would have been spent if the income had remained the same. Of course if there have been increases in wages (or increases in annual income) we can make the proper substitutions for X_3 at the proper times, i. e., stages in the growth of the family (X_2), for a particular family. But we are not so much interested in a particular family as in what takes place on the average. Fortunately we have found another equation which gives us this information, $[X_3] = 932 + 138\ X_2$. We can tell from this equation what the average total annual expenditure is for a family of any size, as determined by the representative sample of families chosen from Philadelphia. Thus for families of three (substituting 3 for X_2 and solving) the average total annual expenditure as determined from our sample of workingmen's families is $1,346, and for families of four, is $1,484. The larger the family, the larger the expenditure. An increase of the size of the family by one (in our equivalent adult male units) increases the expenditure by $138. So from this equation we can determine the appropriate X_3 to be substituted for the particular size of family (X_2) we are discussing.

Following the procedure described in the preceding four paragraphs, we find that what we may term the "net increase" of the family budget for food because of rearing a child to sixteen years, i. e., over what the food would have cost if there had been no child, was $718. The food which the child ate may have cost more than this $718 of "net increase." The husband and wife may have cut down on the cost of their food, or they may have bought cheaper food or less (and perhaps inadequate) food. Or they may have made economies in purchasing or using food. This "net increase," then, would represent not the full cost of food for the child, but only that part of it which was not met by economies or by lessened consumption by the other members of the family.

For purposes of comparison with this "net increase," the actual cost of food for a child up to sixteen years may be estimated in the following way: The average cost of food per adult male per day for the families studied in Philadelphia was $0.51. Now from our equivalent adult male scale it is found that a boy for the first sixteen years of his life eats as much as an adult male would eat in 9.4 years. At 51 cents per man per day the food for 9.4 adult males for one year (i. e., a boy for the first sixteen years of life) would cost $1,750. In other words the actual cost of the child's food, if it cost the same as the average cost in Philadelphia, would have been not $718 but $1,750. The difference is the measure of the economies and adjustments made in the family budget for food over the period of the first 16 years of the child's life.

In a similar manner we can study expenditures for clothing, rent, fuel and light, furniture and furnishings, and miscellaneous expenses. The basic equations for these are the following:

$[X_5] = 8.95 - 0.00569 X_3 - 0.249 X_2$ (clothing)
$[X_6] = 21.59 - 0.00589 X_3 - 0.0577 X_2$ (rent)
$[X_7] = 8.435 - 0.00218 X_3 + 0.0172 X_2$ (fuel and light)
$[X_8] = 2.004 + 0.00517 X_3 - 1.447 X_2$ (furniture)
$[X_9] = 14.199 + 0.00703 X_3 - 1.297 X_2$ (miscellaneous)
$[X_4] = 45.60 - 0.0103 X_3 + 3.132 X_2$ (food)
$[X_{13}] = 92.51 + 0.0235 X_3 - 15.71 X_2$ (deficit or surplus)
$[X_3] = 932 + 138 X_2$

In these equations X_5 equals the per cent of total expenditure spent for clothing; X_6, the per cent for rent; X_7, the per cent for fuel and light; X_8, the per cent for furniture and furnishings; X_9, the per cent for miscellaneous expense; X_4, the per cent for food; X_{13}, the annual deficit (—) or surplus (+) in dollars; X_3, the total annual expenditure in dollars; and X_2, the size of the family in units of the adult male.

From the foregoing list of equations the net increases of the budget for various classes of expenditure in rearing a child to sixteen years have been computed. The amounts are, respectively, for clothing, $265; for rent, $80; for fuel and light, $40; for miscellaneous expenses, $220; and for food, $720. As remarked previously, these are only the amounts added to the expenses because of the rearing of a child to sixteen years, over and above what the family would have spent for them if there had been no child to rear. It is most desirable to find out what the cost was of actual expenditures on the other commodities consumed by the child as was estimated in a previous paragraph in regard to food. This I have been unable to ascertain except for clothing. The actual amount spent on clothing for a boy from birth to sixteen years as computed item by item from families of the working class with incomes around $1,500 and with three children was $525. This sum is to be contrasted with the $265 which is the amount added to the clothing budget of the family for rearing a child to sixteen years of age. Evidently the husband and wife economized on clothing in order to clothe the boy, a good deal more than they would have done if there had been no child.

In conclusion, it will be clear that this paper does not concern the question of what a child ought to have in order to be reared properly. This is a most important question. And no doubt others will develop it. This paper shows rather what does happen to family budgetary costs where children are born and reared. It is a sad story for those families near the minimum-of-subsistence level, as the figures in the preceding paragraphs show. Does the father's wage go up when a child is born, and another, and another? No, as the family grows larger and older, the father's earnings do not increase because of this fact. What does happen? How are the exigencies and needs of a growing family met? And particularly what happens to the children, in the way of commodities purchased for them? The data of this paper throw considerable light on these points. In rearing a child from birth to sixteen years of age, $1,325 is on the average added to what the budgetary costs for food, clothing, rent, etc., would have been if there had been no child. This is the net increase in the total expenditures caused by bringing up the child. But the actual cost of what the child consumes is far more. We have seen that although the net increase of the budget for food and clothing is only $985, the actual cost of the child's food and clothing is $2,275. The difference between the increase in the family expenditures caused by the rearing of children and the actual cost of the food and clothing and other items consumed by them indicates the extent to which the general family standard is lowered by their presence. At bottom, it shows the self-denial of the father and mother.

THE ECONOMICS OF CHILD WELFARE

By DR. ROYAL MEEKER
Commissioner, Bureau of Labor Statistics, U. S. Department of Labor

I suppose that because I am an economist I am expected to point out the relation between economics, the dismal science (so named by those who know nothing about it) and child welfare, incidentally taking up the cudgels for the dismal science.

Whether we discuss babies, baseball, bolshevism, or the binomial theorem, we finally come up against the fundamental philosophy of life —the meaning of creation. What is it all about? Many economic discussions deal with babies chiefly as potential labor power. Now, that is a rather shocking idea when first we come up against it in that crude, brutal way. Shall we nurture our babies and bring them to maturity for the purpose of creating the most efficient labor force? Shall we follow the economic interpreters of history in ascribing all power to the economic motive in the determination of human conduct? Shall we follow the efficiency managers and the scientific experts in laying down the principle that the education of the child must be the education that will make him the most efficient producer so that we may get more product, so that more babies may be brought into the world, so that more work may be done to produce more goods so that more babies may be brought into the world, and so on ad infinitum?

That is the way the opponents of the economic interpretation of history and the opponents of scientific management state the case, and, of course, it immediately arouses every ounce of opposition in all our natures and we say, "away with such theories, away with such doctrines; we will have none of them. We will have the education that will bring the child to its fullest development."

Now, what is the fullest development of the child? You see we are already up against the philosophy of the whole thing. What is it all about? What is our fundamental philosophy of life? Without either subscribing to or opposing the economic interpretation of history it is at once apparent that child welfare is largely economic. If we include in the definition of the economic motive every desire that the human heart feels, then there is no escape from the economic interpretation of history. If we want to give a narrow definition to it, however, and confine the economic motive to the chasing of dollars for the purpose of satisfying our more immediate physical needs, if we hold that there are ethical motives and aesthetic motives and instinctive motives that are more or less antithetical to the economic motive, even so we are bound to acknowledge that child welfare is very largely an economic problem, because ethical teachings, aesthetic appeals, do not go very far on an empty stomach; they do not go very far with the children living under conditions of poverty and distress. We must at least have an economic background, even if we admit without further argument that economics do not include everything in the world and everything in the universe.

We have not put enough scientific study into the consideration of what kind of upbringing children should be given in order to enable them to reach the fulfillment of the purposes of creation. I take it that the Children's Bureau has been established for a purpose quite similar to that which brought about the establishment of the Bureau of Animal Husbandry. For many, many years we have given a great deal of thought to the upbringing of hogs, cows, cattle, and horses. It is a very important thing. I am not saying a word against the Bureau of Animal Husbandry. I am glad it was founded when it was, and I hope it will keep on doing the excellent work it has been doing. I think hogs, cows, and horses should be given every encouragement to attain their fullest self-realization.

Our Children's Bureau is then, in a way, a Bureau of Child Husbandry. In extending its scope statistical studies are of vital importance. Without the statistical investigations that the Children's Bureau has made we would not have a fraction of the knowledge that we now have of the needs for the proper up-bringing of children. I might say incidentally that the statistical work of my own bureau has contributed somewhat to our knowledge of that subject. Take, for example, the cost-of-living statistics. These tables for 22 cities appeared in the Monthly Review of the Bureau of Labor Statistics for May, 1919, and presented many interesting phases. Take the fact that the larger the income the larger the family. Quite obviously the explanation is that the more children there are the more workers. The income increases with the number of income earners.

It is extremely interesting to study the changes in the percentage distribution of expenditures with changes in the size of the family. They show the influence of the babies upon expenditures. A wife when she first marries, according to the tabulations worked out, spends about as much for clothes as the husband, in the workingman's family. Some of you may be surprised to hear that the woman spends *almost* as much as the man. The accepted notion is quite to the contrary. But just as soon as the first baby comes her expenditure for clothes drops. When the next baby comes, it drops again; so eventually the wife becomes absolutely—I do not like to say it but I do not know of any other term in which to express it—a domestic slave. She is absolutely tied to the home, to the house I mean, not the home. She has no clothes in which she can attend a meeting like this to be taught about statistics and all the other things connected with child welfare. She cannot even go to church unless she is willing to go in an outfit that does not lend itself to display.

As a matter of fact in many incomes which I have studied I have noted that with the increase of the family every item of expenditure, except food, declines not simply in percentage but in absolute amounts. This means, of course, that comforts and even necessities must be sacrificed to meet the most pressing need—the need for food. Of course, this is only in the lower-income groups, but it certainly indicates that something needs to be done to bridge this gap. It certainly indicates that it is worth while thinking about this thing so carelessly and complacently called the American standard of living.

FAMILY BUDGETS

By DEAN S. P. BRECKINRIDGE
University of Chicago

There are three items which should be included in any estimate of the pecuniary cost of child care. These are: the cost of the articles needed for the child's physical maintenance; the cost of the maintenance of those persons necessary to the child's existence and care; and the cost of other persons who are necessary to the situation of which the child is a part. For such an estimate of the pecuniary cost, reference must be made, of course, to an ascertained time and place.

The social workers of Chicago have made it easy to answer certain questions with reference to the money cost of child care in a family group in that city at a given time, namely, in February, 1919. Within the past few weeks representatives of the various agencies dealing with families in distress, under the direction of Miss Nesbitt,[1] for some time the distinguished dietitian of the Cook County Juvenile Court, have been working to formulate just that statement; and the result of their inquiry has been laid or will be laid before the responsible executives of these agencies, with the suggestion that these estimates be regarded as a minimum standard below which no family for whose life the agency is in any way responsible be allowed to fall. In this attempt, as is the usual practice, the items essential to the comfort and well-being of the various members of the family are carefully designated by the dietitian, with the aid of the other workers having to do with family problems.

In listing the food requirements, the enumeration corresponds closely with those made by others skilled in the field of nutrition. The needs of the mother and children are estimated in terms of the needs of the adult man per day, taking the 3,000-3,500 calories as the energy basis and 75-100 grams as the protein requirement, with due notice of the mineral requirements. As is commonly done, the proportion allotted to the women and girls is smaller than that allotted to men and boys; but as has not always been done, the food requirements of the older boys and girls are recognized as equal to those of the adult of the same sex.

In general, the estimate of food cost was 43 cents per man per day,

[1] Florence Nesbitt, The Chicago Standard Budget for Dependent Families. Chicago Council of Social Agencies, Bulletin No. 5.

or $3.00 a week for the man, and $1.60 a week for each child under 6, as the younger child should have more expensive food in smaller amounts and the older child should have more food of the cheaper kinds.

The basis of the estimate for clothing is careful inquiry among reasonably well-clothed families where the selection is known to be skilful in the number and kinds of articles used. The estimate is decent and comfortable, in that allowance is made for night wear and for changes required by the alternating seasons. It is, however, far from lavish, although it presupposes independent enjoyment rather than dependence upon charitable gifts or common use.

Assuming that free medical and nursing service are available, a very small estimate is made for expenditure related to the protection of health.

Something is allowed for the recreation of the children over six but not at work and for the school expenditures of those in school.

By adding to these estimates a share of the necessary expenditures for household supplies, we can get totals which express the minimum expenditure thought safe for a child in each of the age and sex groups into which the family is classified.

COST PER YEAR OF NECESSITIES FOR CHILDREN OF SPECIFIED AGES, AND FOR PARENTS.
(Calculated from figures given in budget referred to: not included in these estimates are rent and insurance.)

	Child under 3	Child 3-5 Incl.	Child 6-9 Incl.	Child 10-12 Incl.	Child 13-14 Boy	Child 13-14 Girl	Child Over 14 At Work Boy	Child Over 14 At Work Girl	Father	Mother
Food	$83.30	$83.30	$96.20	$109.20	$127.40	$114.40	$156.00	$124.80	$156.00	$124.80
Clothing	27.00	33.00	45.00	54.00	60.00	60.00	90.00	90.00	90.00	66.00
Increase in household supplies	4.50	4.50	4.50	4.50	4.50	4.50	4.50	4.50	(b)	(b)
Health (a)	3.00	3.00	3.00	3.00	3.00	3.00	3.00	3.00	3.00	3.00
Recreation	....	....	3.00	3.00	3.00	3.00	13.00	13.00	3.00	3.00
Education	....	....	....	1.80	1.80	1.80	....	....	....	....
Total	$117.80	$123.80	$151.70	$175.50	$199.70	$186.70	$266.50	$235.30	$252.00	$196.80

(a) Estimates for health expenditures assume that public doctors and nurses will be used.
(b) Included in common expenditures.
Common expenditures:
    Household supplies (for family of two)..............$48.00
    Fuel 78.00
    Education (newspapers, etc.)......................... 9.00

But there is, moreover, the cost of the father and of the mother. These totals for the rare family, known to the "investigator" as the "normal" family of father, mother, and three to five children under fourteen, range from $842.10 for the family with three quite young children to $1,204.30 for the family with five children scattered through the age groups but all under fourteen.

However, this estimate says nothing of insurance or of rent. According to the housing studies made in Chicago during the past fifteen years, it would certainly not be excessive to add from $7.50 to $12.50 a month or from $90 to $150 a year for rent to this estimate, making the minimum from $932.10 to $1,354.30 without insurance and without provision for the older children's books and magazines, or for extras connected with other emergencies than those provided for in insurance arrangements—christenings, marriages, etc. No allowance is included for charitable gifts or contributions to the church. Of these estimates, the committee says, "the standard set is in the judgment of the committee the lowest one that will furnish conditions necessary for satisfactory growth and development of children and normal adult life, and so in the judgment of the committee no family of whatever nationality, past history, or standards should be allowed to fall below it, if it is possible to prevent them from doing so."

The importance of this estimate in the Chicago situation may be illustrated by the difficulties under which the Cook County Juvenile Court is operating, when under the statute the highest amount which it can grant to any one family is $60 a month, or $720 a year, and then only if there are six children, although for a family in which there are six children, even if they were all under three, the allowance without rent and insurance should be $706.80, without provision for the mother, or $903.60 if her food and clothing were counted in. If there is an incapacitated father, a contingency the Juvenile Court law definitely contemplates, there should, of course, be provision for him, but none is made under the law.

In the same way, the Soldiers' and Sailors' Allowance provision, as generous as those influential in securing the adoption of this method of caring for the families of the men dared to suggest to Congress, contemplates $30 a month for the mother, $15 from the husband's pay and $15 from the Treasury, and allowances for the children of $10, $7.50, and $5, with $50 from the Treasury, or $65 altogether (or $600 and $780 annually) as the upper-limits of contributions.

Three points should be made, of course, in connection with these estimates:

1. They are the estimates of persons whose point of view is that of human well-being. These persons are in daily contact with those whose pecuniary resources fall far below even these slender allowances. They are persons who, while trying to estimate the essential, are accustomed to think in terms of minima and not of adequate or generous or revolutionary allowances.

2. The estimates are based, on the one hand, on prices definitely ascertained; on the other, on uses and practices of careful intelligent managers. In any one of our communities, especially with the shifting and movement of population that has been brought about by the war, there would be many women who might be highly skilled in household arts of various kinds yet not sufficiently familiar with the conditions of retail buying or with the requirements of the season to translate the income thus estimated in such a way as to secure the well-being prescribed.

Estimates similar to the one described have been made in other communities.[1] Miss Nesbitt came to Chicago after formulating a similar budget for Cleveland agencies. In fact, the art of formulating the budget for the family in whose behalf responsibility is assumed for a considerable period of time by the social agency, as for example in the case of the family of a soldier or sailor for whom for some reason the Government allotment and allowance provision is either not available or inadequate, is now being well developed and is practiced by most case-work agencies. Good social case-work agencies must base their work upon such estimates, and the inadequacy of the Government allowance has forced the Home Service Section of the Red Cross to frame similar estimates in order that they may not allow the soldier's family to suffer.

3. Those who made this estimate had in mind the use of charitable funds by responsible social agencies. They were saying nothing of the wage bargain. They were bringing pressure to bear in the service of the weak and inarticulate and not so much in behalf of the individual under care as for the community itself. But if their estimates were placed beside the wage scales of many of the establishments in Chicago, the discrepancy between the estimated minimum and the actual income would become apparent.

There has always been such a discrepancy. If we look back upon the attempts to arrive at such estimates we find, in 1795, David Davies[2], a clergyman of the Church of England, gathering budgets and illustrating from the experience of his own parishioners the connection between the inadequate wage paid agricultural laborers in England and the demoralizing effect of public outdoor relief. At that early date the principle of the minimum wage was urged by the liberal Whitbread.[3]

The economists as well as the statisticians and the students of social well-being have given attention to the problem. In their discussions, it has been assumed that the wage bargain entered into by the employer and the employee, both acting under the motive of enlightened self-interest, would be such as would allow the worker to maintain himself as an efficient worker and to replace himself by an efficient worker, that is, would supply the "cost of child care." The estimates of the so-called necessaries for life, for comfort, or for efficiency, have recognized the complexity of the problem by including the category of "conventional necessaries," in which were grouped those indulgences,

---

[1] See W. Jett Lauck, Cost of Living and the War.
[2] The Case of the Labourers in Husbandry Stated and Considered.
[3] Samuel Whitbread, 1758-1815. See Hammond, The Village Labourer, pp. 134 and 179.

like the pipe and the newspaper, which the workingman would have even if he were thereby forced to do without the articles thought by the economists to be essential to his life, his workmanship, or the perpetuation of the labor supply.[1]

With the eighties came the great effort of Mr. Charles Booth[2] to penetrate the darkest spots of London; and following on his great inquiry into the Life and Labour of the People in London, came Mr. B. Seebohm Rowntree's[3] attempt to furnish an estimate not only of what the depressed classes receive and spend but an estimate of the income necessary in order that the dietetic needs of the household should be met. His minimum for food alone was fixed for a man in York in the year 1899 at three shillings a week, and his weekly income for the family of five at from 18s. to 26s. His estimates are reviewed and revised by Mr. Bowley[4] on the basis of a study of the towns, Northampton, Warrington, Stanley, and Reading, and estimated in 1913 at 11s. 1d. for man and wife, or 17s. 4d. for man and wife and three children under five years of age.

Or turning to the inquiries pursued in the United States, we find, besides the estimates of the social workers, those formulated on the basis of minimum wage determinations. These are rendered, however, far less useful and significant than they might be by the fact that in general under our Constitutional limitations, the minimum wage ideal is thought applicable chiefly, if not exclusively, to women and girls, and so we do not have estimates of minimum family incomes.

The idea of the modern relief-giving agency, that only by adequate regular allowance determined after investigation on the basis of the special needs in the individual case is the responsibility of the society fulfilled, has given rise not only to the practice of budgeting but called for wider studies of cost. These results may be illustrated by such studies as Chapin's Standards of Living in New York City, an inquiry undertaken by the New York State Conference of Charities, and by Miss Winifred Gibb's Minimum Cost of Living in New York City,

---

[1] See, for example, Alfred Marshall's discussion in Principles of Economics, Vol. I, Book II, chap. iv. See also J. S. Mill, Principles of Political Economy, Book I, chap. iii, section 5. "But the consumption even of productive labourers is not all of it productive consumption. There is unproductive consumption by productive consumers. What they consume in keeping up or improving their health, strength, and the capacities of work, or in rearing other productive labourers to succeed them, is productive consumption. But consumption on pleasures or luxuries, whether by the idle or by the industrious, since production is neither its object nor is in any way advanced by it, must be reckoned unproductive; with a reservation perhaps of a certain quantum of enjoyment which may be classed among necessaries, since anything short of it would not be consistent with the greatest efficiency of labour. That alone is productive consumption, which goes to maintain and increase the productive powers of the community."

[2] Charles Booth, 1840-1917.
[3] B. Seebohm Rowntree, Poverty.
[4] A. L. Bowley and A. R. Burnett-Hurst, Livelihood and Poverty.

THE ECONOMIC AND SOCIAL BASIS

based on observation of families under the care of the New York Association for Improving the Condition of the Poor.

All studies of the first of these two groups follow substantially the Rowntree method of laying special stress on the dietitian's estimate of the physiological needs of the individual supplemented by the practices of some public agency[1] which translate those needs into terms of prices as found in the local community. To these estimates of the necessary minimum food costs are added much less definite estimates of the costs of shelter, clothing, the protection of health, and the gratification of the spiritual and intellectual needs.

Whatever the method of approach or the basis of judgment, however, one fact has emerged from these studies. The incomes earned by large numbers of our so-called independent wage-earning men have been far below the amounts estimated by students and investigators as necessary to meet the rational and socially important needs. Chapin concluded that the task of making both ends meet was in 1907 too severe on all incomes under $800 "without a lowering of the standards of living below the normal demands of health, working efficiency, and social decency."[2]

Miss Byington[3] estimated in 1908 for Homestead, Pennsylvania, that $15.00 a week, or $780 a year, was necessary for health, while $20 a week, or $1,040 a year, was required for a reasonably American family life. Kennedy[4] in Chicago in 1914 found that all families earning less than $600 ended the year with a deficit, and estimates that $800 was the least on which a family of five could be supported. Professor Jessica Peixotto in October, 1917, estimated $1,320.[5] And so the estimates might be multiplied.

In all the studies, the deficiency of the wage level as measured by rational estimates of human needs has been made known. Davies showed that reliance on the poor rates was inevitable for the great mass of his parishioners. Eden thought the deficiency might be reduced if the women knew better how to spend. Rowntree and Bowley report appalling percentages living either in poverty or on the brink of the abyss. In the United States, if we recall the suggested estimates, we find great numbers of the workers falling below. The Report of the Immigration Commission appointed by Congress in 1907 and reporting in 1910, contains a hideous mass of testimony to the inadequacy

---

[1] See, for example, Woman and Child Wage Earners, Vol. XVI, Budgets of Selected Cotton Mill Workers.
[2] Robert C. Chapin, The Standard of Living Among Workingmen's Families in New York City, p. 234.
[3] Margaret F. Byington, Homestead, the Households of a Mill Town, p. 105.
[4] John C. Kennedy, Wages and Family Budgets in the Chicago Stockyards District, p. 79.
[5] W. Jett Lauck, Cost of Living and the War, p. 131.

of the incomes received by our foreign-born workers. Great variations exist among the different nationalities, and the different industries, but not only such ancient offenders as the textile industries that have always underpaid women and children, but the great man-employing industries in the newer sections of the country, are shown to have had a wage scale making impossible such life as is described and provided for in the studies referred to above.

Similar facts could be added concerning our southern white mill-workers or the negro wage earners anywhere.

But the question may be put, if there is such a conflict between the estimate placed on the appropriate cost of child life by the social investigator and by the practices of men as registered in the wage bargain, can we be certain that the former are correct? How can this claim be established? There are several pertinent facts to be noted. Some of the most striking are those contained in the reports on infant mortality recently published by the Children's Bureau.

First, as to the source of the income, it should be admitted that a grave wrong has often been done the family situation in the investigations referred to above. Those studies have considered composite incomes made up of the earnings of the father, the supplementary earnings of the mother, and the earnings of the older children. The Children's Bureau made a contribution of incomparable significance when it called us to our senses and pointed out that the income to be considered should be that derived from the earnings or the activities of the father. On this subject the Bureau says convincingly:

"The father's earnings, it is believed, furnish the most reliable index to the economic status of the family because in most cases they are not only the chief support but also the most stable and regular element in the family income. Supplementary sources of income such as mother's and children's earnings are likely to be temporary and fluctuating. A special objection to lumping father's earnings with the earnings of the mother and children is that the gainful employment of the latter indicates a low economic status which would tend to be obscured were their earnings combined."[1]

Second, as to the amount of the income. The Children's Bureau has given us something of a measure of the waste resulting from the low income conditions to which reference has been made in the waste of something no less precious than infant life itself. As the income of the father goes down, the death rate of the babies goes up. In report after report the correlation thus appears. For example, from a report on Johnstown, Pa., the following figures may be quoted:[2]

---

[1] Infant Mortality, Results of a Field Study in Manchester, N. H., Based on Births in One Year, by Beatrice Sheets Duncan and Emma Duke, p. 40. U. S. Children's Bureau Publication No. 20, Infant Mortality Series No. 6, Washington, 1917.

[2] Infant Mortality, Results of a Field Study in Johnstown, Pa., Based on Births in One Calendar Year, by Emma Duke, p. 45. U. S. Children's Bureau Publication No. 9, Infant Mortality Series No. 3, Washington, 1915.

"A grouping of babies according to the income of the father shows the greatest incidence of infant deaths where wages are lowest, and the smallest incidence where they are highest, indicating clearly the relation between low wages and ill health and infant deaths.

"For all live babies born in wedlock the infant mortality rate is 130.7. It rises to 255.7 when the father earns less than $521 a year or less than $10 a week, and falls to 84 when he earns $1,200 or more or if his earnings are 'ample.'"

This connection between low earnings of father and high infant death rate persists if we separate native from foreign born.

"In considering the babies of native and of foreign mothers separately . . ., similar variations in mortality rates according to earnings of father are found, although the foreign infant death rate is higher in each group. The foreign are less numerous both actually and relatively in the higher wage groups.

"The foreigners of a given wage group almost always live in a poorer neighborhood than the natives earning the same amount. The foreigners go where they find their own countrymen, most of whom are poor, and hence even those who earn a fair wage find themselves, until they become Americanized, surrounded by poor conditions and an ignorant class of people."[1]

From Montclair, N. J., the following testimony was taken:[2]

"It is obvious that even the care given the baby by its mother often must be offset by the evils resulting from an income insufficient for the family's needs, since a low income frequently must involve undesirable housing accommodations, an overworked mother, insufficient nourishment for mother and child, and lack of competent medical advice. . . . In Montclair the infant mortality rate was approximately two and one-half times as high among families where the income was less than $12 a week as among families where the income was $23 a week or more."

From Manchester, N. H., the following evidence is obtained:

"Babies born in the homes of unskilled workers where earnings are small face greater hazards than those in more fortunate circumstances. When the 1,564 live-born babies included in this study are grouped according to father's earnings, it is found that among the babies in the lowest-earnings group infant deaths are more than four times as frequent as in the highest-earnings group. * * *
* * * * * * * * * * * *

"The infant mortality rate shows a marked and almost regular decline as the father's earnings become larger. In the group of babies where the father's earnings are less than $450 per annum the infant mortality rate is 242.9, while in the next group, where the fathers earn from $450 to $549, the rate is 173.6. It rises very slightly in the next class, $550 to $649, namely, to 174.5, and thereafter drops steadily with each advance in economic status. The rate, however,

---

[1] Infant Mortality, Results of a Field Study in Johnstown, Pa., Based on Births in One Calendar Year, by Emma Duke, pp. 46-47. U. S. Children's Bureau Publication No. 9, Infant Mortality Series No. 3, Washington, 1915.
[2] Infant Mortality, Montclair, N. J., A Study of Infant Mortality in a Suburban Community, p. 19. U. S. Children's Bureau Publication No. 11, Infant Mortality Series No. 4.

does not fall below 100 until the father's earnings reach $1,050 or more. Babies whose fathers earn $1,250 and over per annum have a death rate of only 58.3."[1]

Or from Waterbury, Conn.:

"The infant mortality rate for Waterbury for babies whose fathers earned less than $450 during the year following the birth of the baby was 153; the rate very gradually decreased in the next two income groups, but it did not fall below 100 until the group $850 to $1,049 was reached."[2]

And finally from Brockton, Mass.:

"The infant mortality rate was highest (132.2) for the earnings group $650 to $849, and lowest for the group $1,050 and over (65.5). Contrary to the findings for other cities, the mortality rates for the earnings groups under $550 and $550 to $649 were considerably lower than for the group $650 to $849. Two explanations for this peculiar showing may be advanced: First, the groups are comparatively small, and consequently may have been considerably influenced by exceptionally favorable conditions in the year selected; second, the earnings as reported in the lowest earnings group do not always reflect the family's standard of living. The relatively high percentage of stillbirths in the lowest earnings groups may be significant in connection with the low mortality rates."[3]

Another testimony to the soundness of these estimates could be found, if we desired to learn the truth, in the records of the juvenile courts and of our truant schools. From the homes of the "poor" and the "very poor," from the low, inadequate income groups, come the processions of children, boys and girls, in whose behalf this Conference is gathered.

A question may be raised with reference to the effect of the war on the conditions described. On this subject, others more closely connected with wide inquiries into changes in price and in wage levels will speak. The testimony of the social agencies to which reference has been made is to the effect that wage levels have not changed with rise of prices. A great employer in a city in which an estimate similar to that I have described was made, said that only one-fourth of his employees earned enough to enjoy life at the level fixed by the social workers.

Miss Nesbitt is willing to be quoted on this subject in the following words:[4]

---

[1] Infant Mortality, Results of a Field Study in Manchester, N. H., Based on Births in One Year, by Beatrice Sheets Duncan and Emma Duke, pp. 38, 44. U. S. Children's Bureau Publication No. 20, Infant Mortality Series No. 6, Washington, 1917.
[2] Infant Mortality, Results of a Field Study in Waterbury, Conn., Based on Births in One Year, by Estelle B. Hunter, p. 64. U. S. Children's Bureau Publication No. 29, Infant Mortality Series No. 7, Washington, 1918.
[3] Infant Mortality, Results of a Field Study in Brockton, Mass., Based on Births in One Year, by Mary V. Dempsey, pp. 31-32. U. S. Children's Bureau Publication No. 37, Infant Mortality Series No. 8, Washington, 1919.
[4] Dictated by her in private interview, May 3, 1919.

"The increase in the cost of living has, so far as my observation goes, been universal since the beginning of the war, and has risen in smaller communities almost as high as in the cities. For example, the cost of staple food materials, including milk, and the cost of clothing are practically the same in the smaller towns of northern Illinois as in Chicago.

"Where workers have been engaged in industries directly affected by the war, there has unquestionably been a large increase in wages. This increase is by no means universal. In communities where there are no war industries, wages are very little higher than before the war. In the larger cities, there are large groups of workers whose wage has not been materially increased."

From such facts as these, a few conclusions may be drawn:

1. The community can learn if it will what the cost of child care is, and this knowledge will be in the possession not only of those who in the past have seemed to profit from the imperfect adjustment between wage levels and human needs, but of the great mass of the wageworkers who will not much longer acquiesce in that maladjustment. They will have knowledge from which they can conclude justly whether the bill if duly presented can be met by industry. The profits taken by the employer will be compared with the gains secured by the workers, and an ampler share in life made possible by higher pay as well as larger share of power in the future control of the product of industry will be demanded.

2. With wider knowledge and greater exactness of estimate will come a wider demand that we judge our common life by our conduct rather than by our professions. As the Chicago committee has said, a level can be fixed below which no one should be allowed to fall. The fixing of that minimum and the giving to all the opportunity to remain on or above that level; the fixing of an adequate economic level maintained by the earning capacity of the father, thus enabling the mother to specialize in the exercise of the maternal function; including in the program native born, both white and black, and foreign born—this is a possible goal for us to seek. Having seen the possibility, we can "do no other" than seek it as a matter of national honor. In fixing this minimum and in raising it as we learn of other elements of cost not now included may be found a field for friendly rivalry. When once quantitative adequacy has been realized, qualitative value may receive greater attention and the peculiar contributions of our variously endowed groups may enrich and beautify the fabric of our national life. Until quantitative adequacy has been attained, however, attention to variety and richness of life must be in considerable measure postponed. But by so much the more is both our present and our future community life impoverished.

COST OF LIVING [1]

By MISS FLORENCE NESBITT
Institute Instructor in Dietetics, American Red Cross

It is practically impossible to avoid the subject of family income when talking about child welfare, because it lies so close to the very root of all work for the interests of the child. If the income of the father is not enough to cover the necessities of life, does not permit a minimum normal standard of living, then either mother and children are driven into industry, and home life is neglected; or else the standard is lowered, and we have bad housing, under-nourishment, and all the other hideous results of poverty.

It is a difficult thing to give any absolutely definite figures for an income below which we do not dare see families fall. These last few years, since the rise in cost of living has focused so much attention upon the subject, have, however, given us increasing confidence that we are able to make a fairly accurate estimate of this sort. When approaching the problem from different points of view, we find that our results when trying to estimate the necessary cost of a normal standard of living closely approximate each other. For example, the estimate which the Bureau of Labor based on a large volume of statistics as to what people really do with their income, differs very little from the estimates of those of us who start from exactly the opposite end, trying to define the elements of a normal standard, and then attempting to discover the cost of maintaining such a standard.

In Chicago, those who have been working on the problem recently figure that it costs approximately $1,500 a year to buy the essentials for maintaining the average family of five—father, mother and three children—at what we might consider a normal standard. That means, of course, a minimum wage of about five dollars a day for the working man.

Last fall I made an estimate of the minimum cost of living for a self-supporting family in Cleveland. The Bureau of Labor had at that time just completed their estimate which placed the cost of living for ship builders' families at something under $1,500 per year. My estimate was almost the same. I asked two managers of Cleveland factories how that compared with the wages of their men. Each one

[1]Delivered at the Chicago Child Welfare Regional Conference, May 19, 1919.

said that not more than twenty-five per cent of their people earned as much as that.

We are so in the habit of thinking about the rather abnormally high wages some people have received since the beginning of the war, that we jump to the conclusion that the whole body of wage earners are earning a great deal more than they are. When it really comes down to figures, we find that there are large groups of workers who have been affected very little by these raises. In the isolated communities where the war industries have not penetrated, there is no increase in wages that even begins to cope with the increased cost of living. If we could raise wages to meet the increase in the cost of living we would be on solid ground, but there has never been a time when the ordinary wage of untrained labor covered adequate living. In 1914, when the unskilled wage was about two dollars a day, it took at least $75 a month to cover the every-day requirements of decent living.

So there seem only three ways out of the difficulty: The cost of living must come down; or there must be a nationalization of financial responsibility which will relieve the individual family of a portion of the cost which they must now bear; or wages must rise to cover the cost of living; so that every child may have his adequate opportunity for normal development.

THE CHILD'S HOME

By MRS. EVA WHITING WHITE
Elizabeth Peabody House, Boston, Massachusetts

This is a particularly opportune time in which to discuss the question of the child's home because every citizen in the United States is now a stockholder in certain housing projects that strike a new note in town and city dwelling. From one end of the country to the other, speakers, writers, chambers of commerce, and public press are bringing home to the American public the significance of the housing enterprises that were undertaken in order to meet the emergency needs of the war period. It may be said without exaggeration that the communities developed by the United States Housing Corporation and the Emergency Fleet Corporation will stand as typifying a recognition of a citizenship rooted in progressive family standards and deepened local ties. Along the Atlantic Coast, and along the Pacific, bordering the Great Lakes, and in the South, are areas where for the first time, comparatively speaking, the workingman has not been disdained in "bricks and mortar"; where artistry has entered into the structural plan; and where the housing problem has been recognized not only as a question of the house, but as concerned also with community life in all its phases. It has been claimed that we cannot be said to have failed to build up wholesome industrial sections, because we have not tried to build them. Heretofore, we have adopted a system of supremely haphazard growth and development which has permitted real estate speculation to such an extent that thousands of lives have been handicapped.

Now, however, we have made a beginning; we have brought complete communities into being—communities of delightful single, double, and row houses, situated on attractively laid out streets and surrounded by green and trees; houses that combine comfort, convenience, and coziness. These houses in the majority of cases either surround or border upon a square or section which includes the store district, the community building which is meant to meet social and recreation needs, the motion picture house, and the church sites. In terms of childhood, compare the advantages of a boy or girl brought up in such surroundings with those of a child living in nearby industrial sections. For example, compare a child living in Buckman, Pennsylvania, which is one of the most attractive communities built by the

Emergency Fleet Corporation a few miles out of Chester, Pennsylvania, with a child living in certain sections of Chester.

If it is true that the home is the foundation of social improvement (and the evidence so far is overwhelmingly in favor of the home), and if we believe that the moral and intellectual fibre of the next generation depends upon home conditions, then certainly there is but one course open to the sincere citizen, and that is to do everything humanly possible to maintain the three great gains in regard to housing that have come out of the war. The first concerns housing as a factor in industrial efficiency. In order to meet the demands of output in manufacturing war material, "Big Business" did everything possible in the way of factory management and the study and regulation of factory processes. It was seen, however, that other factors entered into efficiency; that in order to get the maximum output for given energy good housing was a necessity, so that men might be reinvigorated rather than enervated, cheered rather than depressed; it was seen also that with good housing should go social organization; otherwise neither the men nor their families were contented. The home in a community setting became of prime importance.

This fact should be kept in the forefront of public thought. Until industrial workers in cities are protected as to their living conditions, and until manufacturing and producing centers are established that make life worth the living, efforts in support of improved industrial management, efforts to better fit man to task become almost if not quite an absurdity. That vital force which comes from a sense of permanency and comfort and from a sense of the security of home ties is the plus element and the most telling of industrial efficiency factors. The war brought this out. Peace must crystallize the truth of it in an accepted civic code such that not only shall protective housing laws appear on every city and state statute book, but the movement for better housing shall sweep beyond protective law to demand something more than a shelter, to demand a home.

The second great gain of the war in regard to housing has been the recognition of the necessity of Federal aid. The Government must not withdraw now. In a matter so fundamental as that of the American standard of living there should be Federal oversight of community development as well as monetary aid and Federal initiative in the stimulation of community housing enterprises. No more important matters are to face the citizenship of the United States in the next few months than the establishment of a bureau of housing in the Department of Labor, and the action of Congress on a bill which will be presented, the object of which will be to establish Home Loan Banks so that money may be obtained at nominal rates of interest by the individual home builder. Everyone who believes in action and not in passive good will in such a vital question as that of housing should get a copy of the tentative draft of a bill designed to enable building and loan associations to increase their resources and aid more effectively in financing construction work in their respective localities. This bill can be obtained through the United States Department of Labor, Information and Education Service.

Further, private organizations can do no better thing than to back up an educational campaign on the question of the home and the "Own Your Own Home Movement." The way for home owning must be cleared by local safeguards of city planning, architectural design, consideration of cooperative buying as applied to building material, and copartnership in the operation of enterprises. Every social, educational, and fraternal society should have a series of meetings on home building and home owning led by experts and run on the forum plan of free discussion. There should be clear thinking and public action based on an intelligent appreciation of all that is at stake in regard to the conservation of human energy and the preservation of life, particularly child life. The time is ripe for this. Housing is coming to its own in the public consciousness.

The third great gain that has come from the lessons of the last two years is a quickened sense of personal and social ties. When men were removed from the family circle, when the network of local ties was pierced, that framework which sustains us all and the lack of which leaves us bewildered and alone brought an appreciation of dependence on community forces. Military training had its place. Military strategy had its place. Equally important, even in a state of war, was the weaving of civilian social relationships. Is not the permanency of a democracy largely dependent on the closest possible development of relationships of good fellowship; on the thought exchange between man and man and the welding together of home and home for the protection and encouragement of the young? Surely homes that see themselves in relationship to other homes; that give of their best for good schools; that insist on opportunities for wholesome recreation; and that set a standard of vital interest in community affairs create a situation in which the generations that are coming on cannot but catch the altruism of citizenship based on action for the common good, to say nothing of the assets of health and mental power which proper living conditions always safeguard.

In spite of the hopefulness of the housing situation at present, permanent protection for the home will not be gained by thinking for one moment that someone else will look after housing if we do not. The forces that have held back housing legislation are so entrenched, and the task seems so intricate and overwhelming, that the patient, persistent, constant effort of all is needed. On the one hand there is open opposition to improving conditions, and on the other a kind of apathy due to hopelessness. It is hard to say which is the worse. Then there is a curious kind of contradiction which enters in. Persons will affirm most positively that our widest circles of affairs—business enterprise, matters of government—are not ends in themselves and can be considered as contributing to a given age only in so far as the individual is benefited and the home circle protected and enriched. Yet, in the next breath, these very people will hedge at facing squarely the needs of better housing because someone will lose one or two per cent interest; or, because precedent would be broken, they become suddenly conservative at facing a town layout scheme to forestall bad conditions. Courage and daring are needed, but surely the thought of a happier childhood for thousands of children, to say nothing of the prospect of a lower morbidity and death rate, should furnish these. There is nothing mysterious about good housing. The details of building so as to get light and air and to give privacy and convenience, are in the main solved to a point where it is known that a certain kind of home will safeguard health. Minimum standards at least have been worked out and should be adopted and enforced in every civilized community. The longer the bringing in of the era of improved housing is delayed, the more does society and the state pay the bill in the broken lives of many a man and woman. A parable of the tenements tells its own story. "A little girl living in a court in an eastern city planted a window box in all hope at the beginning of summer. She nursed her seedlings with great care and was elated when the first shoots appeared. From day to day she watched her plants and vines grow, but with each day they grew weaker and more sickly, without symmetry or beauty. Finally they died altogether in the vitiated atmosphere. Yet the child was expected to develop into womanhood under precisely the same conditions."

The moral effect of bad housing is not often as apparent as the physical. It is said, however, that two-thirds of the delinquent children come from homes that no town or city should permit to exist. Overcrowding tends to break down nicety of manner and normal restraint. A young girl cannot be blamed for meeting her friends in the dance hall, park, or street, when home means the kind of tenement that exists in nearly all our cities and towns. Leaving aside all the problems of taxation and land values involved in discussing housing, dark rooms can be eliminated; basement dwellings forbidden; adequate water supply insisted on; homes can be kept in repair and free from rubbish, and in a sanitary condition. Herding can be stopped.

Now, the building of attractive houses and the development of well-planned communities cannot be advocated without taking into account dollars and cents. This leads to a consideration of costs, rentals, wages. At the present time the situation is acute because in nearly every section of the country there is a shortage of homes owing to the fact that in the main commercial building operations were halted during the war. As a result, rents have risen according to the old law of supply and demand, and, since prices of materials continue to be high and uncertain, the construction of homes is still held up. The present cost of materials, combined with the general uncertainty of the financial market and loan rates and the dearth of accommodations mentioned above, has brought about a situation which makes government aid essential at this time. A standardized family budget provides that one-fifth only of a man's income should go for rent. Clearly this is enough if a family is not to be stinted in the way of food, proper clothing, and provision for the education of the children and for safeguarding old age. It is affirmed that at the present rates of labor and cost of material new homes cannot be constructed to rent at prices within reach of the unskilled laborer.

Clearly, then, as a matter of public policy certain problems should be immediately attacked. First is a consideration of lessening the tax on homes; second, the elimination of speculation in building; third, the protection of equities so that an investment will not be lost as the result of depreciation of values when a home district gives way to business enterprise; and fourth, the time is ripe for definitely bringing about the decentralization of industry so that increase of congestion will be stopped. Industrial enterprises should not be encouraged to move into communities until plans are made for housing the people who will come to man them. Otherwise the few gain at the expense of the many. Rents go up. Those who are property owners may gain. Those who pay rent lose, and the community brings upon itself very grave danger of so running up its expenses by the increase of degenerative tendencies that there is an inestimable resultant loss. As to family life, anyone familiar with industrial communities knows of instance after instance where a normal family forced by the lack of housing facilities to live under bad conditions has become subnormal. The father becomes ill. Loss of wages results. Death may follow. The mother may be forced to work. The children are brought up under conditions which are not such as to give them a fair chance. Conversely there is the family that has lived under bad tenement conditions with a history of illness and loss of ambition that after moving into a tenement with sunshine and neatness comes to its own and swings into self-respect and prosperity. Now, if houses cannot be constructed for the unskilled, then let us meet the need for the skilled, and by increasing accommodations take the inflation out of second and third and fourth rate property and thereby permit the family to raise its standards and to better its living conditions.

The time is ripe in America for the development of cooperative enterprise. New York is becoming interested in the cooperative apartment house. The copartnership housing plan which has been developed in England should be studied and experimented with here. If, as in England, the Government should loan part of the capital stock the possibility of developing such a community would be materially increased. Under the co-partnership scheme houses are let at ordinary rentals to persons who own a certain number of shares. Dividends on capital are limited to five per cent. Profits remaining after the payment of the current expenses, interest, and amortization charges on mortgages and loans, and dividends on capital, are divided among the copartnership tenants in proportion to the shares paid in. Houses are leased on 99-year leases as a rule, so that a man is not necessarily held to one spot, as he can dispose of his shares of stock. Vacancies have been rare in England as it is to the advantage of all the shareholders to do what they can to rent property so as to maintain the balance of profits. Upkeep and repair costs have been less than in the case of the average run of property for the same reason; and losses from nonpayment of rent are brought down to a minimum because a man's shares are taken in case rent is not paid. Better accommodations can be obtained for less money. The community safeguards itself and controls its neighborhood enterprises. There is freedom from loss if a person moves. The "unearned increment" accrues to the tenants. If homes could be freed from the deadening effects of rent without value received, one of the great economic burdens would be removed and the insidious circle of bad housing, loss of energy and ambition, ineffectiveness at work, and the "what's-the-use" attitude at home would be broken into. Instead there would be the self-respecting householder; the alert cooperative citizen; the parent who radiates hope and sees before his children not an existence of dull gray, but a future of satisfaction in taking part in the activities of their time.

If the question of rent can be adjusted our next consideration is that of the apportionment of the rest of the family income. Children must have good food. They must be well dressed. They must have the opportunity of training for special talents. Cost of living at the present time is high. Wages are not keeping pace in many occupations. Even in ordinary times the mother has a complicated task indeed in working out her family budget and in running her household so as to live within that budget and maintain the health of her family and provide for their needed change of thought through recreation. Exactly as the home must be protected by eliminating bad housing so the necessities of life must be brought within range of our citizenship. Superneeds can take care of themselves. Increased production of foodstuffs; more economical distribution; the cooperative store; the community kitchen; training in the art of home management—all these challenge our genius and enterprise. For the sake of the American child our entire range of public activity should be gauged by the way in which basic needs are met and by the way in which labor is assured an opportunity for work and an income such that there shall be a margin of saving for security.

Incorporated in the ideals of the race is the ideal of home. Into the ideal of the home enter all those factors of home-making on the part of mothers and fathers which create a background that enables children to grow up true to themselves, stimulates them to carry on the work of the world, and leads them into the wonders of life. The home is still the great educational institution. Every dollar spent on schooling is undercut by bad environmental conditions created by the home and is multiplied many times over by the right kind of home standards. Not only should homes be well constructed and healthful, but beauty should enter in. The family circle should carry within itself the many-sided social obligations of person to person that establish in a child growing up under such influences that involuntary response to the obligations met in the natural relationships of life which means high-mindedness, courtesy, and appreciation of self in relation to others. The physical aspect of the home is only one phase of our subject. The management of the home and the creation of the indefinable atmosphere which means the real home is the second factor. Home management is a science. Moreover, a hearthstone becomes truly a hearthstone only as a result of deep religious sense, ethical outlook, and cultural appreciation. Central in educational procedure should be home training for both boys and girls, and no system of public education is standardized that does not offer extension courses in order that housewives may take advantage of the best thought as to expenditure, household tasks, and child care. Our schools should be imbedded in the home life of their communities. Parents and teachers should know one another, should appreciate their dependence on one another, and should work as one in the educational enterprise. If every boy and girl who is graduated from our schools and higher institutions of learning saw clearly the effect of so-called politics on the home and the result of business exploitation when fathers and mothers are sacrificed to industrial competition, there would be far less need for repressive legislation. If our young people were trained in the principle of thrift, money would give greater values. If they thought through to the things that really count for happiness and well-being, which, after all, in spite of the great variety of modern activities, are very few, greater personal poise would result, as well as greater response to those fundamental direct relationships that have their basis in the family circle and the loyalties of friendship. It is a matter for most serious consideration that with all the gains that have been made so many communities still do little to prepare their young people to meet the responsibilities of the home and the rearing of children.

As trustees of the welfare of our children, our citizens are not living up to American ideals unless they make every effort to secure for each boy and girl the right to a well-ordered home, the best of schooling, free playtime, and the privilege of taking part in the work of the world on a basis of equitable industrial adjustment.

THE LEISURE OF THE CHILD

By L. H. WEIR

War Camp Community Service, Washington, D. C.

and

MISS ABBIE CONDIT

Playground and Recreation Association of America

I shall present to you a statement of the minimum standards which the National Playground and Recreation Association of America feels are necessary to provide properly for the leisure of the children in American communities. This is discussed almost entirely from the point of view of public provision, nothing being said of minimum standards that should be provided through private agencies.

The facts which have become significant as a result of the war, showing that a third of the drafted men were rejected because of physical unfitness, have from the purely physical point of view made it necessary for America to ask herself the question: "How far is the nation responsible for this condition? Has America failed to provide its men in childhood with the essentials for health?" Reports which have come from Great Britain and France and other foreign countries, as well as from America, prove that when, as a result of war pressure, less emphasis was laid on proper recreational activities, there was a great increase in juvenile delinquency and an alarming growth in crime on the part of the youthful population of the countries, as well as a decrease in physical fitness.

That there is a very definite connection between recreation and health, and between recreation and juvenile delinquency, is an incontrovertible fact. In many sections of cities in which playgrounds have been established it has been demonstrated through tests and examinations that in a surprisingly short time a higher degree of health and increased physical efficiency have resulted. The records of the police courts in such districts point to a distinct falling off in the number of boys arrested for misdemeanors. The remarkable progress of the recreation movement in America, showing an expenditure of millions of dollars by municipalities, appropriated not because of a theory, but because it has been demonstrated to these cities that better health and better citizenship will result if the energy of children is directed in the proper channels; the passage of compulsory laws for physical

THE ECONOMIC AND SOCIAL BASIS

education in a number of cities providing for a certain amount of directed physical exercise and play each day as a part of the school curriculum; and the fact that France and England have passed national physical education laws—these are all significant of the important place which recreation has come to occupy in the life of the child, and the recognition which has been given it.

STANDARDS OF PHYSICAL EFFICIENCY

If it is true, as authorities are agreed, that the child must have opportunity for wholesome recreation if he is to develop along normal lines and become physically efficient, what are the minimum standards of recreation which must be maintained?

Organized recreation as a necessary part of the child's development is so new a conception as compared with the health, education, and work standards applied to child life that practically no effort has hitherto been made to establish minimum standards for the leisuretime activities of the child. A possible exception to this lies in the step taken by the Playground and Recreation Association of America, which through a committee of experts, has adopted tests for boys and girls representing the minimum physical standards which boys and girls should reach if they are to be physically fit. The tests for boys are briefly outlined as follows:

The Athletic Badge Test for boys:
First Test—12 years of age.
Pull up (Chinning) ....4 times
Standing broad jump ....5 ft. 9 in.
60-yard dash ....8 3-5 seconds

Second Test—13 years of age and over.
Pull up (Chinning) ....6 times
Standard broad jump ....6 ft. 6 in.
60-yard dash ....8 seconds
Or 100-yard dash ....14 seconds

Third Test—high school boys.
Pull up (Chinning) ....9 times
Running high jump ....4 ft. 4 in.
220-yard run ....28 seconds

NECESSITY OF PLAY AND PHYSICAL TRAINING

In order to attain these standards, which have been demonstrated to represent minimum standards, a child should have physical training and games in the school, and in addition an opportunity for wholesome directed outdoor play in his leisure time. Dr. Henry S. Curtis, one of America's foremost authorities on playgrounds and recreation, has said: "The first requisite of any adequate system is that it must furnish play to every child every day. This needs no discussion. We all realize that outdoor air and exercise are essential to the physical, social, and intellectual welfare of children. They cannot be really well and grow up into vigorous men and women unless they are getting an hour or two of such activity every day."

Dr. Curtis further suggests that play is the first form of education, and should have its largest place in the early years of life, since there is no later time when physical achievement means so much to the child as it does in the period before twelve years of age. His experience leads him to feel that there should be two or three hours a day of organized games during the first few years of the elementary school, and this should diminish with advancing years to a minimum of one hour a day "which is about as little as adults can get along with and maintain vigorous health."

The majority of compulsory physical education State laws providing for compulsory physical education which have been passed in America stipulate that twenty minutes a day shall be the minimum time devoted to physical training. In a number of the laws it is definitely stated that this shall be the minimum and that a longer period is desirable. A large percentage of the physical unfitness disclosed by the draft might have been prevented if the men had had proper physical education in their youth. At least 30 per cent of physical unfitness, according to Dr. Eugene Lyman Fisk, Medical Director, Life Extension Institute, is due to poor general physical condition, remediable by proper nutrition, physical training and personal hygiene.

ORGANIZED PLAY

Everyone is agreed, however, that the child's physical exercise cannot be limited to physical training in the schools. There must be provided for him in his free time the opportunity for well-directed play which will supplement physical training in the schools, and at the same time give a guidance to his energy that makes for citizenship. A large number of considerations must enter into any discussion of the minimum requirements of organized play, and a set of standards which will hold for one community may be ill adapted to communities and conditions of another city. If a child is to have play, however, there are certain requisites which are essential in any community. Of these a place to play is perhaps the first consideration.

Play Space

In determining a standard for the amount of play space necessary, the following factors must be considered:

1. **Distribution of Playgrounds.**—The distribution of playgrounds has much to do with their utilization. For example, two acres of

ground divided in four parts and distributed in congested districts of a large city would do many times more good for small children than the same two acres on the outskirts of a city twelve miles from where the children are. Local conditions must determine how playgrounds are to be distributed if they are to meet distinct needs. The population of a city, its juvenile population, spaces available, their suitability, and the distance children must go are among the determining factors.

As a result of a study made by Henry V. Hubbard, Assistant Professor of Landscape Architecture at Harvard University, it has been pointed out that children under six ought not to be obliged to go more than one-fourth of a mile to their playground, and these playgrounds should be located in such a manner as to make it unnecessary for children to cross car tracks. The average effective radius for children from six to twelve years of age is about one-half mile, and for children from twelve to seventeen who cannot afford carfare, three-quarters of a mile. Boys will go a longer distance than this to reach a baseball field. Experiences differ in the various cities regarding the distances which children will go, but the average effective radii stated of one-quarter, one-half, and three-quarter miles are conservative and represent the minimum of service which a city should offer in the distribution of its playgrounds.

2. Size of Plot.—The only solution for a minimum playground is its maximum use, by having the ground used each hour by different groups and by putting the emphasis on games requiring little space. One acre used six times a day is equal to six acres used once. If there are as many as six hundred children it will not be possible for a playground to be much smaller than an acre. Many authorities feel that there ought not to be more than three hundred children using a playground of an acre. An acre is the minimum size for a school playground according to Dr. Curtis' estimate. For more than 500 children, about 40 square feet per child should be added to an acre playground.

To give the child the ideal expression and opportunity it would be necessary to have for baseball, football, hockey, and skating, four acres; for tennis, two acres; for indoor baseball, one acre; for basket ball, one-fourth acre; for volley ball, one-half acre; for running track, jumping pits, and similar apparatus, one-fourth acre. This makes eight acres of playground for a thousand pupils, but all these activities could be carried on in five acres by playing less football and tennis.

3. Age of Children.—On this depends the use which will be made of the playground. It is possible to handle more children per acre when they are under ten years of age. Little children will use swings, sand boxes, teeters, and similar devices, which, if correctly placed,

do not occupy much space. The games of children up to ten years of age are largely group games, not the real team games which require more space.

4. Number of Children Likely to Use Playground at One Time.—There is always a rising and falling tide of children on the playground during the day. In judging the amount of play space necessary, the amount of the "heaviest load" must be considered, but administrative devices can sometimes be used to distribute the "load." From the playground standpoint, this is the big contribution of the Gary plan of organizing.

5. Density of Population per Acre and Density Range.—The number of children using a playground at any one time is much smaller than the number of children who are served by the playground, and the number of children benefited may be, therefore, two to six times the average daily attendance. A neighborhood may be adequately provided with playground space even if it does not have enough to care for all the children of the neighborhood at one time.

Mr. Rowland Haynes, formerly field secretary of the Playground and Recreation Association of America, from his study of recreation in a number of cities, became convinced that where the density of population exceeded 35 or 50 to the acre, 80 per cent of the children would be playing away from home, because sufficient space was not provided around their own homes.

From Minneapolis comes the statement that there should be one acre of little children's playgrounds for each 15,000 population; one acre devoted to the uses of the neighborhood center for every 5,000 population; and one acre for grounds for special sports for each 10,000 population. This statement affirms that the playground for little children should be at least one acre in area; a play field from two to ten acres; a neighborhood center from two to four acres; and a ground for special sports from two to ten acres.

6. Groups Served.—While the number of children in a neighborhood who need a playground varies according to the density of population and the density range, the size of the group who need and will use the playground depends on other conditions, such as the home habits of the children, the length of time the playground has been in use, and the amount of confidence which the playground leaders have inspired in the residents of the neighborhood.

Equipment

The equipment provided on a playground varies greatly with the amount of money available. Where funds are limited, wise playground officials will expend them for leadership rather than for a large amount of material equipment. There are, however, certain kinds of apparatus which, according to minimum standards, should be included in any playground. These include a sand box, swings, slides, and an adequate supply of game equipment, such as basket ball, volley ball, base ball, bean bags, and similar supplies. Such supplies are considered by many playground workers to be more important than fixed apparatus. As the value of teeters and giant strides is debatable, they may be omitted from the consideration of minimum standards along the line of equipment. Boys' outdoor gymnasium equipment, like many other kinds of apparatus, while desirable, is not essential.

Some sort of shelter, however inexpensive, should be provided on a playground, as should toilet facilities and drinking water.

Leadership

The provision of space to play and a minimum amount of apparatus does not complete the responsibility of the city toward its children. If the utilization of the play facilities is to be made a factor in child life there must be play leadership to insure such use of the apparatus as will make the child derive the greatest benefit from it, to teach the child to play the games that will mean most in his development, and to give the right direction to instincts which, if undirected, may lead the child to the juvenile court. Innumerable instances of splendidly equipped playgrounds little used because they lack the vital element of leadership, while nearby alleys and streets were crowded with children, have demonstrated beyond doubt the primary importance of leadership.

In any consideration of minimum standards it is important to determine what is the largest number of children which one play leader can care for properly. This depends to a large extent, according to Mr. Ernst Hermann, who has had many years experience in playground work, on the amount of self-government which can be developed among the children. This whole question of the number of leaders needed for a definite number of children, he maintains, is a matter of teaching and developing self-management by gradual, persistent, and never-ending organization. The basis of such organization must be the formation of the children into groups or gangs of from eight to twelve members, with a gang leader self-selected and self-propagating, as in the old neighborhood type of gang. The cleverest director can direct continuously only the number of children he can personally entertain. This number cannot exceed sixty children for a certain length of time. If, however, the leader can imbue each small group with the meaning of real leadership and real sportsmanship, he can in a year's time supervise from 500 to 600 children. Mr. Hermahn estimates that with adequate space, layout, and equipment, and with an organization of self-management, the number of individuals under each leader can be multiplied from six to ten times within a year.

There are few leaders, however, qualified to develop such a form of organization, which represents more ideal conditions than usually exist on a playground. The experimentation which such a plan involves would in the great majority of instances probably result in loss of time and in a failure to provide even the minimum amount of leadership necessary. Under the right leadership it might be worked out successfully.

In contrast to this opinion it is interesting to note the statement of another authority, Mr. George E. Johnson, of Harvard University, who maintains that under the most favorable conditions there is a much smaller limit to the teacher's capacity to handle children successfully than Mr. Hermann's outline sets. Many types of play, as, for example, dramatic, need much more intimate leadership than can be given by one person to 500 or 600 children at the same time, though organization and grouping can greatly extend the leader's capacity. Mr. Johnson gives as the maximum number for real leadership the following:

Ages.	INDOORS		OUTDOORS	
	With Equipment.	Without Equipment.	With Equipment.	Without Equipment.
0-2	10	..	10	..
4-6	30	20	40	30
7-9	30	20	50	40
10-12	40	25	50	40
13-15	40	25	50	40

There are certain requirements in leadership which affect even the minimum standard. Among these are the following:

1. The poorer the stationary and movable equipment, and the less effective the organization of the space and equipment, the more leaders will be required and the more vivid and inspiring must be the personal leadership provided.

2. Every play center must have a director in charge of the entire ground. As a minimum standard, no director should be expected single-handed to direct the activities of more than 75 children, unless such a system of organization as has been suggested can be developed. Where there are several hundred children on the playground it is absolutely impossible for one director to handle the situation even on a minimum efficiency basis, and assistants, or such specialists as athletic directors or physical training directors, must be provided.

3. In any system where more than one playground is involved there must be in addition to the directors of the individual grounds a recreation superintendent, supervisor, or secretary, whose task it is to have general oversight of the work, to be responsible for its development,

coordination, and enlargement, and for seeing that play facilities and activities are provided the child during the entire year. No work can be carried on effectively without such a responsible head.

4. There must be a governing body, either a recreation commission, department, or board, to have general charge of the work; or if local conditions make it advisable to have the work conducted by an existing department of the municipality, it should be administered by the school board, park board, department of public works, or some other municipal department. The work should be supported by municipal funds.

Kind of Play and Its Duration

Directed play which stimulates the child into diversified activities of varying degrees of physical and nervous intensity must be handled with great caution, and even under these conditions no two children will be equally benefited. The spontaneous play of children up to nine years of age with an occasional short period of directed play is probably the best kind of play. Indoors the periods must have frequent intermissions of free play. During ordinary school recesses the average child should have from ten to fifteen minutes of vigorous play. According to Mr. George E. Johnson, this period of play should not be less than half an hour.

Active games which demand severe physical and nervous application must be very short indeed, and vigorous and quiet games should be alternated. After the child becomes nine years of age, periods of active play naturally grow longer. But there should still be more or less regular intermissions. Team games should be stimulated among children over ten years of age, and special emphasis should be laid on the development of team games among girls. Each child should be given the opportunity to be a member of some team.

CONCLUSIONS

Any decision regarding minimum standards for the leisure time activities of the child must necessarily be conditioned by the age of the children, local conditions as they relate to play space available, the density of population, layout and equipment of playground, the system of education in the community, and many other considerations which would immediately suggest themselves. A few tentative and very general conclusions may be drawn regarding some of the irreducible minimum standards which should prevail:

1. Irreducible minimum standards for the leisure time of children require that there should be no less than two hours of organized play for every child outside of school hours every day throughout the entire year. The municipality should be responsible for the establishment of playgrounds and play centers financed from public funds raised by taxation.

2. While it is not essential for a city to provide playground space on the accepted basis of the minimum standards of thirty square feet per child, sufficient to enable all the children of a city to play under leadership at one time, there must be opportunity furnished whereby all children shall play under leadership at certain periods of not less than two hours. In communities in which the Gary plan or some modification of it forms the basis of the educational system, such play will be a part of the regular school curriculum.

3. There should be a playground within an effective radius of one-quarter of a mile for children under six years, one-half of a mile for children over six, and baseball fields within the radius of one mile. The size of the playground should be determined by the density of population, number of children to be served, the activities conducted, and equipment provided. An acre for 500 children is the smallest possible space which should be provided; when the same playground must be used for little children and for older boys and girls, the space should be divided. For the most part no attempt should be made to play games requiring a great deal of space on this general ground, but opportunity for such games should be provided in an athletic field containing about six acres, and providing for baseball, football, tennis, and similar activities.

4. The minimum time for play and physical education in schools should be 30 minutes per day.

5. Where lack of funds makes it necessary to choose between a large amount of equipment and adequate leadership, the funds should go into the salaries of trained leaders.

6. Every playground must have one director in general charge of the ground. There should be sufficient leadership so that each play leader will have not more than 75 children under his immediate direction at one time. Minimum standards must permit of constructive play and represent something more than an attempt to keep children from injuring themselves on apparatus. There should be a supervisor or superintendent in charge of the work during the entire year, under a governing board of control.

7. Minimum equipment should include swings, a sand box, slides, and possibly teeters, a giant stride, and outdoor gymnasium equipment. Where equipment is limited there must be increased emphasis on leadership and a liberal quantity of such game supplies as basket balls, baseballs, bean bags, etc. These supplies are even more important than fixed apparatus. Each playground should have some kind of a shelter, toilet facilities, and drinking water.

8. Active play should be carefully directed, and quiet and vigorous games should alternate. Every child who is old enough should have an opportunity to engage in team games, and great emphasis should be laid on team games for girls.

STANDARDS FOR CHILDREN'S PLAY

By JOSEPH LEE
President, War Camp Community Service, Washington, D. C.

Play for grown people is recreation—the renewal of life. For children it is growth, the gaining of life. The problem of children's play therefore is the problem of whether they shall grow up at all, and full opportunity for children's play is the first thing democracy will provide when it shall have truly been established. To state a complete set of minimum requirements would take a long time, but I want to point out some of them that are in danger of being overlooked.

I. The first requirement for the play of the little child is a mother. To him his mother is at once instigator, audience, playmate, playground, and apparatus. If his own mother is dead, he must have another to take her place. There are plenty of women spiritually dying for lack of children and children spiritually dying for lack of mothers. The two must be brought together. A mother is of course of no use to the child when he is locked up in a room and she is working in a factory. By having a mother I mean having one who has time to play a mother's part.

II. The next requirement of the child's play is a home, a place where he can have his own things to play with, his own place to keep them, and someone to share with him and to be interested in what he does. More than half of our child wreckage is due to broken homes, and the disaster to their play life is in great part to blame.

III. Another essential to the child from a very early age is a child-community with established play traditions, games suitable to his age that are immemorial (they need not be more than three months old to possess this latter attribute), games that are taken for granted as what every fellow does and that afford a variety for different seasons and different temperaments and talents. There may be a play leader behind the group and its tradition, but the group is the living medium for the child. Among the plays in vogue for childen over eleven years of age should be the great team games.

IV. Every child should have the equivalent of a tool house, a woodshed, and an attic in his life, whether provided by the home, the school, or some near neighborhood institution. He must, apart from any systematic teaching, have things to hammer and cut and melt and put together, to burn, color, and otherwise deal with as his soul leads him. He must have all the tools, paints, materials, and suggestive objects that have the power to satisfy him and to lead him on.

V. Every child should go through a period of having pets—anything from white mice to horses will do.

VI. Every child should be encouraged to make collections of stones or bones or leaves or some such objects, and should be shielded from the kind of nature study which is to the love of beasts and flowers what the study of anatomy is to social life.

VII. Every child must grow up in the presence of the arts. He must have painting materials and see people painting about him—sketching and carving and expressing their ideas in form and color. He must have a chance to do these things himself, to see pictures incidentally, not having them too much explained or talked about, but finding them, as a matter of course, part of his experience. The art teaching in the schools must, from the first and always, include making pictures from his own mind and imagination.

He must be brought up in the presence of music and of the familiar use of song and of musical instruments—not forced to play the piano until so sterilized on that side that he will never listen again to a sonata if he can help it, but given a chance to learn on some instrument and sufficient training to see whether that is really for him a form of utterance.

He must hear reading aloud and take part in it, not in the inane and stultifying method of reading something to the teacher which she already knows by heart and does not want to hear, but of bringing in things that he has read and wants others to hear because he likes them, or hearing things that others have found worth listening to.

For these purposes there should be in every neighborhood, whether in the school or library or otherwise, a house of the Muses, or rather, two houses, one for music and one for the other arts. The latter should be full of books and pictures and tables and window seats to go off and read at, with perhaps a little stage. The former should also be beautiful and have pictures and a garden besides its music rooms.

The idea that children should be taught to be useful must be supplemented by the idea, equally important, that they should be prepared to live.

VIII. That children should have all the outdoor play that they can hold is too obvious and now too well known to need restating. For children under six there must be a back yard with a sandbox and other things to play with and a little general playground in the block. For those from six to ten there must be a sufficient playground, properly equipped and with the right leadership, within a quarter of a mile, usually connected with the school; and for the rest below seventeen the effective radius is half a mile. The playgrounds and playhouses must be made beautiful. There must be full opportunity for skating, coasting, and skiing in winter where the climate makes it possible, and for bathing and boating in the summer.

IX. Every child must have a garden in his home, or two months a year of country life. In fact, he ought to have the latter anyway, and will have to arrange it with his mother or his aunt or partner to look after his home garden when he is away.

These are some of the things we shall provide when we learn to take either democracy or education seriously.

RACIAL FACTORS

By PROFESSOR KELLY MILLER
Howard University, Washington, D. C.

In the midst of the living truth, statistical facts are mere dead formulas. Mr. Secretary, when you and your trained staff of statisticians get to Heaven, as of course you will, I trust you will put them to the task of determining how much milk and honey are necessary to maintain an adult saint for ten thousand years. And after you have made your calculation remember that it requires just as much to maintain a black saint as it does to maintain a white one.

Every child born into the world is entitled to a fair chance in the race of life. Assertion and exertion of the individual's best possibilities are the birthright of childhood. All men are endowed by their Creator with the inalienable rights of life, liberty, and the pursuit of happiness. Society, by creating harsh conditions and a benumbing environment, may frustrate the fruition of these rights, and deny the enjoyment thereof, but it cannot take away the inherent claim thereto. They are reaffirmed by Nature every time a new babe is born.

Democracy is the watchword of the hour. There is no creed or caste in the cradle. Nature gives each individual a fair start, though society may deny him a fair chance. The Kingdom of Heaven, as portrayed by its Founder, represents the ideal of human relationship: "Suffer little children to come unto me and forbid them not, for of such is the Kingdom of Heaven." Surely there is no discrimination of race or color in this benediction of childhood. Great, indeed, is the condemnation of that social order whose suppressive regime denies this benediction to the least of these little ones.

There is no Negro problem as such. The Negro today represents the acute phase of the universal human problem. The speciality of his needs calls for a special program of treatment. All the topics listed on the program of these several sessions apply to the Negro child as well as to any other. And just as the afflicted member of the body makes the whole system immediately conscious of its suffering, so the Negro in his social distress focuses the attention of the whole upon his acute situation until his condition has become normal.

It is a wise provision of Nature that when one member suffers the whole body suffers with it. If this were not so, the sound members, secure in their immunity from relative affliction, would pay no heed or solicitous regard to the distressed member, however sore might be its suffering and affliction. But the nervous organization of the body is so knit together that pain in one member afflicts the whole system. Thus, the afflicted part transmits its feeling to the central station, which, in turn, pulsates it to the healthy members as a distress call for succor and relief. This sympathetic response is instantaneous. The Negro is a part of the body politic.

The Negro child is born into an environment of economic and social depression which is calculated to crush the just aspiration of humanity. The stress of economic pressure falls heaviest upon the black race, and is felt most acutely by the black child. Insufficiency of nurture blights the whole nature of the growing child. The Negro has come up through the inheritance of slavery where the child through some good hap was supposed to mature his physical capacities as the animals do. The cultivation of the intellectual, moral, and social qualities which fit one for a democratic order found little encouragement in a regime which exploited the black child merely for his animal and mechanical powers. A half century of partial freedom with imperfect provision and facilities is hardly sufficient to overcome the heavy handicap of these traditions. The Negro still loiters at the outer edge of industry and constitutes the left-over man in our economic calculations. He is the last considered for appointment and the first for discharge. The hard exactions of a livelihood make such heavy demands upon father and mother that insufficient time and strength are left for the proper care and rearing of the offspring. The Negro woman must become a wage earner to supplement the meagre income which the man is able to earn. The child is the ultimate sufferer, and bears the brunt of it all.

There is a mistaken conception in the world to the effect that the Negro can maintain a standard of life on a lower level of wage compensation than the white man. This is an economic and racial fallacy. The Negro buys in the same market and pays the same or higher prices for like commodities, and wherever his income is lower than that of the white his standard of life must be correspondingly depressed. We are speaking of standardizing children. You can have only one standard; there is only one ethical standard, there is only one scientific standard, there is only one economic standard, there is only one political standard. You cannot have two yardsticks, you cannot have two multiplication tables, one applied to one race and one to the other. So wherever the Negro is being depressed below the level of economic well-being, the life of the race is depressed correspondingly. The world war has incidentally brought enlarged economic opportunity to the Negro. Let it be hoped that this temporary advantage will be made permanent so that the home life of this race may be correspondingly uplifted.

What chance has the child of the alley, bereft of parental care, whose physical, intellectual, and moral nature is stunted and starved by pinched and impoverished surroundings? Shut in by the murky horizon of this gloomy environment, how can he be expected to become a competent coworker in the new order of things which is being ushered in? The lavishing of wealth beyond reasonable requirements upon the children of the fortunate few is poor compensation for the soul impoverishment of those innocent children upon whom society places so heavy a load. The most pathetic picture from which our boasted civilization would hide its face is the helplessness and hopelessness of the black child farthest down.

But I would not make the picture too gloomy. Not every Negro child is subject to the same degree of disadvantage. There is a rapidly increasing element of the race which is pushing up to a higher level of decency, decorum, and dignity of life, and is providing for its children the advantages and opportunities which are their just due. Unfortunately, like the corresponding class among the whites, this element is not prolific in offspring. The Negro race, like the white race, is still breeding from the bottom.

Encouragement comes from the fact that society's cruelest regulation cannot wholly defeat the purposes of Nature, or take away the birthright even of the Negro child. Frederick Douglass, the slave child, vied with the dogs for the scraps that fell from his master's table; and yet Frederick Douglas, the man, vied with the noblest of the land in the embodiment and appreciation of the higher human values. Booker T. Washington and Paul Laurence Dunbar broke the invidious bar of a degraded childhood and rose to a high level of public honor and esteem. What was accomplished so conspicuously by the few illustrious individuals is being multiplied by thousands in lesser measure in all parts of the land.

The gospel of wealth is paradoxical. The Good Book tells us that "the love of money is the root of all evil"; but experience teaches us that the lack of money is the source of most social ills. Poverty leads to most of the evils that human flesh is heir to. Vice, crime, and degradation are its natural offspring. The child of a degrading environment may possibly escape degradation of character, but the risk is too great for enlightened society to hazard. The child with capacity for decency who becomes degraded, the child with capacity for knowledge who grows up in ignorance, the child with capacity for virtue who becomes vicious, represent a human tragedy the awful responsibility for which society must shoulder.

The cure of poverty may not eliminate all social evils; but social evils cannot be eliminated while poverty prevails. The political turmoil of the world, is, at bottom, economic. The world is convinced

THE ECONOMIC AND SOCIAL BASIS

that the right political order cannot be maintained until poverty has been banished. The Negro will be among the last elements of society to feel the relief from this awful load. The children of the race should not be made to wait upon this slow ameliorative process.

Education is the only practicable partial remedy. The proper intellectual, moral, social, and vocational training will go far to correct the evils which unfortunate social conditions impose upon the Negro child. Educate the child in the way he should go, and he will be likely to lift himself to a higher level. It would be a mockery indeed if this great sacrifice to make the world safe for democracy should fail to make democracy safe for the child, even the child farthest down. There is but one practical program upon which all right-minded and patriotic Americans can agree, and that is the immediate relief and uplift of the Negro child.

The State has assumed the responsibility for education. The performance of the State should be 100 per cent efficient. It is a disgrace to a soverign State to have any one of its functions imperfectly performed. The function of education in many of our States is hardly ten per cent efficient. Every child should receive adequate educational advantages. The Government owes this duty to the child, especially the Negro child whose race has been so loyal to the Government in the hour of its peril. The most effective service that can be rendered the childhood of this race may be done by persuading the Government of the United States to furnish national aid for education in the places where there is need.

At the annual meeting of the Department of Superintendents of the National Education Association at Atlantic City in February, 1918, a resolution was unanimously adopted to the effect that the National Government should render aid to education in those States which stand in need of it. Here is a plan which all can approve which will go farther than any other practicable provision to lift the Negro child up to the desired standard.

Some say that the Negro problem is insoluble; but the American people have never seriously tried to solve the race problem. If the Federal Government will educate every child according to his needs this will be the first important step in this direction.

The Negro child sits in the shadow of poverty and ignorance. His social environment benumbs his higher powers and faculties. He looks at the proclaimed new order of things and longs to enter into its sunshine and joy. But, alas, conditions forbid. The new freedom which the world war has just fought for with countless cost of blood and treasure will prove to be but vanity and vexation of spirit if the least of these is denied his God-given birthright to enter into this proclaimed new order.

When I consider the sad lot of the Negro child I can not refrain from indulgence in the ancient lamentation: "Oh, that my head were waters and mine eyes a fountain of tears, that I might weep day and night for the slain of the children of my people."

BELGIAN CHILDREN IN WAR TIME

By MISS L. E. CARTER, Brussels, Belgium

I understand you are interested in the destiny of the little country, Belgium. Perhaps the little countries serve as links between the great nations in the great international work we are looking forward to, so that I venture to give special details concerning what has been done in my country for child welfare.

I would consider two periods, one ending on August 4, 1914, and the other one comprising the following four years.

The first period comprises eighty-eight years of independence. The jubilee of fifty years of independence was celebrated in 1880. Then in 1905 we celebrated with joy the seventy-fifth year of liberty, and we were looking forward to the celebration of a hundred years of independence. Already some of our large factories were preparing for the celebration.

Long before the application of the law of compulsory education, which took effect in 1914, and which obliges children in Belgium to go to school until the age of fourteen, we had many prosperous schools all over the country—State schools and other schools working in co-operation with the State—and a great number of parochial schools. We are trying year after year to bring those schools into better and better condition.

Among these schools those of Brussels were the best. I have brought with me the annual school report for Brussels for 1913, the last that was printed, because during the war we would not have our matters printed. They were censored by the German authorities, so we were without any printing. The report will show you that we had twenty-three elementary schools for boys and girls, but separated. We have not in Belgium your system of coeducation. We had business schools for girls and manual schools for boys. There were three special schools for domestic science entirely equipped, and our elementary pupils went periodically to those schools which were especially adapted for the teaching of domestic economy. We also had three high schools for boys, three high schools for girls, one normal primary school for boys and one for girls. We had considered, too, the question of defective children and dealt with it as best we could.

In 1913 the law for the protection of children was applied to delinquent children; special tribunals were appointed and very good results came from that organization.

With regard to physical training, our children have at least half an hour a day in exercise, either gymnastic or play games. Before the war we served meals in the schools. We called the several organizations "the cup of milk," "the cup of coffee." There was another one, "the mouthful of bread," because we had many poor children who had not enough food at home. We also provided the children with clothes; and the girls in the high schools in their lessons on needlework sewed on clothing necessary for little brothers and sisters.

One of the things of which Brussels was very proud was a national collection of the principal landscapes and of the principal scenery of the country which had been given to the schools. The schools had copies of beautiful pictures that had been made by our best artists. Many of the places represented have been to a great extent destroyed.

Besides the day schools we had evening classes in all our schools for the children who had left school too early and for those who wanted to progress further in their studies.

Medical inspection is organized as completely as possible in our schools with the help of doctors and of nurses. We send the delicate children into the country; we had five country homes for that purpose —now one has disappeared entirely. Besides these country homes there was a private institution called the Open Air Association which had country houses where our children could be sent.

Everything looked hopeful, although we think that we have still much to do. And among the many things that we must create are, of course, more playgrounds for our children. We would like also to see established the principle of coeducation, and a better understanding of vocational guidance. Our libraries are quite small and our aim is to establish some children's libraries on the model of American libraries. We want also, if possible, if it is not against the interest of the family, to persuade children to go to school until they are at least sixteen.

The beginning of the second period is marked by the invasion of Belgium by the Germans. You know that many of our towns disappeared entirely, schools, churches, everything. Factories and workshops were closed. There was no work, no possibility for child labor. There are workshops for apprenticeships, but all over the country many of these were destroyed. Others were taken by the Germans and used for other purposes.

Brussels being the capital and especially being guided by Mr. Adolph Max, who is I believe internationally noted for his integrity and his sense of justice and courage, was protected. All except three of our many schools (three that were used by the Germans) remained open. But they had to fight against difficulties of many kinds. And among these difficulties was the fact that in the severe cold of the winter our pupils had no fire at all, and in those large buildings made principally of stone the cold was very, very severe indeed.

I want to dwell on these difficulties and on the result of them because there was not only the want of coal, but there was also (in spite of the help given by America) the want of food. Dr. Sand summed up the result of the difficulties against which we had to fight by saying that our school children are one full year below normal in their development. Our boys have lost three pounds in weight and our girls four pounds.

One of the dreadful things for our children was the environment in which they were placed. I have read in an American book on child welfare that "in many respects environment is the dominating factor of human development, and this applies especially to the period of childhood. The physiology of children proves them to be extremely plastic in body, and psychology has rendered a similar conclusion in respect to mental qualities." As to the observations concerning mental life, this is a fact. While our children ought to be brought up in an atmosphere of truth, while our parents ought to teach them the courage of speaking the truth always, during the war parents had the painful duty at times to teach their children to say lies, and to teach them the courage of speaking them out in spite of threats and of bad treatment. I know a sweet mother, of the most noble character, refined, rich, who wanted to do something for her country. Her boys were still too young to serve. She saw the wives of workmen now gone to war in distress because they had no news at all from their husbands or from their sons. With the help of many others she organized a system of correspondence, which was quite forbidden by the Germans. Her little boys helped her, with other persons. These boys met the letter carriers on their way to school and brought back the letters hidden among their school books and copy books. This lady told me many a time how distressed she was because she had to make up her stories with her children so as not to betray the persons who were helping her in this system of correspondence. The system worked out for two years. Then things were found out. She was tried, and she defended herself. One of my friends who has been working in the Red Cross in Paris went down to the place where the judgment took place in the hope of sustaining the courage of our friend, and when she came back she told me that she was not in need of courage; that she spoke so splendidly that the hearts of her judges were moved to tears.

Well, this noble woman had been obliged, as had many others, to teach her children to tell lies. Our children want an atmosphere of calm, of confidence of life. Our children in Belgium for nearly five years have lived in an environment of fear, agitation, worry, and hatred. And though the causes of fear are dying away, worry and hatred are still there at work. The fear and hatred were felt even by little babies. I remember this instance. In a tram car were several persons. There entered a woman who had a baby in her arms. She sat on one side of the car. On the other side of the car was a German officer alone. Nobody sat down next to him. The father of the child had remained on the platform. As soon as the child, who could hardly speak, saw the German, he gave signs of great uneasiness, of agitation, and he was ready to cry. The father was obliged to come in the car to calm the child, and turned his face to the window so he would not see the German officer. In some such cases mothers and fathers have been arrested and considered as responsible for their children. In this case the officer looked grieved and walked out of the car onto the platform.

I could tell you many other tales. Think of the many children who went to bed with their little parcels ready in case they should have to escape during the night. What sweet, restful slumber could these children get? Instead there were heavy dreams and horrid nightmares of rapine and murder. Imagine children escaping with their mothers and having to tramp sometimes during days and nights. I have been told of children who came to our hospital and who died not of any special illness but really of fright, of horror. There was no spectacle more awful than the eyes of those poor little children expressing the greatest fear. The mothers themselves were so desperate and so spent in grief that they were not able to weep. Fancy these scenes repeated at every moment, every day, and acting on the delicate nervous system of a child.

One of my pupils, one of our brightest girls, a very clever girl, at eighteen, broke down entirely. She belonged to a well-to-do family. She was not in need of better food, but she had been worrying about her father who was an officer in the army, worrying about her mother who was ill from the fact of never having a letter from the father, and worrying from having to take the responsibility of the household. She lost in a very short time twenty pounds. Many doctors saw her, and they declared her organs were in good condition, but that her nervous system had been so strained she had given way. One emotion a child may bear, but many emotions, not so. It was not possible for her young nervous system to bear it. Under normal conditions one of these shocks would have been sufficient to break down or to injure forever the nervous system of a child. Now, think that our little children suffered from these shocks constantly during five years.

At home they had the love of their mothers, but they breathed the hot atmosphere of care and sorrow, caused always by the same reason—the father was away or the son had gone to sea trying to reach the front, or sometimes it was the want of money. And even if our poor children were well looked after and if every service was organized to give them the food they wanted, the people of the middle classes, obsessed by a feeling of dignity, would receive no help. One of my pupils had fainted several times during the school hours, and we knew that she fainted on account of weakness. I wrote to the mother as discreetly as I could, asking her if I could help her. She replied expressing her thanks and saying that she and her husband had some savings, and that they would be able to hold out until the war was over, whatever the length of the war should be.

What the child needs is joy, not an existence among these terrible things, seeing the mother grieving day after day. Children were glad to escape sometimes from home and go to school where at least they found companions of their own age. But even school was not what it ought to be. In general, teachers did their duties splendidly, and I am very proud of the fact that we were able to keep the schools open during these long years. But there was the want of liveliness that a certain weakness cannot provide. There is always a touch of dreariness; and the pupil feels that something is wanting. The physical weakness of the staff as well as that of the children could be measured every day. Some teachers used to tell me—and I understood what they had said because I had passed through the same experience—how their heads ached, and they explained, "We feel as if the envelope of our nerves has been wasted away, and as if every movement we make is felt."

Now these children whom we had in our school and in the other schools were helped in every way, but they became weaker and weaker. They ought to have had a change of air. They ought to have had proper food. There was the possibility of sending a certain number of the children to our country homes, but there were not enough country homes, and even children of well-to-do families could not be sent to the country to private homes because in those private homes there was no food to be had. In 1918 we were given fifteen places in these country homes. In ordinary times our children would never have accepted such an invitation, but here it was a very hard task for the heads of the schools to choose fifteen among the mass of four or five hundred children, all needing a change of air. I received many letters which I could scarcely answer from those country homes where the children were going. They went to sleep on mattresses made of hides. They had no potatoes, no butter, no vegetables, no fruit, but they were sent there to escape from a prison, which the town was, and to get the fresh air of the country.

I comment again on the fact that though we were helped, the food given to our children was not sufficient. In schools where the children paid high fees, we had to organize visits of distribution of the little cakes which were made, and we had to give also soup. I will outline another incident. Ernest Solvay, having reached the age of 80 years and belonging to the committee which had done much to help, these children expressed their appreciation by making him an offering; and Ernest Solvay, to thank them, sent to each child a hard biscuit which in normal times they would not have eaten, and a piece of chocolate the size of my finger. When the children saw the biscuit and the little bit of chocolate, it was really painful to us, the elders. But when I went around in the classes to see what had been done with the piece of chocolate, I found that all the children had kept the piece of chocolate with the exception of one little boy who had tasted it—it was so tempting, or else they had given a little piece to the teacher, and they carried it home to their parents. The teachers received the same little piece a few days after, and I received mine. I carried mine home and divided it with solemnity between the four persons who composed my household.

The result of the debility and weakness of our children was very apparent in the higher classes. The possibility of personal work decreased. The pupils understood the message that was given to them, but they were quite unable to do as well their personal tasks at home, and the domestic lessons and the exercises that needed skill had to be left aside.

But play, this was the most pitiful sight. We saw little children stopping in their play. They did not understand what had happened. They were too weak to go on, and many a child had drops of perspiration running down his face. Many were the cases of fits of faintness, and very frequently some of the senior girls who intended to go to the university had to drop their studies; they had not strength to go on. Several were the cases of deaths that might have been prevented if the young people had had what was necessary for them.

I do not exaggerate in the least. For the past few days I have been living in a kind of earthly paradise; I cannot forget and I will not forget that our little children and our people have lived and are still living in a kind of purgatory. If I have dwelt on these subjects it is because I think—although I am not giving a scientific explanation—that the facts are fundamental necessities to help us to discover laws; and I have dwelt on these results as one dwells on the character of a disease in the hope of understanding better the necessities of the situation—as one studies abnormal conditions to understand better what is required under normal conditions. The privation during the war of the elements necessary to the child's welfare and the way in which these privations have acted on the bodies and souls of our children, show more than ever the necessity of giving them what they need—pure air, good food, exercise, liberty, joy.

I come to another conclusion. The children of Belgium have suffered as all the children in the affected countries have suffered, and you, my brothers, you have heard the cry of the children. You have answered the touching appeal, but more is to be done. These awful results, more terrible than can be recounted, are the consequences of war. And if war is to teach us what is the meaning of life, yet I would like that such a lesson should nevermore be taught. I should like other means to be found to come to such conclusions as this that we are discovering, that we should live in a more democratic way. Nations perhaps are going to disappear before the international movement. I am not speaking as a scientific person would speak, nor have I made use of any statistics. But I believe that in the general work of humanity each must bring what he can bring.

I conclude by giving you a message which was given to my school. We had a visit from two American ladies which pleased us very much, and before going these ladies asked if our pupils would take this pledge with them: "May we, the women of America and the women of Belgium and the women all over the world, unite our efforts and endeavor with all our heart and soul to carry out the work of reconstruction and of peace." And I will add only one word: "For the sake of our children."

Section II

Child Labor

(The minimum standards in regard to the employment of children adopted by the Washington Conference will be found on pages 433-435.)

LEGISLATIVE PROHIBITION OF EMPLOYMENT

GENERAL STANDARDS

By OWEN R. LOVEJOY
Secretary, National Child Labor Committee

Hitherto we have more or less unconsciously employed the sliding scale in relation to child-labor standards. We put prohibition of night work in one State, which had an extremely low all-round standard, on very much the same plane of achievement as establishing an eight instead of a ten-hour day in another State, which had relatively high standards. That is, it has been natural to work with almost equal enthusiasm for high standards in States where the demand for them was strong and for much lower standards where the demand was less or where it was lacking. Then when those standards were established we worked for still higher ones. We used the sliding scale in accordance with the age-old theory of demand and supply. This theory in economics is fallacious. It is time to discard it in social work. It is time to consider solely the individual, for what is right for the individual is right for industry and society and the world at large.

Arguments have been used to prove that child labor is not economical; that it is fatal to labor because it lowers wages; that it is not in harmony with efficiency for the manufacturer; that it is not conducive to the education or to the physical health and vigor of the nation. Now it is time to talk of the child, and in turning to the child it is evident that really very little account has been taken of him. We know that work cannot be good for his health, but we do not know scientifically how bad it is for him, nor what are the effects of different kinds of work upon his development, nor at what age it is, physically speaking, permissible for him to enter industry in general.

A few States require by law a physical examination of children when they leave school and apply for work permits, but the fact that these children have not been subject to systematic physical examinations during their school life makes this examination of almost negligible value. Furthermore, up to date not a single one of the 48 commonwealths requires systematic physical examination of children between 14 and 16 years of age who are at work. America has not even had the intellectual curiosity to try to find out what industry does to her children.

Furthermore, though certain studies have been made of child nature, of child psychology, and of adolescence, we really do not know what the child needs mentally and spiritually. I think it is time we applied ourselves to this task. We know that nearly half the children who leave school in order to go to work do so because they are tired of school, because they dislike the teacher, "did not get on," or prefer to work. Why does this common phenomenon of revolt against school appear so regularly at the age of 13 or 14? Is it the fault of the child or of the school? Are we willing frankly to face the fact that the elaborate and formal school system built up by us adults on behalf of children is not acceptable to the beneficiaries? That perhaps they could point a way to its improvement? What in short are the needs of children? It is evident that in order to fix our standards, this question must first be answered. But until the studies can be made—and they never can be finished, for as science advances new light will continually be thrown upon one of its most interesting and baffling problems—certain minimum legislative requirements should be set up, to be established as soon as possible in the more advanced communities, and to be approached for the present as a limit in States whose citizens demand less protection.

A reasonable minimum age for entrance into industry would be 16 years. This should apply to all common work, such as that offered by factories, mills, canneries, offices, stores, laundries, restaurants, and to all the miscellaneous occupations entered by children. It should be a flat minimum, that is, for all gainful occupations with the one exception of agriculture. Eighteen years should be the minimum age for work in mines and other especially dangerous industries, and 21 the age for morally dangerous work such as falls to the lot of night messengers in our cities. There should be periodic examination of all working children to see that they are not being broken down in health, and means should be adopted for their transfer, if advisable, to less harmful industries or their removal from industry altogether. Such an examination, made not less than once a year, would in a short time show just what are the industries and operations which induce excessive fatigue, predispose to disease, or lead to stunted growth.

As to hours of employment the regulations recently proposed by the Commission on International Labor Legislation for insertion in the Peace Treaty and adopted by the Peace Conference in Paris, April 28, 1919, offer a suggestive basis. The Sixth Article proposes "the abolition of child labor and the imposition of such limitations on the labor of young persons as shall permit the continuation of their education and assure their proper physical development." The term "abolition of child labor" is so indefinite that unless light were thrown upon it by other portions of the statement, it would have little more effect than similar declarations in our own national political party platforms. Fortunately, however, the commission speaks with a definiteness that leaves no room for doubt. The Fourth Article proposes "the adoption of an eight-hour day or a 48-hour week as the standard to be aimed at where it has not already been obtained." This limitation of hours does not relate to child labor, which, according to Article Six, is to be entirely abolished. This eight-hour day and 48-hour week refers to labor in general—to the protection of men and women—to those of mature physical development.

The corollary is obvious, and it has already been recognized under existing conditions by the adoption of an eight-hour day for children in States where the limitations of hours for men and women were 10, 11, or 12 hours, or where, perhaps, no limitation existed. The principle underlying this discrimination in the interest of children assumes that the growing, developing child subjected to industry should have the burden laid on gradually rather than all at once, and that if men and women need protection, children need more protection. But now we face a new condition, for certainly America with its natural resources and abundance of enterprise cannot afford to stand on a lower plane than the one proposed in this international labor compact. If an eight-hour day measures a desirable social limitation for the labor of men and women, then an eight-hour day is too long for the labor of children. For the first two years at least—namely from 16 to 18 years of age—no child engaged in ordinary industrial processes should be employed to exceed six hours a day. Therefore we should propose as the maximum industrial burden that restriction of hours to six per day and prohibition of night work under 18 years of age should of course form part of the program.

Obviously this program cannot be put into immediate effect so long as excessive industrial burdens are laid on the shoulders of half-starved mothers, and so long as our schools persist in "teaching" instead of educating our children. It would be absurd to force lawmaking ahead of standards that public opinion can maintain. But these standards are suggested as the ones that in our educational and legislative work should undoubtedly be our object. How soon we may hope to approach them under existing conditions I leave to our statistical experts. Since 1890 our population has increased 60 per cent and our net annual production of wealth has increased 700 per cent. Obviously, therefore, if people were able to exist in 1890 they should be able to exist on a very much higher plane and a more comfortable plane in 1918; and during this period we have produced millionaires more prolifically than anything else except paupers.

Although approximately three-fourths of our working children are employed in agriculture, this is one of the most difficult of all occupations to regulate. Farm work is undoubtedly harmful when accompanied by exploitation as in the Colorado beet fields and the Southern cotton fields, and yet work about the home farm on a variety of occupations, or work for a neighbor, may be highly healthful and instructive. The most serious objection to this form of work is that it almost invariably tends to keep the child out of school for more or less of the short period that rural schools are in session. The child gradually falls behind his normal grade, one year, two years, or three years. He is both ashamed and bored at being forced to study with younger children on matters that are too elementary to hold his attention. Retardation leads to further retardation and to early dropping out altogether.

The trouble suggests the cure. While it might be unfair and would undoubtedly be quite impossible to enforce a law directed against the employment of children on farms, we can raise the educational standard in rural communities, and we must do so at once if we wish to retain our rural population and our agricultural soundness. The condition of our rural communities not only affects our social and civic institutions; it strikes at the very foundation of economic prosperity. Ten per cent of the rural population cannot read an agricultural bulletin, a farm journal, a thrift appeal, a newspaper, the Constitution, or their Bibles; answer an income tax questionnaire; or keep business accounts. Secretary Lane says: "We spent millions of dollars in presenting to the country the reasons why we were at war, and more than ten per cent of the money that was spent was spent fruitlessly, because the people who got the literature, who got the speeches, who got the appeals, could not understand one word that was written."

One thing that draws our boys to the city is the call of life and human intercourse and better facilities for knowledge. If we can in some manner endow our country schools with vitality, man them with teachers earning and getting living wages, introduce the spirit of community effort, and give scope for the instinct of workmanship, and if we can then create and enforce adequate compulsory education laws, we shall have eliminated the worst evil of children's employment in agriculture. We shall at the same time be building up an educationally equipped and consciously effective agricultural and land-minded population.

Continuation schools and laws compelling employers to allow time for attendance by their employees under 18 years of age should be the reverse side of our child-labor laws. But it is very difficult to confine oneself to legislative prohibitions when the whole trend of child-labor effort and education work in this country is in the direction of construction rather than prohibition. Our enforced laws, however good, however effective in keeping children out of industry and in school, will avail very little unless we provide a better substitute than work, and a better school system and curriculum than the one in vogue. And here we return to the question of children's needs. Let us by all means work for the minimum standards which common sense and our industrial experience justify, but let us at once begin the campaign for the scientific determination of the physical effects of work, through regular physical examination of school and working children. Let us by all means encourage educational experiments, especially those which seek in some way to satisfy the craving of youth and adolescence for real work, for learning through doing, and for wage-earning. If we can finally eliminate the two evils of being taught on the one hand and being exploited on the other, we shall have touched the heart of the problem. It is possible that this may be done by bringing work into the schools or taking the schools out into the world of adult endeavor and labor; by substituting for our industrial training, education through responsibility and initiative in different kinds of hand and brain work. Such experiments will inevitably lead to a better understanding of child nature and to an interpretation of its unexpressed demands.

DISCUSSION

Mr. George G. Chatfield, of the Bureau of Attendance of the New York City Board of Education, emphasized the necessity for larger public expenditures in order to pay for the lengthened school period proposed.

Hon. P. P. Claxton, U. S. Commissioner of Education, discussed the significance of calling this conference at a time when the people of the world are deeply interested in problems pertaining to the welfare of childhood.

"There are two reasons for it," said Mr. Claxton. "First, there is great danger now because of the very great losses in life and money, and great destruction of property, that many hardships may fall on children that otherwise would not. An amount equal to one-third of all the wealth of the world in 1914 has been used up. The loss of life has been very great and many families have been left with children without fathers; mothers left to support their families; and frequently the children left in even worse condition.

"There is another great reason. Never before has it been so important as now that humanity should be considered, that no child should grow to manhood or womanhood without the education necessary to prepare it for citizenship in the new democracy of the world, for making a good, honest living, and for attaining the full stature of manhood and of womanhood. The world has paid a great price for freedom and for democracy, but there can be no freedom so long as children are slaves. And Pestalozzi, the great Swiss educator of a century ago, was right when he said that there can be no freedom without the education of man. Democracy cannot be safe in the hands of a people a large number of whom have been stunted in childhood and have failed in the mental and moral and physical development necessary for the duties and responsibilities of democratic citizenship."

MINIMUM PHYSICAL STANDARDS

By DR. EMMA MACKAY APPEL
Chicago Board of Education

Medical inspection was first introduced into the schools for the purpose of preventing the spread of infectious diseases. Later, investigations were made of the physical defects having direct bearing upon a child's progress in school. Inspection with these objects in view continues to be the chief function of the school physicians in many cities, while in others the medical work has progressed, and general physical examinations are made yearly with a view to improving the physical well-being of the child.

With the advent in Illinois of the child-labor law requiring that children going to work be examined by a physician, the physical condition of the child has taken on a new aspect. Medical inspection is carried a step further—to complete physical examination and supervision, in an effort to correct all physical defects and to establish a proper nutritional balance, as well as to inquire into the mental status of the child. Measures for the promotion of the health of the industrial child must be preventive as well as remedial.

The important factors entering into the standard of requirements of physical fitness for industry are:

First—The child must be physically able to perform the work required of him, working an eight-hour day.

Second—The child must be able to perform the particular work contemplated without injury to himself.

Third—The child must be free from any condition which might be harmful to his coworkers.

The placing of the physically fit child in industry, the opportunity of improving the physically unfit, and the placement of the handicapped child in suitable working conditions, have been the very interesting work of the medical examiners of the board of education since the Illinois Child Labor Law went into effect in July, 1917. It has been their aim to direct, suggest, advise, consult, and provide means for treatment, to the end that every child, insofar as is possible, shall be in perfect physical condition by the time he is sixteen years of age.

The methods of procedure in the physical examination used in the Chicago certificate-issuance office are as follows:

CHILD LABOR—LEGISLATIVE PROHIBITION

(a) A routine method of conducting and recording physical examinations is always adhered to. The time required for each examination is from three to ten minutes.

(b) A brief history of the child is obtained covering past diseases, present condition, and symptoms if indicating present illness. The child is questioned in regard to hernia, as to operations performed, and as to maturity.

(c) The child is then weighed and measured. A tentative minimum standard of four feet eight inches in height and eighty pounds in weight for a fourteen year old child was at first adopted, but it has been lowered to four feet seven inches and seventy-five pounds. This standard, while somewhat below the normal for a fourteen year old child, has proved to be a very workable standard and the lowest one consistent with normal health. Occasionally exceptions are made in favor of the undersized child who has no defects and whose weight is normal or above normal for his height.

(d) A careful physical examination is then made. Gait, posture, speech, the color and texture of the skin, the condition of the eyes and eyelids, the nose, mouth, and throat are observed; examination of the chest, heart, and extremities is carefully made. All defects are carefully noted and recorded.

(e) Suggestions are made for the correction of faulty gait and posture, and children having defects in speech are referred to the schools and clinics for treatment. All skin lesions must be treated and cured before a certificate is issued.

(f) When defects in vision are found, the child is sent to a recognized medical dispensary for reexamination and correction. An examination by an oculist is insisted upon—no organ is more vital, and none requires more careful and skillful attention than the eye. Upon the results of its treatment depend not only the child's vision, but to a great extent his general health as well as his industrial value. All glasses obtained from an optician must be checked by an oculist before the certificate is issued, and all diseases of the eye and eyelids must be treated by an oculist.

(g) When defects in hearing occur, a reexamination by an ear specialist is required, also an examination of the nose and throat. Many children who do not respond to treatment are given certificates for suitable work; others are sent to the schools for the deaf for further training. I realize that very little attention has been given to our deaf children, but I recall the case of a very bright, clear-eyed, well-nourished boy who entered my office with a queer hesitating remark: "You don't remember me, Doctor?" I reached for his record to refresh my memory and read: "Hold—absolute deafness, large and infected tonsils and adenoids, under-nourished; referred to school for deaf and

Central Free Dispensary." I asked him in a very low voice—which he heard perfectly—what had happened. "I went to the school the lady sent me to, had my tonsils and adenoids out, and now I hear all right and have gained twelve pounds." At least one child had been helped.

(h) Next in importance to the eye are the teeth, and here we meet our greatest difficulty. In many issuance offices certificates are delayed until all dental work has been completed. In Chicago we require the prophylactic work and a note from a dental clinic or private dentist stating that the child is receiving dental care. All cases of pyorrhea and alveolar abscesses are delayed for treatment. However, upon second and third examinations we frequently find that treatment has been neglected. In this case we again delay the certificate and a fresh start is made.

(i) The mouth and throat are examined, and certificates are delayed for treatment or removal of the adenoid whenever there is evidence of a serious interference in breathing or deafness. We delay certificates for one type of tonsil only, that is, the hypertrophied cryptic, and infected tonsil, complicated by cervical or axillary adenopathy or cardiac findings. The child's general physical condition is also considered in this connection.

(j) In case of the simple goitre of adolescence we advise the child against heavy lifting or strain of any kind. Certificates are delayed, however, where the thyroid enlargement is accompanied by symptoms of hyperthyroidism, and sanitarium care is provided whenever possible.

(k) The examination of the lungs and glandular system is made in detail, careful attention being paid to the child's general condition, weight, degree of anemia, etc. If there are findings indicating a possible incipient tuberculosis, either pulmonary or glandular, the child is referred to the Municipal Tuberculosis Dispensary for observation and treatment. All children who have been patients at either the Tuberculosis Dispensary or Sanitarium, or in whose family there is an open case of tuberculosis, are required to bring a letter from the dispensary stating that they are free from tubercular infection and that they will be kept under observation, reporting at the dispensary at least once in two months. All pulmonary lesions, either acute or chronic, are required to have treatment until definite improvement is shown.

(l) Following major surgical operations very careful examinations are made, and when necessary abdominal supporters or corrective apparatus are provided.

(m) Children having cardiac lesions of a serious nature with symptoms of decompensation, are not given certificates. They are advised of their condition and referred to their family physicians or to a dispensary. Sanitarium care has been obtained for many of them. The mild cardiac case is granted a certificate provided proper work can be secured. The placing of a heart case is most difficult. Finding the proper position where there will be no lifting of heavy packages, where the child is not required to leave home very early in the morning, or where the noon hour is not too short, as well as persuading the child to make the necessary change, often against the wishes of his parents and his employer, calls for both time and patience. The children all work under supervision, reporting at stated intervals for reexamination and advice. They are followed up in their employment by the social service department of one of our large medical dispensaries, where a special industrial heart clinic has been established. Special laboratory examinations, such as urinalyses, blood counts, and Wassermann tests, are required when indicated.

(n) Certificates are granted not only to children who are handicapped by cardiac disease, but also to those who are crippled or deformed, to the deaf, dumb, and nearly blind, as well as to children with varying degrees of spinal curvature, some of them requiring mechanical appliances to correct their deformities. These cases are all gone over very carefully to make certain there are no active processes, X ray pictures are taken when necessary, a suitable kind of employment is found, and they are permitted to work under supervision.

Under the law of the State of Illinois a child is required to have finished the fifth grade in order to obtain a certificate. We have found many retarded and subnormal children. These defective children constitute a special problem and quite an unsolved one. Whenever indicated, mental tests are made, and a few children have been found to be low-grade morons. Others show a moderate degree of feeble-mindedness, and many are borderline cases. These children come from the poorest social environments. They are retarded in school and are frequently advised by the teacher to leave and go to work. Some are delinquents, others stupid, dull, and unsteady in employment. The greatest difficulty is experienced by the vocational bureau in finding positions for these retarded children. They are frequently discharged for carelessness or irresponsibility. They change positions for trifling reasons or just because they are tired of work. Everything possible is done for them by our office to put them in as perfect physical condition as possible. We insist upon antisyphilitic treatment.

This group of children, together with the undersized and underweight group, are at the present time being forced out of industry—first, because of the returning soldier, and second, because of the Federal Child Labor Law, which is forcing the better industries to employ only the child over sixteen years of age.

The following figures, obtained from the employment certificate department of the board of education, show the physical defects found by the medical examiners in examining children applying for employment certificates in Chicago during the four months ending April 30, 1919:

Total number examinations (both first and subsequent)..........10,066
Number physical defects found............................... 1,110

Following is a classification of the physical defects found:

Type of Defect	Number Cases	Per Cent
Nose and throat findings (acute and chronic)....	235	21.2
Defective teeth................................	181	16.3
Defective vision...............................	298	26.8
Skin affections, pediculosis, etc................	83	7.5
Malnutrition, undersize and underweight........	121	10.9
Cardiac findings...............................	100	9.0
Other defects..................................	92	8.3
Total	1,110	100.0

Important as are the physical standards for the working child, of even greater importance is the type of medical examiners. They should be thoroughly trained physical diagnosticians—graduates of recognized medical schools. They must have a definite knowledge of industrial conditions, must be able to judge of the ability of the particular child to do the work required of him, and should also understand the demands of the different industries employing children. Above all, they should be intensely interested in the welfare of the working child.

NOTE

At a later session of the conference Dr. Appel suggested that a permanent committee be appointed by the chairman (Miss Grace Abbott of the Children's Bureau) to formulate definite standards of normal development and sound health for use of physicians in examining working children. A motion to this effect was carried unanimously.

DEFECTIVE VISION AMONG CHICAGO WORKING CHILDREN [1]

By DR. E. V. L. BROWN
Professor of Ophthalmology, University of Illinois College of Medicine

During the past year the Vocational Board of the Chicago public schools has sent some 1,340 boys and girls of 14 and 15 years of age to my clinic for examination of their eyes, preliminary to the issuance of a work certificate under the new Illinois child-labor law. These children were a part of those discovered by the general physical examination given at the issuing office to be suffering from some defect of vision. As the group of these children sent to my clinic were selected at random, the results, I feel, indicate what will probably be found on the average in any such large group of 14 and 15 year old children with defective vision who apply for work certificates in any good-sized American city with a mixed population.

A tabulation of the results of our examinations is not without interest at this time, because it is the first of such surveys.

These examinations were conducted by me personally, and were checked independently by the assistant refractionist of my clinic, Miss Margaret A. Heath. They were made after first one, then the other eye had been put at rest by three days' use of atropin sulphate one per cent solution. This was instilled four times each day before the child returned to the clinic for the second examination.

From the welfare standpoint it is a matter of gratification that the average case of defective vision, as revealed by our tests, can be improved to the extent indicated, namely: 3.5 "visual tenths."[2] This is shown by the accompanying table.

CORRECTION OF DEFECTIVE VISION IN CHICAGO WORKING CHILDREN

29 children who came with less than	1/10 normal vision were improved to 4/10.
75 children who came with	1/10 normal vision were improved to 5/10.
127 children who came with	2/10 normal vision were improved to 7/10.
139 children who came with	3/10 normal vision were improved to 8/10.
160 children who came with	4/10 normal vision were improved to 10/10.
156 children who came with	5/10 normal vision were improved to 8/10.
226 children who came with	6/10 normal vision were improved to 10/10.
134 children who came with	8/10 normal vision were improved to 11/10.
95 children who came with	10/10 normal vision were improved to 20/10.
83 children who came with	12/10 normal vision were improved to 13/10.
100 children who came with	15/10 normal vision were not to be improved.
13 children who came with	20/10 normal vision were not to be improved.
Average improvement per case............................3.5 visual tenths.	

[1]Delivered at the Chicago Child Welfare Regional Conference, May 19, 1919.
[2]A normal eye reads 10/10, or 10 "visual tenths." An eye with only one-tenth (1/10) vision is said to have one "visual tenth"; an eye with two-tenths vision is said to have two "visual tenths," etc.

In plain English, this means that the child who can read the largest letter on the test card at twenty feet (and who should read it at two hundred feet) can be fitted with glasses enabling him to read letters at twenty feet which the normal child can read at from fifty to sixty feet. This definitely takes the child out of the medico-legally "blind" class and places him in the group which sees quite adequately. The average working man or woman with only this 20/50 vision seldom wishes for better vision (except for the movies).

The last four lines of the table illustrate cases where the child's vision was found to be normal in one eye, but examination of the fellow eye showed markedly poor vision. The poor eye was first brought to as nearly normal as possible. Then an examination of the apparently normal eye was made in order to relieve the strain under which it was very probably working. This examination often revealed that further improvement could be obtained, as for instance, from 10/10 to 20/10.

From the standpoint of the eye doctor I can only urge the value and importance of examinations of this type for all children who are compelled for one reason or another to go to work.

DANGEROUS OCCUPATIONS

By DR. D. L. EDSALL
Dean, Harvard Medical School

It is obvious that children are more subject to the dangers of accidents than adults. Everyone knows that. It is equally plain to anyone who has studied the question that children are far more prone than adults to influences of other dangers that occur in occupations; for instance poisons, and especially poisons that affect the nervous system; substances that disturb the gastrointestinal tract; and to a large extent substances that affect the skin. It is obvious also that children, besides being inherently more subject to the effects of such things, are heedless and ignorant as compared with the average adult, and therefore require very much more protection than the average adult.

These dangers are recognized where suitable laws exist, and in some places laws covering these points are fairly successfully developed. I think that one can properly demand the entire prohibition of the use of child labor in any processes in which there is danger of exposure to poisonous substances, or serious danger of exposure to substances that are harmful to the skin, or particularly to the eyes; and also in any processes where there is danger of exposure to irritating dust. Children, and those in the earlier years immediately following childhood, are peculiarly prone to develop a latent tuberculosis, and they must therefore be protected from dangers that are likely to excite tuberculosis, which is the great danger beyond all other medical dangers.

Children are also peculiarly prone to the effects of general physical strain, and to the effect of postural strains—a fact sometimes overlooked in regulations. Some of the most extraordinary deformities I have ever seen in children have been due to the fact that their work caused an unusual strain of some kind. I have in mind a young boy whose work caused pressure on the left side of the chest; he had the most extraordinary chest deformity I have ever seen, due solely to his work. He was not ill in any other way. Such work should be prohibited for children, because the bony structure of the child is extremely flexible as compared to that of the adult, and he is highly subject to effects of strain.

One of the most important things in considering children in relation to industry is what people not accustomed to details of industrial processes do not always apprehend; namely, that you may suspect all you wish about an industry, but you know nothing about its effect on health until you know the detailed processes that the individual may have to meet. You never know whether a thing is going to be harmful or healthful until you have watched the actual process, and the substances used in it. And that can only be done by precise, definite, and detailed knowledge of each process. Making up a code of prohibited occupations necessarily involves precise information as to the particular processes in particular trades. That is an elaborate matter.

All the things I mentioned can be demanded properly as prohibitive regulations, and are already carried out in some of the parts of the world where the best regulations now exist. But even if you have your law it has to be administered, and unfortunately these laws are not very satisfactorily administered in most places.

Beyond that I think it is always essential to have all such statutes drawn so that not only shall certain recognized and acknowledged dangers be prohibited, but the person or body having the administration of the law shall have the power which exists in certain of the States of this country and in England—namely, the power of adding to the designated processess such others as through new investigations appear from time to time to be properly subject to the same regulations. Such new prohibitions should always be subject to hearing on the part of the interested persons. In this way one can cover the matter far better than by having new statutes passed every time a new thing which is dangerous comes along.

I think the number of children in this country who are actually subject to what we can specifically say are serious occupational hazards per se is comparatively small. It is highly important to keep the child from being exposed to them, but if we limit our interest in dangerous occupations to things that are, per se, actual dangers to the child, we have taken up the very minor side of this problem and have left out what is by far the major side. (I have seen very few children who have been damaged by the fact that the process they were working at belonged essentially in the class of highly dangerous occupations. I have seen many a child who has been very greatly injured by the fact that, having some small or large physical defect, he had gone into an occupation entirely unsuitable for him. This is a very complex problem. The fact that a great many children are injured by occupation is shown for example by such figures as those of Teleky, who studied children in Vienna. It was quite astounding to see the results. The figures showed that in the fourteenth year out of 100 children there occurred on the average 22 illnesses in the course of the year that put them to bed. They went to work at fourteen. The next year those illnesses were practically doubled, up to 41, and they stayed around 39, 40, and 41 for the following three years. So that in the early years of their going to work, evidently work in some way practically doubled the morbidity of childhood. This was undoubtedly due to various causes—to the fact that the great majority of these children went to work too early; that in all probability they went to work at tasks that were too hard for them; and to other similar factors. But I have no doubt that a large factor in the increase in morbidity was that a great many of those children entered upon work they ought not to have undertaken when they could properly have been put to work at other things.

The thing we must seek for the benefit of the individual, and for the benefit of society at large, is not to keep moderately defective children out of work when they get to the age where they should work, but to see to it that they do the right kind of work. There is a far greater number of children of this kind than we realize. The Society for the Study and Control of Heart Diseases, for example, makes the statement that there are at any time in New York City alone as many as 20,000 school children who have organic heart disease, and who need special attention in regard to the occupations they undertake. They are capable of being productive members of society with fairly good health, on the one hand, or of becoming cripples, or being killed off, on the other hand.

As to the individual, not only in his economic capacity as a producer but in his happiness and in his good health, it is better for him if he can work that he should work. He stays in health if working at the right kind of work. That has been shown clearly in relation to the heart, for instance. It has been shown that many persons with heart disease do better at work than when allowed to loaf. Tuberculosis is a far greater problem, particularly latent tuberculosis. The number of persons that have the kind of tuberculosis discoverable by physical examination is only a fraction of the number that have potential tuberculosis. Many of those that have potential tuberculosis go to work at weaving, or grinding metals, or blacksmithing, or some other occupation for which they are not suited, just because their fathers or other members of their family have gone into that work. Many such persons have a history of tuberculosis in the family but were supposed to be well themselves. Sometimes they have been examined before going to work, but they have a bad family history and a bad exposure, and where they take up a bad occupation, in a few months they develop a dangerous form of tuberculosis.

Matters of this kind constitute a vastly bigger problem than the specific hazards of industry. Legislative prohibition can have comparatively little effect in regard to them. It is far more an educational matter, and the period when education is of value is before the children enter industry. Two persons have a strategic position in regard to this matter—the school physician and the family physician. The school physicians do not all of them do as careful work as Dr. Appel, and do not all of them take the same kind of interest. I have run across comparatively few of them who know anything about industry or who pay much attention to it. The educational authorities also are in various strategic positions and should be generally educated themselves in regard to this matter. On the other hand, medical professors and doctors should be educated quite differently from what they have been in regard to it. Medical education has been largely, and still remains largely in most medical schools, education for the care of the individually sick. Medicine itself has the potential capacity of being quite as much the preventive care of the community at large, and physicians must be educated in that line.

If those two things are persistently done we may by those means accomplish more than if we devoted ourselves only to the problem of actual dangerous hazards.

Another thing that can do a great deal is the education of industrial managers. I have been deeply gratified to see in this country in the last few years a greatly increased comprehension on the part of industrial management of the economic importance of health. It is calculated that the turnover costs a plant from $35 to $200, according to the character of work, each time one man leaves and another takes his place. I saw figures in one plant where the turnover for several years past had been almost twenty thousand persons. The turnover in that plant costs about one million dollars a year—the loss in training the individual, the loss in destroyed material, and the loss in unskilled work, is enormous. The turnover of a child costs as well as the turnover of an adult.

We can do a little by legislative prohibition. We can do a great deal more by attacking the problem through the school, through school physicians, through medical schools and physicians, through hospitals, and through the service departments of the trades. If the child can be fitted to his occupation before he enters industry and before he must go through that very serious economic loss of changing from one occupation to another, the economic saving and the saving of life and health will be extremely large.

DISCUSSION

In the succeeding discussion, Dr. George P. Barth, Director, School Hygiene Bureau, Milwaukee, emphasized the importance of safeguarding the physical condition of the child when he leaves school to go to work. The need for health supervision, he stated, was shown by an intensive study of the causes of the absence of children from school made in Milwaukee in February, 1917. Of the total of 147,258 half days lost by children during that month, 98,260, or 67 per cent, were due to diagnosed and explained illness of the child. Dr. Barth also spoke of the fact that where working children are required to attend continuation schools an excellent opportunity is offered to find out whether the child is fitted for the job at which he is working and the effect of the job upon his physical well being.

Mr. R. C. Davison, Chief of the Juvenile Labour Exchange, England, spoke as follows: "In our work in the Ministry of Labour in dealing with juvenile employment we have some relation with the certifying factory surgeons who are appointed to examine children. It is the duty of the factory surgeons under the Factory and Workshops Act of 1907 to examine every child or young person under the age of 16 within seven days of the commencement of work in factories and workshops where certain processes are carried on.

"The long list of the trades and processes to which that act applies covers most of the important manufacturing processes. The worker in those processes under the age of 16 must also be reexamined every time he changes his employment. Under our present educational system, that is, until Mr. Fisher's new act comes into force, there is still the half-time system under which children of 12 and 13 may work half time in the factory and go to school half time. Those half-timers are supposed all of them to be examined at the time when they become available for full-time employment. That gives an opportunity for mental examination and advice as to treatment. About 400,000 examinations covering the whole field are required to be made annually. This figure I am afraid is some years old and it is probably larger during recent years.

"The work that I am particularly associated with is the establishment of juvenile advisory committees in connection with employment exchanges, and the point of contact that we have with the certifying factory surgeons is in dealing with the difficult cases that they come across in their examinations, and in trying to find some form of suitable employment for the rejected cases. We have also been able through the juvenile employment exchanges to provide the certifying factory surgeons with special information about children who go into factories and to pass on to them copies of the school medical officer's reports. It is strongly urged by many people that in future the whole work of the factory surgeons should be handed over to the school medical officers.

"Where the certifying factory surgeons find that a child is unsuited to the job into which he has gone of his own accord, then it is for the juvenile advisory committee and the juvenile employment exchange to try to find some occupation, if occupation is necessary, in which the child will not be harmed and will not suffer. The placing of children who are really suffering from some inherent defect, but who are capable of employment, is not, in certain parts of the country, carried on by the juvenile employment exchanges at all nor by the juvenile advisory committees, but these cases are handed over to voluntary bodies known as the Associations for the Care of Physical and Mental Defectives. They have a grant from the Government to aid them in their work, and we leave to them the care of the defective children."

BRITISH EDUCATIONAL STANDARDS

By SIR CYRIL JACKSON
Board of Education, England

I remember nearly 35 years ago when first I went to live in East London, the first job I was given was to try to help a miserable family. There were six children of a widow, the eldest of whom had just passed his standard in school and got exempt. He was the first wage earner who was going to look after that family. He was an extraordinarily bright boy or he would not have passed the standard at twelve years old. Naturally a boy of twelve years old in East London, in a poor family, in one of the worst slums of the place, did not have all the qualifications which are necessary for the battle of life, and a few months later I was visiting him in jail. Now from that moment I have sought and worked to abolish any educational standard that allows any bright boy to get out of school before the minimum age. And the Fisher Act has abolished for the whole nation any such educational standard.

In London we have long had fourteen years as the age at which children may leave school for work. Under the new act fourteen will be the minimum age throughout the whole country, the rural area, or wherever it may be, where the age in the past has been thirteen and in some cases even twelve. That, I consider, is one of the great measures of the Fisher Act of last year. But we have gone even beyond that in the Fisher Act. As you know we in England have had nearly five years of war. Our children have been taken out of the schools before their time. Our boys and girls have been put to work, very necessary work, for the country. And perhaps it was a bold step for the Ministry of Education, at the very moment when child labor was at its highest premium, to bring in a sweeping act forbidding in future any child under fourteen to work, and abolishing at one sweep all the half time which had been considered necessary in the textile factories in Lancastershire since time immemorial. So, as I say, under this bill child labor is not, even in war, going to be exploited in the future.

I suppose you know in the textiles in Lancastershire twelve to fourteen has been considered the normal age for half time instruction of children because it was considered that for half the time they ought to be learning the manipulation of the textile trades and the machines. Of course it was perfectly ridiculous to suppose that these children of twelve to fourteen either were really necessary to the industry or were learning textile manipulation. They were mostly made to run errands for the adult workers, although each had his task assigned to him in the workshop. But the parents, I am afraid, were the people who were the most difficult to move in this question of half time. The present chief inspector of the Board of Education told me not long ago that when he was a Lancastershire inspector one of the parents knocked at his door one morning to know why Tommy had not been let off school. He said: "How old is he?" "Twelve." "When was he twelve?" "The day before yesterday." He said: "Well, has he been in his examination?" "No, there has not been one." "Well," he exclaimed, "we cannot hold an examination the day after every child's birthday throughout Lancastershire." The parent said: "I have lost one lass without getting anything out of her, and I don't want to lose the lad." That was the principle on which that parent was demanding his son's working the day after he became twelve years old.

That is absolutely swept away under the Fisher Act, but the act goes even further, because beyond this raising of the minimum age to fourteen, which is, you know, low enough, it has a permissive provision which allows any local authority to make the lowest age fifteen, either for all the children in that area or for part of the children in that area, according either to their trades or conditions or to the means of their parents, as the local authority may decide. I hope that in the larger and more progressive places we shall at once go forward and make that by-law raising the age to fifteen. In London the age has been fourteen now for a dozen or more years, but there is no reason why we should not go forward and make it fifteen at once. It was said that no boy in the country could learn to manage cows and horses unless he began at twelve. I expect he will learn all the better if he has had a little longer education and shows a little more intelligence, and I hope that we shall very shortly make the general age fifteen or sixteen.

The present act gives us still further the continuation school, although not with quite the same hours as in Ontario. The Fisher Act prescribes that all the young people in the country up to 18 years of age must attend continuation school for 320 hours a year. That provision, however, will not come into effect immediately. For the first few years the age will be sixteen, but at the end of seven years 18 is to be the limit throughout the whole country, and in seven years much may happen. We may raise the required attendance to 400 or 500 hours before the seven years pass. I think 320 hours or eight hours weekly for 40 weeks is a small enough estimate.

I suppose that our industrial conditions are not very unlike yours. Every one has heard a great deal of modern conditions of labor, and it is obvious that the modern conditions of labor which apply to our factory work are not the same as they were when the workmen were able to take an interest in their work because they made something with their own hands. Now the workman is only the human part of a vast machine, doing some small operation of industry. All this means that we have to give a greater interest outside the factory. What we are doing in England I have no doubt you are doing here. We are approaching very rapidly a national basis of hours. Most of the big trades of the country are now fixing their hours at 44 or 48 hours a week. I think we shall very shortly have an eight-hour day and possibly a shorter number of hours as the regular national system, as it is now in Australia.

But if that is so it is all the more important that the working men and the working women shall know how to use their leisure, that they shall have education to enable them to use their leisure, and that they shall have at their disposal further schools which they can attend so that they may become citizens in the true sense of the term.

One of the most hopeful signs, I think, of the progress of England is the latest appointment to one of our oldest universities, Cambridge. The latest professor of Italian is a man who went to the bench at twelve years of age and worked as a basket-maker, and who has taught himself not only Italian but five other languages, and is now an admitted authority on Italian history and Italian literature. I believe that is a true democratization of an old university. But in order that it may not be only the exceptional boy who can do that but that all our lads and girls may have an opportunity of improving their education, we must surely see to it that such a minimum educational standard exists that everybody is able to get up to the top.

There are, of course, many other provisions of the Fisher Act which are very interesting to us. The main interest to us is, of course, its national aspect—the fact that no local authority in the future will be able to fall below the minimum which has been laid down by the Fisher Act. We shall have great difficulty, of course, in getting accommodations and more than all in getting teachers. You have not suffered as we have suffered in that respect. We have had to stop building for nearly five years, and our schools are sadly in arrears. You have not lost so many teachers as we have. The flower of our men teachers went to the front, and some of them will not return. We shall therefore have to come forward with our new Act and do the best we can to make the flesh for the bones provided for us by that Act. The Act itself has given us all a very great deal of hope.

A further provision of the Fisher Act which I might touch upon is that relating to the physical health of the children. We in England have had for some years past considerable medical inspection—practically in all the schools. We have medical inspection and very considerable medical treatment of the children. But that is stopped when the child has left school, except for the examination in factories by the certifying factory surgeon. Now under the Fisher Act there is a very important provision which enables the school medical authority, who will see the boy and girl, of course, in the continuation school, to go into the question of their health and inspect them, and if the employment is such that it is stunting their growth or is unhealthy for them, the school authorities may prohibit such employment. That, I feel, is an advance for the State because never before have we really gone from the educational standpoint to prohibiting employment on the grounds of health.

There are other things in the act on the same line. For example, we are allowed in the future to pay for and to establish holiday camps or any other kind of clubs or physical recreation for these young people up to 18 years of age which may be considered necessary for their physical development. I think, too, all of us who have watched the rejection of men who have come forward for service, as we have in England, because of their low physical development, due to their early going into industry and to the unhealthy conditions of so many workshops, appreciate that these provisions are extremely important to us.

Our Premier, referring to the classification of our soldiers—which, as you know, begins at A and works down to C—pointed out to us not long ago that you cannot make an A-1 nation out of C-3 citizens. And it is that which we have now to take in hand, just as I think we must take in hand the intellectual advance of our citizens if the old British nation is to keep its head above water at all. We shall have keen competition with America in the future. We want it. It will do us all good. But we shall certainly have to "buck up" if we are to hold our heads up. I have been looking, in New York and here, at some of the higher schools, and especially in New York I tried to see some continuation schools and some vocational schools. I am not one of those who think that our continuation schools must be mainly vocational. I think we should run a great risk if we were to say too much about the vocational character of the schools. As a sop to the employer before attendance was compulsory we might have done it, but now that we are compelling the employers to send the child anyhow, I think we will be justified in saying that we who control education must decide what the boy has to learn; and surely it is more important in the future that the citizens of any nation should have a general education and some human education than it is that we should fit them at a very early age for some particular industrial occupation.

I think there is no doubt that we have in the pursuit of vocational education been too apt to consider too little the whole man, and I am hoping that if we give sufficiently good education in our 320 hours the employers may perhaps give the vocational education in the rest of the time. I do not think the boys are going to be nearly as vital to the employers when they have to be taken out of the shops a certain number of hours a week. It is within the possibilities that boys will not be quite so easy to employ, and will not find a job quite so easy to get in the future, when the employer has to take the trouble to have two boys to a job or to let them out certain half days a week to go to school. That will be from my point of view a success, because I do not think that even when we have limited the age to 15 years for full-time employment, or when we have got part-time employment to 18, we have done our duty by the human boy and by the human girl.

DISCUSSION

Miss Julia C. Lathrop (Chief, Children's Bureau): I do not think any English authority can possibly realize the eagerness with which we have watched the progress of the Fisher Bill through Parliament, because we saw at once that somebody in England had had the courage to do a thing which nobody in America had been bold enough to do, which was to try to cut, by an indirect attack, the root of rural child labor. We would like to get a similar scheme in this country, Mr. Chairman, and with the cooperation or by the activity of your division of the Government (the Bureau of Education) to see aid given by the Federal Government to State authorities for elementary education, which would be so universal that in this country also we would at once destroy rural child labor by an indirect attack. I would like to know how much opposition from the land owners of England was experienced in getting this measure through.

Sir Cyril Jackson: I think there was no opposition, simply because we were in the middle of a great war, and we trusted Mr. Fisher. If we had had time to think about it I think no doubt the farmers would have opposed it very vigorously.

Hon. P. P. Claxton (U. S. Commissioner of Education): How many days does this law require of school attendance up to fourteen? Is it 225?

Sir Cyril Jackson: Oh, no. Full time.

Mr. Claxton: Well, that is 225?

Sir Cyril Jackson: 240, I should think.

Mr. Claxton: I wish you would take note of that. In the United States it is usually 180 days or less—180 for our cities, and an average of 140 for rural communities. The Fisher Act does not, however, prevent children from working when they are not in school on their fathers' own farms, does it?

Sir Cyril Jackson: We have limitation of hours in the act. Children over 12 years of age may work one hour before 9 a. m., if they do not work after 6 p. m., I think it is.

Miss Lathrop: Is it true that this act is recognized as a measure which is absolutely as much a labor measure as it is an educational measure? Was it put through under the delusion that it was purely to teach children to read and write better, or was it recognized that it was going to revolutionize child labor in England?

Sir Cyril Jackson: We all knew that it was going to make a tremendous difference in labor, because the fact that these continuation schools would take half time away from the factories was a direct challenge to the employer. It has been, I think, accepted by the employer as such and agreed to. I am a very old friend of Mr. Fisher, and I talked over the bill with him before it went to the House. I also talked with certain chambers of commerce, and on the whole I think the employers recognized that under modern conditions it was necessary for them to allow the children to have time off for school. Therefore I think it is true to say that it is recognized as a labor bill as well as an educational bill, and that from the child-labor point of view it was welcomed by everybody.

Mr. Claxton: I would like to ask Miss Lathrop a question. With the giving of Federal aid to the States for education in the rural communities and elsewhere, would you couple some requirement in regard to child labor? Otherwise it would not be effective except for the hours that the children were in school.

Miss Lathrop: I would always in the matter of special subsidies take a leaf from an English book. They are the only people speaking the English language, granting that they include their own colonies, who know how to give a subsidy. We hand out money and run away. They hand out money and stay by. They say: "You can have this money if you do your duty according to the standards agreed upon between the Federal Government and the local authority." Is not that true?

Sir Cyril Jackson: That is true.

Miss Lathrop: It would be a disaster if we began this effort to standardize education by getting rid of child labor without setting up new standards of educational effectiveness. The great advantage for us in a discussion of this English measure is that it shows us a way to standardize education in the interest of the future and at the same time to get rid of the one thing we have never dared attack—rural child labor.

One reason I have said this is because I have seen in one country in this world, and under the American flag, schools so well managed that the children clamored to go to them. Eight years ago I saw the schools in the Philippines, and found they did not dare have a compulsory education law there because they had not enough schools to take care of all the children, and that the children were eager to go to the schools because the schools were agreeable and taught them to do all sorts of things they had not known how to do before. The schools were steadily lifting up the standard of life. Children were taught to cook; they were taught to raise poultry for eggs and food instead of for cock fighting; in a hundred ways directly contributory to the happiness of life they were being educated.

Mr. Claxton: Will taking the children off the farms until they are 12 or 14 years of age, except for this hour a day, seriously interfere with agricultural production in England?

Sir Cyril Jackson: I do not see why it should. I was some time in Australia as head of the Education Department, and we had there a very large agricultural population. I had a freer hand there than I have had in England, and I raised the age to fourteen for everybody at once directly I got there. The only allowance

I made for the farmers was that they might have an exemption for children during harvest time, but I do not remember that we ever had any applications. The difficulty of coming to the central department was enough to deter them from asking for the exemption. I do not think that agriculture suffered in the least degree.

Mr. Claxton: I am quite sure that in this country with our modern methods of farming we could produce all we do and might produce much more if children were not required to work their lives away on the farm. There is one other thing about it that it is worth while considering, that there are some things that can be done on the soil, on the farm, about the home, that have just as great an educational value as anything a teacher can say to the pupil in the schoolhouse. Work has educational value if it is properly directed and in the right measure, and if it is done intelligently. I think we shall realize that the whole matter is not merely one of prohibition, not merely one of negation, but one of positive direction in the right way.

Robert C. Deming (Connecticut State Board of Education): I would like to ask as to the effect of this law upon street trading.

Sir Cyril Jackson: We have long had by-laws against children working at street trades. In London, I think, the minimum age is 14 for boys and 16 for girls. The new act does not make any exception there in favor of children of school age. It only forbids any child trading on the streets below the age of 14. That has been the by-law in London for a long time. Now it is a national law and will have to be enforced, but we shall still have the right that we had before to raise the age to 16 years if we wish to in certain localities.

Mr. Claxton: Do you contemplate using the system of half time in alternate weeks, so that two boys or two girls may hold the same job—that is, so it may be possible for all the children to have a good half-time school attendance through the period of adolescence up to 18?

Sir Cyril Jackson: I have seen and noticed that system in force in the schools in New York, and we shall, of course, be only too glad to get that sort of hint.

Mr. Claxton: Have you done anything of that kind?

Sir Cyril Jackson: We have not done it by legislation. We have done it by practice. We have had boys in London who have been doing silversmithing work on half time in the artcraft schools and half time in the shops.

Mr. Claxton: But none where they have the privilege of general vocational work?

Sir Cyril Jackson: No, I do not think we have had that yet; I hope we may.

AMERICAN EDUCATIONAL STANDARDS[1]

By CHARLES E. CHADSEY
Former Superintendent of Schools, Chicago

I am much impressed with the necessity of having a higher standard than exists at the present time in Illinois, where we allow a fourteen-year-old boy or girl to go out of the Chicago schools as soon as he or she has completed the fifth grade. It is well for us to have certain ideals. I do not want those ideals to be so high they can never be realized, but I do want them high enough to give us something definite to work for. It seems to me that it is not unreasonable to say that here in this State no child shall have his formal education come to an end until he is sixteen years of age, whether he has finished the eighth grade or the university.

I think further that we are not doing the right thing for our young people under twenty-one, who have reached the age at which the law permits them to go to work, if we allow them to separate themselves entirely from school opportunities, unless they have completed high school. For that large group there should be continuation schools, offering the work best fitted to the individual needs.

So I have these two ideals to set before us. A few years from now I may have a higher ideal, but I think these standards are reasonable: first, that education shall be the chief and only occupation of all children up to the age of sixteen, because no child can have gotten too much education during that period; and secondly, that those young people who have not finished high school at least, and who are at work between the ages of sixteen and twenty-one, shall have an opportunity—yes, shall be compelled by State law—to go on with their education, that education being related definitely and especially to the work they are doing. Under those conditions, I think we can say the condition of childhood in our State would be tremendously improved, and eventually the citizenship of our country would reach a perceptibly higher standard than it has reached at the present time.

Now, during that interval between the present time and the time when such an ideal may have been brought about, what should we do? I think we should always be taking the next step. In Illinois we have regarded as the perfect condition our law that no child shall leave

[1] Delivered at the Chicago Child Welfare Regional Conference, May 19, 1919.

school until he is fourteen and has finished the fifth grade, no continuation work being compulsory. In this we do not compare favorably with certain other States in the United States. Our law is not as good as that of Michigan or Ohio, or as the laws of a number of other States. It would be quite simple for us to take one step forward and say that the compulsory education law shall be changed so that no individual shall receive a permit to work until he is fifteen years of age and has finished the sixth grade. Let us put this into effect for a year and get adjusted to those conditions, and a year from that time let us take another step, perhaps making the completion of the seventh grade compulsory; then the eighth grade; then perhaps extending the age for leaving school to sixteen years. It may be wiser to spread this over a number of years if there is a necessary economic and business readjustment to new conditions.

I do not recognize, as some seem to imply, that the great obstacles in the way of higher standards for compulsory education and child labor are found in the schools. I think they are found rather among those very sincere social workers who see in an extension of these laws the danger of a sufficient decrease in the income of deserving families to make them dependent, where they are now independent. I have discussed this question scores of times with social workers of the highest standard, of whose sincerity there can be no question. It is true that there are many homes where the wages of the child mark the difference between dependence and independence. It is true that it would be unfortunate to do anything which would increase the number of those who may become to some extent pauperized. We have a complicated problem. But at the same time we must remember that it is more important to conserve the rights of the child than to perpetuate the rights of some person who will deteriorate from semi-pauperization.

However, I see no reason for such a result. We should recognize the rights of these children, and where there is financial necessity, provide scholarships which will measure the difference between the earning power of the family with the assistance of the child, and the earning power of the family without such assistance. I see no more reason why that should be pauperization than the mother's pension laws which are in operation in many States. It is justice, not pauperization.

I remember a few years ago when I was in Colorado that I received a letter from the then mayor of the city, urging me in the strongest language of which he was capable that a certain child, eleven years of age, should be given a permit to work because the mother was a widow. That mayor thought he was doing a kindly thing. He thought I was doing a rather unjust thing in not giving a permit to a child eleven years old. That is something I cannot conceive as being possible at the present time. But we all know of States where perhaps the majority of the people believe that there is nothing unreasonable in allowing a twelve-year-old child to leave school and go to work.

We have come to assume in a number of States that under certain conditions a fourteen-year-old child should be allowed to work; that failure to permit him to do so brings about an injustice to a family; and that a complete withdrawal of all of that kind of labor might have certain detrimental effects upon the industry and commerce of the community. That is not so. A community can adjust itself to the idea that the entire time of young people is needed for education up to the age of sixteen exactly as easily as it has adjusted itself to the idea that fourteen is a proper standard. It is very easy for industry and commerce to adjust themselves. It is usually very easy for the economics of the home to adjust itself, and in the comparatively few cases where there must be relief it is quite possible for the child to be taken care of by a private organization, or preferably, in my judgment, by the State itself.

I mentioned as my ideal that young people under 21 years of age, who have not finished high school at least, shall be compelled to attend continuation schools, especially designed to meet their needs. Perhaps the first step in the way of compulsory continuous education may be to have continuation schools only for that comparatively limited group of boys and girls who are working under permits, at present those from fourteen to sixteen years of age; but let us extend that compulsory continuation school education with the requirement of a permit to eighteen years instead of sixteen. Let us see that no child shall leave the public schools until he is eighteen years of age unless he has received a permit. And then let us see to it that we have compulsory continuation schools for that group of individuals who are thus released from school to work.

Here we have a practicable plan. Perhaps it should not come into operation too rapidly; possibly continuation school education may be made compulsory first for those fifteen years of age; the next year for those sixteen years of age; the next year, seventeen; but within a reasonable time let us have such a law actually on our statute books and actually in force. Then I believe we can say that we have accomplished something definitely worth while, and that we will have placed our State among the most advanced as to the broad-mindedness with which its citizens look upon this great problem of conserving the lives of our children, so that when they cease to be children they will be fitted as effectively as possible for life.

DISCUSSION

Miss Grace Abbott (of the Children's Bureau) read the minimum standards adopted by the Washington Conference with reference to child labor and education. She added:

"I wish, as a citizen and voter of Chicago, that Illinois standards were so high that these standards meant nothing to you. Personally, I will say that Illinois is far from leading in child-labor legislation; there is a very definite necessity for all of us to go to work. And I want to guarantee to Mr. Chadsey here and now, as a social worker for many years in Chicago, that social workers will not hinder but help him in accomplishing this program; that every one of them, whether working with a relief agency or not, will assume whatever additional burden is involved in raising the standard for the education of children. They are not worthy of the name of social worker unless one of their principal jobs is seeing that that thing is accomplished. I am sure there is no one here who is not ready and willing to join with the school authorities in elevating at once the requirements of education of the children of Chicago, of Illinois, and of the Nation."

LEGISLATIVE REGULATION OF EMPLOYMENT

STATE CONTROL

By THE HON. ALBERT E. HILL
Former Lieutenant Governor of Tennessee and Speaker of the State Senate

In the discussion of the legislative regulation of the employment of children I shall take for granted it is a foregone conclusion that the following have been established as minimum standards of child-labor laws:

(a) That the employment of children under sixteen years of age is prohibited in any mill, factory, workshop, laundry, telegraph or telephone office, or in the distribution or transmission of merchandise or messages, or in any form of employment that interferes with regular attendance at school.

(b) That no minor shall be employed for more than eight hours per day nor more than forty-eight hours per week.

(c) That no minor shall be employed before 7 a. m. nor later than 6 p. m.

(d) That no minor shall be employed in any occupation where there is more than the ordinary hazard to human life.

With these standards agreed upon, I shall briefly comment upon a few of them.

In the eight-hour day for children there should be a break in the day—a period of real recreation. No child should be employed in any concern that does not furnish a clean, wholesome place for the child to eat his lunch, stretch himself, and wash his face and hands.

The 7 a. m. to 6 p. m. limit for minors would prohibit them from carrying routes of morning papers. This should be done. It is work that is of serious detriment to the child physically, morally, and from an educational standpoint, as any public-school teacher can testify. Boys doing this work must arise not later than 3 or 4 o'clock in the morning, and usually start out without breakfast and poorly protected against the weather. They hang around in groups, in all sorts of places, waiting for papers to be given out. They come back from their routes hungry, tired, and sleepy; it is then almost school time, so there is no time for rest; and they are physically and mentally unfitted for school attendance. This work, like the street trades, should be left for adults.

Then comes the perplexing question of a minimum wage. Certainly a child employed eight hours a day for six days a week ought to be earning a living—that is, he should be fully self-supporting. His wage should furnish him housing, food, and clothing, and leave a little margin for recreation and emergencies. A smaller wage would be a social crime. What this wage should be must be worked out by experts and accepted by us.

We should take into consideration, however, that it would be hardly fair to enforce this wage where a child is employed only part time, as when he works only after school hours or during vacation, or at an employment where he is clearly serving an apprenticeship whereby he will learn a useful skilled trade by which he can make a living for himself and family when he reaches manhood. If all labor were organized, this problem would solve itself, or at least each organized trade would solve the problem for its trade, and then see that its requirements were enforced. But all labor is not organized, and we must deal with conditions as we find them.

There is also the subject of the administration of child-labor laws, for the administration of a law is as important as the provisions of the law itself. A law of minimum standards administered in an intelligent manner and rigidly enforced, will accomplish better results than an ideal law poorly administered. It is one thing to get a law passed and another to have it enforced. In each State it is necessary to have a department of factory inspection, charged with the duty of carrying out these laws. Factory inspectors should be men of practical experience, in full sympathy with the laws. Every concern employing minors should be compelled, under heavy penalties for failure, to file with the factory inspector monthly reports showing for every minor employed, the name, age, name of parents, nature of work, hours employed, and wage received.

There are certain other laws so necessary in the proper enforcement of child-labor laws that they may well be called companion laws. Among such laws is a vital statistics law. Unless the State is required to keep a record of births, the factory inspector is compelled to rely on the word of the employer or the parent as to the age of a child, and experience has taught that this causes the greatest confusion.

Laws requiring attendance at school for the full school term are also necessary to prevent child labor. Compulsory school-attendance laws, backed up by free text books, are, in fact, great preventives of the child-labor evil.

Mothers' pension laws are also closely related to child-labor laws. Without doubt the poor widow has been made the excuse for child labor more often than she has been the cause, but she is a cause often enough to make it essential that the State should make provision for the mother of a family of children left without support. These children become the wards of the State. They can be cared for much more economically at home than in institutions. If the State will provide mothers' pensions to meet this need it will save for future use one of its greatest assets, the lives and well-being of its future citizens.

The only connection that I have had with child-welfare work has been nearly twenty-five years' experience as a member of a legislature that has had this question up for twenty-five years. In that State when we started out we could not get any support, but we made a standard, and we have progressed until today we have almost reached that standard.

The law of 1911 prohibited the employment of any child under 14 years of age in any mill, factory, workshop, laundry, telegraph or telephone office, in the distribution or transmission of merchandise or messages, or in any business which interfered with the child's attendance at school during any part of the school term. Under the same law children under sixteen years of age were prohibited from employment on dangerous machinery, and children under eighteen years of age were forbidden employment as messengers for telegraph or messenger companies between 10 p. m. and 5 a. m.

In 1915 a law was passed excluding canneries from the operation of the 1911 law, but again in 1917 canneries were by law brought under the regulation.

In 1917 the 1911 law was further amended so as to require a working certificate issued by the county superintendent of schools before any child between 14 and 16 might be employed.

The hours of work for minors under sixteen years were first regulated by law in 1907, to wit: That after January 1, 1908, no child under 16 years of age should be employed longer than 62 hours in one week; after January 1, 1909, not longer than 61 hours, and after January 1, 1910, not longer than 60 hours. In 1913 a law was passed reducing the hours to 58 per week and $10\frac{1}{2}$ per day. By another act of the same year, it was provided that no child under 16 years should be employed between 6 p. m. and 6 a. m. An amendment passed in 1915 reduced the weekly hours for such minors to 57. The law of 1917 finally amended former laws so that no child under 16 years of age may be employed between 7 p. m. and 6 a. m., nor more than 8 hours per day or six days per week. So the 8-hour standard was reared, covering a period of about seven years.

The Compulsory School Attendance Law was passed in 1913, requiring that all children between 8 and 14 years of age shall attend school for 80 consecutive days each year, or, in the larger cities, for the full term.

In 1915 the Mothers' Pension Law was first passed authorizing the expenditure of $4,000 by the county courts in certain larger counties.

In 1917 the amount was increased to $8,000. The only counties availing themselves of this privilege are Shelby and Knox. So you see we are progressing very slowly in regard to mothers' pensions.

In controlling the labor of children Tennessee is well to the front except in three particulars. It has no law controlling street trades, no law requiring physical examinations and no law fixing a minimum wage. These are considered essential by students of child-labor conditions.

HOURS

By MISS AGNES NESTOR
President, Women's Trade Union League, Chicago

We feel today that we have come to a real point of departure from old standards. Those we drew up a few years ago, perhaps five or ten years ago, are no longer considered standards for today. The standards which were set up in the child-labor law were various safeguards that we all felt were well worth while and necessary. We all felt very proud of them a few years ago, but I think we feel today that we must depart from them and go on to what may be considered by some groups, I assume, as very radical.

As we go over the laws in the various States we feel without particular examination that we have fairly good laws, that we have various safeguards thrown around the children at the ages they are permitted to work. As we go down the list of States we find the maximum working hours[1] for children under sixteen years in nineteen States and the District of Columbia to be eight hours a day and forty-eight hours a week, and in eleven additional States the same hours but with certain exemptions; in ten States[2] a maximum working day of nine to ten hours but not more than fifty-eight hours a week; and in seven States ten hours or more a day with sixty hours a week.

After the age of 16, children are permitted in many States to work ten hours, in some States even longer. In Indiana, which is one of our important industrial States, there is no regulation of the hours for women. Thus after children reach the age of 16—and girls of 16 are children—they can work 12, 14, in fact any number of hours that the employer may choose. Our safeguards are left off at that very tender age.

I was glad to hear Mr. Lovejoy suggest raising the age to 18 and limiting the hours of work of children between the ages of 16 and 18 to six hours a day. I am glad to subscribe to that standard because we have to face this question as a health question—we must face the fact that the child must go through life. Are we going to permit him to work such long hours and under conditions so injurious as to handicap him for the rest of his life? I feel that I can talk critically of the various States, of the legislation they have now and the safeguards which neither you nor I feel are adequate, because in my own State I

---
[1] These hours do not always apply to children at work in all occupations.
[2] In one of these States the law applies only to children under 14.

feel that we are far behind in the matter of protective legislation. In Illinois we permit our girls over 16 to work ten hours a day and six days a week. Worse than that, we permit night work. We have no prohibition of night work at all except for the children between the ages of 14 and 16. We are not sufficiently stirred or alarmed by the conditions we are permitting. We must have an educational campaign to present certain facts; yet when we present these facts to our legislators we seem unable to make them feel that we are doing more than just talk, as they say, sentiment to them.

Dr. Sand spoke about basing the campaign on science and experience. Two years ago in Illinois we were agitating for an eight-hour law for women, a law we had been trying to get for many years. Our legislators felt that we did not have sufficient evidence to present to them. They felt that we ought to have a scientific investigation made, that we ought to have experts study the question so that we could come before them later with testimony to convince them that our contentions were true; to support them with sufficient facts and base our demands for this legislation on such a report.

There was a commission appointed about two years ago, upon which I had the privilege of serving. It was made up of two representatives of employers, two representatives of women workers, and three physicians. Of course, they do not consider seriously what the women workers say—they say we are not scientific—but we were feeling quite cheered by the thought that when the testimony of the three physicians on this commission was brought in some attention would be paid to it. This commission had a limited time to work and a limited appropriation. It was not appointed until January, 1917, and did not get down to work until about April, and had to make a report by December. But even in that time there were a number of very interesting studies made. That report was submitted to the Governor the first of December.

Experts told us that to make a study of fatigue you must measure fatigue by output; so we made studies of output. We were able to find certain factories and particular industries where hours had been changed and to make comparative studies. We sent out charts to employers; we examined the cards in the factory inspector's office; we sent out questionnaires; we got the testimony of industrial physicians. We got information from as many sources as possible. We found that long hours are not justified by output. We found, for instance, in one study covering a period of four years, that by reducing a 54-hour week to a 48-hour week the total output was increased two per cent and the hourly output was increased seven per cent. In another industry the same reduction of hours in a period of nine months increased the total output 3.9 per cent and the hourly output 11.8 per cent. In still another industry, covering a year and a half, with the same decrease in hours, the total output increased 13.4 per cent and the hourly increase was 31.5 per cent. We found in studying seasonal trades that it did not pay to have long hours over the season. The shorter length week, while it eliminated the big spurt at the beginning, tended toward a steady production throughout the entire season. A 66-hour week raised the output at the beginning of the season, but brought it down at the end so that the total output did not justify the long hours.

If the employer would look at this matter from an economic standpoint it would be to his advantage. We ourselves have a bigger question to consider, the health of the child.

We presented this report to the Illinois legislature. Some of the members are disturbed because we have not come in with a scientific classification of industries. But every one admits that in factory work where speeding-up takes place there is a great strain which necessitates regulation. Work in the stores, which is considered a light occupation, we know includes the strain of standing steadily and the pressure of the public. The fatigue at the end of the day is as great as factory fatigue. So it is when you go to other occupations. We believed we were justified in asking that the limitation of an eight-hour day be set on all the occupations that we have included under our present law until some other study or other evidence is brought before the legislature to justify a different regulation.

We studied the question further. We were eager to know what effect the long working hours of the mother had upon the health of the child. We made studies at some of the welfare stations in Chicago, where the Children's Bureau in its Children's Year Campaign was weighing the children, getting information, and giving advice to the mothers. Out of 110 babies registered at one branch, 67 were found in good condition and 43 in poor condition. Among the 67 well babies there were only 3 whose mothers were working mothers; among the 43 undernourished there were 10 whose mothers were working. We find, no matter where we go, that if long hours exist they affect the health of the women and eventually the health of the children, and thus the health of the future race.

I am glad to subscribe to and suggest as a standard for today that no child should be permitted to work under the age of 16, that no child between 16 and 18 years of age should be permitted to work more than six hours a day, and that no woman over 18 should be permitted to work more than eight hours a day. I should like to see the eight-hour day universal throughout the country. We ought at this conference to put forward advance standards, standards that all people, not only of our country but of all the countries of the world, are prepared to meet today.

WAGE PRINCIPLES [1]

By PROFESSOR F. S. DEIBLER
Northwestern University

I have been asked to speak on the principles underlying wage standards of working children. I do not know that the principles determining the wage of the working child are essentially different from the principles which should determine the wages that any individual worker should receive. There is no subject in the field of economics concerning which it is so difficult to lay down principles on which one can stand with perfect assurance as that of wages. It is one thing to lay down general principles governing general conditions; it is quite another thing to say what a particular wage shall be.

There are, however, certain general principles that should at least narrow the ground for dispute. Two general principles contend for supremacy in all wage matters. One, known as the "Productivity Principle" is that before a wage can be paid, a product must be produced. In other words, wages must come out of product. While there may be differences of opinion as to how much of the product shall go to labor and how much to profits of capital, unless, as Secretary Wilson says, there is something to divide there is not much use in having a dispute. This is only another way of expressing the idea that economists put in more formal terms. Along with that as a principle of determining wages, there is the principle of the living wage—the minimum cost of what is necessary to maintain the individual in physical efficiency. There is not only the question of whether a concern can pay the wages, but there is also the question of whether the individual can live on the wage.

Unfortunately so far as the application of these principles is concerned, they operate somewhat differently when we are dealing with material goods from what they do when we are dealing with labor. Ordinarily, in the case of material goods, if the price does not cover the cost of production, the goods will no longer be produced. But unfortunately we already have a supply of labor, and we will continue to have a supply, even though the cost of maintaining it in a state of physical efficiency is inadequate; even though that cost in the form of wages is not sufficient to maintain laborers in a state of physical efficiency. Excessively low wages will result in a gradual deterioration of the character of the labor supply and will result eventually in a depreciation of the productivity of industry.

---

[1] Delivered at the Chicago Child Welfare Regional Conference. May 19, 1919.

Fundamentally these two principles—that of the living wage, and the productivity theory, or the principle of what the product will afford—apply as much in the case of the employment of children as they do in the case of adults. It is true that some industries will be carried on for a time during which the returns from the product are not adequate to cover the cost, that is, during a promotional period, while a market is being found. But beyond that time the industry will not continue unless the returns cover the cost of production. So in some cases, for those entering industry there may be, for a certain period at least, a kind of training which is in the nature of promotion. Apprenticeship, where it really means learning a trade, has something of that character. Moreover, employers say that it takes a period of time for the individual to become worth his compensation; to a certain extent, no doubt, this is true.

I find at the present time that there is a very encouraging symptom to be found in the discussions of employment managers—how far it is a real sign of development it is too early to say. There is an increasing sentiment in favor of insisting on a careful job analysis of all the work in a shop and the arrangement of these jobs in such a way that there is a definite chance for everyone who comes into the factory or into the industry to have an opportunity for promotion. If that form of handling industry continues and becomes a permanent part of the conduct of industry, those who are entering, say, from the schools, do in a measure start to work at a profession. They have something definitely ahead of them. It is somewhat in the nature of an apprenticeship, not the old apprenticeship in which a single trade is learned but one in which the industry is learned. Under those conditions the wage at the start might perhaps be even less than the keep of the individual, if the job actually leads to a permanent position giving adequate return. That is a possibility. There are other jobs, however, that never lead anywhere in particular, the child being hired because his wage is lower than that of an adult. In case of that kind of a job I see no justification for less than a living wage. An industry that pays less is probably a parasitic industry and should not be in existence.

How are the principle of cost and the principle of product going to function? In some places the product may be adequate to pay the boy or girl a large wage; but certainly no larger wage will ever be paid than is necessary to get the worker. How can the functioning of these principles be directed? I see no other method than one similar to that of collective action. It may be that a method can be worked out through advisory committees composed of school officials, labor exchanges, representatives of industry, and social workers. Such committees might work out a satisfactory scale of wages under which children leaving school might enter industry on a satisfactory basis. This seems to me the most practical way of solving the problem.

MINIMUM WAGE

By DR. JESSICA B. PEIXOTTO

Professor of Social Economics, University of California

In this company there is no need to urge the merits of minimum wage legislation. Here at least, the case for such legislation has been finally won. In all circles, it is gaining ground.

For a century, facts slowly accumulated and assembled have shown that a large proportion of working people were being paid wages that demonstrably could not give them a bare subsistence. As consequence, for more than a generation the industries paying such wages, the so-called sweated industries, have been the focus for a rising tide of protest. Few persons in a modern community would not shudderingly protest the woman who stitched and stitched and starved, but equally few realize the hard fight necessary to eliminate the type; few trace the connection between legislation for a minimum wage and that process of elimination.

For minimum wage legislation has made its way in opposition to well-established opinion. Unquestioning acceptance of the speculative psychology that inspired individualistic doctrines led orthodox economists to insist that the operation of economic forces alone could determine the wages of labor. Any other method, they declared, would in the long run work to the disadvantage of the laborer and all other elements in society. Even collective bargaining has fought an uphill battle not yet won. Minimum wage legislation was for a long time altogether prevented. Not until a wave of new conviction swept over the civilized world, not until it came to be fairly well-established thinking that low wages are an injury to the worker and especially to the rising generation, and that the closest interrelation exists between a living wage and the health, the strength, the skill, and the intelligence of the working population,—not until then did the movement for a dead lift in wages through legal enactment get any headway. Dreariest fact of all, not until business interests came to see that well-fed labor spelled intelligent labor and thus labor that paid, did effective opposition to the passage of such laws cease. Then, in spite of the economist, because of the dread of physical deterioration that agitation and investigation had aroused, and because of a recent "business" principle that "cheap labor is dear labor," minimum wage legislation began. Though the emphasis, speed, and clearness vary, the leading nations are now all legislating on the principle that holds destitution socially disadvantageous and therefore intolerable and declares it a social safety device to secure for all workers, from industry, not from philanthropy, the means to buy a minimum of food, shelter, and clothing.

This public legalized interest in the cash nexus between employer and employee began in 1894, when the New Zealand Industrial and Conciliation Act was passed after considerable agitation and investigation. In spite of a continuing opposition, by 1915 all the Australian States had minimum wage laws that have gradually been extended to apply to all industries. Great Britain took the first step in this direction when the Trade Boards Act was passed in 1909 and put into operation in 1910. This act authorized four trade boards to fix minimum rates in four trades especially subject to sweating. Though all seem to have been more interested in home work and earnings of home workers than in factory workers and their wages, France, Belgium, and Germany have also taken steps toward legal control of the wages of female workers. The States of Canada have interesting minimum wage laws actively enforced.

Massachusetts passed the first minimum wage law in the United States in 1912. In 1913, California, Colorado, Minnesota, Nebraska, Oregon, Utah, Washington, and Wisconsin enacted laws touching wage-fixing. In 1915, Arkansas and Kansas; in 1917, Arizona; and in 1918, the District of Columbia followed. Thus, twelve States and the District of Columbia now have laws that aim primarily to fix the minimum wage which may be paid to women but which also take into account the wages of minors and in some cases also regulate the conditions under which they may work. Arizona, Arkansas, Utah, and Colorado have been practically inactive since passing their laws and Nebraska lacks appropriation for enforcement. Wisconsin and Minnesota have scarcely begun active enforcement. Thus, at best, five States, Massachusetts, Oregon, Washington, California, Kansas, and the District of Columbia, are actually enforcing minimum wage laws. The active States are Massachusetts and the Pacific Coast States, Washington, Oregon, and California.

In all of the States except Arizona, the law covers all industries. Only the Arizona law limits protection to certain industries. The District of Columbia specifically omits domestic service. None of these commissions in any State have yet used their full legal powers. Each commission is proceeding slowly, industry by industry, covering first those industries proven most menacing to the life and to the happiness of the workers. All the laws cover females of every age and minor boys. Arizona and Arkansas do not specifically set minors apart. The other States make four classes for awards—adult experienced women, adult inexperienced women, experienced minors, and inexperienced minors.

The work of young persons in industry is characterized by abuses with which most of us are all too familiar: low wages or no wages; long hours, night work; the apprenticeship period unduly prolonged; apprentices discharged at the end of the learning period; too many apprentices; young workers entering the trades with no vocational guidance.

The minimum wage laws under discussion aim to correct some or all of these abuses. In general, it may be said that all the States are meeting some of the evils, but that none are meeting all of the evils. Obviously all profess to correct the abuses of low wages or no wages. In California at least, the commission is also given special power to standardize hours and conditions of work; it can regulate night work and the length of the working day and can set the length of the learning period so that it shall not be unduly prolonged. It can also control the educational quality of the apprenticeship, but thus far has not done so. California, Massachusetts, Washington, and Kansas limit the proportion of apprentices who may be employed in any one business. California has a rather futile ruling that no more than 33 1-3 per cent shall be of this class; Washington and Massachusetts limit this group to 25 per cent of the force; Kansas limits it to 20 per cent.

Awards for minors are made at the same time that all other awards are made. In all these States, except Wisconsin, where the age is fixed at twenty-one, minors are persons under eighteen. Arizona makes its award on the flat rate basis. The $10 a week rate fixed as the minimum by the Act of 1917 applies as has been said to all workers in all industries. Unfortunately the Arizona law is not being enforced.

Two other states, Utah and Arkansas, fix rates on something like a flat rate basis. Utah has a graduated scale according to age and experience: $0.75 per day for all workers under eighteen; $0.90 for adult learners; and $1.25 for experienced workers. Arkansas fixed a flat rate in 1915 of $1.00 a day for the first six months; thereafter for women and minors the rate is $1.25. After investigation and public hearing the commission may raise the rate. In 1919, in spite of rising prices, this low rate is unchanged.

In all the other States, minimum rates for apprentices and learners are regularly below the "cost of living" rates for adults. They are also graduated according to age and according to industry and are ordinarily increased at regular intervals to the end of a period whose length is fixed from time to time by the minimum wage boards. It might excuse though not justify low wages, were educational opportunities legally provided to offset low pay. But I have found in the laws no rulings regarding educational opportunity. When apprenticeship was a status, the law and the contract dictated nurture and training for those indentured or otherwise bound. The advantage of the master dictated the same thing. Modern apprenticeship, however, is ordinarily a farce. It has no real likeness to medieval apprenticeship where the master "obligated himself to teach the apprentice a trade" until he could make a masterpiece. The educational opportunities provided by most mercantile and manufacturing plants travesty the name. "Apprenticeship" cannot now bear comparison with medieval usage. Therefore, if a two or three year apprenticeship period is allowed, as it was until this year in Washington and still is in California and Massachusetts, commissions that make such rulings must either be influenced by the interests of business or be paying unthinking homage to outworn traditions.

Minimum wage laws should consider the work performed, irrespective of the age of the worker. To make painstaking "apprentice" exceptions for minors is merely concession to an outworn custom and to shortsighted business enterprise. These exceptions made for minors are disadvantageous to the adult worker and to the community. Granting minors less than a subsistence wage is likely to protect them from the worst abuses only; the abuse of low wages continues unchecked.

The minimum wage set for women by any one State is nowhere as yet a wage that permits them to live well. It is still only a rate that, as Walter Lippman says, "gives just enough to secure existence amid drudgery in gray boarding houses and cheap restaurants." The Pacific Coast rulings of April, 1919, announced a minimum of $13.50 as against $10 previously paid; in the District of Columbia the rate is $15.50 for the printing trades. Encouraging as these figures are when viewed retrospectively, they mean little actual advance in real wages. When equated with a rising scale of prices in 1919, it is plain the subsistence standard of 1913 has merely been maintained. Since the standard which sets the minimum wage of women is such that the wage covers little more than physical necessities, obviously wage rates for minors that are uniformly below this sum are in no real sense living wages. In existing rulings, the pay of young persons of sixteen to eighteen is regularly one-fourth to one-third below the bare subsistence level set for women. Customary? Yes! Satisfactory? No!

It may be objected that raising their wages would probably exclude minors from industry. This is a desideratum, not an objection. Any wage, high or low, tends to tempt minors to leave the schools too soon. The nation needs its children in school long enough to prepare for the demands of democratic social order. A theory of education sent the child into industry. One hundred and fifty years ago it was thought wholly desirable that children should be at work as early and as long as possible. We who gather here to-day in connection with these problems of child labor are as eager to get them out of work. It would be a poetic justice, would it not, if a theory of education takes them out of that deteriorating discipline to which a theory of education consigned them. In the United States—for that matter in all civilization—nothing but ignorance or penury sends children to wage work. Upper class standards have long followed the practice of prolonged schooling. In the so-called middle classes, parent and child are alike ambitious for it and make sacrifices to give it to their children. In a democracy, upper class standards so penetrate that all the "Americanized" have one standard of living though perforce different planes of living. It is sober fact that all Americans would give their children prolonged preparation for life if income permitted, and that even now all Americans, however small their income, strive to give it to their children. The free public school and the university are forever whetting an ambition for knowledge that today is felt by little less than the whole population.

To rule that minors must be paid as adult workers are paid, according to experience or inexperience, would doubtless lower the demand for young workers because business could not long afford any but trained and intelligent help. Thus the child would be kept in school with added incentive to get a little technical education, while at the same time his parents' demand for a living wage would be proportionally sharpened. Experience and investigation have become basis for a public opinion that in the United States favors the elimination from all industry, and especially from dangerous occupations, of all minors until their eighteenth year.

As they relate to minors, these minimum wage laws, these adventures into the no-man's land of wage-rate fixing, are the latest comers in the group of regulations designed to protect children from the wastes of the industrial process. The child-labor laws which preceded them aimed fundamentally to remove young children from industry. They touched but slightly the destiny of the adolescent children. In most civilized countries many minors are still at wage work. We find them in larger or smaller proportion in industry, where they receive money wages, or in agricultural or domestic service, where they receive the better part of their pay in kind. Characteristically, the young person in industry goes there from a wage-earner's home to supplement family earnings. The child of philanthropy as well as the child of its own parents will be found at wage work after fourteen. Though domestic or farm service is known to be the service the least promising, the worst paid, and the most unprotected of any class of work, yet the 1910 census tells us that one and one-half million of the children between the ages of ten and fifteen years are listed as farm laborers, and even though the majority of these are reported as "working at home," they are still doing a work that limits their opportunity to prepare for life. The cant about young children at fourteen "saved from the city's strain" by being sent to the country to work survives in despite of findings. A study in a rural section of North Carolina made by the Children's Bureau in 1916 showed two-thirds of the white and three-fourths of the negro children between 5 and 15 years of age doing chores and working long, hot hours in the cotton fields, over a third of them under ten years of age. Farm work and house work then seem to compete with poor school curriculum and poor attendance laws in developing illiterates and incapables to be underpaid minors.

With all the facts reviewed, it would seem fair to say that minimum wage commissions have as yet failed to take a consistent stand in legislating for minors. Created to work out wages on a cost of living basis, they still—even in the Pacific Coast States and in the District of Columbia and despite the intention of the acts in all but Massachusetts—allow business interests ("the financial condition of the occupation" as it is phrased in Massachusetts) to keep awards below subsistence levels. Apparently either the courage or the power is still lacking to say frankly through law enactment that men who cannot run their business without cutting wages below a recognized living cost shall not cloak their own inefficiency by using up young people's lives.

Minimum wage legislation for minors is undoubtedly making some progress. An excessive number of apprentices is no longer permitted, and the period of apprenticeship begins to have limits. Some wage as against no wage at all is now available for inexperienced workers. Finally, the whole question of apprenticeship has been raised to an issue that is being met progressively though slowly.

Through these laws, minors at work are protected in some seven commonwealths from the most aggravated forms of exploitation, and in the Pacific Coast States from the most unfortunate conditions of work. But the apprenticeship period is still too long; the whole field of agricultural labor and domestic service has not yet been brought within the law; a true educational opportunity during the apprenticeship period has not yet been legally provided. Therefore the current legislation by countenancing the practice of lower wage to minors continues a situation disadvantageous to the adult worker and to the community.

Since the wage award to adults by these commissions is a subsistence wage and nothing more, to pay less to any worker is to continue an evil practice of subsidizing industry out of the health of the nation and encouraging the employment of the untrained. Minors are best protected by school laws rather than by labor laws. Legislation for compulsory school attendance; for prolonged schooling; for continuation schools; for juvenile labor exchanges that provide the machinery to register the desire for work, and the current demand for workers, and give vocational guidance; and finally, legislation for a minimum wage for the bread winner of a family group, so that mother and children shall not be obliged, despite the proven disadvantage, to supplement the earnings of the father—these things will do far more to protect minors than minimum wage legislation.

Therefore I submit these standards of legislation for young persons. As immediate steps, minors are best protected by laws for compulsory school attendance, for continuation schools, vocational guidance and the like. Minimum wage legislation should take cognizance of only two classes, the experienced and the inexperienced workers. Given the simple initial work in most industries, a six months' period of learning is all-sufficient. In the few employments where the work is exceptionally hard to learn, a bona fide apprenticeship period may be provided for, but as soon as the output of the minor equals the ordinary output of the adult, the minor should receive the minimum wage provided by the award.

ADMINISTRATIVE STANDARDS

By MISS TRACY COPP
Wisconsin Industrial Commission

A few years ago the advanced employer was the man who had established the eight-hour working day and provided for decent wages and good working conditions. But today an employer to be advanced must have established some acceptable plan of joint control in his shop. A few years ago we said that a child who had lived fourteen years and who had certain minimum educational qualifications was legally qualified to enter industry. Today, however, all that can be said of permitting children to go to work at the age of fourteen is that it is better than permitting them to do so at an earlier age.

We have seen in Wisconsin the operation of a good law. We have seen industry organized to meet it. We have seen the development of special agencies to take care of the unusual child. We have seen the procession of children who come into the permit office for their first working permits and for the reissued permits for each new job. We believe that when the time comes—and I am not sure that it is not here now—to improve our child-labor law, it should be improved by raising the age at which children may enter industry, and by raising the educational qualifications for such entrance.

In Wisconsin the responsibility for the enforcement of all legislation affecting the relation between management and labor is given to the industrial commission. In the city of Milwaukee (which is half of the State so far as the employment of children is concerned) the industrial commission issues the labor permits. It has been my privilege to have, as supervisor, authority in that department for the last seven months. I have prepared for you a practical outline of our office procedure, our methods of enforcement, their relation to the continuation school, to the inspection service, and to the other departments of the commission.

The Wisconsin law requires all children between the ages of 14 and 17 who are employed, other than in agricultural pursuits, to secure labor permits. Issuing labor permits for children has many significant aspects other than their legal entrance into industry. For instance, the permit represents a change in educational experience for the child. Upon its issuance he leaves the regular school and enters the continuation school on an eight-hour-a-week basis, which time is taken out of his working hours. The permit also represents, for the boys especially, an opportunity for a program of apprenticeship, which begins at the age of 16. The apprenticeship contract takes the place of the labor permit for children between 16 and 17 years of age, but the continuation school education continues at least to the eighteenth year.

The permit should mean that a child has had the advantage of competent counsel and advice in relating his tendencies and abilities to the job opportunities in the locality. The permit also means to the child that he shall be followed into the factory by the State inspection service for the purpose of enforcing the hours of labor and the prohibited employments clauses of the child-labor law, and that substantial violations of the law at least shall be corrected.

The permit has an added and serious significance to the employer. It means more than simply a means of classifying young people into age groups for the purpose of arranging their working hours to comply with the law. Upon the employer of children who have no permits, or who are at work at prohibited employment, the Wisconsin Compensation Act makes a heavy pressure. Under this act, the industrial commission must award treble compensation to minors of permit age who are injured while employed without a permit or while working at a prohibited employment. The employer must himself pay the extra compensation, or two-thirds of the whole amount, which is added on account of the unlawful feature of the employment. He cannot insure against this hazard.

Every phase of child-labor legislation is negative. All the elements of such labor are clearly undesirable. The legislation is designed to throw about the children all types of protection. Provision is made by which certain educational training may continue. There is restriction as to employment—the whole scheme being to limit the opportunities rather than to extend them. Child labor is wasteful, and a burdensome thing. It is quite proper, therefore, that the features of the child-labor law which contemplate the protection of young persons in industry become at once the hazards to the employers of these children.

The correct handling of the permit business of the State is imperative. It is also necessary to develop the closest cooperation and harmony among all the agencies with which the child deals in making his entrance into industry.

The legal proofs necessary for a work permit are: proof of age, proof of educational qualifications, proof of physical fitness, and proof of a job. We do not require the child to obtain a job before coming to our permit office; rather, we encourage him to avail himself of our counsel in securing his job.

On the educational certificate we have provided for the personal recommendation of the school principal regarding the issuance of a permit, and we have further said that no permit shall be issued when the school principal recommends adversely, except in special cases, and then only after a hearing at which all interested persons may participate. The health record is used in the same way. The school physician is asked to make recommendation also as to the issuance of the permit. The school physician may recommend adversely, or affirmatively with limitations on the kind of employment. The issuing officer issues the permit as far as practicable in a manner consistent with the school physician's recommendation.[1]

It is clearly necessary that the greatest care be given the mechanical end of the work. Modern conveniences in office fixtures are quite as essential in a permit office as in any other big business institution. The handling of various legal records which cannot be duplicated requires a peculiar kind of office housekeeping. The permits contain transcripts of important documents that may later be used in court cases; hence a mistake on the permit means more than merely an embarrassing recognition of inefficiency.

The need of a sympathetic and friendly atmosphere in the permit office cannot be overestimated. Under the present arrangement in Milwaukee a child may make his first request at the issuing office or at the office of the school principal. Much depends upon the attitude of the interviewer at this time. If the child has already secured his work, he has experienced a very vital event in his life. At this time, the kind of job, his hours of labor, his wages, and shop supervision mean very little to him, but the fact that he has a job is a very real thing to him. He makes his first acquaintance with the big, abstract thing known as the State. I cannot emphasize too much the necessity of having this phase of the State's business make the most wholesome impression upon him.

For the children who have not been persuaded to continue their education, or for whom readjustment of their educational program has not been made, and who are legally qualified for work, the labor permit may be issued. The industrial commission, however, has the power to refuse a permit to a child if by so doing the best interests of that child are served. The child must sign the permit, and if he is between the ages of 14 and 16, his parent or guardian must come with him. The permit is issued to the employer and is sent to him by mail, and the child is told that he may report for work the following day. For the children who are interviewed in any day and for whom

---

[1] In the ensuing discussion, Dr. George P. Barth (Director, School Hygiene Bureau, Milwaukee) emphasized the fact that in Milwaukee no child can secure a permit to work until he gets a certificate of physical fitness from a physician.

permits are to be issued, the permits are issued and mailed out on that day.

When issued, the permit is used as a means of enrolling the child in the continuation school. Subsequently he is assigned to classes. It is used also to maintain attendance. In aggravated cases of non-attendance the permit may be revoked for such a period of time as is necessary for the child to make up by continuous attendance the time lost.

At the expiration of a child's employment, the permit is returned to the issuing officer by mail, and the child must come to the office with a letter from the new employer to whom the permit is to be reissued. Before it is reissued, approval from the attendance department of the continuation school is required. If there is school time to make up, the permit is held and not reissued until a clear school record is reported. The employer is notified by us that the permit which he has requested will be held for a specified time. In the event, which is not infrequent, that the job is not to be held open for the child, the permit is not granted until a new job is secured.

Permits coming into the office each day represent the number of children who have left their work. Many of these permits are reissued within a day or two, as it is quite customary for a child to withhold his quitting notice from the employer until a new job is secured. Other returned permits represent the groups of children who have left the city, entered agricultural work, or returned to school; or who have been committed to public institutions; or who have secured employment on a false statement of age. All these children are known as "unemployed" for the purposes of office records, though our own surveys indicate that many of the so-called unemployed are actually employed without permits. As soon as a child between 14 and 16 years of age is unemployed, he becomes a full-time or part-time school problem, though those employed without permits are clearly a responsibility for the industrial commission.

The temptation for the child between 16 and 17 years of age to secure employment without a permit, and the ease with which it is accomplished, together with the hazards to the employer under the compensation act, have made us feel that a very prompt follow-up of these children is necessary. Their homes are visited, the place of employment determined, and the employer notified by telephone immediately. Reports are kept in the office of the commission showing by historical record the attitude of the employer toward employment of children on no better evidence than their own statements of age, and also the employer's attempt to improve the employment system of the shop following the discovery of violation. The survey of unemployed children has been made and supervised by volunteers who have had special social-service training. All children applying for reissues to new employers, who have been loafing or employed without permits, or who have been otherwise outside of the supervision of the permit officers for a period of four weeks or more, are especially interviewed. The purpose of interviewing these children is, first, to get a list of employers who habitually accept children into their employ on their own statements of age, to advise the children of the danger of making false statements as to their age, and to attempt to reduce as far as practicable the high labor turnover among juvenile workers. Attempts to reduce labor turnover, however, should not eliminate the opportunities for children to use judgment in selecting their jobs. The things that make work desirable for juveniles are frequently identical with the things that make work desirable for adults, and many times in changing their jobs children use mature judgment.

A junior employment department, dealing with children between the ages of 14 and 17 years, has been established in the Milwaukee permit office. The agents are engaged in placing children in employment, filling positions in the local establishments, encouraging children to return to school, adjusting their educational programs to fit their needs in individual cases, taking part in the usual routine work of the child-labor department, and assisting in making all employment of children of permit age legal. Children who are found to be illegally employed by public and volunteer agencies are brought to this office, counseled and advised on the law, and given assistance by the employment department in securing new jobs under proper legal conditions. Children who change their work frequently and seem to be unable to get on in any particular line are advised in relation to their tendencies, equipment, and the job opportunities, by both the junior advisor and the apprenticeship supervisor.

Our aim is to encourage all the social agencies that are concerned with the welfare of young people to use the permit and employment department as a clearing house. It is not our wish to discourage in any way the fine personal work being done by these agencies with children and employers, but simply to see that whatever placements they make are legal, giving the employer no other burden than the special one in connection with the unusual circumstances of the employment, and also to see that the placements are made in a manner consistent with the permit office procedure; by that I mean, children should be placed, so far as is practicable, in the shops of the advanced employers where the housekeeping and supervision are best, and not in the shops in which difficulty is experienced by the commission in maintaining the legal standards. It is especially desirable for an agency wishing to serve the employers along employment lines to have available the equipment and personnel of the permit department and the continuation school. No placement of a child between 14 and 17 years of age should be made unless both the child and the employer are thoroughly protected under the law.

The relation between the permit department and the factory inspection department in Milwaukee is clearly the strongest feature of the present arrangement. The women factory inspectors survey the shops employing women and children with careful attention to their special problems. The agents of the industrial commission, who inspect the shops where children work, study the surroundings of the employees with a view to further extending or limiting the employment opportunities of children.

The industrial commission may, after thorough investigation, refuse to issue child-labor permits for occupations in which there is great danger. The commission refuses to issue child-labor permits for occupations in which there are obvious hazards to young people, and to employers whose attitude toward their responsibility under the law is such that the commission feels such employment to be unsafe. The issuing of permits to such employers is temporarily suspended until reasonable assurance is given the commission that the manner of employing children is to be improved.

Employment of children in establishments where the management shows repeated indifference to its obvious responsibility in connection with children which it employs, is considered undesirable. Every effort is made by the commission to make clear to the employers their obligations under the child-labor law, and also the penalties imposed under the compensation act for failure to comply with the child-labor law. When these efforts fail to secure a proper compliance with the law, the commission feels justified in imposing severe penalties upon those employers who persistently disregard warnings. In most cases of first offense, where it is clear that an employer has been careless through no desire wilfully to violate the law, he is given an opportunity to correct the condition with the understanding that he will be held strictly to account for subsequent violations.

The commission recognizes the necessity of bringing these matters before employers repeatedly. Employers are burdened in many ways and frequently handicapped by the mistakes of their superintendents and foremen, who are already overburdened with production problems. The commission has endeavored to show employers that it is advisable to give the responsibility of the legal employment of children to one person in the managerial department. Wherever this has been done, it has been found that the firm has been reasonably secure from unintentional violations of the child-labor law. Further to assist employers, the commission has published newspaper stories, written many explanatory letters, and endeavored in every way to give publicity to typical kinds of violations of the law and their serious consequences, which may serve as warnings to other employers.

Employers whose records in the commission's office show a constant repetition of minor violations, are requested to meet a representative of the commission and to show cause why they should not be prosecuted. These conferences frequently result in a better understanding of the law by the employer and a better understanding by the commission of the employer's problems. When an employer is thus put upon probation with the department, and for subsequent substantial violations is prosecuted, a clearer understanding of the necessity of such action is evident.

It is clearly desirable for all the agencies affecting the employment experience of permit children to be physically so located that a minimum of the child's time is spent in adjusting his entrance into industry. There should also be the closest harmony and cooperation among the directing chiefs of these departments, with no jurisdictional jealousy, but with a working plan built around the interests of the children.

In a community that is not poverty stricken and that has educational institutions of high grade, with decent employment opportunities for adults, the child-labor situation should be much above the standards set by law. Heroic efforts should be made to keep children in school, to adjust their educational program, and to make continued education profitable and possible, whatever the minimum standards of law may be. A social administration of a law is the reasonable forerunner of a better law. Honest administration and wise use of discretionary power, however, should not be accepted as a substitute for better law, for, after all, the raising of the standards for leaving school and going to work, and the further limitation or extension of job opportunities for children, can be accomplished effectively only by statute.

DISCUSSION

A Member: Will Miss Copp tell us what to her mind are the advantages of having the permit office connected with the industrial commission rather than with the school system?

Miss Copp: I have not been able to compare them, but in our special case the advantage is that the industrial commission has a local office in Milwaukee where we have the necessary office equipment and the clerical help. In the other parts of the State the work of issuing permits has been done by the continuation-school or the public-school authorities without compensation. I see no reason why our inspection service and our methods of prosecution would not be as available for the school authorities as for another department of our own office.

VOCATIONAL GUIDANCE AND PLACEMENT

JUVENILE PLACEMENT IN GREAT BRITAIN

By RONALD C. DAVISON

Chief, Juvenile Labour Exchange, England

We shall all agree that in the contest between school and wage earning we should wish to see the claims of the school advanced at the expense of wage-earning. But juvenile employment is still with us, and it will remain even when these changes are made. It is, therefore, important to secure that the nature and conditions of that employment are made as worthy of the education which preceded it as possible.

My special business is to tell you something of the methods by which we have tackled this problem in Great Britain. Since 1910 we have had a national system of employment exchanges which correspond to the employment offices set up by the Federal Government in this country. At the present time we have about 400 main employment exchanges and about 1,200 branch employment offices attached to the main exchanges. All the main exchanges and some of the local offices deal with juvenile applicants and with the vacancies notified by employers for juveniles. The juvenile age limit in England for this work is now 18. The employment exchange system is divided into ten divisions, each being controlled by a divisional office, and each divisional office containing an organization section especially concerned with juveniles. Finally, the whole service is controlled from the central office of the Employment Department in London, where again there is a special Juvenile Branch in charge of juvenile work.

The ordinary functions of our employment exchanges are to provide a market place for labor and to carry out the system of unemployment insurance. We have realized that far more than this comparatively mechanical work—though it is not wholly mechanical as regards adults, and it is becoming less so—is needed where juveniles are concerned, and we have endeavored to secure that the juvenile exchanges or bureaus should be used in the interest of boys and girls themselves, and with the main object of helping them to make the best possible start in their careers as wage earners. In this way the juvenile bureaus were to be the means of improving some of the evils resulting from the industrial system. And I think we can claim that we have been able to bring about some improvement in the conditions of juvenile employment as a whole, and to render the whole system of real benefit to the community.

I will state briefly some of the problems which the juvenile exchanges and juvenile employment committees have to meet. Boys and girls when they leave school at 14 are faced with a variety of opportunities of wage-earning. Many of them are attracted by the deceptive promise of independence which is offered by a small wage rather than by the need of looking to their permanent careers and of taking a job which gives them prospects. They are pathetically ignorant of the task that is before them and of the world into which they are going. There was one boy who came to an exchange who, when asked what he wanted to be, thought carefully for a little time, and then said, "What I really want to be is a retired merchant." Boys and girls are also liable to ignore conditions which may be harmful to their health or may be wasting the educational advantages which they have obtained. Again, it is necessary to find some way of dealing with the boys or girls who cannot hope to take up the employment which they desire or to get skilled jobs, either because they are too young, being under 16, or because there is no suitable vacancy at the moment and is not likely to be one perhaps for a month or two. Those cases have to be dealt with specially.

In general, one may assume that it is altogether too easy for school leavers to get jobs. I do not know whether that is the condition in America. But in England in normal times there is a surplus of juvenile vacancies, many of them necessarily being of the blind alley type. The demand for juveniles is greater than the supply. This leads many children to be indifferent about keeping their jobs and to be careless as to whether they secure jobs which offer them permanence.

Of course parental guidance ought to play a part here, and to a large extent it does. But as regards specialized advice about a job or about a trade, I think there are very few parents in any class of society who are really able to estimate the exact prospects of any trade except the one in which they happen to be themselves engaged, and it is very often the one trade into which they do not advise the boy or girl to go. What is wanted is expert advice from somebody who is in continual contact with all the employers in the district, and is giving his whole time to the placing of children. This is highly technical work, worth doing for its own sake and for the social benefits which can be obtained.

It is not suggested that, by the establishment of our juvenile bureaus, we have been able to remedy all these ills. But we have satisfied people that the work is valuable, and it has been a popular feature of our employment exchange work. Not the least of the advantages to be gained from the establishment of machinery of this kind is the detailed knowledge and experience of the local conditions of employment and of all problems affecting juvenile welfare which may be obtained at this one center dealing with the employment of boys and girls. Information collected in this way has already been a powerful factor in leading up to important legislative changes and other provisions. For some time before the war the juvenile exchanges, and the juvenile employment committees attached to them, were able in many areas to obtain better by-laws which restricted the conditions of juvenile street trading by raising the minimum age at which street trading was allowed and by securing that no license should issue except through them. And coming to a far more important matter, one of the factors which led up to the new Education Act, which has now passed into law, was a big inquiry conducted through the juvenile employment committees all over the country, which produced information for the use of the Board of Education.

Further, during the war we made an elaborate investigation of the war conditions of juvenile employment. Over 3,000 firms were visited, and the conditions of juvenile employment reported upon. A report was published on the results of this inquiry, and in that report were outlined the schemes which should be adopted for dealing with juvenile unemployment when the time should come at the end of the war. The time did come, and these schemes were to a large extent put into operation, providing for an out-of-work donation for juveniles in the same way as for adults, although at a lower rate, and providing that as a condition of the receipt of the out-of-work donation they should attend at juvenile unemployment centers provided by the educational authority in each district.

Another inquiry which is being conducted now is an inquiry into the hours of juvenile employment all over the country, especially employment in those trades not at present covered by restrictive legislation. I understand that a bill is in draft to put into effect certain higher standards.

There are, I think, valuable benefits to be secured by concentrating through one agency and one agency only the filling of as large a proportion as possible of all the juvenile vacancies in any district. Not only can the experience of people who have knowledge of education and of employment, the two sides being equally important, be brought to bear upon the problems of individual children, but also this is probably the only way of achieving something like the right distribution of the juvenile applicants for employment among the available supply of vacancies. So long as you have juvenile employment, it is important that the best vacancies should go to the best children, and that the less desirable vacancies should go to those for whom the best prospects cannot be entertained. A central agency also gives the child a wider range in selecting the employment in which he will make his start in life.

I could give instances showing how we have been able to approach one of the most difficult questions, namely, the placing of children at a distance from their homes, a thing to be touched with great hesitation. But where there is no skilled vacancy for a boy in his home district, and there is a demand at a distance, we have been able to satisfy ourselves that it was desirable and in the boy's best interests that he should leave home and take such an opening. We have been able to transfer to one big shipbuilding firm about a hundred apprentices, securing that their lodgings and leisure were carefully provided for and their general welfare assured.

Further, I think it is better for boys and girls to obtain their jobs under conditions of comparative publicity rather than in an obscure and casual manner, as when they go to see a foreman or manager or an employer at his own works.

We have always regarded as the principal feature of our work the functions associated with the juvenile employment committees, which have been set up in gradually increasing numbers during the last nine years. Over a hundred were set up in the last year of the war in preparation for the crisis which we knew was coming. When I left England there were some 250 of these committees, and hardly any important industrial area was left uncovered. All these committees were closely associated with the juvenile exchange, although about a hundred of them were set up not by the Ministry of Labour, but by the local educational authority in cooperation with us. In this connection, I might explain that where the Ministry of Labour sets up a committee that department on its side secures the cooperation of the local educational authority and arranges for the appointment by that authority of a minimum of six members on the committee. The link is complete in all areas where we have an effective and successful committee.

Every district is left to work out its methods according to local needs, subject to a certain general plan. In the first place it is necessary to get a full report from the school on the child's school career. Such an arrangement enables the juvenile bureau to exercise a useful supervision over those who have obtained employment independent of the bureau. You can then arrange for after-care supervision; you can be ready to deal with the child when he comes back later and asks for assistance in obtaining employment. The school-leaving forms show the result of the medical inspection before the child left school, so that the considerations of health are not overlooked. In cases where the assistance of the bureau is desired the secretary of the committee asks the parents to come up and discuss the future of the child. This arrangement tends to quicken the sense of parental responsibility rather than to relieve parents of any interest in this important stage of their children's lives.

In most areas we have committee meetings once or twice a week, at which one or two members of the main committee sit, attended by the officer of the exchange, in order to interview juveniles who need special advice.

Then there is the system of after-care supervision, and without some system of that sort we could hardly claim to have an effective organization. Some supervision is needed over a great proportion, but not necessarily all, of the boys and girls who obtain employment. I do not think we wish to make a purely mechanical business of the supervision where it may amount to nothing more than fussy interference, but we must have some system of keeping in touch with those who need it.

We work with the existing agencies in every district; with the school care committees (an organization under the educational authority, which has known the child during his school career and is willing to keep in touch with him afterwards); and with the voluntary clubs, scout troops, guilds, and other associations of endless number. Recently we have had an interesting and important development known as the juvenile organizations committees, which now exist in most large towns for grouping together all the juvenile organizations and looking after the recreation and social welfare of the boys and girls who belong to the different bodies. They will perform a very valuable function, I think, in connection with after-care supervision. Such arrangements do much to secure that the committee will have due notice of any cases where their intervention is desirable, or where a child should be advised to change his employment. Also this system of after-care supervision should provide a point of contact with the certifying factory surgeons who have to see the children when they start to work in a factory.

No account of the work of our bureaus, our exchanges, or our committees would be complete without reference to propaganda. The personal influence of a committee including representatives of the local educational authority and of leading employers, representative trade unionists, and representatives of all other agencies interested in the welfare of boys and girls, cannot fail to be of very great importance in attracting sympathy and notice to their work. In many districts they hold separate meetings for employers and for works managers, and again in some cases experiments have been tried of holding meetings with foremen and interesting them generally in the work. Teachers' meetings, of course, are held, and meetings with parents. Every committee, when it organizes, and at intervals afterwards, circularizes the employers in the district on matters of importance, particularly for the purpose of securing their cooperation in reporting vacancies to the juvenile exchange.

This function of carrying on propaganda in the district is an opportunity for influencing juvenile employment as a whole, apart from the individual work of advising or assisting children. Some of our committees have been able to call into conference a group of employers in a certain trade or a group of firms in a certain district, and have been able to get trade unions concerned in those trades to meet with them, and then with this three-sided conference they have worked up a new scheme for juvenile employment in the trade concerned, with improved conditions, possibly better wages, shorter hours, or better provision for attendance at classes or for securing the permanent absorption in a trade of all the boys and girls that enter it. This results in uniform standards among all employers covered by the agreement, and these employers take it on themselves very often to persuade other employers not covered by the original agreement to adopt that general standard. Obviously they have to do that in self-protection.

In case of an apprenticeship scheme, such an agreement has a special interest, because the terms of apprenticeship are almost always a matter of individual bargaining between the employer and the parent, and here we now have something like a collective apprenticeship scheme with uniform conditions. I am not sure how far that may lead us. We may find it possible to do a great deal on those lines.

In conclusion, I should like to give you a few figures. First, as to the number of registrations of juveniles that we have in the exchanges in the course of a year, the most recent figure I remember was rather over a half a million. The number of placings was rather over a quarter of a million. Second, there are about 6,000 members of juvenile employment committees. And perhaps we have even twice or three times that number of after-care supervisors giving some of their time to look after a certain number of boys and girls in the different districts.

DISCUSSION

Mr. W. E. Hall (National Director, Boys' Working Reserve, United States Employment Service): I understand, Mr. Davison, that you operate under two acts—the Employment Exchange Act and the Choice of Employment Act. Are these advisory committees appointed under both of those statutes, or is it merely a voluntary organization? Is the employment of these committees provided for in the statute?

Mr. Davison: The two acts do exist and they practically amount to dual legislation for the same purpose. Therefore the Ministry of Labour and the Board of Education got together and arranged a system which would prevent useless confusion. That system has been in force since 1911.

The solution adopted is that where local educational authorities wish to set up committees in connection with the Ministry of Labour Exchange they may do so, and they receive certain financial assistance from the Board of Education amounting to half the cost.

We have for eight years let any of these educational authorities take the initiative if they wished to, and that arrangement still obtains. Where they do not wish to set up a committee, then the Ministry of Labour has undertaken to set up a juvenile advisory committee arranging for not less than six members to be appointed by the local educational authority. So cooperation is secured in either case and the method of working is not seriously different under either of the two systems.

Mr. Hall: At the present time is there any control of the applicant so that he must go to one place in order to get a position? In other words, is there one place of hiring in every district, or may a child go to seek employment at the factory gate?

Mr. Davison: No, there is no such control. We have not got compulsory notification of vacancies or compulsory registration. And on the whole I will say that the balance of opinion is still against it—I do not state my own opinion. In fact, we simply rely on the contact with the schools and with the public to get children to use the Juvenile Exchange and to ask for assistance. The existence of such agencies has gradually become known until now we can say that over a third of the children leaving school come to the exchanges for advice, or information about them is reported to the exchange, and over another third come at a later date for their second or third jobs.

Mr. Robert C. Deming (Connecticut Board of Education): Do they have in England a system by which they follow up the child; in other words, a permit system by which to locate the child, identify him, and know what he is doing?

Mr. Davison: That is the after-care supervision which I was trying to explain. There is no official visitation so far as we are concerned, but it is done by keeping in contact with the child in a voluntary capacity.

Miss Julia C. Lathrop (Chief, Children's Bureau): For what purpose are funds used by the advisory committee? Are they used for supplying a salaried officer under the advisory committee, or what are the legitimate expenses of these advisory committees?

Mr. Davison: They do not administer any funds. The only expenses which they may charge are their own personal expenses in certain very restricted and limited circumstances, when they are required to travel on the work of the committee. The secretaries are paid in the same way as all the other officers are paid throughout the employment service. They are not specially paid by the committee.

Mr. Frank M. Leavitt (Associate Superintendent of Schools, Pittsburgh): Dr. Claxton has made a distinction between education and the schools. It seems to me that the trouble with our schools, and I speak as a school man, is that they are confined too largely to the education which they can actually give themselves. I am interested also in the education that the schools may direct.

So when the Employment Service of the United States Department of Labor came to Pittsburgh a few months ago and asked the public schools if they were willing to cooperate with the Employment Service in the field of guidance and placement, I grasped the opportunity to help run the Government, or the little portion of the Government that was willing to do some work in my community.

We started out with the assistance of the Junior Section of the United States Employment Service to create something in Pittsburgh that we think ultimately will be of value. We have talked to several hundred employers and asked this question: "Provided we can tell you how many young people will come into the labor market year by year from the schools and can give you information regarding the physical, mental, and temperamental characteristics of those young people, are you willing to use the service which we can give you? In addition, are you willing to give us a certain amount of information; will you tell us the number of young people you have in your employ now under 21 years of age; will you tell us what wages you are paying and what are the opportunities for advancement in those positions now held; will you tell us approximately how many young people you are ready to employ each year?"

We feel very confident that we are going to get that information. We sent out last week in the hands of a personal representative a letter asking those questions. That letter was presented to forty employers. Out of the forty employers thirty-nine said: "We should be delighted to use such service as that if you can give us that information." We are sending out now 400 similar letters by mail.

On the other hand, inside of two weeks there will go to every school principal in the city instructions that he is to send to the office of the superintendent of schools a report on every child who leaves school. If a child over 14 years of age chooses to leave the school there will come automatically to the office of the superintendent a statement regarding that child, his age, his standing in school, his special likes and dislikes, his ambitions, his physical characteristics, and his mental characteristics. We shall then send a school visitor to the home of the child to get all the information we can from the parent as to why the child is going to work, and so forth. In brief, we are going to get as good a picture of that individual child as we possibly can. We have taken this statement to the parochial schools, the University of Pittsburgh, the Carnegie Institute, the Duquesne University, and other educational institutions, and said: "This is what we are going to do with our students; are you willing to do the same thing for the United States Employment Service with regard to your pupils?" We have their promise to give us all possible information with regard to their students. In fact, for some of these schools we now have on file the number of children who will leave by graduation and the number who will leave by dropping out.

We believe that in a very short time we shall have collected an amount of information about this particular body of junior labor that will be so valuable that the employers will have to consult it. The better employers are already consulting it. We are already making placements of boys and girls; but we were not so much interested in the first instance in making placements as in developing a system that we hope in the course of five or ten years will bear fruit.

I believe that ultimately this matter of vocational guidance and placement is one of education, and particularly the education of the young people themselves so that they will know enough to avail themselves of the service. We may have a very good placement bureau, we may have an excellent United States Employment Service, but if the people do not know enough to use that service it is of no avail. I believe it will take some years to teach the young people and the older people, the employers and the employees, to use intelligently a placement bureau, or an employment service, or a labor exchange.

Hon. P. P. Claxton (U. S. Commissioner of Education): Mr. Davison said to me as he sat down, "There was still another point." I want to ask what it is.

Mr. Davison: Really it was only to give a rather more extended description of the arrangements we made after November 11th when the Armistice came upon us. The inquiry which we made was the first step that I have already described. The next was to provide a complete network of committees throughout the country, and I have already referred to that. The next was to raise the age of juveniles for our purposes to eighteen, because in England the military age begins at eighteen. We did not want to have some of the boys between seventeen and eighteen going into the department where there were soldiers and older people, and the problems of the boys between seventeen and eighteen, owing to the special circumstances of the war, undoubtedly would be juvenile problems.

Then when the suggestion of the out-of-work donation was decided upon by the Cabinet, provision was made to include juveniles from fifteen years of age upwards, not below. For the children between fifteen and eighteen years of age the donation was fixed at $3.60 per week to boys and $3.10 to girls for a period of thirteen weeks, on condition that they reported regularly that they were unable to obtain employment and were available for work. You cannot give money away without imposing some conditions, and those were the conditions. There was a third, namely, where the educational authority set up a school, which was called a juvenile unemployment center, we would not pay that out-of-work donation to any child unless he attended regularly at this center. That system has been carried out.

Mr. Claxton: I should like to make a statement and ask a question. Some of us in this country, and the number is increasing rapidly, believe that education for citizenship in the larger democracy which is coming, not only for us but probably throughout most of the world, will require a kind of education that cannot be given to children under fourteen or even under sixteen years of age.

At twenty-one years of age, men and women, but yesterday boys and girls, go to the polls and decide by their vote the policies of the local community, of the State, and of the Nation, and very soon thereby the destinies of the world, because there will be some closer association of nations, and the action of one cannot help influencing, more than it has in the past, the destinies of others. And these problems are more difficult, more complex, than they have ever been before.

Many of us also believe, and the number is increasing, that you cannot give the education necessary for industrial life, the knowledge of the underlying principles of chemistry, physics, biology, and mathematics, that are necessary in our modern industrial and commercial life, before fourteen or even before sixteen years of age. It requires education through adolescence. And all of us like to believe that in a democracy like ours, in a time when with labor-saving machinery it is possible to create wealth, that all children have a right to whatever education can be given them until the years of manhood and womanhood, for culture, for life, for humanity, because after all everything exists for that.

Now, with that understanding must we not find some means of giving systematic formal education at least up to the age of eighteen and possibly longer?

One other statement. Some of us have come to believe in this country that vocational guidance is not a very easy thing, that it is not something that one can do without knowing the child and knowing him well; and that another, possibly an outsider, can never do it to full satisfaction for any individual. Therefore the child himself must have some part in his guidance. He should not choose his occupation or have an occupation chosen for him until he knows something of the round of occupations, in general at least, and probably not until he has had some experience, some knowledge of them through actual contact.

For that reason these people that I have referred to—I think it includes now the larger number that are responsible for guiding educational policies—have come to believe that we should have some kind of half-time instruction (I use that term instead of part-time), some means by which we shall have an all-year-round school, let us say, of 48 weeks; they believe that arrangements should be made so that children over a certain age, fourteen, fifteen, or sixteen, as the case may be, may attend half the day, alternate weeks, by the fortnight, or probably by the quarter, if necessary; they believe that there should be formal instruction not only in the things that have reference to the child's vocation, but in those equally important things that have reference to citizenship in a world-wide democracy, to culture, to manhood, to womanhood, to all the opportunities and all the duties of life.

There have been experiments in this country that have shown that this is at least possible—some of them in universities, some of them in the last year or two years of high school, and some for children as young as fourteen years of age. Usually these experiments have succeeded.

I have come to believe that we must find a means of doing this, and to feel that with our constant improvement of labor-saving machinery, and the possibility of larger production for the individual man, it is not necessary that most children shall begin making a living, or give all of their time to making a living, at sixteen years of age.

Section III

The Health of Children and Mothers

(The minimum standards for the protection of the health of children and mothers adopted by the Washington Conference will be found on pages 436-439.)

MATERNITY AND INFANCY

STANDARD REQUIREMENTS FOR OBSTETRICAL CARE

By DR. J. WHITRIDGE WILLIAMS

Professor of Obstetrics, Johns Hopkins University, Baltimore, Maryland

Taking into consideration the varying conditions obtaining in different localities, it is not easy to lay down universal standard requirements for obstetrical care; for it is obvious that the problem will differ in large cities, in small urban communities, and in rural districts. Furthermore, the problem will vary in large cities according as they contain medical schools with their attendant students, who may be utilized in solving some of the problems, as well as by the proportion of the population that employs midwives.

Broadly speaking, it is not difficult to lay down standard requirements for cities, which for the present must be of such a character that they can be carried out by general practitioners of average intelligence. In such a standard the following requirements seem essential: (1) Monthly prenatal visits during the second half of pregnancy, with examination of the urine; (2) a careful preliminary examination four or six weeks before the expected date of confinement, which should include a general physical examination, as well as pelvimetry, mapping out the position of the child and the determination of the existence of any serious disproportion between the size of the head and the pelvis; (3) reasonable care at the time of delivery by one who will observe the ordinary rules of aseptic technique and who knows enough to abstain from meddlesome midwifery, with the understanding that suitable hospital accommodations are available for all patients presenting such complications as cannot be satisfactorily treated in their homes; (4) a careful postpartum examination four weeks after the birth of the child, for the purpose of relieving or treating minor abnormalities and of detecting the existence of such lesions of the birth canal as may require operative relief; (5) supervision of the baby for the year following its birth.

It will be noticed that I have not included the Wassermann test as part of the routine prenatal care, nor the determination of the blood pressure at each monthly examination. This is not because I do not fully appreciate the serious rôle played by syphilis, but because I consider that such examinations are feasible only in institutions with well-equipped laboratory facilities, or in communities in which the health department maintains an efficient laboratory and is willing to cooperate in the work. Of course, it is understood that such an omission will result in the birth of a certain number of syphilitic babies, as well as in the development of hereditary syphilis in others who survive. But, at the same time, I feel that under average conditions the Wassermann test should be obligatory only for patients who present a suggestive history, or in whom the repeated occurrence of premature labors or stillbirths strongly suggests the existence of syphilis. Routine blood pressure determinations were omitted for the reason that in the vast majority of cases the subjective symptoms and the presence of albumin in the urine permit a diagnosis of pre-eclamptic toxemia to be made without their aid.

At the present time I think that it is conservative to estimate that even such standards as are here outlined will not be applicable to more than one-half of the population of most communities. A more liberal estimate might be made in the case of large cities, which are abundantly supplied with hospital facilities and other philanthropic resources; but, on the other hand, they would prove difficult to carry out if any considerable proportion of the population were attended by midwives. Furthermore, under present conditions, such standards could not be maintained in many rural districts, and particularly in the open country, as is evidenced by the reports issued by the Children's Bureau concerning the conditions in certain counties of Kansas and North Carolina; for in many such localities physicians are not available, and the woman is often fortunate if she can avail herself of the services of even a partially trained midwife.

It appears to me that progress in this regard can be made only along three lines: (a) by a campaign of education, in which the women and their husbands are taught that it is their right and duty to demand reasonable care during pregnancy and at the time of labor; (b) by the institution of State aid and by National subventions, partly for educational purposes, but particularly for the carrying out of such minimal standards as seem essential; and (c) by legislation requiring local health officers, in localities in which midwives are generally employed, or in the open country where they represent the most available source of assistance, to assume charge of the situation and to lay down certain regulations which the midwives must be compelled to follow.

I take it that the first step in such a campaign of education for the improvement of obstetrical conditions must consist in the compulsory registration of pregnancy through the local health officer. In this event, it will be possible for every pregnant woman throughout the entire country to be supplied gratis with certain of the publications of the Children's Bureau, and thereby, if able to read, to be convinced of the importance of insisting upon adequate care. Furthermore, it should be the duty of the local health officer to see that the women who register should promptly arrange for suitable care during pregnancy and at the time of labor. If a physician were engaged, the health officer's responsibility would end, but if the patient is to be cared for by a midwife, it would be his duty, or that of a paid substitute acting for him, to see that certain examinations and requirements were carried out.

Thus, I believe that it should be stipulated that midwives could attend only such patients as offer every prospect of having a normal labor. This could be effected by providing that they could not assume charge of a patient until a certificate had been procured from a properly qualified medical man stating that he had made a suitable preliminary examination and had found everything in order and that he considered a normal outcome likely. This could be further checked by the health department providing suitable blanks for the purpose, and stipulating that they must be returned when the birth certificate is filed. Furthermore, the midwives should be required by law, even in cases which had been certified as presumably normal, to call a physician whenever labor lasts for more than 24 hours, or when any unexpected abnormality develops.

Such a procedure would have a highly educative effect upon the patients, especially upon the foreign born who are accustomed to believe that midwives are thoroughly competent; it might also teach the midwife something, and it would certainly constitute an important step toward her eventual displacement. In cities, the midwives might bring their patients to the obstetrical dispensaries, when such are available, where the certificates could be filled out gratis for the very poor, and for a small fee in the case of women in more comfortable circumstances.

On the other hand, women who present some abnormality at the preliminary examination should be referred directly to a physician, or be sent to the hospital at the county seat for treatment.

Of course, the general adoption of such regulations would necessitate a revolution in the methods of medical practice in rural districts, and could only be carried out if funds were available for the employment of suitable persons to regulate the midwives, as well as for the institution of hospitals at the county seats, which would be available for the reception of patients urgently needing hospital care.

The suggestions here made do not cover in any way the supervision of the child during the first year of life, and I imagine that in rural communities this can be effected only by the employment by the county of visiting trained postnatal nurses, who would make tours through their districts at regular intervals and see the children under their care. I take it that radical reform in these directions can only be attained after a campaign of intensive education, for we have learned that the most efficient method of safeguarding the interests of the child is by teaching the mother how to care for it. No amount of supervision will accomplish the greatest good unless at the same time the mother is taught what her duties are to herself, and how they can be best carried out.

DISCUSSION

Sir Arthur Newsholme (Late Principal Medical Officer, Local Government Board, England): In regard to the notification of pregnancy we have in our country hitherto preferred to make provision to induce prospective mothers to come, rather than to make notification obligatory. Therefore we have set up in our centers prenatal consultation clinics and have tried to induce mothers to come, and at the same time have used our official machinery in connection with the midwives, who assist in 75 per cent of the births, to induce them to bring mothers to these clinics.

THE CONTROL OF VENEREAL INFECTION

By DR. PHILIP C. JEANS

Associate Professor of Pediatrics, Washington University, St. Louis

The Importance of the Subject

Gonorrhea.—Though gonorrhea plays a large rôle in the sterility and general ill-health of the mother, it has, with the exception of infection of the eye, usually but mild effects upon the newly born infant. Occasionally gonococcal arthritis may be observed, but this condition, though quite painful, usually ends in complete recovery without loss of function. Vaginitis may occur in the newly born, but more frequently occurs at a later time as a result of contagion. Vaginitis at this age is frequently quite painful and always disagreeable, but it does not have the serious sequellae that it has in adults. Infection of the eye in the newly born is serious in that it frequently results in permanent blindness, and unless treated early and vigorously it may result in impaired vision even with good treatment. It has been estimated that from 25 to 30 per cent of blindness as found in adults is due to gonococcal infection of the eyes at birth. This alone makes the condition one of common interest.

Syphilis.—In syphilis we have a much more serious disease. In the study of a large number of syphilitic families, it has been found that 75 per cent of the pregnancies result in syphilitic offspring; one-fifth of these die at or before term from the infection; one-fourth of those born alive die in infancy as a result of syphilis; and but one-sixth of all the pregnancies result in non-syphilitic children who survive the period of infancy. The waste in infant and child life in a large group of syphilitic families is over 60 per cent as compared to less than 25 per cent in a similar group of non-syphilitic families of the same social plane. The list of serious disabling lesions of syphilis is a long one. Those infants who do not die as a result of the infection frequently suffer from a long period of malnutrition, and the maintenance of their nutrition becomes a difficult matter. Most of the serious affections other than those mentioned appear as later manifestations, but for purposes of prophylaxis should be considered as a part of the subject under discussion. One-third of these surviving children sooner or later develop an inflammation of the cornea. This condition if untreated or neglected frequently results in blindness, and under the best of treatment there is usually a prolonged period of loss of function. In one-third of syphilitic children the nervous system has been seriously invaded by the spirochete of syphilis. It is perhaps going beyond our knowledge to say that all of these sooner or later develop some outward evidence of such invasion, though it is certain that a large number of them do develop paralysis, dementia, blindness, or other neuro-syphilitic manifestations. The numerous painful and disagreeable lesions of syphilis need not be further enumerated. Enough has already been said to emphasize the seriousness of hereditary syphilis.

A proper question, and one which can not be answered accurately, is with what frequency does syphilis occur. Statistics from four cities of this country show that about 10 per cent of married pregnant women are actively syphilitic as shown by the Wassermann reaction. It is to such women that syphilitic children are born. Statistical studies made in St. Louis and New York indicate that from 5 to 6 per cent of our infant population is syphilitic. These surveys among the mothers and infants were all made among the poorer classes.

It is obvious that any disease affecting in so serious a manner such a large number of families is worthy of our best efforts for prevention.

Preventive and Curative Treatment

Gonorrhea.—Gonococcus infection of the infant occurs during or after birth, the infection occurring directly or by contagion from a localized open infectious process in the mother. In most instances ophthalmia neonatorum occurs as a result of infection of the eyes during the birth of the infant. For this, the most serious gonococcus infection for the infant, there exists a means of prevention both harmless and easy of application, i. e., the instillation of a 2 per cent solution of silver nitrate into the eyes immediately after birth. Credé, who first advanced this method of prevention, was able by its use to reduce the incidence of gonococcus ophthalmia in his hospital practice from 136 to 1 per thousand births. This measure is universally recognized as effectual in prevention and all that is needed is some means by which those attendants at confinement who otherwise would be negligent may be compelled to take such a precaution. In many States this matter is well looked after by follow-up visits and prosecution by the health boards under State law. The details of methods of checking and follow-up need not be enumerated. Propaganda through lectures, motion pictures, and leaflets intended for the people in general makes a very useful adjunct to legislation and health-board activity. The Federal Government is already carrying on such propaganda to some extent. The rather obvious next step would be to have suitable laws passed in those States which do not have them and to activate those State boards of health that need it.

Syphilis.—Except in rare instances, syphilis of infants and young children is a congenital or hereditary infection transmitted to the infant before birth by way of the maternal blood. It is generally agreed that germ transmission does not take place and in order that the child be infected before birth it is necessary that the mother first be infected. Though this view may be shown later not to be entirely true, preventive work based upon this conception has been demonstrated to be effective. It is probable that the fetal infection occurs in all instances by way of the placenta and that the spirochetes reach the placenta by way of the maternal blood stream in which there occur occasional small showers of spirochetes from a more or less active focus elsewhere in the body. Whether or not the child will be infected depends upon the activity of the process in the mother, which in turn depends in a large measure upon the length of time which has elapsed since the maternal infection. Those children born soon after the maternal infection are severely affected. Even without treatment the infection in the mother in many instances tends to subside to such an extent that it is not transmitted to the offspring. This is not necessarily so at an early date. In some instances a syphilitic mother has non-syphilitic children eight to ten years after her infection, while in others she continues to have syphilitic children 25 years after her infection. In a few instances the period between the infection of the mother and the birth of the first child is of such a length that none of the children are syphilitic. It may be stated as a general and probable truth that the Wassermann reaction will be positive in any mother whose infection is active enough to allow the infection of her child *in utero* and that a mother whose infection has subsided sufficiently so that the child will not be infected will give a negative Wassermann reaction. The exceptions to this rule must be very few. From this it is seen that a Wassermann reaction on the serum of a prospective mother may be taken as a criterion, not as to whether or not she has syphilis, but as to whether or not she is likely to infect her infant. Some such criterion as this is necessary for the reason that nearly 90 per cent of the mothers of syphilitic children honestly deny all knowledge of infection or later manifestations of such infection. In many instances a history of abortions and stillbirths may lead one to suspect syphilis, but this alone is insufficient evidence upon which to make a diagnosis. The one most constant and reliable symptom of syphilis is the positive Wassermann reaction.

It has been fully demonstrated that adequate antisyphilitic treatment of a mother throughout her pregnancy will result in the birth of a non-syphilitic infant. It is probable that this treatment acts to cause a retrogression of the maternal infection or at least in its being held in check to such an extent that the fetus is not infected. Based in part upon laboratory studies of the products of conception, it is thought that—in most instances at least—fetal infection does not take place until the later months of pregnancy. Upon this basis may be explained the fact that even if a mother is treated only during the latter half of her pregnancy the infant in the great majority of instances will not be infected. The shorter the period of treatment prior to birth the more likely is the child to be syphilitic, but even the shortest periods of treatment are not without benefit. The cure of syphilis is at best a laborious process, and it would seem greatly preferable to prevent infection of the infant in this way than later to treat the infant for the disease even though eventually it may be cured.

The treatment of the mother during one pregnancy does not protect the subsequent pregnancies unless that treatment is continued to the point of "cure" of the mother.

In the prevention of inherited syphilis, we are confronted with a somewhat complicated problem. It is necessary first to make a diagnosis of syphilis in the mother at a fairly early period of her pregnancy, and it is necessary in our present knowledge to depend in a very large measure upon the Wassermann reaction for this diagnosis. The conscientious physician will try to verify the diagnosis made in such a manner in as many ways as possible. Serological and physical examination of the husband and of the other children would be very useful not only for this purpose but also as a public-health measure. In this connection it is well to remember that many husbands, though the source of infection, will give a negative Wassermann reaction at the time of such examination, for relatively few men will marry with a known active infection. The standards for good prenatal care should include an examination of the blood just as they include urine and other examinations. The diagnosis of syphilis having been made, the mother should be treated according to the best recent standards for the treatment of this disease.

In those instances in which the infection has not been diagnosed until the puerperium there is the added factor of management of the syphilitic infant. The first goal in the management is the diagnosis. It is necessary to realize that a very large number of syphilitic infants show no outward signs of their infection either at birth or during the customary period of obstetrical observation, and any infant that does show marked signs at this early date has a relatively poor prognosis. The Wassermann reaction on the infant's blood is also unreliable in this period to the extent that fully one-third of actively syphilitic newly born infants give a negative reaction, though the reaction if positive means syphilis as much as at any other time. These same negatively reacting infants will a few weeks later give positive reactions. Though the obtaining of blood in sufficient quantity for a Wassermann reaction is a relatively easy matter in expert hands, the practical difficulties are such that many physicians would not undertake it as a matter of routine.

Nor is it a procedure that would be universally tolerated by parents unless some urgent need were shown. As a substitute for taking blood from the infant, blood might be taken from the placental end of the cord at delivery. This procedure has the advantage of ease of accessibility. The same objection holds for this blood as for that of the infant, that only about two-thirds of the infections can be diagnosed thus. In the hands of a competent pathologist, a much larger number of infections may be diagnosed by histological examination of the placenta. Perhaps 95 per cent of the infections may be diagnosed in this way. This method of diagnosis is but little trouble either to the obstetrician or to the pathologist. It also has the possible advantage of avoiding what might be awkward explanations. A Wassermann reaction on the mother's blood has the same advantage in diagnosis as it does earlier in her pregnancy, and the agreement between this and the infection of the infant closely approaches 100 per cent unless the mother has had antisyphilitic treatment during her pregnancy.

Except in small towns and rural communities, the obstetrician does not ordinarily undertake the treatment of syphilis. Since the nutritional factor is often a very large one in syphilitic infants, it is desirable to make extraordinary efforts, if necessary, to have the baby breast fed. The patient should be referred at the earliest possible date to those who are competent both in the management of infant nutrition and the treatment of syphilis. In the absence of nutritional disturbance and intercurrent disease, infantile syphilis may be completely cured, according to our present standards of cure, in the great majority of instances, and the policy of "why not let them die" apparently held by many is entirely unwarranted.

The Control of Syphilis

Having means to diagnose and treat syphilis which are on the whole fairly adequate, it becomes necessary, in order to apply these measures, to locate infected individuals. For successful prevention it is necessary to bring the mothers under observation early in their pregnancy. The public is more and more becoming educated to the desirability of obstetrical supervision throughout pregnancy. Further propaganda along this line is needed. It is not necessary to advance any arguments here as to the desirability of such care. The encouragement and wider distribution of prenatal clinics will reach a large proportion of those who most need such care. A "blood examination" should be made a part of the general examination of each such patient and the finding of a positive Wassermann should be the signal for anti-syphilitic treatment, enforced if necessary. This whole idea must be carried out largely by publicity, since it is scarcely feasible to require legally a Wassermann test on every mother.

Failing in prevention it becomes desirable to diagnose syphilis in the infant at the earliest possible moment. Though good obstetrical standards should require a Wassermann on the mother, a positive reaction is merely presumptive evidence of infantile infection, though in most instances the presumption is correct. A negative Wassermann on the infant at this age may lead to a false sense of security. The most constant evidence of infantile infection is found in the placenta. Since the examination of the placenta requires so little time and at the same time reveals such important information, it should be a part of proper obstetrical routine in every case. Before carrying this plan out on a large scale, however, its reliability should be better founded. In case it proves to be satisfactory, it could be required that all placentae or proper pieces of all placentae be sent to the board of health. Material from stillbirths and miscarriages should be included in this requirement. One pathologist with one or more technicians could easily examine promptly material from all the births of a city. The details of the follow-up by the health board could well be left to depend upon local conditions within certain limits, but there should be some means provided by which the infant would receive prompt and effective treatment either voluntarily on the part of the parents or enforced if necessary. The diagnosis made in this manner should later be checked by serological examination of the infant.

For those patients handled by prenatal and obstetrical clinics, the logical sequence is to refer the infant to postnatal clinics whether suspected of syphilis or not. In such clinics overlooked infections would be diagnosed as symptoms appear.

In conclusion, the chief points to be emphasized in the control of hereditary syphilis are as follows:

1. Infection of the infant can be prevented by treatment of the mother during pregnancy.

2. The Wassermann reaction, checked by other observations, if possible, is the one most dependable criterion as to whether or not a mother should receive treatment.

3. In about 95 per cent of instances of infantile syphilis placental examination will show evidence of such infection. Of the various clinical means of diagnosis of syphilis in the newly born infant this examination indicates the presence of infection with the greatest frequency.

4. Both a Wassermann reaction on the serum of the mother and an examination of the placenta should be included as a part of good obstetrical standards.

DISCUSSION

Sir Arthur Newsholme, M. D. (Late Principal Medical Officer, Local Government Board, England): The question of venereal infection has been mentioned. In regard to that I think we can claim to have done some very important work. Regulations were issued by the Local Government Board, about three years ago, which made it an obligatory duty on the part of the sanitary authority in every large center of population, to provide clinics at which anyone (millionaire or pauper) could obtain secret and gratuitous treatment for syphilis or gonorrhea. And we have in our country now a complete system of free clinics for the treatment of venereal diseases. Having provided free treatment, we endeavored to insure that these diseases should be treated only by regular practitioners, and to this end we persuaded Parliament two years ago to pass an act prohibiting any druggist or other unqualified person from treating them. In view of the facts we have heard as to the importance of venereal disease in the destruction of child life and child health, in the impairment of the health of the mother, and in the sterilization of potential mothers, I am quite sure you will agree with me that this is an important step forward in regard to child welfare.

Dr. Dorothy Reed Mendenhall (Children's Bureau): I have made some estimates from the percentages Dr. Jeans has given us[1] in regard to the prevalence of syphilis, and the result is rather startling. We have two million and a half estimated births in this country, and 234,600 estimated deaths under one year, in 1916. We had therefore, using Dr. Jeans' estimate, 125,000 stillbirths, and of these 41,700 were caused by syphilis. We had 125,000 live births, the victims of congenital syphilis, and 31,300 of these died as a result of syphilis. This gives 41,700 stillbirths and 31,300 deaths in infancy, a total of 73,000 infant losses in one year due to congenital syphilis.

Dr. S. Josephine Baker (Division of Child Hygiene, Health Department, New York City): I hesitate to question Dr. Jeans' figures on the number of babies under one year that die from syphilis, but they are of extraordinary interest because they are so entirely contrary to anything we have experienced in New York City.

Syphilis as a cause of stillbirths is universal, I think, but with us syphilis as a cause of infant deaths does not figure largely at all statistically. It is a minor consideration. Inanition, congenital debility, and those vague titles it is possible may have syphilitic origin, but if anything which would prove they have has been done in New York it is unknown to me. I do not know of anything which would warrant us in saying that there were any such extensive deaths from syphilis under one year of age as these figures would show. In fact it is quite contrary to our general opinion.

Dr. Jeans: The figures that I gave were averages from a large number of cases from a great many sources, some from New York and some from other places. It was my impression that the averages were somewhat near the correct figures, but I may be mistaken.

Very often syphilis is an indirect cause of death. In an article published by Dr. Holt, using material from New York City, he stated that about 25 or 30 per cent of the syphilitic babies studied died from syphilis, and that, in all, more than

---

[1] These percentages were given in a paper read by Dr. Jeans before the Association for the Study and Prevention of Infant Mortality at its ninth annual meeting, December, 1918. Paper published in The American Journal of Syphilis, Vol. III, No. 1, Jan., 1919.

50 per cent of them died. Whether or not syphilis was the cause of death in the remainder of those instances is difficult to say. But certainly it is not a factor to be ignored.

Dr. Baker: I did not question the number of syphilitic babies that died in proportion to the number of cases of syphilis. I was questioning the number of syphilitic deaths in proportion to the total number of deaths.

Dr. Jeans: The fact that 10 per cent of mothers among the poorer classes give positive Wassermann reaction would seem to make the subject of considerable importance, as well as the fact that 90 per cent of those mothers will give no history nor show any signs of syphilis.

THE CONTROL OF MIDWIFERY

By DR. CHARLES V. CHAPIN

Superintendent of Health, Providence, Rhode Island

The only midwife problem with which I am familiar is that of our manufacturing cities with a large foreign population, of which my own city, Providence, is typical. In Providence the midwife is not indigenous. She came to us with our recent immigrants, from Russia, from Austria, from Poland, from the Azores, but chiefly from Italy.

Medical practitioners in general, and obstetricians in particular, denounce the midwife; social workers and public health nurses do not like her; and health officers do not consider her an asset to the community. The latter, however, while desirous of replacing her by something better, admit that she is not so inimical to public health as are many physicians. Thus in some cities the midwives report births and cases of ophthalmia better than do the physicians. They report births more promptly. In Providence, though there are no accurate data, midwives certainly report births more completely than do physicians. Last year 10 per cent of physicians' reports were late and only 1 per cent of the midwives'. For the prevention of infant mortality prompt returns are necessary, and the health officer is grateful to whoever makes them. There are very many physicians who know little about infant feeding, and their babies die and the health officer can do nothing about it. With the midwives' babies it is different. The nurse engineers them to the welfare station, where they are cared for by specialists. No wonder that in Providence, in 1917, the infant mortality rate of midwives' babies was 77, while of all others it was 117. It cannot be argued that this is because the midwives care for a stronger stock of women and healthier babies. About 85 per cent of the midwives' babies are of Italian mothers. In the years 1902-1909, before there was any instructive nursing service for mothers, the infant mortality rate among Italians was 138. In 1917 it was 93. The midwife, therefore, does not thus far seem to have been a hindrance to the prevention of infant mortality.

Objection to the midwife is based almost entirely on *a priori* reasoning. In the biological sciences this mode of reasoning is dangerous, though I doubt not that in this instance it is valid. Midwifery is a branch of medical practice, and we have abundant evidence that training and knowledge make for better practice. Nevertheless, there is some truth in the old adage that "a little knowledge is a dangerous thing." We are safe in assuming that imperfectly educated physicians and imperfectly educated midwives are not as useful members of society as those who are well educated. In medicine we need the best. Even this, owing to the limitations of human knowledge, is far from the ideal. In knowledge the midwife must always be far below the physician, and it is a safe deduction that she is not an institution to be fostered, but is rather to be tolerated only until such time as an acceptable substitute can be found. We allow non-medical individuals to provide glasses for our eyes and to attend women in confinement, but in no other specialty is this permitted.

Nevertheless, it would be desirable to show by comparative statistics whether the practice of the midwife results in sickness and death. When comparison is made between the results of midwives' practice and that of physicians, it is at times apparently unfavorable to the latter. Dr. Williams, a few years since, aroused great interest by his argument that poor doctors have more deaths against them than do the midwives, and that there are many poor doctors. The majority of teaching obstetricians were of his opinion. Dr. Baker of New York says that the morbidity and mortality, both of mothers and of babies, is greater among those attended by physicians than among those attended by midwives. Dr. Van Ingen has presented figures, relating to the lower East Side of New York, which show that stillbirths are much more frequent in the practice of physicians than in the practice of midwives. The great fallacy in all such statistics is that there is a selection of cases. Difficult confinements gravitate to the physician or the hospital, while normal confinements remain with the midwife.

There are several reasons why there is a demand for midwives:

1. They are cheaper. In my own city at the present time the prevailing rate for midwives is $15, with a dollar or two thrown in the baby's bath for tub money, and for physicians $25 and upwards, though a number of physicians will take cases at the same rate as midwives. Such physicians, however, are likely to be below the average. It is believed by many that economy is the most potent reason for the retention of the midwife.

2. Many foreign women do not wish to have a man attend them in confinement, or what is probably much more common, their husbands do not wish it. This is a custom or fashion, but I cannot believe that it will prove very difficult to change it as soon as good medical service and other care is available within the mothers' means. When one sees the remarkable change in customs, clothes, food, drink, etc., among foreigners, after only a few months' residence, one can be confident that the preference for a midwife must yield to the force of American public opinion. The Italian will, in time, substitute the doc-

tor for the midwife, just as she has substituted the milliner's hat for the bright colored handkerchief that formerly covered her head. In this process of education the public-health nurse must play an important part. Her influence with a family is very great, and she can do much to teach the importance of the best medical attendance. The woman physician, too, can be utilized to give medical service to those who object to a male attendant.

3. The midwife performs more or less household service for the family, "tidying" the rooms, preparing the meals, and caring for the older children; but apparently there is a tendency for the midwife to do less and less of this sort of work.

There is evidence to show that midwifery is decreasing. Dr. Woodward stated that in the District of Columbia, between 1896, the date of the adoption of the law regulating midwives, and 1915, the number of births attended by midwives in the District of Columbia fell from 50 per cent of the total births to less than 10 per cent. In 1918 it was 5.5 per cent. This was due chiefly to the elimination of midwives by examination. In New York, in 1905, 42.1 per cent of all births were attended by midwives, while in 1917 the per cent was 33.5. The decrease has been especially rapid since the opening of the war, which is interpreted as indicating that it is the newcomers who are most inclined to rely upon the midwife. In Providence the proportion of births attended by midwives increased with the increasing tide of Italian immigration up to 1913, when over 33 per cent of all births were attended by them. In 1918 the percentage was 27.5. An encouraging feature in Providence has been the almost complete disappearance of the Jewish midwife. Ten years ago nearly 150 births annually were attended by Jewish midwives. Last year there were but four so attended, although we have a Jewish population of nearly 20,000. This seems to be due largely to the appreciation on the part of Jewish women of the value of medical service. In Rochester the number of midwives and the number of births attended by them has decreased during the last eight or ten years. In other cities, as Newark, it is stated that the proportion of births attended by midwives has remained quite constant.

Various plans have been adopted, or proposed, for solving the midwife problem. One is absolutely to forbid her practice by statute law. This is true of Massachusetts now and was true in Rhode Island up to last year. In neither of these States was any serious attempt made to enforce the law and to drive out the midwives. When I saw that the midwife was to remain in Providence I tried to secure her cooperation, with the result that her births are more completely and promptly reported than before, as are her cases of ophthalmia, and her babies are promptly brought under the care of public-health nurses and physicians, so that the infant mortality rate of midwives' babies has been reduced nearly 70 per cent.

Another plan, which may be developed in different ways, is to license the midwife. This has as yet been attempted in only a few States. The statutory provision should be as broad as possible so as to allow opportunity for experiment and the development of new methods of control. The Rhode Island law provides that "the State board of health is hereby authorized and directed to make rules for the regulation and practice of midwifery, and for the licensing of midwives." The New York statute, authorizing the enactment of a sanitary code by the public health council, provides that this code "may contain provisions regulating the practice of midwifery."

Under such general provisions the licensing may amount to a mere registration, or it may develop into an elaborate system under which midwives are carefully examined, educated, trained, and supervised.

The advocates of licensing are divided into two groups. One of these believes that the midwife is but a temporary institution, is unnecessary, and can sooner or later be eliminated. They would issue a license annually, perhaps establish moderate standards of conduct, and gradually eliminate those midwives shown to be careless, dirty, ignorant, or neglectful. They would not attempt to teach obstetrics to the midwife, or to raise her social or economic status, fearing that, by so doing, her position would be made more permanent. The midwife who is educated in a school and who has a diploma will be independent and will resent efforts to draw away her clientèle. She will believe that she has rights which she must defend. On the other hand, the midwife who is made to feel that she has no real status, that she is allowed to practice only on sufferance, and that she is dependent on the good will of the health officer, will not dare to make much fuss if she sees her patients leave her. Dr. Stone, our superintendent of child hygiene, finds that our best qualified midwives are the least tolerant of advice and correction. If the midwife has no real status, she can the easier be made to obey the rules of the department; thus such midwives can often be made to report births and inflamed eyes more promptly than the physicians. Perhaps they may even be made to report pregnancies. Under control, such midwives are not dangerous to the babies, as is shown by the Providence figures previously given. That they are not dangerous to the mother is indicated by data from Philadelphia, where there were only 17 deaths in about 12,000 confinements attended by supervised midwives.

Others think that the midwife will surely remain with us for a long time and they prefer to attempt to improve her status. They would fix educational standards, and by definite supervision of her work see that these standards are lived up to, thus following the ideas of most

European countries. Thus the New York code requires that midwives must possess a diploma from a recognized school or must have received personal instruction from a licensed physician, of which instruction he must make a report. A school for midwives had previously been established at Bellevue Hospital in New York City in 1911. The New York State Department of Health has planned for the supervision of midwives through the medium of nurses. These nurses cover chiefly those parts of the State outside the great cities. New York City had previously undertaken similar control in 1911.

New Jersey has adopted much the same plan as New York.

In Pennsylvania midwives are licensed by the bureau of medical education and licensure, and are also supervised by the same bureau. The system is best developed in the district in which Philadelphia is situated. In this district there is a supervisor, a specialist in obstetrics, who has under him a number of women physicians who act as inspectors. The midwife must call upon the inspector for advice in every abnormal delivery, and definite rules are given to guide her judgment. In practice nearly every patient is seen by the inspector. The midwives receive considerable systematic instruction, but, as I understand it, the authorities look to the ultimate extinction of the midwife and think that this result will be endangered if the requirements are such that women of some education will be led to prepare themselves, at some expense, for midwifery as a "profession." In Pittsburgh close supervision of the midwives is maintained by nurses.

In Providence the "baby nurses" of the health department have, for some time, sought, by personal instruction given to each midwife, to make her more cleanly and in other ways to take better care of her cases. She has been made to report births and sore eyes promptly. She is shown the necessity for sending for a physician in case of any abnormality and is warned of the danger of delay. Many midwives secretly prescribe medicines, and the endeavor is made to break up this practice. Very much was done along these lines before we had a license law, and now it is hoped that the State board of health will refuse licenses to those women who do not follow directions.

If midwives are to be supplanted, some substitute must be offered which appeals to their patrons as desirable. Perhaps the most important reason why the midwife is preferred is because she costs less than a doctor. If the midwife is to be supplanted by a physician, the latter must not cost more than the former, and the supplanting process will be more rapid if he does not cost as much.

A free out-patient obstetrical service certainly draws cases from the midwives. Wherever there is a medical school, such a service is necessary for teaching purposes. Even if the patient is able to pay a midwife, I consider it entirely legitimate to draw her away by free treatment, particularly as the patient is to be used for teaching purposes. Moreover, some compensation may be received even from this kind of a service. Thus at the Boston Lying-in Hospital the out-patients contributed on the average, in 1916, $1.38 each, which was an appreciable help in meeting the low cost of the service. That such a service pays from a public health standpoint is shown by the fact that maternal mortality in the last 5,000 out-patients was .04 per cent. That this low rate was not secured by sending an undue number of difficult labor cases into the hospital is indicated by the mortality of the house cases, which during substantially the same period was 1.1 per cent, certainly not abnormally high.

Unfortunately, or rather fortunately, most of our cities are not supplied with a medical school, so some other means than the utilization of medical students has to be found to provide obstetrical service for the poor. An out-patient service would seem to be best provided in connection with a maternity hospital. The country certainly needs a much larger maternity service than it now has. Many general hospitals are, however, now adding a maternity service, often because a number of States are requiring of their licentiates in medicine a hospital internship with a prescribed obstetrical training. This will certainly draw cases from the midwives, and will at the same time, by the training thus secured, make the young doctor a better obstetrician, a most desirable result.

The cost of out-patient obstetrical work is a matter of much moment in these times when there are so many demands on philanthropy and so many lines of municipal health work. We must all admit that it is a great injustice to ask so much gratuitous public service of physicians. Many of us are trying to draw away from this practice, though it will probably be a long time before all such public medical service will be adequately paid for. The tendency in some places is to utilize internes, or other members of a resident hospital staff, for out-patient work of all kinds. In this way the out-patient worker is likely to be paid something besides his board, and he may even be paid a fair compensation, yet I am sure that less money will be required in this than in any other way, and that this arrangement will better satisfy the medical man. The utilization of a resident staff for out-patient work also makes for efficiency, as the work can be supervised by the hospital management and the service is sure to be more prompt and regular. Hence out-patient obstetrical service would seem to be desirable in connection with maternity hospitals whenever possible.

At Manchester, N. H., a city of about 80,000 people, out-patient obstetrical service is carried on by the district-nursing association, which has a medical man for director of the service. Young physicians, just coming to the city, do most of the work, and they are glad to do it, as they are thus brought in touch with the more influential people. The city has many textile operatives, and it is estimated that about 10 per cent of all confinements are in need of free service. About 6 per cent are now served by the dispensary.

The "pay clinic" has, for various types of medical service, been strongly advocated in Boston as a means of securing efficient treatment for a class of persons who can pay only a moderate sum, but yet sufficient in the aggregate to afford modest compensation to the physician. It was deemed advisable in East Boston to establish such a service in connection with the Maverick Dispensary, a private institution, not connected with any hospital. This has been running only a short time, but is drawing cases from the midwives. A charge of $15 is made, just the amount charged by midwives, and of this $10 goes to the physician. The physicians are men who are glad temporarily to take this service to perfect themselves in obstetrics.

Enough has been said to show that in the United States a variety of views prevail as to the midwife and that there are various ways of dealing with her. Those who would dispense with her service have different plans for doing so. This is the period for experiment, and our Federal system, with its forty-eight legislatures, favors experimentation. It is too early to standardize and not a time for dogmatism. It is not unlikely that different plans will be found best for different parts of the country. Meanwhile my own conclusions, applicable chiefly to our cities with large foreign populations, are as follows:

1. The midwife is unnecessary and can gradually be eliminated.

2. There should be an annual registration, and supervision should be maintained.

3. The foreign population must be educated, the most valuable agencies being nurses and clinics.

4. Prenatal clinics are needed and especially an enlarged out-patient obstetric service, partly free and partly pay.

5. More maternity wards are needed.

6. There should be better obstetric training for medical students, which will be made possible by greater opportunity for clinical instruction.

DISCUSSION

Dr. Julius Levy (State Board of Health, New Jersey): I want to recall some of the points that Dr. Chapin made very tellingly and clearly. He made the point that midwives are not so bad as some doctors; he made the points that births are reported more frequently and more promptly by midwives than by doctors, that there is less ophthalmia than in cases handled by doctors, and that midwives are more disposed, under advice and instruction, to use silver nitrate. He also made the point that infant mortality is lower among cases handled by midwives; and then he wants us to believe that we are to eliminate midwives!

As far as our studies can show, experience has proven that under regulation and supervision and proper instruction our standards are better maintained by midwives than by doctors as they exist. And I may add that where that does not occur it is not the fault of the midwife but of the public-health officer. I will not claim that with the same kind of regulation and supervision of doctors the results would not be better, but Dr. Chapin also stated that he discovered it was much easier to regulate and supervise the midwife than it was the doctor.

Dr. Chapin also pointed out that as the midwife became educated she was more difficult to handle. You notice she is getting a little like the doctors and the results are not always as good.

I ought to suggest that I do not think that obstetricians need fear the existence of the midwife in perpetuity. Elevating her status I think is a sly way to eliminate her, if you really wish to eliminate her, because as you elevate her standard she demands more for her service, and when she demands more for her service, she is in competition with the doctor. By the law of the survival of the fittest, if the doctor is a superior individual, he will survive.

Sir Arthur Newsholme (Late Principal Medical Officer, Local Government Board, England): So far as England is concerned, at the present time 75 per cent of all confinements are attended by midwives, whose practice on the whole is satisfactory. Favorable statistics could be quoted similar to those that Dr. Chapin has quoted as regards Providence. But we have midwives in England under absolutely complete control. Midwives that are on the register to practice can be removed from the register if they are guilty of malpractice or inefficiency. They are so removed frequently. They are subject to regulation and systematic inspection by local supervising authorities; so that any midwife who gets a bad reputation or has an excessive number of complications is sure to be hauled over the coals and her practice will diminish very seriously. In those various ways we have secured that midwifery is a fairly safe profession.

Moreover, the Local Government Board has arranged for Government grants to fifty per cent of the total expenditure for the employment of midwives, these grants being given to the rural authorities and to the poorer districts and towns where midwives are located, the other half of the total expenditure being paid by volunteer subscribers or by the local authorities.

In addition every midwife is required when any complication occurs to call in a doctor. There has been great difficulty in the past in providing a fee for this doctor, and now it is made obligatory upon the local authorities to pay this doctor's fee, so that no doctor can be excused for not going at once when the midwife requires his assistance in any complication, however minor that complication may be. I think you will agree that, if the practice of midwifery by midwives is to continue, we have in that way safeguarded it.

In the last twelve months I have also been advocating that an additional duty should be imposed on midwives, to which I personally attach the greatest possible importance. This is that if for any reason during the time (ten days or a fortnight) that the midwife continues her attendance after confinement, the mother proposes to give up breast feeding, it is the duty of the midwife to notify the medical officer of health of that fact at once, so that he or his assistants may visit that house at once to see that breast feeding, which is the most essential element of the welfare of the child, shall be continued if it be possible to continue it. This has now been secured by a regulation of the Central Midwives' Board.

Furthermore, the Local Government Board has given grants for the formation of maternity homes and maternity hospitals, and it has been prepared, **and expressed its anxiety, to pay fifty** per cent of the total cost of these hospitals and homes without any limit of the total amount which is thus payable. Such maternity hospitals and homes, I am glad to say, are springing up in many parts of the country. They are, in my view, one of the greatest needs of town life. It is a great shame that it should be so, but it is the fact that in a large proportion of the tenement houses of our big towns it is not possible for a confinement to take place under conditions that can be regarded as anything approaching satisfactory.

The Local Government Board pays doctors' fees; we pay for maternity homes and hospitals; and we also pay for the provision of home helps. We were glad to have the help of the Women's Cooperative Guild in securing that additional boon. We were pushing it at the same time, and we eventually succeeded in getting the Treasury to give money without any limit of the amount for the provision of home helps. That is somewhat similar to domestic service; the helpers visit the homes of women who have been recently confined; provide assistance during confinement and afterwards; and, if the mother is ill during pregnancy, see that she has a physician or nurse to attend her.

Dr. S. Josephine Baker (Division of Child Hygiene, Health Department, New York City): It is a very great pleasure to have heard Sir Arthur Newsholme speak of the control of the midwife in England, because it is exactly duplicated by our control in New York City. We have a six months' preliminary education at municipally controlled schools for midwives.

By the constant supervision of the midwife, and the elimination from practice of every midwife who violates our regulations, the number of practicing midwives has been reduced in ten years from 3,000 to 1,600. There is one sure way of eliminating the midwife, and that is to educate her. Midwives are a condition and not a theory. In seeing what can be done with midwives it is essential to remember that poor people who have to deal with them are guided by practical considerations rather than by academic theories.

I think Dr. Chapin quite unwittingly did us a little injustice when he said the infrequency of stillbirths and the low mortality among mothers and babies attended by midwives were due to the fact that hard cases were transferred to the doctors. That is true, but they were counted against midwives. Every case that had a midwife in attendance at any time was counted as a midwife case. Of course the complicated cases went to the doctors and were reported by them as deaths, but not reported against them in the final sense. But that shows what have been the practical results of the control of midwifery in New York City.

I think that we can grant that whatever improvement has been made in obstetrical practice in New York has been counterbalanced by the improvement of obstetrical practice in every other large city in the country. Why is it then, that in a study of the maternal mortality rates in seven large cities of the United States, made by the Children's Bureau, these rates were shown to be increasing or stationary in every one of them with the exception of New York City, and New York City showed a decrease? The only difference between New York City and the other cities is our method of control of midwives.

Beginning ten years ago with no method of finding out whether there were cases of blindness, we had literally thousands of cases of ophthalmia, and literally hundreds of cases of blindness—no way of computing how many we had. Last year—we do not claim these are exact figures—with the most painstaking methods that we could devise by a follow-up of every case of sore eyes reported by the midwife, by a follow-up at the hospitals where ophthalmic cases might come, by every means we could devise to control the situation, we found that out of 135,000 births in New York City we had 35 cases of ophthalmia and one case of blindness.

Nothing that I know of has changed in regard to the practice of doctors, but a very great deal has changed in regard to the practice of midwives. I am an advocate for the strongest kind of supervision, the most thorough control, and above all the education of the women to such a high standard that only a woman of extraordinary intelligence and ability will be able to be a midwife.

Dr. Mary Sherwood (Baltimore, Maryland): It occurs to me that possibly we might look at this from another angle. There is no topic that provokes so much discussion as this question of the midwife. And after all it is not the question of whether the midwife is better than the doctor, or whether the doctor is better than the midwife. The question is, is the midwife or the poorly trained doctor good enough?

Is there anyone who will discuss the practice of obstetrics from the point of view of surgery? Is not obstetrics a branch of surgery, and is it not entitled to the kind of care we are inclined to give, and always do give to a hospital matter—surgical operating room, all the appliances of modern surgery, all the precautions of modern surgery? Is obstetrics something that can be compromised with poor doctors and with midwives?

Dr. Helen MacMurchy (Department of the Provincial Secretary, Toronto, Canada): I think the best way to make students understand that it is a matter of surgery is to make them realize that at the time of birth we have to care for what is really an enormous open wound. Of course it is quite true that that wound is physiologically produced. It is quite true that the danger of infection through that wound is very much reduced by the wonderful provision of nature for shutting these gaping avenues of infection. But nevertheless that is what it is.

ESSENTIALS FOR PUBLIC CARE OF MATERNITY AND INFANCY

By MRS. ELEANOR BARTON
Women's Cooperative Guild, England

At the present time most countries are turning their thoughts to the question of child welfare. I am sure that we are at the beginning of a new era which will also recognize the mother of the child. Someone has said that to have a healthy child you must begin with its grandmother. If we today can start with the mother we shall be making a real bid for public health in the best possible way.

In the old days the Grecians would not allow a pregnant mother to look on anything unpleasant, let alone feel it. What a difference between their ideas of the expectant mother and those of our world today. A campaign to reduce the death rate among infants under one year of age has already decreased the death rate by nearly one-third, showing very clearly that many of our social evils are amenable to treatment. Bad housing and sanitation are responsible for a good deal, but ignorance and the absence of medical advice and help are also responsible for much suffering. It is vital to the welfare of all countries that an enlightened and generous care of maternity should replace the present indifference and neglect.

The Women's Cooperative Guild of England has for several years given special attention to this subject. When our Insurance Act was before the country, and before it became a law, the Guild specially asked that a maternity benefit should be included in the act, and it was included. Some of us were astounded to find that this maternity benefit was the husband's property, especially after we had had our cities placarded with huge placards portraying the mother with her child in her arms. However, when the act was amended we had the maternity benefit made the property of the mother.

Since then we have gone on inquiring and getting information, working out a scheme which we placed before our Local Government Board in 1914. As the outcome of all the inquiries we have issued a book giving an account of the suffering of the working women themselves at the time of pregnancy and of childbirth, showing very clearly to all thinking people the great need of the care of maternity. It has been so common for children to be born that the large majority of people have not considered the question at all. Most young mothers today turn for advice to older women, and very often when she is suffering they tell her, "Well, it is just a symptom of pregnancy and you will not be better until you get through with it."

We realize today that pregnancy is not a nine-months disease and that women can be cared for and can be helped. A very pathetic case some time ago came to my notice. A young woman who was pregnant for the second time came to one of the Cooperative Guild members saying that she would not go through with her pregnancy, that it was impossible for her to do so, that she had suffered in exactly the same way from her first pregnancy, and that she would prefer to make a home in the water, that is, to commit suicide. She was finally persuaded to go to a doctor, and her suffering was much relieved throughout the period of her pregnancy. The physician said that if she had consulted him during her first pregnancy he could have cured her.

We have all sorts of information, all sorts of reasons, all sorts of statistics before us which show that we must have better care for maternity in the future than we have had in the past. One of the features of the work of the Cooperative Guild is this: Whenever we take up a question we go into it thoroughly, through all the branches throughout the country, and having got all the information we can and pronounced on it, we at once decide upon some practical campaign in connection with it. We never leave a subject that we have taken up without trying to get some practical results from it. As a result of our inquiry concerning maternity we decided that it was best for the local health authorities and the national health authorities to be the people to carry out the great maternity help that was to be given to the large majority of women in our country.

So we set out to form public opinion. I suppose it is true in America as in all countries that the governments will go just as far as they are pushed from behind, or from underneath, shall we say, and that what must be done is to arouse public opinion. In order to do that we published and distributed widely some attractive little pamphlets, each one on some subject relative to maternity. The women in our local branches cooperated with the women in their areas and arranged deputations to their health committees and to medical officers of health, pushing forward these questions of maternity. During the war, especially in the early days, we found many women were suffering because they could not get food and milk, and we pushed in that way also.

In 1915 we had secured compulsory notification of births. We have a good scheme of health administration, and every mother, directly she gives birth to a child, is visited and advised by a health visitor who follows the case up, and when the mother is ready to come out advises her to bring her child to a public clinic. So because of the act of 1915 we are in touch with births at the present time. Finally in 1918 we had a maternity act passed by our House of Parliament, and we are very proud today in England that we have got so far because we do realize it is a great step in the right direction.

We have maternity centers where advice and minor treatment are provided. Where there are complicated cases or where real medical attention is needed, the patient is always told to consult her own doctor. Where treatment is provided for mothers during prenatal and postnatal periods, health visitors visit the mother in the home. Food and milk are supplied for expectant and nursing mothers—the amount of milk given being determined according to the advice of the person who has the case. Hospitals or wards are provided for complicated maternity cases and for babies up to five years; also maternity homes for normal cases and convalescent homes after maternity. Homes are provided for mothers and babies in fatherless, illegitimate, widowed, or deserted cases; or grants are made to such mothers to enable them to stay at home and care for their children.

The service of home helps has also been organized. Perhaps I ought to explain what the service of home helps is. I believe this is a great outcome of our inquiry. We found that when the mother was in bed practically the whole of her household was disorganized, and that many of our women got up at the end of three days, or before they should do so, to attend to their household duties. We found that in many cases the mother had her bed carried down into the living room where she could lie with her purse under her pillow and direct the younger children or neighbors to make purchases. Under the system of home helps women are to be trained to go into the homes, not to do any medical work or to do the nurse's work, but to work under the direction of the nurse or midwife who is attending the case, performing the mother's household duties, such as getting the children off to school and preparing the food. We feel that this is one of the greatest essentials to our working-class mothers. Our bill at the present time makes provision for it only in this way, by providing that the local authority may adopt the scheme after approval by the Local Government Board.

Services of midwives, and of doctors when the doctor is called following the midwife, have been regulated under the Midwives' Act. We have had very many sad cases where women's lives have been lost because there was no doctor to follow the midwife. Sometimes a doctor has been sent for but refused to attend the case because he was not sure whether he would get his fee or not. The Government gives a grant of 50 per cent of the net cost of all this service I have outlined, provided the local scheme has been sanctioned by the central authority.

Where a local authority adopts a scheme of this kind they must appoint a maternity committee on which there must be two women. The Cooperative Guild is very anxious that working women should be on the maternity committee as they will understand the lives and homes of the women who will be treated under this scheme. Mr. Hayes Fisher, of the Local Government Board, himself has expressed the hope that working-class women will be appointed. In recent years they have become articulate and have been able to give very valuable service and information to all committees of this kind. Now we are hoping that all local authorities will take advantage of this scheme and will make this provision for mothers and babies.

I ought to say that the maternity benefit is 30 shillings to the child. This maternity benefit is given to the wives of men who are insured and come under the income tax limit. And the women who go out to work, if they themselves are insured, would also receive benefits in their own right, thus making a double maternity benefit.

We must remember that under the present industrial system the wages do not permit women who are bearing children to get the medical attention or the help in the home which they need. We must try to relieve their financial burdens. We have had some excellent lessons during the war period in the allowances paid to mothers and children, and many people today are hoping that we shall be able to outline some scheme for an endowment under which the mother will not be so worried because of the coming of another child into the home and will therefore be able to bear her children better.

We believe that the whole question of maternity should come under the Ministry of Relief, now in the process of formation, instead of being managed largely by insurance societies and organizations of that kind, as it is at the present time. We have had cases which have shown us that these are the very worst institutions under which our maternity benefits can be paid. At the present time, therefore, we are considering a Ministry of Relief in which there shall be a maternity department with a woman at the head of it. We are asking that there should be women adequately represented on all those committees. We are asking, too, that in addition there shall be what we are calling a council of men and women representing the people who have to be treated by our public-health officers because, as we found in regard to our food supplies during the war, these are the people who know the difficulties and these are the people who can best deal with them.

What I feel that we want now in all countries is to raise the standard of maternity. We want to be proud of our expectant mothers; we want to alter the idea that we have had, and instead of thinking about material things, think more about human things; instead of building up huge industries and huge warships, let us build up able-bodied men and women. I think it was an American who said that where the greatest number of able-bodied men and women stood, there stood the greatest city. Now, it is up to each country to see where the greatest city shall be.

It will be good to have competition in that direction. It will certainly raise the whole standard of life. It will raise the standard of women and children; and we must remember that when we raise the standard of women we raise the standard of the race.

DISCUSSION

Dr. Helen MacMurchy (Department of the Provincial Secretary, Toronto, Canada): May I take this opportunity to say one thing? Do you think we pay enough attention to the father? I would say to him, "Now, you are the whole thing, we are just acting under your orders. It is for you to take care of the mother; it is for you to provide for the child." I do think that the education of the father is a most important thing for us all to attend to. I do not know just where you would insert it in the very excellent outline that has been prepared, but I do not like to see the father neglected.

Mrs. Barton: There are many people who say today, "Yes, the husband and father should provide in this way," but we in England, at any rate, have got a free elementary-school service and recognize that our elementary-school service is very much better than in the days when the father did provide individually. We should have this system in exactly the same way as we have public libraries for the use of all citizens, whether rich or poor. The fathers cannot do it. The money that comes into the working-class home, even with wages up as they are, is not sufficient. Has not everything else gone up, and are the wages very high in proportion? Not at all. The working-class home is not fitted to receive a confinement case in a proper way. There are thousands of homes unfit for a woman to lie in, even if it were a question of policy and not of wages.

We want exactly the same thing applied to our maternity service. It is not enough for us to say that the man should provide. We want the public service. After all, the child is the asset of the nation, and we want the nation to recognize that the welfare of the child is its business. During the war when the State wanted the boys they put their hands on their shoulders and took them, without any questions being asked. Now we want the State to realize that it is responsible in exactly the same way for its children.

The thing you must consider is whether you can get a better service by a communal service, as it were, or by leaving it to the individual. I think the individual system has broken down absolutely, and now we want to put in its place municipal and national service.

If we are going to have a system that will work efficiently and do the best for the mothers, we have to make it a national thing, so that every woman can feel that she is accepting that service as a right and as a citizen. If there were anything that savors of a charitable institution, our women would not accept it.

While I am on this point I want to emphasize that it should be national and free. The book we have issued (Maternity) shows terrible examples of suffering, and yet we have to recognize that our working women are the most self-respecting, the better class of working women. The Guild would not advocate anything that savors of charity.

What we have to do at the present time very largely is to educate the mother to take her baby to the child-welfare center. The women are gradually seeing the advantages of this, and are coming to these centers more and more, feeling that it is their right, as much as it is the right of the elementary-school child to receive its education in the free school. I want to emphasize the fact that we wish to put the whole question of maternity under national supervision, so that a woman can receive maternity ca e and nobody shall ask whether she is rich or poor.

A Member: May I ask how the English women appreciate the nurses? What has been the experience? Do they enjoy having the nurses come to them?

Mrs. Barton: I saw a case in Wales, in the mining district, where the husband, a miner, was objecting to the nurse telling his wife, who had had several children, what to do. I think on the whole that this attitude is gradually being gotten rid of, however.

Mrs. William Lowell Putnam (Boston, Massachusetts): We have a scheme somewhat similar to that of the mother helps of which Mrs. Barton has spoken, that is, provision for the care of sickness in the homes of persons of small or moderate means. They cannot possibly afford trained nurses, and yet they must have care in sickness as well as during confinement. Accordingly we undertake to provide trained helpers, giving them a course of study. These women are supervised by trained nurses, who visit the homes and see that the work is being done properly. We can furnish these women with supervision for $18 or $20 a week. That is not a small sum, but is very different from the price demanded by trained nurses, and I believe there is a very great future for that sort of care.

Dr. S. Josephine Baker (Division of Child Hygiene, Department of Health, New York City): Although I am a strong American, and advocate our form of government, it is refreshing to get the message that Mrs. Barton brought us. It would be a wonderful thing if the Federal Children's Bureau, or any other national organization could solve this entire problem of infant mortality by one stroke of the pen in the way that England has done it. But we have to do it 48 times.

Their method of home helps is practically new to us. The idea of having one visitor to every 500 children, as I believe they have in England, is something that we ought to copy. The fact that the Government gives grants to help these women during the period of pregnancy, and to see that their children have the proper care, is something that we should give heed to. England, I believe, has set us a very high standard. And England has reaped its reward because England's infant death rate, as we all know, is extraordinarily low and has gone down very much in the last few years.

SERBIAN EXPERIENCE

By DR. RADMILA MILOCHEVITCH LAZAREVITCH

Legation of the Serbs, Croats, and Slovenes, Washington, D. C.

The question of child welfare is an urgent question to us. How urgent it is these few words will show you, which were spoken in Parliament in Belgrade on the 24th of February, this year, by one of our prominent members, an ex-minister, Mr. V. Veljkovitch. He said: "We have in Serbia 100,000 invalids, 100,000 children who need immediate care, and 50,000 orphans." I would ask you to remember that these numbers are taken from a country that had before this war 4,500,000 inhabitants.

I want to try to tell you something about the urgent conditions prevailing among our children in Serbia because I love my country, and knowing the great generosity of the American people toward all oppressed nations and all who are in misery, I wish to awaken your interest in our children.

In attempting to tell you what we have done in Serbia for the protection of the child, I shall not be able to compare it with what you have done here, but I shall try to give you a little picture of the history of the country which will explain to you why we are no further advanced in this respect. For 150 years my country has been fighting for her deliverance, during which time we have had about ten wars and fifteen revolutions. Fighting always for our liberation, we neglected many other important matters, among which was the scientific study of child welfare.

Our country holds a high place in the percentage of large families. Our birth rate proves this record, but alas, our infant mortality rate is also very great. Why? Because notwithstanding the fact that our people are very strong and healthy, bad hygienic conditions exist and ignorance of the fundamental rules for the proper care of the expectant mother and the baby prevails. The State, which has been obliged to buy guns and munitions to insure its very existence, has had neither the time nor the money to devote to hygienic conditions and the care of the mother and the baby.

Our women in the country give birth to and bring up their children with only God's help. The pregnant woman works in the household and in the field until the last moment. It often happens that the baby is born in the field, when the mother picks up her little one and carries it home. On the morrow you can see her again in the field, but this time with her baby so she can nurse him.

Our mothers in the country always nurse their babies; they know of no other kind of feeding. But in the cities the mothers have adopted bottle feeding. Although the country mother nurses her child, she knows nothing about the technique of nursing and preparation and technique of artificial feeding if breast feeding is not possible. The mothers are healthy, however, and the newborn baby is usually healthy, too; he weighs from eight to twelve pounds. Although I speak in the present tense, this splendid condition existed only before our last two wars. Now after seven years of hard fighting, which have brought misery and privations, we have lost the one good thing which we had, namely, the healthy newborn baby. Epidemics (especially typhus), hunger and misery, and their companion, tuberculosis, have nearly destroyed our nation. We have lost one-fourth of our population through epidemics and war, and those remaining are mostly tubercular.

If you are interested, I beg that you will allow me to read you a few statistics that may give you a better idea of what we have been called upon to meet in this war.

The population of Serbia before the war was 4,500,000

1. Number killed or died from wounds from August, 1914, to December, 1915 170,925
2. Deaths in civilian population from epidemics 350,000
3. Soldiers killed during the retreat in the autumn of 1915 150,000
4. Soldiers dead from hunger and starvation in Albania during the same period 60,000
5. Boy recruits dead from hunger during the retreat 80,000
6. Deaths from hunger and cold among civilian population during the retreat 250,000
7. Prisoners and interned in Bulgaria, Austria, and Germany 130,000
8. Number killed (hanged and slaughtered) by the Bulgarians, Austrians, and Germans 60,000
9. Number killed during a revolution in Nish, Prokoupile, and Leskovatz 40,000
10. Soldiers killed on the Saloniki front 40,000

Total 1,330,925

So you see we are not what we were before this terrible conflict. Our mothers can give no more little giants to their country. The women as well as the men have deteriorated in health.

Before the war we had begun to devote some attention to the welfare of the child, but only through private associations, without the help of the State. Now we are beginning to realize the importance of the health of the child to the nation. In 1917, after our retreat, we started in Vodena the Society for the Protection of Children, with Dr. Popovitch as president. The aim of the society was to look after the physical and moral health of the children; to find out the causes of all sickness and if possible to provide remedies; to reduce the mortality among children, and also to care for the abandoned children of refugees and soldiers. Now our United Kingdom of the Serbs, Croats, and Slovenes started on the 5th of February, 1919, the State Department for Child Welfare. The vice-minister president is in charge of it, which shows how earnestly the State takes the problem. The number of children without both parents is about 120,000; the number with only one parent lost, 500,000.[1]

---

[1] The statistics are not yet complete.

URBAN PROBLEMS

By DR. HENRY F. HELMHOLZ

Medical Director, Infant Welfare Society, Chicago

The care of infants in a city falls logically into three divisions:
1. The care of the unborn infant.
2. The care of the infant during and immediately after the birth act.
3. The postnatal care of the infant.

At the present time in most communities the prenatal care of the infant is almost entirely neglected. The postnatal work has reduced the death rate from diarrheal diseases and respiratory infections very markedly, but has not affected that of congenital diseases, which has remained practically constant. One-third of the total deaths of infants under one year occur in the first month of life. Two-thirds of these deaths occur in the first ten days. They are caused largely by conditions that are preventable by prenatal care. Prematurity, syphilis, stillbirths, and birth injuries can in a large measure be overcome by good prenatal care. The supervision of the mother should include (1) advice as to diet, (2) control of the urine and blood pressure, (3) pelvic measurements, and (4) a routine Wassermann examination of all mothers. With adequate treatment during pregnancy the ravages of syphilis would be very markedly reduced. Laws to prevent mothers from working in factories during the last months of their confinement would increase the weight of the newborn baby by pounds and so reduce the group that are at present dying from prematurity. Furthermore, the examination and measurement of the pelvis would cull out that group of mothers that would probably need hospital care and should not be taken care of in the home and be rushed at the last minute to the hospital when it is too late to save the baby and probably the mother also. Constant watching and control of urine and blood pressure will reduce materially the maternal as well as the infant death rate.

As a minimum to do this work one nurse to every three hundred births would be required. This very important period has received relatively little attention and deserves very much more. The results of prenatal care will become especially evident if the work is done in close cooperation and coordination with the actual birth care of the child. Only when proper facilities in hospital and home are at hand can the results of prenatal care manifest themselves. If the lying-in hospital facilities are insufficient to care for the probably difficult cases that have been discovered in the routine examination of the prenatal work, then naturally much of the work will go for naught. It is therefore important that adequate hospital facilities are at hand to care for all difficult cases and an ample obstetrical out-patient service to care for the mothers who remain at home. What the ultimate outcome of the midwife or obstetrical nurse question will be I do not know, but certain it is that if the busy general practitioner alone is in attendance there will be entirely too many forceps deliveries. We must have someone whose duty it is to carry through the watchful expectancy necessary to a normal labor.

Important as is the close coordination between the prenatal and the obstetrical work, still more vital to the welfare of the infant is constant uninterrupted supervision from birth. Too frequently at present valuable time is lost, and instead of bringing a normal breast-fed infant to the infant-welfare station the mother brings an infant that is weaned and is suffering from some gastrointestinal disturbance. In our work in Chicago over two-thirds of all babies come to us for the first time when they are over two months old. As the death rate is highest during the first month of life, our postnatal work has missed this very valuable period for its work.

The postnatal work must begin early. There must be a regular transfer of the case from the obstetrical nurse to the infant-welfare nurse. As is quite generally accepted at the present time, the most successful postnatal care is given in the infant-welfare station to which the mother brings her baby at regular intervals to be weighed and examined, and to receive instruction from the doctor regarding the care and feeding of her child. The station nurse follows up this instruction by visiting the mother in her home and showing her how with her utensils she can prepare the baby's food and arrange her home hygienically. With regard to feeding, the emphasis must be placed first and foremost on breast feeding. The closer the cooperation with institutions doing the obstetrical work the greater will be the number of mothers that can nurse their babies. In our experience, improper teaching and technique of nursing, and not the unwillingness to nurse account for the large number of artificially fed babies.

The artificially fed child must have good milk, constantly controlled and supervised. It seems to me likely that in the not very distant future powdered milk will in a large measure replace the fresh milk because it is safer and cheaper. The supervision of the milk, the housing question, water supply, garbage disposal, and flies are of great importance to the child of the city. They must be closely watched by our health departments. The housing question is one that needs more attention than any of the others because the public has not been educated up to the importance of this factor in its relationship to infant mortality.

The hygiene of the home, on the other hand, the ventilation, the bath, the sleep, the clothing, and the fresh air must be looked after by the station doctor and nurse. In the postnatal work the nurse can care for not over 150 babies. In close cooperation with the infant-welfare stations we must have ample dispensary and hospital facilities to which the sick infants can be referred from the stations. Just one word with regard to the preschool age. The care of the child from two to six can in all probability be best looked after in connection with the infant-welfare station. We have at present in Chicago six such stations in operation.

In every city we ought to have an organization that is doing both the prenatal and the postnatal work, this organization to be closely affiliated with the various organizations that are doing the city's obstetrical work, connecting and consolidating the work which is being done for mother and child so as to keep them constantly under supervision.

MATERNITY CENTERS IN NEW YORK CITY

By DR. R. W. LOBENSTINE
New York City

We are considering today the momentous question of providing this country with the means of more adequately safeguarding motherhood. Upon our decisions may rest the ultimate fate of millions of women and children, who are dying or who are crippled because of poor medical and nursing care, or no care at all.

Never before have nations been brought to such a keen realization of the value of the mother and her child. With the frightful losses at the front, with the startling ravages of the world plague continually before us, and with the inevitable injuries wrought in the home by the strenuous efforts of war, conservation of life stands out as the pressing need of the hour.

Our aim should be to furnish every mother during pregnancy with intelligent oversight, to protect her from the dangers incident to industrialism, and to render childbirth reasonably safe. Reckless sacrifice of infant life should stop. Childbearing has long been regarded as merely the natural lot of women, and its hazards have been either neglected or accepted as inevitable. Can a function, however, that kills thousands of women annually, that cripples many thousands more, and that is responsible for a very large infant mortality, be called safe? Childbearing still possesses for the mother many dangers—some of which are avoidable and some of which are not; but this we know, and we know it very definitely, that the closer the supervision during pregnancy and the better the care at the time of delivery, the fewer will be these complications and the more satisfactory will be the results.

We find, moreover, that approximately fifty per cent of gynecological operations are performed for injuries resulting at the time of labor—injuries many of which are preventable and most of which could be fairly satisfactorily treated at the time of their occurrence or soon after. The truth is that we cannot estimate the number of partial or complete invalids who are invalids as the result of either poor nursing, inefficient medical attention, or meddlesome midwifery at the time of miscarriage or at the time of labor. Furthermore, spontaneous and criminal abortions occur with astounding frequency. The great majority of women have little or no care at such times. As a result of ignorance, thoughtlessness, and the failure to grasp the real significance of unnatural termination of pregnancy, thousands never recover their health.

Turning to the newborn child, we find that although the loss in life due to stillbirths is unduly high, and that although approximately forty per cent of all deaths of infants under one year of age are due to congenital causes, nevertheless, progress in remedying such a deplorable state of affairs is very slow. In New York City during the thirty-year period from 1884 to 1914, the death rates from diarrheal, respiratory, and contagious diseases have been markedly reduced—approximately seventy-five per cent, fifty-three per cent, and eighty-eight per cent respectively—while the death rate from congenital diseases has been reduced by only one and one-half per cent.[1]

Since the first year of the war our birth rate, as in Europe, has gone down everywhere, while our mortality rate has steadily gone up. Actual death is one thing, but what about the child that lives for a short time, or for many years immature in body and mind or actually deformed? These abnormal or subnormal beings are so in part because of causes over which we have more or less control, and in part because of factors arising in the course of pregnancy or during labor, over which we may at times be almost powerless. The studies carried on by the Federal Children's Bureau, as well as by certain public and private organizations in this country, all strikingly reveal the fact that "the nine months of intra-uterine life coupled with the first month after birth represent the high mark of danger in the life span of every individual." It is high time that every community should be roused to the fact that the logical time to begin guarding infant life is not after birth, but rather in the earlier periods of development.

This is the era of preventive medicine. It is because we believe in prevention, coupled with coordination of effort, that we meet in conference at this time. With properly organized clinics, such as can be established in progressive communities, we feel justified in stating that there should result a reduction of from thirty to thirty-five per cent in the deaths under one month of age; a material lowering in the number of stillbirths; a reduction in premature births of at least twenty-five per cent and in the maternal death rate of from sixty to sixty-five per cent below the general rate of unsupervised cases. This great conservation movement is, aside from its medical and nursing aspects, a great social undertaking. It is a fight against poverty, filth, rum, tuberculosis, and ignorance of the barest fundamentals of health. These are the hostile forces that are ever busy, ever eager to accomplish the physical and moral undoing of the community. Expectant mothers and young children fall easy prey to their attacks. As Mrs. West, of the Children's Bureau, has well said, "One of the reasons which es-

---

[1] Jacob Sobel, M. D., Department of Health, New York City: "Instruction and Supervision of Expectant Mothers in New York City," in New York Medical Journal, Vol. CVII, No. 2 (Jan. 12, 1918), p. 49.

pecially justify the necessary expenditures for giving prenatal care, is that in studying the problem of the mother we get closer to the fundamental causes of suffering than in almost any other way." In passing, we should recall that approximately forty per cent of the labors throughout the country have been handled, in most part, by careless and unclean midwives; and that a very considerable percentage of the other sixty per cent of the women have been in the care of physicians poorly trained in obstetrics, who have been graduated from the medical schools with only a minimum amount of practical equipment for this branch of medicine.

The problem of the city differs in many respects from that of rural districts. On the one hand it is easier because distances are less great than in the country, thus offering greater accessibility to doctors, to nurses, and to hospitals; on the other hand, it is more complex because of the overcrowding, the frightful poverty, and—in many cities at least—because of the great mixture of races.

In New York City we began two years ago to develop a plan for the coordination and extension of maternity care among the poor. After thorough investigation, it was found that while much good work was being carried on by the department of health, by maternity hospitals, and by a few lay organizations, yet on the whole the situation was unsatisfactory. This was due in part to the inadequacy of the care given, in part to the confused standards of medical and nursing supervision, and perhaps especially to the evident lack of coordination and to the relatively small number of expectant mothers reached. We therefore began to look at the needs of the obstetrical community not from the standpoint of the individual clinic or of a particular society, but from the standpoint of communal interest.

The first question to present itself was one of distribution of hospital cases. By means of a map, the house location of every woman cared for by the different maternity hospitals in the Borough of Manhattan during the year 1915 was graphically shown. By studying the distribution of these cases in their relationship to existing clinics, and at the same time computing the total number of births in different sections, there was developed a zoning system. As it now stands, the borough is divided into ten zones, each zone comprising a group of official census districts. The plan itself, however, is not an official one. The Borough of Manhattan has, roughly, two and a half million inhabitants with from sixty to sixty-five thousand births annually. The districting has many advantages: First, it encourages the hospitals to draw their patients from their particular zone rather than from a great distance, thus rendering prenatal oversight of their registered cases far easier, by economizing the time of both patient and visiting nurse; second, it encourages patients to seek hospital aid more readily because of their greater familiarity with the hospitals in their own neighborhood; and third, it forms the basis for our entire maternity center plan. The Maternity Center Association early in its career decided on a broad, far-reaching program. The difficulties were in a large measure foreseen, but the great call for help could not go unheeded. The originators of the movement had in mind three fundamental purposes:

First, the coordination of the work of those agencies already in the field engaged in maternity welfare.

Second, the awakening of community interest in the needless sacrifice of health and life and in the value of prenatal care both to mother and child.

Third, the providing of additional nurses for field work, and the establishment of new prenatal clinics in the several zones whenever existing agencies should prove unable to cope with the demand.

With these definite objects in mind, we felt that the most satisfactory method of attacking the program was through the establishment of a maternity center in each zone.

In the Borough of Manhattan about thirty-three per cent of the births were cared for by the indoor and outdoor services of maternity hospitals; yet at the beginning of this movement most of these either had no follow-up system during pregnancy, or had at best a very inadequate one. By arousing community interest, we hoped not only to reach gradually the remaining sixty to seventy-five per cent of expectant mothers, but we confidently looked forward to the time when the hospital boards would be aroused to the need of systematic social and nursing service in the homes of their registered mothers.

During this first year of definite organization, nine of the ten zones have maternity centers; the tenth zone, having but a small annual birth rate, has been left for later development. One of the great difficulties in New York City, as in most other communities, lies in the fact that there are available all too few "free or moderately priced" obstetrical beds. In the large Borough of Manhattan, with its great congestion, we find that there are not more than 725 available beds to accommodate the many who are really in sore need of hospital attention. In the Borough of Brooklyn, with approximately two million inhabitants, a careful survey made by some of the physicians there recently showed that they had scarcely 275 available beds. Think of it, and we are progressive!

There are engaged in this prenatal work, at the present time, about 58 nurses and perhaps a half score of social workers. The numbers employed fluctuate somewhat, from month to month. Several of the hospitals are now giving their undergraduate nurses, through the maternity center, a number of weeks' training in maternity care in the tenements. Furthermore, a certain number of student nurses, who are taking the public-health course at the Teachers' College, and at the Henry Street Settlement, are likewise receiving post-graduate training in the care of obstetric patients under the difficult conditions presented by tenement-house life.

There are at the present time, twenty-one clinics for expectant mothers in the Borough of Manhattan, in addition to the regular hospital ones. All of these aim to follow the same general standards, and all, I am sure, are looking forward to continued improvement in the service rendered the community.

A maternity center should be the center of an educational campaign for prenatal care of the mothers of the district. (The fathers, too, need education and should not be neglected!) It should be the coordinating agent or clearing house for the expectant mothers in the zone. It should keep records of every case coming under the care of the clinics in the neighborhood and follow up each case so that no woman who registers will be allowed to slip out from under medical care by reason of illness, carelessness, or other causes. It is this follow-up system, after all, which is the chief point of the whole scheme. Nurses and social workers should be used as follow-up visitors in order to keep in touch with each expectant mother in the district. How important this is may be realized from the studies of the Bureau of Child Hygiene in New York City, which has disclosed the fact that from thirty-five to forty per cent of the population of childbearing age of a given section move during the year, and that some of these families move as frequently as three or four times during the year.

The center should promote and extend the work of every agency working within the zone, that is engaged in the problems of maternity and child welfare. It should secure the opening of new prenatal clinics conveniently located when not enough of these clinics exist to serve the needs of the district. The district doctors and midwives should be urged to bring their cases to these clinics for consultation. It should be open day and night for emergency calls and should see that a doctor or midwife is supplied for all cases of labor, and a nurse for abnormal labors. This beyond question is perhaps our hardest problem to solve, and on it but very little work has as yet been done. In the districts in which there is no hospital with an out-patient obstetrical service, the problem of supplying the patients with even fair medical attendants (either doctor or midwife) is a difficult one. The midwife situation in New York City is greatly improved, but the medical aspect is less satisfactory. In the new prenatal clinics that are being developed by the Maternity Center Association, we are endeavoring to provide women physicians as far as possible, in order through these clinics to reach the large class of foreigners who go to the midwife because of their prejudices towards the male physician. These prejudices may be considered unimportant, but they can only be broken down slowly and cautiously.

All the clinics are standardized so far as records, nursing care, and medical oversight are concerned, and an effort is being made to encourage all "abnormal cases" to go to the hospitals for supervision and delivery. Such a system will gradually extend its benefits to a large part of the poorer classes in the community; in time it should gradually and effectively eliminate the midwife; it should raise markedly the general average of obstetrical knowledge among the doctors who most need this experience; it should lessen the maternal invalidism so often a result of poor obstetrical care; and it should do away with many of the evil results affecting the child due to immaturity or injury during labor.

This is a comprehensive plan for the guarding of infant life from the prenatal state through childhood to young adolesence. If carried out it offers a progressive, systematic scheme for the compilation of accurate statistics in this country. We need national, state, and municipal action. The machinery must be provided by which the poor can find it possible to raise families without undue sacrifice of health or unreasonable financial strain.

Standards of prenatal requirements for both hospitals and maternity center clinics were formulated by the Maternity Service Association of Physicians. These requirements are:

1. Patients should be urged to register at a clinic early in pregnancy. This is of great importance in order to obtain prenatal care at an early date, and in order that the physicians may determine the presence or absence of abnormalities. Strange as it may seem, two of our leading obstetrical hospitals have until recently been unwilling to examine applicants until in the fifth and seventh month of pregnancy, respectively.

2. At the first visit patients should be given printed instructions for their general guidance during pregnancy. The instructions given are simple and concise and will be read when more elaborate ones would be disregarded.

3. Patients should be urged to return every four weeks (every two weeks for maternity center patients) up to the end of the sixth month, and every two weeks thereafter (for maternity center patients every ten days up to eight months and every week thereafter). If they do not do so, a postal should be sent, and if there is no answer within two days, a nurse or social worker should visit the house. In case the patient's condition is not entirely satisfactory at the time of any one visit, and in case she does not return on any appointed day, the visit to the home should be made at once. By such watchfulness a considerable number of complications may be avoided. These

home visits are of particular value in obtaining the confidence and interest of the patient. They enable the visitor to familiarize herself with the particular social and economic difficulties of each family under her care, and afford an opportunity of teaching the fundamentals of personal hygiene.

4. The patient should bring a specimen of the urine at each visit.

5. The medical examination shall include:

(a) Thorough physical examination.

(b) Urine examination every four weeks up to six months, and every two weeks thereafter (maternity center cases every week during the last month).

(c) A blood pressure estimation at each visit.

(d) A Wassermann test in every suspicious case (this can be carried out through the board of health).

DISCUSSION

Mrs. William Lowell Putnam (Boston, Massachusetts): I have a very strong belief that the people of moderate means are the people who are least cared for in this matter of protection of the health of mothers and children. For five years we have carried on an experiment in Boston to try to bring this care within the reach of those mothers who cannot afford the prices required by the best physicians, and yet who should not be offered charity, and who under no circumstances would consent to accept it. We have not yet made this experiment pay, but we have made a start. We have been given the use of two rooms at a hospital for our clinic. Our plan requires at least two visits by the patient to the clinic for medical care; then every ten days a visit to the home by the nurse from as early in the pregnancy as the patient can be persuaded to apply. The nurse is also present with the doctor at confinement, which, if possible, takes place in the home. If there is any complication, the patient must be taken to the hospital. After confinement follow two to four more visits by the doctor, according to the need; visits twice a day for three days by the nurse; once a day for the next two days, and then less frequently until the mother is able to get up, by which time she has had a good opportunity to observe the proper way to care for her child.

We have thought that we could supply such care with thoroughly trained physicians and nurses for $25 a case for the whole period. As I say, I am not sure of this; we may have to raise the price. The only thing I am sure of is that we shall not take a case for charity, because the whole object is to provide care for those of limited means and to provide it without dependence on medical schools where students can be used without expense.

I think that if this can be done, our experiment ought to be worthy of being copied in other places. If we can prove that this care can be given for $30 or even $35 a case, that ought to be of value to the community, and I hope we shall be able to bring this about.

RURAL PROBLEMS

By MISS ELIZABETH G. FOX
Director, Bureau of Public Health Nursing, American Red Cross

The rural mother needs the same prenatal, natal, and postnatal care and advantages as the city mother. She needs to be kept well, protected from avoidable complications, provided with adequate medical and nursing care during the lying-in period, properly instructed in infant hygiene, and guided in caring for her infant.

Translated into concrete terms, she should have at least one thorough medical examination including pelvic measurements and urine and blood tests. Where a venereal disease is discovered, suitable treatment should be available. She should be visited frequently by a public-health nurse who would teach her how to care for her health and to prepare for confinement, would help her to arrange for medical care, and would make urinalyses. Some arrangement should be made to relieve her of her more arduous duties such as washing, carrying water, and milking. A hospital should be within reach for the care of all complicated cases, and possibly also for those normal cases that might be able to take advantage of it. After confinement the mother should continue to be visited frequently by a public-health nurse, who would watch and guard the baby's growth and would teach her how to give it intelligent care; who would encourage maternal nursing, and would show her the relation between this function and her own health. It should be possible for her to secure advice from a doctor familiar with modern pediatrics if the baby shows any departure from normal or if it becomes necessary to resort to artificial feeding.

It is one thing to outline these essentials; it is quite another thing to provide them. A number of difficulties lie in the way of such provision, some of which are now slowly being removed while others remain. One of the chief difficulties is the inaccessibility of adequate medical care. In many rural localities, the distance between farm houses, poor roads, and the large area covered by one doctor make his attendance at confinement very uncertain and often impossible, and also partly account for the frequent absence of prenatal and postnatal visits. It has been shown that many country women do entirely without medical supervision both before and after confinement, relying entirely upon their own resources except for the actual delivery.

Furthermore, many country people, unused to handling much ready money, are unable or not inclined to afford the cost of good medical care. They have not yet learned to regard childbirth as a serious and important event and do not understand the justice of the seemingly high price which the doctor places upon this service. Even should they recognize his fee to be a proper one, poverty would make it impossible for some of them, perhaps a good proportion of them, to pay it. Many country doctors, moreover, are not informed concerning the best obstetrical practice, to the great and sometimes fatal disadvantage of the woman whose pregnancy or delivery may be complicated.

The result of all this is that many country women are cared for entirely by neighbors, who may or may not have acquired some skill from experience; or by their husbands; or in some parts of the country, by midwives. Normal cases usually survive this amateur assistance, but abnormal cases suffer a high injury and death rate. Except to those living near small towns or cities, hospital care is practically unknown. Complicated cases no matter how serious remain at home. Very few farmers' wives would find it possible to leave their homes well in advance of confinement in order to travel to a hospital in some distant city.

Many counties and communities have not as yet installed a public-health nursing service. Moreover, even where public funds are available for maintaining a public-health nurse, her work is often directed toward the development of school nursing. Where there is but one public-health nurse in the county, as is usually the case, and she is expected to make school nursing her primary duty, she cannot undertake also to develop a prenatal and maternity service. If she is allowed to develop a general service, she can give prenatal, natal, and postnatal care and can eliminate many of the dangers which now surround childbirth in the country.

Another condition which causes many miscarriages and undermines the health both of mother and baby is the heavy work which the mother must perform. Many a farmer's wife does her daily chores, even to carrying water long distances, up to the very eve of her confinement; and she resumes them within a very few days after it. These duties must be carried on, and servants are hard to secure even when the family budget permits of their employment. Relatives and neighbors are generous with their services, but usually have families of their own, and cannot be expected to assume household duties other than their own for any length of time.

Another foe, usually more beforehand than the doctor or the nurse can be, is the patent-medicine vendor, who finds all too ready a sale for his wares. And finally, behind all of these difficulties lies the ignorance or the indifference of the farmer and his wife. Although there is a great awakening everywhere—as a result of the lessons taught by the war and the work of the Children's Year Campaign—to the importance of safeguarding pregnancy, maternity, and child life, much must still be done to translate this new knowledge into conviction, determination, and action. This problem has been discussed for a number of years, and various partial remedies have been suggested. No definite experiments have yet been reported to prove their worth.

The rapid development of rural public-health nursing seems to offer one of the most immediate and tangible remedies. In order to make the nurse's work at all effective, counties must be divided into districts with a general nurse in each district. She will then have time to teach the rural women the hygiene of pregnancy, to visit them frequently, to watch for symptoms of complications, to make urinalyses, to care for women during and after confinement, and to teach them the principles of infant and child hygiene. She too can convince them and their husbands of the necessity for proper care throughout this period and may be able to find ways to help them lessen their household burdens.

Some way must be found of providing adequate obstetrical service. As such service must be of the best it will necessarily be costly. It must be put within the reach of all, nevertheless, through health insurance, mothers' pensions, or some form of State aid, or else through a more just economic distribution of the profits of labor. Cottage hospitals or county maternity hospitals are necessary for the proper care of complicated cases. The attention of a child specialist must be available for all country babies in need of special treatment. Some form of itinerant children's clinic might make this possible. Some provision must also be made for supplying mothers with household help before and during the lying-in period. The public-health nurse might be able to arrange, direct, and supervise an attendant or practical nurse service.

It has been suggested that all of these agents might work together as a unit on the county basis, radiating out into the country from a center. Dr. Grace Meigs Crowder has described this plan in her paper, "Rural Obstetrics," given before the Association for the Study and Prevention of Infant Mortality in 1916. She says: "The fundamental provisions necessary to meet this problem naturally vary with the density of the population and with the differing living conditions found in various parts of the country. It is probably safe to say that the county would in general be the unit in any plan, and that county centers of maternal and infant welfare could be established, ordinarily at the county seat, but accessible to all the women of a county, where they could obtain free or for pay simple information as to the proper care of themselves and their babies. The plan for such a center would naturally include, first, a county nursing service; second, a cottage maternity hospital or beds in a general hospital, for the care of complicated cases or for normal cases where women can leave home for confinement; third, provision for skilled attendance for normal cases at their homes, with access to especially skilled assistance for complicated cases; and lastly, provision for obtaining temporary household help for mothers whether confined at home or at the hospital."

Had not the war drawn away so many of our doctors and nurses, some such plan would undoubtedly have been tried out and its practicability proved or disproved. Let us hope that the new and universal interest in health and the protection of child life resulting from the war will make many such experiments possible and successful.

The Red Cross through its plan to promote rural health nursing hopes to contribute toward the protection of maternity and infancy in the country.

DISCUSSION

Miss Mary Power (Director, Child Welfare Bureau, Ontario): I am greatly interested in rural problems because I come from the Province of Ontario where the cities so far are fairly well organized and the chief concern of our bureau is the extension of medical and nursing service to the rural communities. By rural communities I mean communities other than the large cities, from towns of less than 5,000 population to strictly isolated country districts. Our Bureau is at the present time considering the possibility, and we hope the probability, of demonstrating public-health work for rural communities in our province. We hope to use the county seat or some other convenient point as a center for the surrounding country. The staff might consist of at least a physician and a supervising nurse. The physician in charge might perform the duties of medical inspector in the schools, and might hold weekly baby clinics. The supervising nurse might direct the nursing service in the district. Thus we will be able to do the follow-up work in connection with medical inspection, and in addition take care of maternity cases and general sickness cases which require visiting nurses. It may be that we are asking a great deal for a small unit, but we want to show what can be done. Before organizing this unit we desire to secure the hearty cooperation of every practical nurse in the district and to enlist certain volunteer workers who might be called "home helpers" for the aid of the supervising nurse. In addition, we should like to have a dentist to follow up the medical inspection work, who might hold weekly or at least biweekly clinics for children of preschool age and for adults.

In this way we are hoping to accomplish something in the reduction of maternal mortality, maternal sickness, and infant and child mortality. At the same time we hope to bring the whole community, through this health center, to a higher plane of general health.

We have felt that whereas our diarrheal diseases and respiratory diseases have decreased slightly, we have not yet by the means we have used been able to make any impression upon the large group of deaths under one year due to congenital causes; and we trust this new departure will be a help in reducing the large mortality from those diseases, which in 1917 constituted 50 per cent of Ontario's total deaths under one year, excluding stillbirths from both births and deaths.

An inspector of education with whom I talked recently and who was interested in the provision of hot lunches for children in rural schools said that he had been working at the problem only since last September but had been able to accomplish a good deal in that time. In 100 rural schools they are now serving hot lunches to the school children. He mentioned, however, that a grant of $40 is given to the school and $20 as a special bonus to the teacher. I asked him if he thought he would have been able today to report the same results had no grant been offered, and he said absolutely, "No."

I am hoping that as a result of this meeting we shall be able to arrive at the point where we can say that grants in aid from central authorities will be the greatest help we can have in our work. Mrs. Barton says that in some cases where the agency has been approved by the Local Government Board, the Board grants 50 per cent of the net cost; on the other hand, the municipal government will give 50 per cent of the net cost. In other words, the entire cost of a maternity and child-welfare scheme in England can be met, half by the central authority and half by the municipal authority.

Mrs. Edna Hatfield Edmondson (Field Secretary, Indiana Child Welfare Committee, and Field Worker, Indiana University Extension Division): I come from a State where our problems are strictly rural. We have one city of approximately 250,000 population and only 25 cities of over 10,000 population. The rest of the State is made up of small cities and towns of less than 10,000 population and country districts. Our problem is one of providing machinery to get this service into the rural districts.

Miss Lydia Holman (North Carolina): Twenty years ago a call to a special patient took me into a remote mountain county in Western North Carolina, a county one hundred per cent American. Before my patient had fully recovered, I discovered that mothers and babies were dying at such a rate that I felt that the matter should be investigated and that something should be done for these neglected Americans. There was not an organized State board of health at that time, Dr. Lewis being a volunteer secretary. There were no vital statistics.

Though I told the people I was only a nurse they insisted upon calling me a doctor. I have been obliged in this work to do many things which as a nurse I was taught not to do. Fortunately, in my training I had observed the methods of first-class doctors and surgeons and in consequence met many emergencies successfully. Grave necessity has even driven me to perform minor operations. In fact I have been brought before the court for practicing medicine, though there was but one practicing graduate physician in the county, and he was frequently incapacitated. But our judges are our most enlightened men, knowing usually the needs of a district, and they rarely interfere with an essential for the betterment of the people.

The work grew. Doing careful maternity work, I had more calls than one person could respond to in such rough country. Teaching careful and cleanly methods at each place helped the situation and stamped out of my district "childbed fever." It can be done.

In my travels there were times when the rivers were up and the trails so bad that it was impossible for horses to travel fast; naturally, we were not always in time for the birth. However, out of 500 maternity cases there were no losses of mothers or babies.

We have by publicity secured more and better things; great is the need still. Our doctors have taken postgraduate work. The expectant mothers are so well instructed that they demand good clean service. Their husbands are ambitious to secure the best attendants.

At first we were 28 miles from a railway station. Twenty years is a long time to talk about, but at last we are ready to put up a new building—a community center with a ten-bed infirmary for mothers and babies and for emergency cases.

The work of the State board of health has not yet reached our county. Will the mountain counties be reached by the State? In my estimation only the government can make possible right conditions and give such service as will remedy the long neglected problem of rural mothers and babies.

Mrs. Kate Brew Vaughan (North Carolina State Board of Health): I do not want you to think that there is no public-health work done for mothers and babies in North Carolina. We have a very vibrant State board of health. We have, of course, that lack of funds from which, I presume, nearly all State boards of health suffer. The different agencies for child welfare in North Carolina have usually heretofore been of the philanthropic kind—usually the mission church and the mission nurses. This past year, however, the Governor of North Carolina proposed some excellent health bills which were passed by the legislature. We have now an appropriation of $50,000 for school inspection, which, to some of you, must seem like a drop in the bucket, but to North Carolina it seems like a great deal. We have a traveling dental clinic and our adenoid and tonsil clubs which will give relief not only to the children but to the parents as well. Incidentally, they teach hygiene as they go along. We have also rural nurses. Four nurses are already installed, working directly under the State board of health doing the work that Miss Fox spoke of as necessary. We have two cooperating with the Red Cross and four cooperating with the philanthropic organizations.

The biggest problem we have to contend with is our midwives. Eighty per cent of our colored mothers are delivered by midwives. They are ignorant, they have no idea of cleanliness. Educated women would hardly undertake the work of these midwives, for they are paid so little. Forty per cent of our white mothers are delivered by midwives, a few of them white women of not very excellent status. That is one of the problems we have to meet.

We have started something in the way of hygiene. For three years there has been a movement with regard to soil pollution work in the South, which is the biggest work there, since it removes the hook worm and the diarrheal diseases.

Referring to infant hygiene, nearly one-fourth of the deaths in North Carolina are infant deaths, and most of these are attributable to congenital diseases and diarrheal diseases.

I want you all to know that North Carolina has big possibilities. For instance, it has the highest birth rate of any State in the whole Union in proportion to its population; and since we are going to reduce the death rate North Carolina may soon come to the front.

Dr. Julius Levy (New Jersey State Board of Health): I think it is important to realize that the real solution of the rural problem lies in the responsibility of the State department of health. I believe that the most worth-while effort of the Red Cross or any other organization is merely to insist that the State department of health shall perform its proper function in protecting the health of the rural population and that the function of private organizations is not to do in piecemeal the things that are needed in rural communities.

Miss Holman's experience serves a magnificent purpose if it is used properly. I do not think that any group of citizens could listen to her without being ready to say: "Here is something that the State department of health ought to solve." To-day child-hygiene and the general health work is sufficiently advanced so that we do not have to demonstrate how it should be done. We have passed the demonstration stage. We know sufficiently what we ought to do and that it can be done. We have a right to say that we know what we ought to do.

In New Jersey we obtained this past year, available July 1st, an appropriation of $125,000 for the child-hygiene work. The Council of Defense was of considerable help. Our plan calls for applying to every city in the State a proper preventive hygiene program. I personally believe we should forget somewhat the distinctions between rural and urban population, recognizing the difference wholly in the application of details. You need the same kind of work in the rural population in North Carolina and New Jersey that you do in the city of Newark. We must do it differently in order to put it across.

I think I heard mentioned the question of traveling clinics. In New Jersey we prefer the idea of having a motor car which will bring the people to a permanent station. I will not go into the reasons why, but I think you will find it will have many advantages. We are so distributing our stations—whether they be infant-welfare clinics or mental-hygiene clinics—as best to adapt them to the roads and transportation conditions, and get the cooperation of motor cars so that we can bring the women and children to the stations; and then we divide the community up among nurses in order that each one may get the greatest possible benefit.

New Jersey intends to put on 100 workers July 1. This staff is paid for by the State. In addition, the city of Newark has nurses of its own. I treat that as I would any part of the State, since the nurses are there and we do not have to put them there. We should stimulate the city to carry on its own work. The rural communities can not carry on their own work unless we can make large communities.

Dr. Andrew Wilson (Wheeling, West Virginia): We are talking about stimulating the State board of health, stimulating the social organizations, stimulating this organization and that organization. We are considering the problem, when the thing we should consider is the specimen. We take it coldly; we do not consider, apparently, that it has brains. The fundamental thing to do is to teach people to take care of themselves. We have organizations enough to do this already, in the public-school system of the United States. It is the most far-reaching organization for the teaching of health that we have. The organization is made and is here. Why not use it? Why not have the department of public health teach public health in every public school in this land?

Dr. Dorothy Reed Mendenhall (Children's Bureau): I think that the rural problem is the most vital and interesting health problem that we have to face, and I believe that we are going to solve it in the next ten years. I do not agree with Dr. Levy on one point, and that is that the rural problem is the same in the different communities. The rural problem in New Jersey is very different from that in Wisconsin, for one thing because of the difference in size of the two States. The largest counties in Wisconsin are about one-quarter of the size of the State of New Jersey; and there are 71 counties, large and small, in Wisconsin. There is not a public-health system in any of the counties. We have an excellent State board of health, but we cannot, with the small appropriation we have, expect to do very much work in States as large as most of the Middle Western States.

We all know that rural communities should have the same opportunities that cities now enjoy. We want every child to have proper care at birth, proper prenatal care, proper care during infancy and during the preschool age, as well as proper schooling and care during the period of adolescence. Safeguarding the social welfare as organized for city children is also needed. How is it possible to bring this about in the country? What is the short cut? I believe we have found it in the public-health nurse. I believe that Wisconsin in making it mandatory to have public-health nurses in its 71 counties is paving the way towards a solution of her problem, for where you have a public nurse, if she is a visiting nurse and not a school nurse only, there is the beginning of a health center and there is the beginning of the best educational work in the home.

Miss Holman has shown what a public-health nurse can do in one of the isolated counties in North Carolina. I think her splendid work shows what can be done elsewhere. If you can put the right sort of a nurse into a rural county, she will soon have a public health center and perhaps itinerant clinics started such as they are having in Minnesota and such as they have also started in New York, so that we can begin to safeguard the life of the mother and her child in rural districts. It is continuity of care that we must work for—from conception to adolescence.

I believe the best way we have to educate the public in these isolated counties to want this work is to start with a public-health nurse. She will bring in a public center, a maternity center, a social center, and pave the way for the best school work; and we want all these features in our health work.

I want to refer for a moment to a bill that was presented at the last Congress for the protection of maternity and infancy in rural districts. It was favorably reported by the committee of the House to which it was assigned, but did not go any further. In this bill the attempt was made in a way to adopt the principle of the Smith-Lever Bill for the promotion of agriculture and to copy what the Department of Agriculture has carried out so successfully. The bill is for the purpose of promoting the care of mothers and babies in rural districts, and of providing instruction in the hygiene of maternity and infancy. It provides for Federal aid to be given through State authorities to rural counties to help them carry out this work through public-health nursing, consultation centers, the provision of medical and nursing care for mothers and infants at home or, when necessary, at a hospital, and other methods. According to the bill a certain sum of money would be given outright to each State; the remainder of the sum to which the State would be entitled would be given only after an equal sum had been appropriated for the purpose by the State. It is, as you see, a matter of giving Federal aid on a fifty-fifty basis. If such a bill is passed, there might be a center of public-health nursing in every county. I think that this bill is one of the most important proposals that have been made in connection with the welfare of the women and children of this country, and that, of course, means the welfare of the nation.

THE PRESCHOOL CHILD

HEALTH CENTERS FOR PRESCHOOL CHILDREN

By DR. MERRILL E. CHAMPION

Director, Division of Hygiene, Massachusetts State Department of Health

A health center, within the meaning of this paper, is a place where people may come to learn how to keep well. The term "health center" is gradually coming into use and replaces, in part, the less desirable one of "clinic." To many persons the word "clinic" means nothing at all, while to many others it carries an unpleasant connotation of sickness and medical treatment of one sort or other. There is danger, however, that the term "health center" will, for a time at least, carry to many persons a less definite impression than does the older term. This is only another way of saying that as yet the idea of disease prevention, and especially health preservation, is less clearly defined in people's minds than the idea of medical treatment and disease cure. Nevertheless, the health center will be a positive force in the future.

While this paper is entitled "Health Centers for Preschool Children," I do not mean to imply that a health center for children of this age should be considered to have any peculiar attribute not possessed by one for children of any other age. It may safely be said, however, that at the present time the public is not sufficiently awake to the fact that the child of preschool age is being considerably neglected. The reasons for this are indubitably that the high infant mortality and the general helplessness of the baby call attention to his needs; and on the other hand, the somewhat better organized activities for the protection of the child of school age detract attention from the younger child. In the State of Massachusetts we have annually about 3,500 deaths among children over one year and under five years of age. This represents about one-fifteenth of our total mortality of all ages. Apart from the death rate, many of the defects and disabilities discovered in children of school age take origin in the earlier age group.

It may well be said that under our modern conditions strait is the gate and narrow is the way which leadeth unto good health, and few there be that find it; and wide is the gate and broad is the way that leadeth to self-indulgence and neglect of health, and many there be who go in thereat. As far as the child is concerned, this is due to the ignorance of the parents; hence the great function of a health center is to radiate an educational influence. The work done there should be positive; the workers should deal in "do's" rather than in "don'ts." This being the case, a different type of nurse and physician is needed from that often found in clinics for the sick. They must have the enthusiasm to inspire in people the desire to pursue an ideal, without having the advantage of the keen incentive which goads to action the sick man in his pursuit of health.

To repeat, a health center, then, is a place where people may come to learn how to keep well. This does not necessarily call for any particular machinery. Like the college which consisted of Mark Hopkins on one end of a pine bench and a student at the other, a health center for preschool children might well consist only of a roof sheltering an enthusiastic public nurse or physician, and a mother with her child of preschool age. In fact, I think the emphasis in the past has often been laid too much on the surroundings and too little on the essentials.

The ideal should be that of the benefactor of the New Zealand Society's Baby Hospital, quoted by Dr. Truby King: "I specially desire that, so far as possible consistent with doing full justice to the babies admitted, the hospital will continue to be so directed and managed that any mother in ordinary circumstances visiting it may feel that almost everything done in the institution could be effectively carried out by herself in her own home after receiving the necessary instruction. As conducing to this end, it is hoped that strict economy and simplicity in regard to buildings, furnishings, appliances, clothing, etc., will be maintained as heretofore, and that the treatment will continue to be conducted, as far as possible, on broad, simple, practical, scientific lines, easily comprehensible by the ordinary mother." Two or three rooms in any central location, even in a business block, will furnish an office and examining room for the doctor, a waiting and weighing room for the children, and an office for the nurses; on occasion even one room is enough. Accommodations can be varied to suit the circumstances of the case.

This brings us to the question: "Who should conduct the health center?" I may as well say at once that I believe this to be the plain duty of the municipality. The health of the citizen is of vital importance to the community. The community calls upon the citizen to perform certain duties; it is equally important that the community furnish the citizen the opportunity to fit himself for the performance of these duties. This principle is well recognized so far as cultural education is concerned. Furthermore, it is recognized that as a matter of self-protection the community handles communicable disease, spending money in the process without legally pauperizing the persons involved. Why should this not be equally true of physical education and noncommunicable disease? To quote Truby King again, "They (the workers of the Special Health Mission) have recognized throughout that the need for more light and higher standards is as essential for one class as for another—a matter for friendly cooperation and free education, not a matter for patronage or charity."

It will be noticed that I use the phrase "duty of the municipality" rather than that of the State or county. In my State, Massachusetts, the principle of home rule is highly cherished. There, the town or city is the unit rather than the township or county. But whatever the unit, it would seem that the ultimate community responsibility should be on the collection of homes rather than on the collection of municipalities, subject, of course, to a certain unifying control on the part of the larger body—the State. In many instances, however, the individual community is too small or too poor to maintain the proper agencies for the well-being of its citizens. Theoretically, such a community has no excuse for existence, but nevertheless it does exist. The only recourse, then, is for such a community to combine with one or more similarly situated to get the service both desire; or a county made up of such towns may assume the responsibility. Often the question of transportation in winter must be a governing factor.

Too often, on the other hand, the community as a whole is not awake to its duty of seeing that physical education is available for its citizens. Under such circumstances, private organizations must furnish a demonstration of the value of such service in the hope of educating the municipality to a sense of its obligations. This, I presume, has been the usual method of procedure in the majority of places. Of these private bodies, the hospital would seem to be the least suitable for clinics for well children or for health centers. It is far better from a psychological point of view to emphasize the value of health as an end in itself rather than as a means of avoiding disease. There are, however, many private organizations suitable for this work of establishing health centers. Visiting nurses' associations, those which lay the emphasis on public-health nursing rather than on bedside nursing, can do it well. So can child-welfare committees, women's clubs, settlement houses, and other such philanthropic agencies.

An unusual example of the health center as conducted under semi-private auspices is afforded by the so-called Health Demonstration at Framingham, Massachusetts. The prime object of this demonstration is to show what can be done in the way of control of tuberculosis by a well-financed private enterprise working in cooperation with the local health authorities. All modern methods are employed to this end: physical examinations of various age groups, with special reference to tuberculosis; school inspection; child-welfare work; and educational work along public-health lines. The Framingham demonstration is, however, an unusual instance, in view of the amount of money available from private funds, and in view of the national interest in the work. Another well-known example is the work done through the National Social Unit Organization in Cincinnati.

There is, however, one very real danger in much of this. It is that there will be a multiplicity of organizations, each with its own overhead expense, running a variety of poorly supported enterprises, each in competition with the other. This is fatal to good work and is utterly inexcusable from an economic standpoint. The municipality can do the work much better. It is often argued in favor of private organizations, that they can conduct such enterprises more efficiently and with less political interference than can the municipality. The claim is made, furthermore, that such projects, sponsored by aggregations of allied private interests, are conducted in an especially democratic manner. I do not agree with this view. If public health were to be looked after in this way permanently it would represent a reversal to the earlier days before self-government became an accomplished fact. The venality of certain forms of municipal control is no valid argument against municipal control. If the same amount of effort were put by the public into correcting municipal abuses as is often put into well-meaning private enterprises, there would be no occasion to lament such abuses, for they would not exist.

It will be seen, now, why I have not gone into great detail as to plans for a center for the child of preschool age. It is because we may say that there should not be any such thing, per se. We should have health centers which should include all, from the baby to the adult. The day is not far distant when even adults will seek periodical health examinations. These health centers for all ages should be conducted by the municipal board of health, whose duty it is to guard the health of all the people. In small communities the whole health center will be under one roof. In large places there should be one main center, preferably in some municipal or county building, with as many branch offices as are necessary to reach all the people conveniently and to give a sense of neighborhood proprietorship. I believe this neighborhood proprietorship is absolutely essential.

This plan saves overhead expense and makes for economy as well as efficiency. Under this roof could be grouped the branch of the health work having to do with prenatal care; the infant could be brought here to be weighed and measured, and to have his feeding supervised; the older child, not yet of school age, would also have his place and consultation days here. The school work, of necessity, must largely be done in the school and the home, but the special examinations needed might well be made at the health center. The child in industry, too, need not be excluded from such a center; regular physical examinations would check up the healthfulness of his work. Lastly, the adult could learn here how to live a little longer.

I have purposely left out the obstetrical work. I doubt if it is wise to combine a hospital with a health center. This same objection would hold good for nose and throat operations. I do not see that they belong in a health center. Eye and dental examinations, however, might be included with propriety. Dental treatment would be on the border line and, at first at any rate, would be included simply because people demand it.

Needless to say, the center would serve as headquarters for the public-health nursing force of the city or town, since adequate public-health work would now be unthinkable without the services of the public-health nurse at the center and especially in the home. Indeed, one may say paradoxically that the real work of the health center must be done by the nurses in the homes. This phase of the subject, however, is being treated elsewhere. Proper medical social-service work, too, would be included as an essential factor in the success of the center.

Such an outline as I have presented belongs partly to the present and partly to the future. A center is sketched from which would radiate all effort directed toward keeping the citizen and his family physically and mentally fit. It would recognize community responsibility and yet, with a little State regulation, would not be unduly narrow; it would be economical both in money and in time; it would be simple. Best of all, it would serve as a great educational center, comparable only to our public schools.

THE PUBLIC HEALTH NURSE

By DR. C.-E. A. WINSLOW
Professor of Public Health, Yale School of Medicine

When the modern movement for health protection began in England fifty years ago it was chiefly concerned with the sanitation of the environment. Sir John Simon and his followers were occupied with the purification of water supplies, the supervision of foods, the disposal of sewage, and the elimination of "accumulated obvious masses of filth," which threatened the health of the community through the exposure of excreta and the incubation of insect carriers of disease. It is true that Sir John Simon himself had a wider vision. He said:

"Long before our modern codes of public sanitary law had begun to shape themselves, elaborate counsels of personal hygiene had become current in the world; counsels as to the ways and habits of life which would most conduce to healthful longevity; counsels, above all, for moderation in life—'the rule of not too much'; and those counsels for personal self-government, enforced from age to age by the ever growing common experience of mankind, are not now to be deemed superfluous because boards of local government have arisen. In relation to the sexes and their union, and to the many personal influences which are hereditary; in relation to eating and drinking; in relation to work and repose and recreation for mind and body; in relation to the charge of infancy, and to proper differences of regimen for the different after-periods of life; there are hygienic rules, perhaps not less important to mankind than the rules which constitute local authorities."

At the beginning of any public-health campaign, however, it is necessary to deal first with the great sweeping pestilences whose origin lies primarily in the environment. When General Gorgas went to Panama his first preoccupation was necessarily with the engineering difficulties involved in obtaining a supply of pure water and eliminating mosquito-breeding marsh lands. After a time, however, these engineering problems are in a measure solved and become matters of routine, and the primary interest of the public-health official is then focused on another type of problem, that of the community infections, due not to defects of sanitation but to the spread of the germs of disease from person to person by the more or less direct routes of contact. On the first period —the period of the engineer—follows that of the bacteriologist; and the detection of carriers, the isolation of infected persons, the disinfection of discharges, and treatment by the use of sera and vaccines occupy the most prominent place in the health campaign.

The control of community infections in its turn is gradually being accomplished, although the recent pandemic of influenza makes it clear that we have yet much to learn in this field. The statistics for even 1918, however, when the figures for the last three terrible months are merged with those for the rest of the year, show that other causes of death are quantitatively more important than even influenza and pneumonia. After all the death rate for the year only carries us back about ten years; it was only about the normal death rate for ten years ago. The greatest problems which we face, day by day, require for their solution not merely the sanitation of the environment, not merely the control of community infections, but in addition, and in an even more important degree, attention to daily individual habits of hygienic living. In the future the sanitary engineer and the bacteriologist will, I believe, both yield to the physiologist the premier rôle in the drama of health protection. I may say that my confidence in this analysis of the phases of public health is strengthened by the fact that a year or two ago Dr. Chapin and I both independently presented the same analysis of the history of the health movement at two different meetings within a week or two of each other. So since he agrees I think probably the analysis is correct.

Take for example the problem of infant mortality with which we are here specially concerned. There is no other line of activity in the whole field of public health that will yield more definite and tangible results than can be obtained by well-directed efforts at the reduction of the infant death rate. Infant mortality may be reduced in part by sanitation, by the pasteurization of milk, by the removal of conditions which facilitate the breeding of disease-carrying flies, and by better housing, which will make possible the maintenance of lower room temperatures during the hot summer weather. Infant mortality may be reduced in part by measures of isolation and disinfection, which tend to protect the infant against the germs of communicable disease, so much more deadly to the infant than to its elders. Yet even greater is the need for hygienic instruction of the mother, for the training in the knowledge of child physiology and child hygiene which is the primary essential in keeping a well baby well. Sanitation and the control of community infections may be accomplished by official regulations; but the inculcation of hygienic habits of living and hygienic methods of infant care can be accomplished only by education of the individual mother in the individual home. The great tasks of modern public health are educational tasks.

We have found in this country that by far the most effective agent for the conduct of this type of educational work is the public-health nurse. Her hospital training gives her not only a fundamental knowledge of the human body and its needs, but a discipline, a loyalty, and a tradition of service that fit her in an unusual degree for the arduous tasks of her profession. Above all, the fact that she is able to bring immediate physical relief in a thousand emergencies ensures her a welcome, and makes it possible for her to deliver her message in a way that is quite beyond the reach of one who enters the home merely as a teacher. There are others who think differently about this question. There is a tendency abroad, and to some extent in this country, to introduce a new type of health educator, and we are all interested to see how that works out. Personally, however, it seems to me that the wisest tendency is in the other direction, to combine more and more closely the educational work and the bedside care in the person of the health nurse.

The public-health nurse is always in attendance at the infant-welfare station to weigh the babies and prepare them for examination and to give instruction to groups of mothers in the preparation of artificial feeding and in the other essentials of infant care. By far the most important part of her work, however, is accomplished in the home. The infant-welfare nurses spend a day or a half day each week at the welfare stations and devote the rest of their time to visiting in the homes where they teach the mothers how the food of the baby should be prepared, how it should be clothed and bathed, and where and when it should sleep, and do these things with the actual utensils and under the actual conditions with which the mother must deal. As Dr. J. H. Mason Knox said:

"All the work hinges upon the better care of individual babies coming under our influence, and it is here that the trained nurse should be given the first place, both because of her unique opportunity and because of the good results which she has and does accomplish. It is she who enters the home, a welcome visitor, but one armed with expert knowledge and kindly tact. It is she who can open the closed windows, remove superfluous clothes, prepare the baby's feedings, give it a bath as an object lesson to the mother, and perform a hundred other services which together mean the difference between life and death."

The development of public-health nursing in the infant-welfare field has been a rapid one. According to a study made by the Children's Bureau in 1915,[1] there were in that year, in 142 cities of 10,000 population or over, 539 infant-welfare stations in operation, maintained by 205 different agencies. In the summer these stations maintained a corps of 866 nurses, reduced to 604 in winter. In the same year 466 nurses, not connected with infant-welfare stations, devoted their entire time in summer to infant-welfare work, while 122 were assigned entirely to this duty in winter. In addition, 460 nurses in summer, and 491 in winter, were employed for a part of their time in the infant-

---

[1] A Tabular Statement of Infant Welfare Work by Public and Private Agencies in the United States, by Etta R. Goodwin. U. S. Children's Bureau Publication No. 16, Infant Mortality Series No. 5, Washington, 1916.

welfare educational campaign. In other words, there were in these cities, in 1915, nearly 2,000 nurses engaged in whole or in part in infant-welfare work, and that number has been since greatly increased.

We are still very far from the ideal, however. The infant-welfare nurses of the visiting nurses' association in New Haven care for approximately 400 babies each, but it is the conviction of those most familiar with activities of this kind that the number of babies assigned to one infant-welfare nurse should be not over 150. On this basis we should have something like 16,000 nurses devoted to this type of public-health activity in the United States.

This calculation is based on the assumption that infant-welfare nursing is to be conducted as a specialty, by public-health nurses who devote all of their time to this particular task. Personally I am far from convinced that this is the wise policy. It is the opinion of a majority of those who have had experience in the public-health field that specialization in public-health nursing has in the past been carried too far. Friction and confusion result from the visit to one home of several different public-health nurses, and the large area covered by a nurse doing only infant-welfare work, or only tuberculosis work, causes waste of time and militates against intimate personal knowledge of family and social conditions. Public-health nursing should be organized on the lines of localities rather than specialties. This is one phase of a problem which seems to me to be confronting us in almost every field of social organization, the problem of functional or regional organization. We are meeting it even in the question of instruction in medical schools. Shall we go on teaching physiology, anatomy, and histology, or begin to teach the systems of the body? And so here: Shall we organize this work functionally or locally? In business the functional organization is replacing the local organization. In health nursing, however, I believe the organization will have to be local with a functional staff for consultation. I think the ideal way is to have your local nurse doing all the work in your district, and have her backed up by various kinds of special nurses who will assist her when she gets into difficulty.

In this way the nurse may know her district thoroughly in all its aspects, and may come to be a sort of community mother, a trained and scientific modern representative of the good neighbor who nursed the sick and helped out in all sorts of emergencies in the village life of earlier days.

I am inclined to think that the most successful public-health education in the future will be done by the district nurse working with a small population unit, ready to do ordinary visiting nursing, infant-welfare work, or tuberculosis work, and combining in every field the care of the sick with the educational activities of the modern public-health campaign. I do not agree with Dr. Champion here. I do not believe in separating this educational work from the medical work. I believe, on the other hand, we have got to absorb medical and nursing work into public health and keep them more closely combined than ever before.

Under average conditions a public-health nurse can perhaps care in this way for a population of 2,000 persons. That, it seems to me, is the program we should set for ourselves—50,000 women of this type, public-health nurses, devoting perhaps on the average, very roughly, a third of their time to infant-welfare work, a third to tuberculosis, and a third to the general task of visiting nursing. In addition, of course, school nurses and factory nurses are necessary. These are special lines that must be organized functionally, but these nurses could turn their home work over to the district nurse, I think.

The program is an ambitious one; but in New Haven, a city of 160,000 population, our visiting nurses' association has a budget for the coming year of $100,000, and will employ a total of approximately 50 nurses, about two-thirds of the ideal number indicated by the calculation above. So that this ideal is not beyond the limits of achievement.

And I may say that this visiting nurses' association in New Haven in order to get this budget went out for a four-day drive for $80,000. At the end of three days they had a hundred thousand. That shows the popular support that you can get for work of this kind. There is absolutely nothing you cannot secure for a visiting nurses' association which is doing its job well.

It is evident that for the conduct of educational work of this character we need women of a high type with a sound and broad education. You see, we are outlining a program which calls for 50,000 public-health nurses, and we want good ones. We must go further than this. We have to create the demand, on the one hand, and we have to do something to create the supply, on the other. What does the public-health nurse need to know? What do we need for this work? I am not discussing what the doctor needs for bedside assistance with sick cases. We are talking about a public-health nurse. For her work she should be well grounded in the fundamental sciences of chemistry, physics, and biology, for these sciences form the basis for all scientific thinking and all scientific applications. She should know something of the principles of sociology and economics, for her work is closely related at every point with that of the social reformer. A knowledge of foreign languages is very helpful. In some cases the ability to speak Italian or Polish or Yiddish may be essential, and I heard recently of a case where Chinese was a prerequisite. The requirement of high-school graduation before entrance upon the course of the nurses' training school should represent a minimum of preliminary general education for the nurse who is planning to enter the field of public health, and a full college course would furnish the most desirable preparation.

The course in the training school itself must be fundamentally reconstructed in order to supply the type of training that is needed by the public-health nurse of the future. Training schools in the past have grown up in a haphazard fashion and have often been actuated rather by the need for obtaining unpaid help in the hospital than by any educational ideals. Hours are too long and formal instruction too casual. The lengthening of the training-school course from two to three years was inspired by the hope that the third year would be devoted primarily to education, but such has not been the case, and we are at present in this country face to face with the need for a radical reform. The first essential, as I conceive it, is the complete divorce of the training school from hospital control. It must be independently endowed and governed like any other educational institution by authorities primarily interested in education, the relation to the hospital being essentially the same as that maintained by the medical school of the present day. Much progress has been made in this direction by the establishment, at some dozen different places, of training schools as an integral part of universities, and at the best of these schools two years of college work are required for entrance and the bachelor's degree is conferred for the completion of the training course. I am personally of the opinion that for women who have had two years of college, a six months' course of theoretical instruction, followed by eighteen months in the wards and a year of special training in public-health nursing would probably furnish the ideal type of education. In any case, the independent endowment of the training schools is a fundamental need, and there is no problem in the whole field of public health that seems to me more urgently pressing than the obtaining of endowments of this sort.

As soon as you get educational authorities interested in the education of the nurse, rather than solely in running the hospital, these things will come. This question of the endowment of training schools is the biggest single problem in public health and the biggest opportunity for philanthropy. I have nothing to do with training schools except delivering fifteen lectures a year in one, and I am not interested in the question personally, but if anybody asked me where to give a million dollars, I would say, "Don't give it to a department of public health; give it to endow a nurses' training school," because the first person that endows a nurses' training school will do what Johns Hopkins did for medicine, and what William Barton Rogers did for engineering when he established the Institute of Technology.

Finally in closing let me point out the significance of such developments as have been here discussed in relation to the broader problem of organizing the resources of medical science for efficient service along preventive lines. As I pointed out at the beginning of my address, public health is becoming more and more preoccupied with the human machine and its efficient operation. We must not be satisfied to teach merely the broad principles of personal hygiene as they apply to one and all alike, but rather to bring to each individual the particular knowledge that he needs in order to use his own body, with its physical defects and limitations, to the best advantage—just what Dr. Edsall pointed out in connection with employment and factories. In speaking of dangerous occupations, he suggested that we should ask "dangerous to whom?" Is it dangerous to John Jones? Perhaps. Is it dangerous to Simon Smith? Perhaps not.

Sound instruction in personal hygiene can be based only on a preliminary diagnosis which will reveal physical defects in their incipient stage. The line between public health and private medicine must be broken down in the interests of both; for the physician as well as the public-health worker realizes that under our present organization the resources of medical science are generally applied too late. We in America are far behind some of the other nations represented at this conference in the development of an organized system of social medicine; we can boast of relatively slight accomplishment in making the resources of medical science available for the prevention of disease; but the organization of public-health nursing by our best visiting nurses' associations furnishes a striking lesson of what may be done to attain a similar end in a related field. The accomplishments of the public-health nurse are not only fruitful in themselves but pregnant with inspiration for the task of organizing the knowledge of the physician in a similarly effective way.

DISCUSSION

Dr. Julius Levy (State Board of Health, New Jersey): I shall discuss Professor Winslow's paper in particular, because he raises a very important practical question in the conduct of preventive child-hygiene work. I believe we ought to make a distinction in the very beginning between public-health nursing work and district-nursing work. To my mind public-health work deals with the prevention of disease and not with its treatment or cure. If that is true, that phase of the nurses' work which deals, for instance, with the bandaging of an ulcerated leg cannot be included in public-health work. Therefore the greatest development of public-health nursing work must not be expected to come from district nursing associations, although I realize that sick-nursing work makes an especial appeal in raising funds and for philanthropic support.

The next point is that a logical and well-organized public-health child-hygiene program cannot be combined with district nursing, because in public-health work you wish to reach as many babies as possible and help maintain them all in health, and you must lay out a systematic program. Sick nursing does not permit that system. It is of necessity emergency work.

For instance, in a rural district you can not say you are going to give a certain nurse a district covering four or five small communities, and that she is to be on a certain day in each one of these communities, because if she had a confinement case in one town she would have to stay there, and work that she expected to do in another town would have to go by the board. I know that those of you who are in practical work will understand the reasons why emergency sick nursing can not be combined with a logically developed preventive health program.

In the second place, I do not believe that the nurse as now trained is the best person for public-health work. Professor Winslow has fully realized that, as evidenced by the program he has laid out for her proper education. I want to stress particularly the defect of the hospital training of the nurse as a public-health worker. She has been taught that her greatest function is not to think independently but to do only as she is ordered by a superior person, the doctor. Public-health nursing in a broad child-hygiene sense can be done properly only by a person who has developed independent thinking in the solution of problems connected with the family and who is willing even to tell the doctor that he does not know how to feed a certain baby.

Now, in regard to the specialized and the generalized nurse, some distinction should be made. I think we can approve of the specialized nurse in child-hygiene work if we will include under child hygiene prenatal care, infant care (but not actual maternity obstetrical care), preschool work, and school hygiene. I believe that a child-hygiene nurse ought to be specialized in that way. I see no excuse in placing school hygiene under a board of education. A board of education can not protect the health of the school child; that is part of a health program and belongs to the school nurse. That is to me a very important point. Moreover, in State work we ought to have a specialist instructor in prenatal care, infant hygiene, and school hygiene, who will help the nurses to stimulate that particular phase.

Dr. S. Josephine Baker (Director, Division of Child Hygiene, Department of Health, New York City): Sometimes practical experience is of more value than the most delightful theories. As a matter of fact, I agree perfectly with Dr. Levy that public-health nursing is not nursing the sick. Public-health nursing is nursing the well; it is the prevention of disease and not the cure or correction of disease or the treatment of disease.

And secondly, from a practical point of view the two cannot go together. When I say that, I say it not because I believe it and always have believed it, but because I have tried it. For two years in New York we tried out a system of combined nursing in one of our large boroughs, the Borough of Queens. It was a total failure for the reason that, just as Dr. Levy has said, the emergency work always took precedence. Weeks went by when no school children were visited. Weeks went by when no babies were visited. Why? Because it was not essential; they could wait.

In a well-evolved program of public-health work for children the work is not ready-made to your hand. You have to go out and make it for yourself, and if you have other duties especially pressing and essential, you are not going out to make it for yourself, and necessarily the baby work, the child work, will always be neglected.

One of the great arguments against this so-called overspecialization—and in my view there is just as great a danger in overgeneralization as there is in overspecialization—has been the question of what we call overlapping. People have said that at times you may see a tuberculosis, a school-hygiene, a district, and a child-hygiene nurse all visiting the same family. I know of investigations in Detroit, and in Grand Rapids, covering a great many cases, to settle that point. In New York we investigated 25,000 consecutive visits for the same purpose. In no one of those cities was there three per cent of duplication. That is, not three per cent of the families had had more than one nurse visiting them at any time. There was practically no duplication.

If there is no duplication the next question is the cost, and careful studies that we have made to determine as nearly as may be the expense of the matter have shown that it is not more costly to employ a nurse who knows her business and who goes to the house with a definite purpose, than it is to send the general-utility nurse who does everything and perhaps not anything very well.

It is a specialized thing to care for children. We are quite sure of that. We have bureaus of child hygiene, and in that connection I do not agree with Dr. Champion that we can have a health center which will take care of babies and take care of adults. We must specialize if we are going to accomplish anything. As long as child welfare was considered a part of the generalized work we did not get results. If we are going back to this old idea of doing everything, and expect to do everything equally well, I think we are going to be disappointed in the outcome.

As to the need of professional training for nurses for child-hygiene work or for preventive health work, there can be no two opinions. Dr. Winslow has expressed the opinion of every one who knows anything about public-health nursing, that we are not getting trained nurses; we train them after we get them. They are trained to treat disease, to cure disease, and I think I am not exaggerating when I say I have rarely ever found a nurse—and we have some 350 doing child-hygiene work in New York—who upon her entrance into the department knew what preventive health work was. We have to begin at the beginning and give them the entirely new point of view of which Dr. Levy spoke, the point of view of initiative, of the prevention of disease, of keeping the child well, of looking at the work as a unit.

When we talk about specialization as confined to children I am agreed that in certain places we are overspecialized, and it is possible that when our work is a little better developed we can have nurses who will take care of the child during the entire period of childhood. That is most essential in rural communities now. In large cities with large staffs we seemed to get better results if we kept to specialization and did not have the school nurse do infant-welfare work. However, we are open to argument upon that point. It may be that in time we shall feel that it is better to consider the child as a unit, for I firmly believe that it is time for us to stop thinking of activities and turn our thoughts to the child. We have talked entirely too much about child school life, child recreation, child physical training, and a hundred other things that affect the child. We have worked from the activity inward, and it is time for us to work from the child outward.

Sir Arthur Newsholme, M. D. (Late Principal Medical Officer, Local Government Board, England): On this vexed question of the public-health nurse, it appears to me that the description given of this official as a "nurse" rather begs the point at issue. We call her a health visitor, which indicates her hygienic functions as contradistinguished from nursing functions. And in England her functions are almost entirely, if not solely, hygienic. It is true that during epidemics, especially of measles, she is sometimes diverted to actual nursing, but that is the exception and not the rule. We have heard a great deal, as Dr. Baker has, of the overlapping of different visitors, but the overlapping is not so considerable as is commonly supposed. But we personally prefer that health visitors should be confined at the present, at any rate, in the main to hygienic work.

We have adopted in the cities the specialized plan. As a rule the health visitors visits only mothers and babies. But in country districts we have adopted the more generalized plan for the sake of convenience of travel. Indeed, in some places the health visitor is also tuberculosis nurse and school nurse; and sometimes, in scattered rural districts where difficulties of travel are great, the health visitor is the district nurse of the district, doing actual nursing, and sometimes is also the village midwife. But those cases are exceptional.

I think the best solution of the problem is not to solve it but to let each case be decided on its local merits—in scattered areas combining different functions, and in crowded areas specializing or not, according to circumstances.

As regards the kind of training which is wanted I am quite clear that the usual nurse's training is not the chief or the only qualification needed. Much more hygienic instruction is required, as well as some of the knowledge of a sanitary inspector; and a great deal of social knowledge is required if the health visitor is to bring back to the child-welfare center information which the physician needs in regard to the cases under his treatment. Personally, I regard the sympathy of the health visitor as quite as important as special knowledge. The health visitor who does the best work is the one who manages to instil the mother with confidence and to make her feel that she is a friend. That is a principle which is impressed on all of us in England. A technical knowledge of any kind will not suffice.

I entirely agree with what Dr. Winslow has said, that health visiting is the major part of the child-welfare work. The centers in England never have attracted more than about a third of the mothers, a third of the babies. More than half of the mothers must be visited at home if they are to receive the proper instruction.

Now with regard to the question as to whether ignorance is the chief enemy which we have to fight, I gather from Professor Winslow's paper that he rather leans to that view. Unless a very wide view is taken of what ignorance means, I cannot agree with that. I am quite certain that to suggest, as many high authorities have done, that all we have to do is to instruct these poor ignorant mothers, is to take an erroneous view of the matter. We have to think of these people living in the homes in which they have to live, of the bad housing conditions; we have to think of the bad sanitation which still exists in many of our municipalities. Infant mortality is largely determined by the degree and the quality of municipal sanitation and by the quality of the housing. We have to think of the fact that a large proportion of these mothers are overworked; they have no nurses when their children are sick; that they have no domestic servants, must attend to the family without any of the helps with which all of us are familiar. And unless we provide help as well as advice I am quite certain that we are not going to get the results which are necessary. I personally attach very great importance to that, and the Local Government Board, as representing the Central Government in this matter, also attaches great importance to it.

We have gone so far as to subsidize to the extent of half the total cost the provision of nurses when required, both during the lying-in period and afterward, the provision of nurses for sick children, and the provision of hospital beds for children and their mothers. If the mother can not go to a lying-in home, we arrange for the children to be taken away from the home in order that the mother may be quiet and not be disturbed by the little children whom she is not able to attend to. Furthermore, we have begun to subsidize the provision of home helps during the confinement of the mother, superior domestic helpers who have been partially trained for the purpose and who will give not skilled nursing attention but help in the domestic circle, so that the mother may feel she can lie quietly in bed until she has completely recuperated. I am confident that mere skilled, enlightened nursing does not cover the ground, and that when we can combine health and instruction we will obtain the best results.

Miss Elizabeth Fox (Director, Bureau of Public Health Nursing, American Red Cross): It may be interesting for you to know that at a recent conference of about 75 State supervising nurses, directors of the Red Cross, and other nurses engaged in executive work, we almost all swung around to Dr. Winslow's point of view. A number of these nurses had had Dr. Levy's and Dr. Baker's point of view and had been working at it for some little time. They have concluded that general nursing including nursing care is more practical, especially in smaller cities and in the country.

It seems that Dr. Baker and Dr. Levy have both uncovered the failure of administration and not the fallacy of a principle. If it is not possible, as Dr. Baker and Dr. Levy seem to think, to combine nursing and instruction, if the nurse is not at the place she is needed at the time she is needed, that is because the management of the work is not properly done; it is because there is not a sufficiently large staff of nurses, or because there is no arrangement for floating nurses who can take care of the emergencies when they arise. It is quite possible to arrange staff and work in such a way that instruction and teaching will not be neglected or poorly done.

About the poorest way to teach people is by the printed word—by dispensing pamphlets and circulars. If we tell them a thing by word of mouth, a considerably greater impression is made, and if we actually do it for them we are employing the most valuable teaching method of all. There is no better way of teaching hygiene than by the actual repeated giving of nursing care. We seem to think that our American people are most anxious for advice. I do not think public-health nurses would agree with that point of view. American people think they know how to run their own affairs pretty well, and are not anxious to be told by some one else how to do it. But when the nurse who comes into the home and nurses them when they are sick, and does something for them when there is suffering, tells them what they ought to do, they are going to take her advice, because it is not advice, but friendly counsel from a person who has helped them out in time of need.

We have all gone into homes and tried to tell mothers about the care of the family, and when we have gone back we have found that we had not made much impression. They have said politely, "Yes," but they did not do what we told them to do. It is the person who has been there repeatedly, who has done something for them, and who has dropped these little kernels of advice as she went along in casual remarks, who really gets the thing over to the family. This may not seem to be preventive medicine, but in this way the nurse may work a revolution in the home which she could not possibly bring about in any other way.

I should like to say also that if there is no overlapping there ought to be; the nurses have not done their work if they have not found in the homes occasion for bringing in all the other nurses in the city.

Dr. H. J. Gerstenberger (Babies' Dispensary and Hospital, Cleveland, Ohio): In Cleveland we made an investigation of overlapping, and we found that it occurred in not more than one per cent of the homes. This investigation included the visits of social workers as well as nurses.

Personally I take a middle stand between the two groups. I believe that in the future we shall have a general practitioner nurse, but I do not think that the older cities are ripe for that development at the present time. I have advocated in my own city the use of one district for a period of ten years for the gaining of experience in this field.

I think it is absolutely essential to develop first properly trained heads. We have not the institutions where we can train them at the present time, and therefore we have not enough men and women to take the positions that would necessarily have to be filled. Secondly, we have not the funds to pay the salaries that would be necessary to hold such workers permanently.

Dr. Baker: Public-health nurses do not by any means merely talk to the people in the house. They teach by doing, quite as much as the nurses who care for the sick. They go in and bathe the baby, and clothe the baby, and instruct the mother. In fact, the nurse who goes to the home simply to make a social call very soon finds herself out; we do not keep such nurses. I do not think that point should go unchallenged because I am sure that any one who has anything to do with public-health nursing knows the work is practical, instructive, and educational.

FRENCH EXPERIENCE

By DR. CLOTHILDE MULON
War Department, France

To obtain a clear understanding of what has been done in France in connection with children's welfare, it is well to record the main lines of the situation created in that country by the state of war.

Two very different periods are to be considered. During the first period, general unemployment was caused by a real economic panic. Three days after the beginning of the mobilization, there were in Paris alone 100,000 women out of work. This occurred to a greater or less extent all over France; all our industries suddenly and completely collapsed. But as soon as the end of 1914 people began to realize that the war was not to last for a few months, as was thought in the beginning. Ammunition was running low on account of the great loss during the Marne battle. A rapid industrial reawakening took place, but only for the manufacturing of ammunition. A Ministry of Armaments was established, which, with M. Albert Thomas at its head, succeeded in creating a great number of new works. The increase was constant, and even at the time of the armistice factories were being built. A tremendous amount of manual labor was of course needed for all these establishments, and the number of trained mechanics and workmen that could be called back from the army was much too small to meet this emergency. Ninety per cent of this labor had therefore to be done by women.

City women were the first to enter upon this work—unemployed workers of all kinds, especially those whose livelihood depended more or less on luxury, as well as servants, teachers, governesses, and housewives. But this was not sufficient, and train loads of women coming from the rural districts poured into the factories. Most of these women were cantoned near big towns, under scarcely better conditions than soldiers at the front; they had to live in huge provisional wooden huts, without any physical comforts, and—far worse for creatures thus suddenly deprived of their homes and families—without any moral support or protection. This very hard life was nevertheless borne by these girls, not only by reason of the high salaries, but also on patriotic grounds.

Now, what about maternity in these conditions? We find here, also, two very different periods. Up to the beginning of the industrial mobilization, not only did infant mortality remain within its normal limits, but it underwent a marked decrease. Although this may seem paradoxical, it has been observed, more or less, in several allied countries, and even in invaded Belgium. The explanation lies in the fact that, being out of work, the women remained at home. As a consequence, breast feeding became much more common. Bottle feeding became at the same time very difficult owing to the scarcity of milk. Now, although the absence of the husband, the hard moral and material conditions, and the great anxieties of these first months had injured the health of many mothers and severely strained their nerves, and although in consequence the infants did not receive as good milk as formerly, they did not, nevertheless, die in such large numbers as usual. This, by the way, constitutes a most interesting physiological experiment, and goes far to prove the crushing superiority of breast feeding. During this first period, the most important thing was therefore, as far as child welfare was concerned, to support the mother herself. For that purpose, all existing charities increased their work, and new ones were started.

Let us now consider the second period, which corresponds to the industrial mobilization. Its characteristics were, first, the great decrease in the birth rate, and at the same time, the increase in the infant death rate.

The first condition is readily accounted for: All our young men were rushed to the border, and no leaves were granted before the middle of 1915. That "strike of the newborn children," if I may venture to call it so, reached such an extent that, in Paris, several of the lying-in hospitals were closed. This is all the more to be noted because, most of the obstetricians being mobilized, even the women of the well-to-do classes had to be delivered in hospitals. The granting of leaves as well as the return of some workmen after a while slightly increased the natality; but, as already stated, the infant mortality increased too. The reasons for this we shall now examine.

First, it can not be denied that abnormal conditions of life during the war have in too many cases resulted in the lowering of the standard of morality. Not only did the practice of criminal abortion become more common, but the proportion of illegitimate births reached much higher figures than formerly. Worse still, desertions of children became more numerous, and it must be borne in mind that children thus deprived of their mothers and taken care of by the "Assistance Publique," died at the appalling rate of 50 per cent. Second, as another consequence of the state of war, all those working women were very soon overworked, especially in the beginning, when nothing had yet been done, as it was later on, to adapt the machinery to feminine labor. So overworked were they that there is practically no case on record of one of them being able to bear it for more than eight or ten months, without breaking down so completely that she had to be admitted into a hospital. A great number of premature births ensued, these children being naturally weak. Even among those who were neither abandoned nor prematurely born, a heavy mortality was caused by the impossibility of breast feeding by the mothers at work.

When we realized the full danger of the frightful fall in the birth rate, and women's mobilization, a great emotion was felt in all medical and social circles. Three main opinions were put forward on the subject. The first one was that every power must be used to repulse the invaders. Therefore no women should be taken from the ammunition works, whatever the consequences might be for the children and for the race.

The second opinion was defended by Professor Pinard, at the Medical Academy, who said that expectant mothers ought to be replaced in the works by other women (chiefly, in his mind, of the well-to-do classes), and be compelled to rest for 5 months before their confinement, and 8 months after, during which time, of course, they were to receive an allowance from the State, the figure of 5 francs (one dollar) per day being proposed.

A third opinion was: "It is true that we must resist till the end, and true also that any shortage of ammunition may be responsible for the death of some of our soldiers; but, while they are sacrificing their lives in order that France may survive, how can we bear the thought that even one of our children shall die if we can prevent it? Let us make the women work, but at the same time let us do it in such a way that they may be able to bear children and to nurse them. The nation needs both labor and children."

This last opinion, I firmly believe, was the best under the circumstances and will probably prevail in the future. I quite agree that it would be better if mothers could stay at home; but their work will become more and more a necessity both to enable them to earn their livelihood and for the prosperity of the nation.

Pardon me for expressing an opinion which is not yet very widespread in France and might seem a trifle revolutionary: There is some injustice in attempting to forbid a woman to work for the reason that she expects a baby or that she just had one. Experience shows that six weeks of rest before the confinement, and six weeks after, is generally quite sufficient to safeguard the woman's health and prevent premature births. Moreover, if the husband does not earn enough, or if he has escaped his duty, the State must support her. This it never does very generously, less than the husband's salary being granted, and the woman is compelled to live in a restricted way, because she is about to make the gift of a new citizen to the community. Most women hate the idea of living at the expense of the community, and I think they are quite right. Work carries with it the joy of action and independence. Has the community the moral right to deprive a woman of it? Has it not struck you that these regulations always apply to the poor woman? Nobody ever thought of making a law to keep at home a rich woman who wishes to travel, to ride, to dance, or forbidding a lady doctor to visit patients with contagious diseases. This, however, is as dangerous for the baby as industrial work.

I hope that future laws will be based on the principle that the health of the poor or the rich woman alike must be protected, not only because she has a right to it, but because she represents all the future of the race. Let us struggle against all sorts of evils that threaten the child through his mother's ignorance, exhaustion, or overworking, whether its cause be the care of the home or work outside. Let us adapt woman's labor to her physiological characteristics; let us reserve for her those professions which need less physical effort. Let us ask for short days of work; not only do they exhaust the workers less, but they leave to the mother, to the father, too, more time to spend at home. Let us protect her in a special way when she is pregnant or feeding her child.

Medical inspection is indispensable, but is not sufficient. These women ought never to work unless sitting. They ought never to work during the night or carry heavy loads. They ought to rest six weeks before and six weeks after confinement. But we should not be satisfied with giving that piece of advice. We should endeavor to enable her to follow it. Every woman working at a gainful occupation ought to receive the whole of her salary during those days of forced unemployment. It is not at the time when the expenses are increasing that the salary ought to decrease. And furthermore, if because of her pregnancy the mother becomes ill or is compelled to give up her work as too hard, let us give her a decent indemnity.

And when at last the child is born I am convinced that it must not be deprived of its mother. The mother's milk belongs to the child, as Dr. Pinard says, and I add that the child needs its mother's care as much as it needs her milk. The new-born is not a finished being; the mother must finish her work with all her love. Whenever the mother is obliged or even prefers to work out of her home, let us allow her to do so, and let us manage things so that she can feed her baby while she is working.

But let us return to the situation in France. The maternity benefit law of 1913 compels every working mother to rest 4 weeks before and 4 weeks after her confinement if she wishes to be paid an allowance; this allowance varies from 0.90 to 1.75 francs per day (16 cents to 31 cents) according to the towns; 10 cents per day is added if she nurses her child. During the war it was seen that this was too little to prevent the expectant mothers from working as late as they could; therefore, the aim of this law, which was to prevent premature births, was not attained.

The allowance could not possibly be raised for all the mothers, but the Government decided to raise it at least in all the factories which were directly under its control. One month of rest with a full salary was granted before the confinement and one month after with half of the salary, plus a fixed sum of 50 francs (10 dollars). Moreover, if the mother could prove that her health needed it and that she was nursing her baby, she could have three months more rest, being paid one-quarter of her salary.

A great number of women asked for this extension, which gave very good results, but many others preferred to go back to work because they needed all their salary. So it was necessary to make some provision to enable the mothers to continue breast feeding in order not to compel them to have their babies boarded out, which so often meant the baby's death. As the employers did not realize the situation quickly enough, the law of 1917 was passed, in accordance with the wishes at the meeting of Bordeaux for the protection of infancy of the Committee of Women Labor and of eight very important women's associations. That law gave the right to all nursing mothers to leave their work twice a day for thirty minutes. All employers of more than 100 women had to provide nursing rooms in their factories. A similar law exists in Italy and in several countries of Europe.

What have been the results of the establishment of these nursing rooms?

Before the war 52 of them existed in France in textile factories. A very charming one was established on the roof of the biggest trade shop in Paris. They all have been entirely beneficial for the child, and the mothers bore well the double burden, work and maternity. In a factory near Lille the same young woman bore and nursed two children in three years without any harm to her health. During the war many more nursing rooms have been created. Even before the law of 1917 I myself was asked by the Surgeon General of the French Army to organize one in a military factory where twelve hundred women were doing camouflage work.

It is, of course, very difficult in such a troubled period to account quite scientifically for the influence on mothers of breast feeding carried along with industrial work, so numerous have been the other factors of their material and moral life. Here, however, are some of the results.

Three of the 53 mothers in my nursing room have been ill. One of these had lost a good deal of weight since her husband was killed but ultimately regained her former weight without ceasing breast feeding.

Two others had tuberculosis; the first, aged 17, had lost both parents and several relatives from tuberculosis. The second's husband, a soldier, died by her side of the same disease. She was depriving herself of her food in order to feed on her little salary her husband and two other children. All the other 50 mothers were in good health in spite of the difficulties of their life. I therefore think that in normal times well-supported mothers properly examined by doctors could fulfill both duties without harm. Of the 53 babies of these mothers none died, and there was no case of transmission of contagious disease.

But I also believe that my duty is to show you the dangers of these nursing rooms. According to our experience a very careful inspection of the babies is absolutely necessary every morning on their arrival from home to prevent the spreading of contagious diseases. All the babies that do not look quite well must be put into the isolation room until the doctor has visited them. This inspection only serves its purpose if it is done by a nurse who has been specially trained in a hospital for that work. All the day nurseries or nursing rooms which did not comply with that rule have had epidemics. In my nursing room, where it was strictly enforced, although in several cases children were brought from home with contagious diseases such as scarlatina and bronchial pneumonia, there was no case of transmission.

Perhaps it might interest you to know some French definitions. We call nursing rooms, those which are reserved for breast-fed children in the factories. We call day nurseries the ones which only keep children up to 3 years. The maternal schools are those which take children up to seven years of age. We have 300 public maternal schools in Paris.

I must say that, as regards day nurseries, most of our pediatrists call them a necessary evil and ask for important improvements. The nurses receive only 6 francs per day for fourteen hours work with the result that their technical knowledge is too little and the babies suffer. We felt the need of creating a special course of instruction for them, and in 1916 I was asked to organize it. The American Red Cross organized others in 1917 in several towns. The same year a central school for the teaching of child welfare was established in Paris. The teachers are the best pediatrists in Paris. The courses are supplemented by practical training in day nurseries.

During the war, too, we adopted a long-sought-for measure in order to raise the standards of the midwives. They all have two years' training, but from 1916 on the schools of midwifery have accepted only girls having completed the high school course.

I will show you how the war has benefited France in other ways, although in the main it has affected her so terribly.

First, the unemployment which became quite general after the mobilization, and impoverished hundreds of thousands of workers, led to the excellent result that the principle of the unemployment compensation was applied for the first time and has come to stay with us. The allowances are paid by the State Labor Exchanges when there is no work, in order to avoid voluntary unemployment.

Another happy result of the war is the downfall of the barriers which used to keep people of different classes apart from each other. Since August, 1914, a national committee for relief has centralized the gifts and distributed them among the different relief agencies. It was organized by the dean of the Science College in Paris. French union leaders sat in the committee together with the Archbishop of Paris. That may be quite usual with you, but such a thing was not very often to be seen in prewar days in our country.

The children have become better protected. I must of course except those refugee children who had to flee, pursued by the enemy. I shall never forget those poor little ones who were brought to the hospital only to die there without any definite symptoms of illness. They really seemed to have been killed by the terror that still widened their eyes. Their mothers, standing by their death beds, looked hardly less overcome by fright. But if war has been responsible for the death of many children, it has, on the other hand, shown the necessity of cooperation. The Bureau for the Assistance of Mothers and Children gathered together all the experienced workers. The number of maternal and prenatal centers grew considerably. Social service was introduced into the lying-in hospitals, even though so many doctors and nurses had to leave for the front. I hope this will not only survive the war, but also develop considerably, thanks to the efforts of the many women who have become experienced in the war hospitals. The women now can no more lead the useless lives which satisfied them formerly. The American Red Cross has helped considerably in this movement, in Paris as well as elsewhere.

The bombardment of Paris began in March, 1918; I would not go as far as to say that it was agreeable to the Parisians. It came together with the German drive and the air-raids, so that it was especially disastrous for the children, who caught many diseases in the cellars. The consequence was that, for the second time, we sent as many children as possible to safer places, 75,000 in less than six weeks. The municipality paid two-thirds of the boarding expenses; the relief agencies made up the rest, and the American Red Cross gave $20,000 for clothing. The children stayed four months away from their homes. This cooperation between the open air agencies and the municipality will survive the war. Paris will send more children than ever to the country. War has also helped to create a favorable atmosphere for the establishment of a health ministry. Many efforts are made to centralize study and action in the lines of medico-social questions, and at this very moment an international conference is meeting to consider the hygiene work related to reconstruction of the devastated areas. The American Red Cross has organized in Cannes a meeting of the committees of the Allied Red Cross. Out of this meeting a lasting benefit will accrue to mankind.

I do not want you to think that because of these benefits I like war; yet one of the great benefits that war has brought to France is the brotherly love of America, which is more evident to me from day to day as I become familiar with your country. I ardently hope that our countries will understand and help each other better every day, that more and more French people will come to this country, where they will find again the love of life and learn much. I hope that we shall more and more exchange the children of our schools and the students of our universities. I hope, indeed, that all the citizens of the future will spend several years far away from their own homes. By that means only will they learn to know other civilizations, to respect other ways of thinking. By that means only will they become more conscious of human solidarity.

DAY NURSERY STANDARDS

By DR. S. JOSEPHINE BAKER
Director, Division of Child Hygiene
Department of Health, New York City

Day nurseries as conducted in the United States generally furnish day care for babies and children from a few weeks to five or even six years of age. The day nursery not only is a day home for infants, but, because it also cares for the child of preschool age, frequently includes a kindergarten as a prominent feature. As a rule, these nurseries are under the auspices of private organizations, or are endowed by individuals. They exist almost entirely as separate units and they may be located in buildings erected for the purpose or they may occupy rooms in a family dwelling or tenement house. Because of their diversity of location and control and the broad age group of the children under supervision, it has seemed of distinct importance to establish some method whereby their administration and maintenance might be standardized and definite and responsible supervision maintained.

The purpose of this paper is not to trace the history of day nurseries, nor, indeed, to discuss the extent to which they have been organized. It is proper, however, to speak of their importance with relation to the preschool age. It is well known that this age—from two to six years—is the neglected period of child life. Comprehensive public-health programs have been formulated and carried out for the benefit of infants and children of school age, but the child of preschool age has had no such advantage. The possibilities of this age group in preventive health work are of vast importance, but they have attracted little attention from public-health authorities. Even superficial investigations and surveys, however, will show that not only does this age period offer the best opportunity for constructive work in child health, but it is also in itself the time of life where many of our common preventable diseases are most likely to occur.

It has been estimated that in the United States 81 per cent of the deaths from contagious diseases and 85 per cent of the illnesses from contagious diseases occur under five years of age. Physical examinations of children of this age group reveal a prevalence of physical defects from 10 to 15 per cent in excess of those found in children of school age. Undernourishment has been found to be at least one-third more prevalent in children between two and six than in children from six to fifteen years of age. These statements are a mere indication of the necessity of competent health supervision at this time.

It cannot be claimed that the day nursery as at present constituted is a predominant factor in the care of the preschool age child, but its possibilities are almost unlimited. This has been recognized in England, particularly, where provision was made in 1918 for the establishment of nursery schools under Section 19 of the Education Act, which went into operation August 8 of that year. Carefully drawn and most comprehensive standards are established by this act.

In the United States there are no universal standards at the present time. In fact, very few of our States or cities have established any standards at all and the day nursery, in a number of instances, has come to be looked upon as a commercial proposition, maintained for gain, and sometimes to the actual detriment of the children who are cared for.

Public-health authorities should not lose this opportunity to reach children of the preschool-age group. Day nurseries should be maintained under proper and competent supervision, which can best be carried out by governmental authorities. For this reason all communities should include in their public-health laws provision that no nursery shall be conducted without a permit therefor, issued by the local board of health, or otherwise than in accordance with the terms of this permit and with such regulations as the said board of health may issue from time to time. This permit should specify the number of children that may be received by the day nursery, and this number must not be exceeded in any instance.

Such supervision has been tried. In New York City the enforcement of such an order has resulted in standardizing the conduct of day nurseries in that city, and they are at present an active and potent force in the public-health program for child welfare.

Standards for day nurseries must take cognizance of the construction and equipment of the building in which the day nursery is to be located; the provision of the necessary rooms and their proper furnishing; general hygiene and maintenance of nursery routine; medical supervision of the children for the purpose of controlling epidemic diseases, as well as the prevention of disease in general and the correction of existing physical defects; and general physical care, including rest, exercise, and proper diet. In addition, the day nursery must offer to children of the two-to-six age group some mental and social training.

Construction and Equipment

Wherever it is possible the day nursery should occupy a separate building constructed for the purpose. It may be assumed that the location of these nurseries will always be where the need is greatest, which generally means in the more crowded parts of communities. For this reason separate buildings are rarely feasible or available and changes in construction must be made in already existing tenements or dwellings. Frequently, day nurseries can be made part of community health centers or social settlements. As parents have become accustomed to these neighborhood houses, they are particularly desirable for this purpose, giving the mothers a sense of security when leaving their babies or very young children.

Adequate space, fresh air, and sunshine are the main requisites to be considered in the selection of day-nursery premises. If possible, outdoor space should be provided and outdoor life encouraged through the greater part of the year. If yards are not available, roofs can often be utilized.

Necessary Rooms

The minimum requirements for rooms are: (a) kindergarten or playroom for children from two to six years of age; (b) nursery with cribs for children under two years of age; (c) dining room; (d) kitchen; (e) lavatory and bathroom; (f) cloakroom; and (g) isolation room.

Kindergarten.—The kindergarten or playroom for the children from two to six years of age should provide at least fifteen square feet of floor space for each child. Adequate ventilation, lighting, and heating should be provided. Except in extremely cold weather, the ventilation should be maintained by means of open windows. The rooms should have the necessary kindergarten furniture, and, in addition, wooden or iron bed frames or bunks, so arranged that they may be let down from the wall and form low, easy day beds for the children.

Nursery for Children Under Two Years.—Separate iron beds or cribs must be provided for each child. They should be so placed that there will be a space of two feet on all sides except where the head or sides of a bed or crib touch the wall. Woven iron springs should be provided over which a folded blanket, protected by a rubber or oilcloth sheeting, must be placed. Mattresses should never be allowed. A minimum of two hundred cubic feet of air space for each child should be provided.

Dining Room.—The air and floor space requirements heretofore mentioned must be maintained in the dining room, and adequate light and ventilation are essential.

Kitchen.—The standards in kitchen equipment relate to simplicity, accessibility, cleanliness, and ease with which both utensils and equipment may be kept clean. The exact type of equipment does not need to be standardized, but should be adapted to individual requirements. Order and cleanliness, however, must be insisted upon at all times.

Lavatory and Bathroom.—Washbasins should be sufficiently low to be easily used by the children. Running water should be provided, and each child should have for his exclusive use a towel, toothbrush, drinking-cup, and comb. The toilets should be of a child size so that they may be used by the children without assistance. They should be of modern type, easily flushed, and in the ratio of one toilet to each twenty children. The use of common washcloths, towels, combs, and hair brushes should be prohibited.

Cloakroom.—A well-ventilated room for children's outer garments must be provided. In this room the clothing removed from the children in the morning must be placed, and unless all clothing worn by the child on admission is clean, it should be changed for clothing belonging to the day nursery, or a suitable overapron, the property of the day nursery, should be worn through the day and each individual apron marked for identification unless a clean apron is provided daily.

Isolation Room.—An isolation room for cases of suspected contagious disease should be provided in each day nursery.

General Hygiene and Maintenance of Nursery Routine

The purpose of the day nursery is not merely to provide a shelter for children during the daytime. Its ideal must be further, to afford them complete protection from disease and to establish necessary health habits. The health control, therefore, resolves itself into several parts:

1. The control of contagious diseases. Such procedure should be:

(a) The department of health and the nursery physician should be notified immediately by telephone of any suspicious rash or illness occuring among the children at any time, and children so affected should be placed at once in the isolation room.

(b) The matron must make daily inquiry of each mother or other person bringing a child as to whether or not any sickness exists in the child's home, and if suspicion is aroused as to the possibility of such home sickness being of an infectious nature, the child should be excluded and the department of health notified.

(c) Each child as it enters the nursery must be inspected by a competent person, either the matron or the nurse.

(d) The physician of the day nursery must make a systematic examination of every regularly attending child at least twice a month, such examinations to be made at least two weeks apart.

(e) When any child who has not previously attended the day nursery applies for admission the physician should examine such child at once and exclude it from attendance at the nursery if any suspicious signs of infectious disease are present. If no infectious disease is found to exist, the matron in charge of the nursery should be given a certificate to that effect and the child admitted.

HEALTH—THE PRESCHOOL CHILD

(f) Whenever, in the case of female children, there is evidence of any vaginal discharge on the clothing, a smear for bacteriological diagnosis should be made and examined to determine the presence of gonorrheal vaginitis.

2. Medical inspection and health supervision:

(a) There should be on file in the office of the nursery an original certificate of health, signed by the nursery physician, for each child who is a regular attendant.

(b) There should be on file in the office of the nursery a record for each child regularly attending, showing that it has been examined by the nursery physician at least twice a month, such examinations being at least two weeks apart.

(c) Whenever, upon examination, a child is found to be suffering from any physical defect or abnormality or from any condition which requires health supervision or instruction, the case should be referred to the nurse, whose duty it should be to supervise the health care of the child until proper treatment has been obtained.

3. A nurse should be attached to each such nursery whose duty it should be:

(a) To assist the doctor in the physical examinations;

(b) To make daily visits to the nursery to treat minor ailments, make regular health inspection of the children, and give health advice or aid when indicated;

(c) To be responsible for the cleanliness of the children and the maintenance of the health regulations of the board of health with regard to sanitation, hygiene, and health care;

(d) To visit the homes of the children at regular intervals, instructing the families as to the individual needs of the children, with reference to home hygiene, feeding, and physical care.

4. Care of infants:

(a) Adequate care must be taken of the milk, bottles, and nipples used in infant feeding.

(b) Individual formulae should be prescribed for each child after examination by the nursery physician.

(c) Proper infant care and hygiene must be maintained at all times.

(d) Each infant on admission must have its clothing removed, be given a bath, redressed in fresh clothing belonging to the nursery, and kept in such clothing during the day.

(e) All diapers that may become soiled during the day must be immediately placed in water and thereafter thoroughly washed and boiled. No diapers in an unclean condition should be removed from the premises.

5. Care of children from two to six years of age:

(a) Each child from two to six years of age should receive one hot meal in the middle of the day. This meal should include one hot meat or vegetable dish, with soup, and cocoa or milk. Bread, fruit, and eggs should be included in the dietary.

(b) Each child should have a morning lunch at eleven o'clock and an afternoon lunch at four o'clock, consisting of a glass of milk and bread and butter.

(c) The total amount of milk supplied to children between two and six years of age should not be less than three pints per capita per day. Part of this may be given to the child in the form of soups, custards, or other types of food.

(d) Each child should have a suitable rest period at a regular time each day. Experience in the open-air classes has seemed to prove that the morning rest hour is the most desirable. Children may be given their morning lunch at eleven o'clock and then required to lie on the cot beds which, when not in use, fold up against the wall. They should be encouraged to sleep during this period, and sitting up or talking should not be allowed.

(e) Regular and systematic exercise is essential. Group games, simple setting-up exercises, or unrestricted play may be allowed. Biologically, children of this age need much activity and opportunity for free action. Lesson periods, therefore, should be short, and children should not be required to sit still for more than a few minutes at a time. Chairs should be movable, and the child's interest should be kept up through the type of educational games which allow free movement and free interpretation. Whenever exercises such as deep-breathing drills, setting-up exercises, or other vigorous forms of physical exertion are practiced, the windows of the playroom should be open, except in severely cold or stormy weather. Whenever possible, the exercises mentioned should be taken out of doors, either in the yard or on the roof. In warm weather, practically all the classroom work should be done in the open air.

(f) Children must be kept clean at all times and particular attention should be paid to the condition of the hair.

During the past few years it has become evident in some of our large cities that the work of the day nursery must be extended to provide a certain amount of night care in emergency cases or for short periods of time. Health visitors have long felt the need of some place where little children might be temporarily cared for, day and night, while the mother was temporarily incapacitated by illness or necessary absence from home. In New York City appeal was made to the day nurseries to meet this problem, with the result that several of them set aside one room for a night nursery. A nurse was placed in charge and children were kept at the nursery, day and night, for periods not to exceed one month.

The possibility of thus utilizing the nursery plant is a valuable addition to our program for child health. Such use, however, needs careful supervision. If unrestricted, it may easily lead to making the day nursery an institution taking entire care of children for long periods of time. It would thus, in great measure, defeat its own purpose by detaching the child wholly from its home environment. Properly restricted and supervised, however, the need for temporary night care of children can be met by utilizing the day nursery plant at a time when it is generally idle. No such work, however, should be carried on without a special permit which indicates the purpose and the extent to which such care may be given.

The development of properly supervised day nurseries or nursery schools for children under six years of age may well be considered as an important contribution to the solution of our present problem as to how to care for the child of preschool age.

DISCUSSION

Dr. Mulon (War Department, France): I should like to say that the day nursery will be a simple failure, and worse than any bad conditions in the families, if it is not placed under the supervision of a physician. And not only that, but it must be under the supervision of a nurse, and a sufficiently paid nurse. We had a long experience with those things in France; and if we had not changed conditions in our day nurseries we would still have, as we formerly had, a very high mortality in those institutions.

Miss Myrn Brockett (Mary Crane Nursery, Chicago): The standards outlined by Dr. Baker present a basis for care of children, which, if adopted and practiced in day nurseries and other institutions caring for children, would mean much in the lives of the children under such care.

The entrance physical examination should result not only in the exclusion from the nursery of children with communicable affections, but also in the formulation of a health program for each child, the nursery assuming the responsibility for carrying out the plans. This involves intimate and more or less individual attention to the diet of the children, which, in day nurseries, makes necessary also a knowledge of the home diets. If surgical or hospital care is advisable, the nursery should see that it is provided. There should be also, as the test of effective treatment, the monthly weighing and measuring of each child, with careful note of gains or losses and provision for corrective treatment when needed. The children whose physical examinations result in their exclusion from the nursery should be referred to the proper agencies for treatment. When an infant-welfare station is available, it is an excellent plan to register the nursery children of suitable age and to cooperate with the infant-welfare nurses in carrying out the health plan.

Dr. Baker's recommendation of home visiting is a recognition of the fact that effective service to the child must be based upon a knowledge of his home environment and that the family rather than the individual child must be made the unit of effort. Such a plan, in my opinion, involves the assumption by the nursery of the care of the older children of the family. If the nursery accepts the young children of a family, thus releasing the mother from the home, and does not accept the responsibility of the care of the older children, its social contribution is likely to result in more harm than good to the general family situation, because it deprives the older children of the mother's care and also of their interest and responsibility in the care of their younger brothers and sisters and leaves them to the dangerous influences of the streets and alleys. In a nursery which has been planned for the care of young children only, this work presents a difficult problem but one which the nursery can and should accept.

The contact with the home and family, besides furnishing a basis for nursery effort, should also make clear the financial situation of the family, so that if the income of the working mother is cut off by illness of herself or of a child, the relief-giving agency will be prepared with data at hand to formulate a definite plan for relief, if necessary, during the period of distress.

The object of day-nursery effort is fundamentally to raise the standard of home and family life, and follow-up visits to the home will readily reveal whether or not the nursery service is helping to accomplish this result.

Any adequate service to a normal child must include a plan for his mental development through suitable occupations and play. Most of the day nurseries of good standing provide a brief kindergarten period for children of preschool age, either at the nursery or at a near-by school or settlement. The day nursery, however, offers a most excellent opportunity for the enlargement of the kindergarten plan to include the activities of the child for the entire day. The program for the day should be carefully planned under the advice of experts in the various lines of nursery service. The kindergarten teacher, the food economist, the nurse, and the physician should all be consulted in determining the plans for the hours of sleep, the mealtimes, diets, playtimes, and the character of the occupational work and of the play.

The participation of the child in the work involved in his care is of great interest to him and is valuable educational material. The enlargement of the day-nursery ideal to include that of the all-day kindergarten, giving the children opportunity to express themselves in pleasurable and helpful activities, should be accomplished under the direction of the trained child teacher and with definite educational intent. The technique of the child's activities—the setting, serving, and clearing of the tables; the washing, drying, and setting-away of the dishes; the toilets and baths—should be as carefully worked out as is the rhythm, circle, and table work of the short-time kindergarten session. Such a plan requires the all-day services of a kindergarten teacher of a high type. Further, if this work can be conducted under the inspiration and supervision of a good kindergarten college, it is of great value to the nursery and offers to the kindergarten students an opportunity for the most advanced type of kindergarten experience in their work as cadets. For the past two years the National Kindergarten and Elementary College and the Mary Crane Nursery of Chicago have been working out such a plan with most gratifying results for both the college and the nursery.

The organization of day nurseries has usually been the result of the efforts of a group of philanthropic women who have sought, by providing daytime care for children, to enable mothers who must work outside the home to keep their children with them rather than place them in institutions. The initial efforts have been conducted as a rule on a small scale, an old house or apartment being adapted to the purpose, with equipment partaking of the same makeshift character. The gratifying returns in child welfare and happiness have had a tendency to make these makeshifts acceptable, and the need of a better type of housing and furnishing has often been lost sight of. A careful study of ideal housing and equipment for day nurseries would be most helpful in making a differentiation between expediencies and ideals and would be a great help in the work of standardization.

A similar condition has existed in regard to the nursery staff. The opportunity for intimate and effective service to the families under nursery care is quite worth the efforts of the best-trained women. There should be a capable graduate nurse to supervise the carrying out of the health programs and other matters pertaining to nursing and hygiene; a child educator with ability for creative work to develop and standardize an all-day program for the nursery child; a trained household economist to direct the selection and preparation of food, the buying of furnishings and equipment, and the general household plans; and, further, a trained social worker to bring about effective cooperation between the nursery and home life. To secure such expert service a cooperative plan might be worked out by a group of nurseries. With the exception of the kindergarten teacher, part-time work would seem to be sufficient for the other services. This group work would also have a tendency toward consonancy of day-nursery effort, the supervision of the educational work of the group by the kindergarten college accomplishing a similar result along that line. These expert workers might be affiliated with a central organization of day nurseries, acting under the direction of a general supervisor or secretary, who would coordinate their work and interpret it to the members of the governing boards of the various nurseries and to the central organization.

There has been in day-nursery work the whole-hearted purpose of bringing happiness to the child in kindly, loving service. At the same time there has been a proneness to isolation and a too great reliance upon sentiment for guidance in methods. The past few years, however, have marked a distinct progress along this line and have resulted in a more cooperative and intelligent effort to bring real happiness to the child through a broad interpretation of his needs in terms of the highest standards of child welfare.

Mrs. Eleanor Barton (Women's Cooperative Guild, England): I am going to take an entirely opposite point of view from that which has been given you this evening. I am absolutely opposed to day nurseries. I think that day nurseries are part of the great industrial problem. I wonder, if we asked each person in this room what is the greatest need of a child, how many varieties of answers we should have. I think we could all agree upon one thing, that the child needs most of all its mother; and that is the position I take. Dr. Baker did mention that the day nurseries in New York had been especially helpful during the influenza epidemic. I will bow to that statement; I think that is right. I think there ought to be some provision for those women in the working-class homes, where the mother is everything—work-mate, washerwoman, cook, and everything combined; when she is stricken down, there should be some provision for the care of her children.

But if that means that we are to take care of children whose mothers go into industry for someone else to make a profit out of them, then I am totally opposed to it. With all the troubles we had in England during the war, with all the women in industry, I consistently took this stand. I took this stand, not because I am afraid of women going out to work. I am a suffragist. I believe a woman should do the work she is best fitted for. But Dr. Mulon has told us of the difference between the industrial mother and the other mother. I want to see the industrial mother more like the other mother, and in regard to the welfare of her child, it seems to me that she is not becoming so through the setting up of day nurseries.

We had during the war rather an interesting experiment in the town that I came from. We have a very progressive medical officer of health, with his staff, and a very good welfare center for the children, where the babies are weighed, where they are inspected, where their mothers are advised as to the feeding of the children, and so on. The children are weighed each week, and their progress watched. This town is a large munition-manufacturing center, where many of the women worked. A day nursery was established there, in a good house, with an adequate number of attendants for the number of children, and so on.

They carried on the same experiments that we do in our child-welfare centers; they weighed the children, and advised with us as to the food, and so on. But those children, in spite of being well cared for in this well-equipped day nursery, did not make the same progress as did the children of the mothers from our poorest quarters who brought their children to our welfare center. So we were forced to the conclusion that, even though the child was being cared for in the day nursery, with fresh air and baths and all the proper care, there was something that was lacking; it did not come up to the same standard as the child in its own home and under the child-welfare direction of our medical officer of health. It is not only the fresh air and the cleanliness that the child needs; there is something else, and that something else the mother alone can give.

I wonder if we have considered these things? When we consider them we ought to go down as deep as we can, because there is no doubt that the work of this conference will carry great weight in the States. We have all sorts of opinion here. We have really intellectual opinion, and people are going to watch what we do. I do not want to make a false step, if it is possible for us to do otherwise. It seems to me that we must consider keeping the mother and the child together. To separate them during the war might have been allowed, from the fact that our women were wanted in industry—though I never was convinced of that, because I found many women, who had no children, that might have been out in industry. They could have helped the mothers to stay at home and attend to their children. But now we have no longer war conditions. We are setting up new standards, and we are having new ideals—and ideals precede practice. So let us get our ideals right, and the practice will be right; let us not separate mothers and children.

Some people will say, "It will help industry." They told us that in the early days, when very young children were going to work in the cotton mills; and when we tried to raise the age of the children, the cotton manufacturers opposed us. They said: "We must have these children in the cotton manufactories, because their fingers are more supple than those of adults." Well, we succeeded in taking our children out of the mills; we did not listen to what the cotton manufacturers had to say; we took the children out, and the cotton mills are now flourishing. The very same people who made that complaint have made their fortunes, and others have made their fortunes, out of cotton mills. The same will apply very largely if we take women out of industry. I am very certain, at least, that we have no reason to force mothers into industry.

Now, if you are going to have day nurseries, what sort are you going to have? If you are going to have them, you must have the very best. None of us, even if we were convinced that day nurseries are necessary, would approve of anything not the very best possible. You must have them under public-health authority; you must have gardens, and baths, and everything that will make them thoroughly equipped. In addition to that, the people who attend the children must be well trained. And with regard to the health visitors, it is not only training that is important; it is their sympathy and their way of approaching the family. Now that all means money; you must have money to set up your day nurseries, and you must have money to train the people who take care of the children. Well, why not spend your money on the mother? Why not give it to the mother, and let her stay in her own home? We in England at the present time are discussing some of these problems. We are discussing family endowment, which, it seems to me, will solve the problem of these children.

And it seems to me that if we have found during the war that it was good to give the mother an allowance for herself and an allowance for each child, and if we are able to prove, as we are able to prove, that during the war children have been better kept and better fed, and more healthily nourished, and have had more working ability, and that people have been able to send their children from the elementary schools to the secondary schools through this allowance, why not continue this allowance in peace times?

I am against day nurseries, because I do not think we should send our women out of their homes to go into industry. I am not against day nurseries when they are necessary. But I do agree with Dr. Mulon as to the great difference between the industrial mother and the other mother. The other mother may go out to work if she is a doctor or a teacher; but she has her own time each day. The working-class mother has not. And I know that all the country will benefit, and the children will benefit also, if the women do not go out into industry. Do not let us advocate things that will be detrimental to the children of the future.

Dr. Mulon (War Department, France): Perhaps we are too timid in France, but we never put in the same room a nursing baby and an older child, because we are very anxious to prevent contagious disease; and if we put the two classes of children together contagious diseases would spread. For the same reason we keep apart the baby that is bottle-fed and the baby of the same age that is breast-fed, because we very often find that they are not of the same standard; a baby that is bottle-fed gets contagious diseases more easily. In the day nursery that I should like to have, we should have many rooms—rooms for bottle-fed babies, nursing babies, babies between two and three years, and so on. Every room should be different—the personnel, the food, and the education, if we can talk of education for such young babies. And education has to begin from the first.

I perfectly agree with Mrs. Barton that mother and child must not be parted. And it is for that reason that we have nursing rooms. But if the mother is obliged to work, what can we do? You say: "Do not spend the money on the day nursery; give it to the mother." Well, the day nursery may cost a great deal, but the money would not be enough for the mother; it would be only enough to keep her from starvation. So if a mother is not supported by her husband, she must choose between the best for herself and the best for her child. There is only one other thing that she may do. She may send the child away to a peasant home; and in 50 per cent of the times she will have no chance to see it again.

We have nursing rooms not only for our factory workers, but for the shop girls. We have a charming nursing room now in one of our biggest shops, on the roof, and the babies there are beautiful. Before it was established, those girls were obliged to send away their babies and the babies died. A large portion of the babies sent away to boarding homes died. But all these children are very beautiful; and their nursing at those rooms means not to separate the mother from her children.

Mrs. Barton: I have just one other point. This relates to our big industrial centers, where our women are going out to work. In the cotton mills they go out at six o'clock in the morning. It is notorious that in those northern towns of ours, where married women go out to work, there is a heavier infantile death rate than in any other part of England. And it is not only that the death rate is very high, but a number of the children are weakened. And I remember that a gentleman living in the South of England said to me, "Do you know what impressed me most when I first went to the North?" I said, "No, what was it?" He said, "The small stature of your people." "How do you account for it?" I asked; and he said, "It is their mill life"; and I said, "Yes, because their mothers were not able to give them what they needed in their child life."

By putting day nurseries in the munition centers, what is going to happen? The hours are even worse than in the cotton mills. In the cotton mills, it was from six in the morning to five-thirty in the evening; but in the munition factories there are three shifts; and the woman would be taking the child to the day nursery at five in the morning, and taking it home at two; or taking it to the nursery at two and taking it home at ten; or taking it to the nursery at six in the evening, and getting it back the next morning. A suggestion was made by Dr. Baker that the day nurseries take children for the night, as well as for the day. Of course, Dr. Baker said that should be limited to one month. But our women have been working that way for nearly five years.

You will have to remember this also: I think Dr. Mulon said that the French women could not work more than seven or eight months on war work without a breakdown. Think of women working under those arduous conditions! If a woman works those eight hours, she does not go home and rest; she goes first to the day nursery and gets her baby, and then she has to go home and provide a meal and take care of the baby until the next day, and so on.

If you will look into the matter, it is very pleasant to talk about the bath for the children, and the kindergarten, and all those things. I agree with our friend from Chicago; I think taking the older children off the streets is a good thing.

But it seems to me that the people who are studying this question are too timid. Let us not be nervous. If we think a thing is right, let us not consider present manufacturing and industrial conditions; let us have an ideal. If you do not get your ideal, you will at least have the satisfaction of knowing that you yourself have worked the thing out in what you think is the right way; and if people do not carry out your ideal, theirs is the blame, and not yours.

Dr. Mulon: I should be glad to answer that. When we speak of the ideal, I agree with Mrs. Barton; but I cannot foresee the future. I live in this time, and I speak only of our actual present conditions. I know that it would be better to have a very nice home, and that the mother should stay at home; but I speak only for the mother that can not stay at home. However, the working of mothers at night must be absolutely prohibited. No woman must work at night, under any conditions. In our country the mortality among the children of working mothers is very high, just as in Mrs. Barton's. In all industries it is the same. About 80 years ago, around 1830, a man that had a factory in France, who was very generous, installed a day-nursing room in his factory. That made conditions better than they had been.

It is not my own opinion merely, it is the opinion of many doctors who have the supervision of factories, that the death rate among children in the industrial cities where the mother is obliged to work, is appalling. One year the police board's figure was 86 per cent among the babies whose mothers had to go out to work and leave their children to be taken care of by some old woman. But when those children went into nursing rooms, there was practically no mortality among them. I have had no child that died except one who died two months after having left the nursing room.

Dr. Jessica B. Peixotto (University of California): I venture to speak because I come from the State of California, which is, I think, one of the few States that license day nurseries; and I am a member of the State board of charities and correction, which has the power to do this licensing. California is not an industrial State in the strict sense of the word; and yet we have our industrial centers, and in those centers day nurseries have tended to grow. I take emphatically the position of Mrs. Barton, and when I went on the State board of charities I resolved to see that something was done so that day nurseries should not grow in our State. If the board of management of the nursery really investigates the family it finds often that the situation that seems to require the mother to add to the income can be worked out in some other way than by separating her from her home and her family. Perhaps I am speaking for a more prosperous State, and for a less crowded part of the country; California is not what the Atlantic coast is, I know. But ordinarily it has been found that the people who send their children to the nurseries are following the traditional notion that if the income is at all weak they must not fight to force up the man's income, but must see that the mother ekes out the family income and that every child who can be pushed into industry also ekes out the income.

As an entering wedge between the practice of kindly, friendly, cordial care of other people's children, which is the ideal of the day nursery, and the idea which I share with Mrs. Barton of abolishing the day nursery as fast as possible, it seems to me that it would be of great benefit to require every case in a day nursery to be treated exactly as a case in any other type of relief. That is, a definite inquiry into home conditions should be made, and a plan devised for improving the family conditions so that an adequate living wage is received.

The responsibility is put upon a board of managers, and, if they are the kind of people that are running nurseries in our part of the world, they will face it. And facing it, they will reduce the population of nurseries wonderfully. It may be that in other parts of the world more crowded conditions will not permit early adoption of this plan. In that case it seems to me that every worker for children ought to join the fight for a living wage for men, and to see that the women do not go into industry. Thus the children of this country may at least have a potential home through an income which is reasonable.

Our children's agencies fight the nurseries, because they say that they definitely bring about increased infant mortality. The little children coming together touch each other, play with each other; the children cannot be examined every day. The theory of nurseries is good, but the practice does not work out. So the best agencies think that the nurseries are a mistake, and do not place their children in them.

In San Francisco we have a widow's pension system, which gives $12 for each child, $12 for overhead, and $12 for the mother. Even if there are four or five children, the family is taken care of out of county and State funds; there are county funds for deserted women.

Dr. Mulon: We have been told about contagious diseases, and that it is not possible to prevent them, because when the child goes home he is in contact with his brother or his sister, or the rest of his family, and so gets contagious diseases which he may bring to the day nursery. That is perfectly true. That is the greatest danger of the nursing homes and the day nurseries. But it is a point on which I ask permission to insist, that if you have the proper personnel you will not have that condition. Every morning the child must be inspected before entering the nursery. In the interval when he is undressed, when the nurses see him completely, they can examine him. We have never had a case of transmission of contagion in my little home. And because my nurses were very well trained, they have been able to discover diseases in the children coming to the home which a mother would never have seen or asked for medical advice about. And some of them were diseases that could have compromised all the future of the child. So that the children need supervision. I am very sorry that I cannot show you my children; I think that would be the best argument.

Miss Julia C. Corcoran (Factory Inspection Department, Connecticut): My experience has been very similar to that of Dr. Baker, because I work with working women. And I would like to ask when you would consider a day nursery not a day nursery? I would consider it not a day nursery when it is a room in a factory set apart for the care of the children of the working mothers. And I think that public sentiment should get back of the movement for mothers' pensions. I have investigated a great many cases of what were supposed to be worthy widows, and just as Mrs. Barton said, they have their housework to do, and of course their housework is neglected. During the war I pleaded with many men and women who wanted to put money into day nurseries, to put the money into these different families and keep the mothers at home. In looking up the family budgets, we found in many cases the income was ample to keep the mothers at home. But the pressure for these war workers was so great, and is still so great, that now we have our industrial day nurseries supported by our manufacturers; and I am afraid they have come to stay. And I am afraid that is what the manufacturers want—just as Mrs. Barton said as to the textile industries.

If there is still a need for the married mothers to enter industry, a visiting housekeeper should be employed to cook their food and keep their homes in order; the mothers must not be obliged to go home and do their housework. I am very much opposed to the industrial nursery, although I am afraid it has come to stay, unless you work to secure mothers' pensions or State aid for widows; and even then there may be day nurseries, because there may be women who will not accept the pension, but will go out to work. In Connecticut provision for such State aid for widowed mothers who can give good care to their children became a law at the last session of the legislature.

Miss Lydia Burcklin (Friendship House, Washington, D. C.): I think the fact that we have had practically no standards for our day-nursery work in this country is giving some worth-while work a bad name. I have been connected with a day nursery for ten years. We have never taken a child from its home when there was any other possible plan. We cooperate with every agency that we have, and we believe that the best place for the child is in the home. We have no mothers' pensions; but in a case where a mother can give good care to the child, we take that child away only temporarily, or while we are working out some plans so that the mother can remain in the home.

I feel that it is too bad that there should be nurseries connected with industries. That is all wrong. I have visited nurseries in many cities, and I have been heartsick over the conditions I have found in some of them. Their one idea seems to be how many children they can take care of. They have no idea of proper supervision, physical or moral. Now, that is not the kind of nurseries we should have. The best possible examination should be made, and the thing should be done that seems to be best for the child and for the family. I am sorry to say that day nurseries are a necessary evil in our present state of social development.

Miss Brockett: I wonder whether the conditions cited by previous speakers would hold true in a nursery operated on the plan which Dr. Baker gave us? I should like to ask Mrs. Barton whether the statement which she made in regard to the health of the day-nursery children as compared with children in their homes referred to children over nine months of age, which is accepted as the minimum age of nursery children in this country?

Mrs. Barton: I could not say what the ages were, but at any rate, the ages of both classes compared were alike. Children visiting the child-welfare center were compared with children of the same age who went to the day nursery. Everything was done in an impartial way; and, although I was against day nurseries, I was surprised at the result.

I am against day nurseries, because I think they are at the center of everything that is wrong. It seems to me that it is not the socialists who are going to break up the homes, but it is industry which is going to break up the homes. It was with that point of view that I was watching the result of the comparison, and I was very much surprised to find what it was. The people who conducted the test were very impartial; they took children of the same ages in each case.

Miss Brockett: I thoroughly agree with you about children under nine months old; and I do not know but that I would put the age at a year. But I cannot believe, from my own experience at least, that it is true of older children, or of children over one year old, who receive nursery care; I believe the nursery children over a year old are better children than the average children cared for in the home—at least, that is true in our city.

Mrs. Barton: That may be true as to children receiving the best of care in a well-equipped nursery.

Dr. Mulon: We can compare only the child that is boarding out and the child in the factory nursing room. I think everybody is of the same opinion, that the home is superior to any other solution. But we must bow to the necessity for the mother to work; and decide whether it is better for her to have the child boarding out, or to have the child in the day nursery. If you can give the mother a sufficient allowance, that is very well—so that the baby will be in a beautiful house, with a bath, and under hygienic conditions; then I am sure that the baby will be better off than in the nursing room.

DENTAL CLINICS

By MAJOR LEWIS TERMAN
Leland Stanford Junior University

I was especially impressed by one of Dr. Winslow's remarks, that America has progressed not nearly as far along certain lines of socialized medicine and hygiene as some other countries in the world. I am afraid that is true. In regard to dental clinics, before the war the promise was that before very long we would be among the leading nations in the world. I understand that the tremendous expenses along other lines, the large amount of energy that had to go to other things, have, for the time being, prevented further developments in dental clinics, and in some cases even lost us some of the clinics which had been established. I hope that everyone here will make it a point to use his influence to restore that kind of work and to bring about its increase.

Perhaps many of you remember from your childhood reading of Don Quixote, that the author in telling about one of the hero's unfortunate adventures, in which he lost a number of teeth, put into his mouth these words, "Alas, a tooth is more precious than a diamond." I suppose Cervantes meant that as a humorous exaggeration, and doubtless we so took it when we read it, but after all these years of development along lines of preventive medicine, we can now hardly take it as exaggeration. I am sure that no one here would exchange his thirty-two teeth for an equal number of precious diamonds.

You may remember, too, that a few years ago Dr. Osler stated that in his opinion the evils which came from neglect of dental hygiene were more serious in the long run than the evils produced by alcohol. That, too, we probably took as a pleasant exaggeration by that prince of all jokers, Dr. Osler, and I am not sure whether Dr. Osler himself meant it literally. When we think of it, however, it does not seem so unreasonable, because the affections of the teeth concern practically ninety per cent of the population, while the evils of alcohol affect immediately perhaps only a fourth, or a fifth, or a tenth of that number. Dental caries at any rate is said to be, by the best authorities, the most widespread of human diseases, one from which probably ninety per cent of the people suffer. At least, extensive investigations in our schools have shown that ninety per cent of school children have one or more decaying teeth. More than that, these investigations have shown that something like twenty per cent of all the teeth of school children are in a more or less serious state of decay. That is a very serious, humiliating admission that we have to make, considering the progress which scientific medicine has made; especially humiliating since dental caries is a disease the cause of which is perfectly well known.

We know that it is theoretically a preventable disease. We know that a clean tooth, a tooth that is kept clean, cannot decay. We know that probably something like forty or fifty millions of dollars would put all the teeth of all the children in order as nearly as dental science is able to do it. We know that something like twenty-five or thirty millions per year—it might run a little higher—would be sufficient to keep them in order. And yet the conditions which I mention still exist, although of course cities here and there have done and are doing a good deal to better the conditions.

I shall not spend time in enlarging or in emphasizing the evils which are produced by decaying teeth. You know the facts as well as I. But I would like to emphasize the fact that dental caries is a disease which affects predominantly children and youths. Teeth which are kept clean and sound until the individual is 25 years old are likely to remain sound until a good old age. Teeth which are neglected until the age of 20 or 25 are very often past salvage. I think there is nowhere else another case in which an ounce of prevention will come as near literally being worth a ton of cure.

Besides dental caries I want to emphasize ulcerated teeth because we are likely to overlook the seriousness of that disease, and especially its frequency. Of course we know how serious it is in a way. We know that it is the cause of a very great deal of rheumatism, heart disease, and many other ailments. We know that by this condition children are frequently kept in a chronic state of ill health, and their very lives even jeopardized. We do not as a rule know so well how common it is. In two or three school surveys I found (many others have found the same thing) that approximately one child in a hundred at any one time in an ordinary school has an ulcerated tooth. It may not be an acute ulceration at the time but it is one which involves a condition present that is productive of injury.

The only way I know to get the teeth of all the children put in order is to do it in connection with the schools. If there were any other way I should not in the least hesitate to champion it. I am not one to urge the schools to take up duties which could just as well be performed by some other institution or means. The plain fact is that in the very best communities as a rule something like 60 to 75 per cent of the school children have never gone to a dentist. This, in addition to the fact that approximately 20 per cent of all the teeth of our school children are at least in initial decay, is sufficient argument for the extension of dental clinics.

Then how different is the problem of getting the work done in a dental clinic from that of persuading parents to hunt up a dentist, and have the work done at their own expense. Probably 20 to 40 per cent of the families in the United States really can not afford the services of a good dentist. Having school nurses go over and over again to the home to persuade the parents to take appropriate action, involves an almost inconceivable amount of lost motion. It can all be done in the schools with a fraction of the expenditure of energy and at no very great expenditure of money. The time will unquestionably come when the school dentist will be considered just as necessary a part of the school system as the school principal himself. The work can be carried on in the schools wholesale and therefore very cheaply compared to the price that must be paid the private practitioner.

I want to protest, too, against the custom which is common in a good many cities of putting the matter on a charity basis; having the associated charities, for example, investigate a family before the children are allowed to go to the school dentist, and thereby branding the parents as paupers if they cannot afford to secure the services of a private practitioner. There is absolutely no justification for this, and in a good many cities an entirely different method is adopted. The dentists are employed, and all children who want to go to them are encouraged to go.

Of course there are people who will say even yet—it was very common for it to be said ten years ago—that this is an undue interference with the rights of a great profession, the profession of dentistry; that dentists have spent a great deal of money in their education and deserve an opportunity to make a living from the profession for which they have prepared. Of course the same argument once was brought against free schools. There were many private teachers who had invested a good deal of money in private schools, and education at public expense was in a way a transgression on their chosen profession. Of course we no longer consider that argument for a moment. We will not consider it for a moment in connection with dentistry or even medicine, when we have once put the question in some such form as this. And I would like you to put it this way in your thinking, namely, Is disease a resource to be conserved for the benefit of a profession, or is it an evil to be gotten rid of?

There is one other point I want to make, namely, that in our school dental work we ought, wherever we are unable to take care of all the teeth of all the children, to emphasize especially the work with the younger children. It is too bad that we have to neglect any, but if the schools in the city cannot afford to take care of all, they ought first to take care of the teeth of the children in the first two or three grades. Thus after a while the task will have been pretty well accomplished for all children.

DISCUSSION

Sir Arthur Newsholme (Late Principal Medical Officer, Local Government Board, England): I should like to express my hearty endorsement of what Major Terman has said as to the extreme importance of the public dental services. I am sure those would be best established in most instances in connection with our dental school service.

I happen to have been a member of a departmental committee dealing with the question of dentistry in the United Kingdom, and I would like to read to you two sentences from the report made by it. The first sentence runs as follows:

> "The evidence before the committee as to the condition of the teeth of most of the people presents a picture of almost hopeless neglect, except in so far as it is relieved by dental work established by grants from the Board of Education and the Local Government Board."

In regard to those grants I should say the Board of Education have been doing a large amount of work in the treatment of teeth in the school child. It is only a small fraction of what needs to be done, but rapid progress has been made. In addition, there are grants to public-health authorities of half the total expenditure for the dental treatment of expectant mothers who attend prenatal clinics and for the dental treatment of the young child in the preschool period; and these three services are being linked up together so as to provide something towards a public dental service.

In that connection I will read you another recommendation of this committee which is far-reaching and which I think will show to you how far we are advancing towards the socialization of medical service in Great Britain. The recommendation is as follows:

> "The provision of adequate dental service to meet the existing needs is impossible at present, owing to the shortage of dentists, but your committee are strongly of opinion that simultaneously with the enforcement of prohibition of the practice of dentistry by unqualified persons, the nucleus of a public dental service should be set up, and dental treatment for such service should be available free of charge for persons needing it. We think that service should be established as a definite branch of public-health work and should be entrusted to the public-health authorities."

Dr. H. J. Gerstenberger (Babies' Dispensary and Hospital, Cleveland, Ohio): Major Terman, in his address, emphasized the importance of cleanliness in preventing caries in teeth. I should like to call attention to the very great importance of the state of nutrition of the child. I believe that the dental work, that is the curative work, is going to be reduced more by the protection of the proper nutrition in the child than by the cleaning of the teeth. I think that if we will prevent rickets, we shall reduce dental caries to a minimum.

THE SCHOOL CHILD

NUTRITION CLINICS

By DR. WILLIAM R. P. EMERSON
Boston, Massachusetts

All children of preschool and school age may be divided for the sake of discussion into three groups: the sick, the well, and the malnourished. The sick are cared for at home and in the hospitals. The well are inspected and receive a certain amount of preventive care from school physicians. The malnourished, about a third of all, receive no treatment for their malnutrition as such because they are considered well by both private and school physicians. These under-par children make it impossible for the schools to reach reasonable standards of achievement. At the same time the system of school organization compels the teacher to attempt to crowd the pupils through the various grades at high pressure, thus adding to the burden of the under-developed and delicate child. As a result 20 to 40 per cent of those graduating from elementary schools are physically unfit.

It is remarkable that this group of children has received so little medical attention. They pass through hospital clinics unnoticed because malnutrition among older children is not considered a pathological condition.

Weighing and Measuring

The simple procedure of weighing and measuring each child will identify all but the border-line cases. All children habitually 7 per cent or more underweight for their height are not only undernourished but malnourished, retarded in both weight and height from one to four years.

Nutrition Clinics

The object of the nutrition clinic is to identify this group of children, and then on the basis of physical, mental, and social examinations to make a diagnosis of the cause of the malnutrition, thus leading to its proper treatment. It is of as much importance to make this accurate diagnosis in malnutrition as it is in other illnesses. It would be absurd for a physician to ask a group of nurses to care for a ward filled with patients affected with various diseases without informing them of the diagnosis in each case. Yet we are asking school nurses, health workers, and parents to carry out general directions with practically no attempt at diagnosis, resulting in an enormous waste of time, energy, and expense. The nutrition clinic corrects all this by determining the cause of the malnutrition in each instance and then indicating measures for its treatment.

Physical and Mental Examinations.—The physical examination reveals an average of more than five defects in each child. When defects interfering with nutrition, especially obstructions to breathing, are corrected, the child is considered free to gain. The mental examination is made in most instances during the course of the physical examination, when it is determined whether there is any question of mental deficiency or retardation. An essential part of the mental examination is to learn the child's disposition and reaction to his environment.

Social Examination.—The home life of the child is investigated by a 48-hour record of his program, which includes a list of food taken during that time, his hours of sleep, of work, of play, time in the open air, and in fact all his various activities.

Simple causes, such as the following, are found adequate to explain malnutrition of the most severe type: fast eating, insufficient food, the use of tea and coffee, late hours, closed windows at night, too little time in the open air, poor hygiene, over-pressure and long hours in school. Such definite diagnoses are essential to successful treatment.

Nutrition Classes

Having then found the causes of the malnutrition by means of these physical, mental, and social examinations, it requires the cooperation of the child, physician, teacher, and parent to remove them and at the same time to secure for the child the essentials of health. These essentials are the removing of physical and mental causes of poor nutrition, getting the children to take sufficient and proper food at frequent intervals, securing fresh air by day and night, preventing overfatigue, and establishing sufficient home control to insure good food and health habits. If these results are accomplished, the child should rapidly gain weight and become well and strong, because of a powerful force in nature that makes for health.

Preparation for the Class.—Cooperation for the essentials of health is best obtained by means of nutrition classes of not more than twenty children in each. The nutrition worker prepares for the class by the weekly weighing of each child and the recording of this weight on a chart. The chart shows the average weight line, corresponding to the child's height, and also his actual weight line as he gains or loses. The worker also checks up the diet lists which are carefully kept by pupil or parent in a small record book for two consecutive days of each week. On these days each article of food taken is recorded; the amounts are indicated in tablespoonfuls or ounces. At this time errors in diet should be corrected and helpful suggestions made, especially in regard to taking milk and cereals. The 24-hour amount should be large enough for gain, usually 2,000 or more units (calories). A blue star is given for rest periods and a red star for lunches, if each has been taken every day of the preceding week. In case of failure to gain, personal conferences are held with each pupil in order to discover an adequate cause, which always exists, and therefore should be found by either the nutrition worker or the physician.

Class Conduct.—The charts having thus been prepared, the children are assembled by the nutrition worker in a room by themselves where two rows of seats are arranged, ten seats to each row. The child gaining most is given a gold star and is placed at the head of the class. The other children are arranged in order of their gain. The weight chart of each child is hung opposite his place in the class. The nutrition worker keeps a history and record card of each child which contains the doctor's directions and her own follow-up notes. These cards are used by him in considering each child.

When the class is in order the doctor conducts the exercise in such manner as to leave a clear idea in the mind of each child as to what he is to do the following week that he may gain. The room should be quiet and free from interruptions. Parents should occupy the back seats, but the teacher and nutrition worker should be seated in front where they may show by their attention lively interest in each child's progress. The physician praises the children who have gained, but it is his special duty to discover the causes for loss in those who have not gained. These causes are usually failure to take regular lunches or rest periods, overtime, late hours, etc. This gives an opportunity to show the importance of these factors in the gain or loss of the particular child. A half hour is sufficient time for the physician to take for this exercise. The nutrition worker makes notes and explains the recommendations to each child or parent. Usually the child losing one week is at the head of the class the following week. Where there is complete cooperation and the essentials of health can be wholly obtained, the child should reach his own normal standard of weight in ten or twelve weeks. From 5 to 10 per cent of the children present serious medical problems requiring most careful study by the physician. Even in these cases, however, the class method provides the most satisfactory method of treatment.

Cooperation with the Home.—The nutrition worker should visit the child in his home in order to gain the cooperation of his parents and to learn his health habits, especially with reference to eating and sleeping. Plans should be made for open windows at night and for plenty of time in the fresh air by day.

Prevention of Over-fatigue.—During the period of treatment the children should be placed in open-air or at least open-window classes and school pressure should be reduced. Some children will need only sufficient additional time for rest and lunch periods; many will work to best advantage on a half-day schedule; a few will need to be reduced to two hours a day, while certain cases cannot profitably attend school at all for a time. One rest period of at least half an hour should be taken before the midday meal. The child should lie flat on his back, thus correcting his usual fatigue position of stooping shoulders, retracted chest, and prominent abdomen. In the mid-afternoon a similar rest period should be taken but for a longer time.

Food.—Mid-forenoon and afternoon lunches should contain about 250 units of such food as will not destroy the appetite for the following meal. Sweets should be avoided at this time. Children gain faster on less food taken in small amounts five times a day than when a larger amount of food is taken in three meals.

Authority of the Class Method.—The class method appeals to the imagination of the child and makes him do for himself what no one else can do for him. It teaches and inspires him to "train for health" in the same way he trains to be a boy scout or a good athlete. Therefore ask him what you will and he will do it cheerfully if he is convinced it is good "dope." The boy of seven or eight years steals off by himself, wraps up in his blanket, and takes his rest periods, or teaches himself to take and to like foods to which previously he had an aversion. He stops drinking tea and coffee, goes to bed early, prepares his bed with hot water jug and papers between blankets, that he may sleep with his window open on the coldest night. All this he does that he may see his weight line go up each week and the stars registered on his chart.

Successful treatment in the majority of cases is both easy and sure, provided either the physician, nutrition worker, or teacher has sufficient vision to paint true pictures in the child's imagination, thus securing his complete cooperation.

THESES ON NUTRITION CLINICS AND CLASSES

1. In the present organization of hospital clinics, school medical inspection and child-helping agencies there is little provision made for the care of a large group of malnourished children—fully one-third of all—who are not sufficiently sick to require hospital care nor are they "well," although they are reported as such because their true condition is so little understood.

2. The work of these nutrition clinics and classes, although fundamentally medical, is for the most part educational. They furnish a medium for the inspection, examination, and treatment of children in the schools, and should be an integral part of school organization.

3. These clinics and classes are especially adapted to make better use of the resources of the family and afford a means of giving training to mothers by teaching them how the child may become well.

4. All children found to be seven per cent underweight for their height require special consideration and treatment. This rule does not identify all cases of malnutrition, but it furnishes the best single standard of selection which we have been able to formulate.

5. The first step is the identification of the members of this group This can best be done in the schools where all children should be weighed and measured periodically.

6. Those children who are found to be seven per cent underweight for their height should be given special treatment and relieved for the time from a part of the usual school pressure.

7. To each of these children should be given an intensive examination. This examination should be made in so far as possible in the presence of the child's parents.[1] All clothing should be removed at least to the waist in order that no defects may be overlooked.

8. The data coming from this examination should be put in form so that they can be used by the specialists to whom the child may be sent for further examination and study. For the same reasons all data accumulated by the specialists should be available in duplicate form for the physician in charge of the nutrition clinic. The amount of time required for these records will be found to be less rather than more than that now used in reports and records which, on account of their lack of standardization and definiteness, are often of very little value.

9. The same plan should be followed with reference to the records growing out of the mental and social examinations and the agencies which these have brought into the case. No defect of any kind should be considered in isolation.

10. An organization similar to that used for open-air classes will be found most serviceable in caring for the malnutrition group. Even from the standpoint of the child's studies it will be found to be economical to reduce the pressure of school responsibilities and work on a program which without delay will make it possible for him to be brought up to his own normal standard.

---

[1] In England as well as in our clinics it has been found possible to secure the attendance of mothers at the greater number of examinations conducted in the schools. It is the testimony of medical officers in that country that the results of the presence of the mothers are the most important of the many valuable outcomes of the work.

11. It will be found that some children in this group will be able to attend school both morning and afternoon, provided adequate arrangements are made for rest periods. In other cases an alternation can be arranged placing one group in school mornings and another afternoons. Those who are excessively underweight cannot afford to attend school for more than two hours a day. Of course individuals may need to be removed from all school pressure for a time.

12. Children should be made free to gain by having all necessary medical and surgical attention given to them promptly. This should include the removal of diseased tonsils and adenoids, the proper care of the teeth, et cetera.

13. From 20 to 40 per cent of the children of school and pre-school age will be found to be in the seven per cent underweight for their height group.

14. It will be found that a reasonable program such as we have outlined will make it possible for the greater part of this group to return to their regular work in from three months to half a year, and that practically all will come up to their own normal standards by the end of the school year.

15. The open-air class organization will serve best as a clearing house for the various types of health-need cases. It will accomplish more as a station in which these special needs can be met than as a more or less permanent retreat for chronic cases.

16. A certain number of problem cases will require a special station for diagnosis in which they can be under constant observation.

17. Special consideration should be given to children who are convalescing from any attack of severe illness so that it may become a custom in the school to help such children reach a state of complete recovery before they are allowed to return to the heavy pressure of the regular classroom work.

18. Relations should be established with summer camps to avoid children being sent to them without diagnosis.

19. It is desirable to keep the responsibility for improving the growth conditions of the child upon the parents. Permanent results require control by the forces nearest to the situation.

20. Under conditions of sympathetic cooperation between the members of the clinic staff, the school corps, and the other agencies involved, it should be possible to do some valuable experimental work with reference to the most favorable hours for school work, the length of school sessions, the conditions of recess periods, the value of school lunches, training in hygiene, et cetera.

21. Many of the conditions of the nutrition clinic are especially favorable for the work to be accomplished in the examinations given for working certificates. The most serious problems met at this stage

of a child's life are those of growth. The more the results secured at this period are interpreted in terms of school life, the better will the school be able to work out an economical and efficient program.

22. There are many reasons why the work to be done with children of the preschool age should be in the hands of those agencies which have had charge of the period of infancy. Much of the waste met in the school years could be eliminated during these earlier years by means of more adequate provision for this most neglected period of growth. It is not infrequent to find serious cases at the school age who have excellent records with reference to nourishment and growth when they were infants. It is important that there should be close cooperation between those who are working with members of the school and preschool groups. It is especially desirable that the latter group should not have a third set of agencies built up to compete in its demands upon the time of the mother with those already caring for the needs of the school children and the infants.

23. The nutrition clinic is especially well adapted to care for dependent, delinquent, and defective children. Nutrition classes for State wards having foster mothers have proved to be remarkably effective.

DISCUSSION

Dr. David Mitchell (Bureau of Educational Experiments, New York City): I do not like to be pessimistic about nutrition classes in public schools, but, having been connected with the bureau which has been responsible for the New York nutrition classes, I should like to present several facts which I think it is well for us to think about. During this past year we have had approximately ninety children in four nutrition classes; two of them were open-air classes, the other two, regular grade classes.

One of the open-air classes is composed almost entirely of children who were included in our nutrition classes last year. They had the instruction and the care which was given to all those children during approximately nineteen weeks. Of twenty-three children who were in last year's nutrition classes, eleven have failed to increase as much as the average child in the ordinary school groups. Taking the results for all the children of the class, we find that they have increased about seventeen per cent faster than was expected. For the children who made gains in excess of the normal or expected gain, the average increase in excess of normal was about thirty-two per cent. These children have few of the so-called physical handicaps. All for whom it was recommended, have had operations for the removal of enlarged tonsils or adenoids. But they are still a problem for us; they are still almost as much underweight as they were when the classes were first organized.

Here is another fact: During the last week of September, 1918, we weighed and measured approximately one hundred and twenty-five fifth grade chilen. At that time we found that thirty-nine or approximately thirty per cent were seven per cent or more underweight for their height. Owing to the conditions in the school system and to the epidemic of influenza, it was impossible to organize nutrition classes for a period of seven weeks. At the time of the first session of the class, these thirty-nine children were again weighed and measured and we found that twenty-two had come up to within seven per cent of the average weight for their height. Some of these children had come up to within one and two per cent of the average weight for their height. This result came about without any training, without any attention to removal of physical defects, and without any instruction in health habits and hygiene. In other words, we did not need to do anything with these children to make them what we call fairly well nourished children.

This led us to the question as to what we should do in order to find out which of our school children are undernourished. It seems to me extremely important that groups of children should be weighed and measured frequently, weekly if possible, monthly if weekly weighings are not feasible, and the amount of variation which these children undergo in weight should be determined. It is now about twenty-three weeks since the classes were organized and in that time those children have not increased more rapidly, in fact have increased less rapidly, than they did during the seven weeks between the original weighing and the first meeting of the nutrition classes.

There are exceptions to this general rule. One child, who was considerably underweight in the beginning, has made almost a continuous and rapid increase in weight. He is now as much overweight as he was underweight at the beginning of the class. This result has come about despite the fact that he has consistently ignored practically all the recommendations made. He has refused to rest, he has refused to give up the use of tea and coffee, he has refused to go to bed early enough to get what we consider a requisite amount of sleep, he has refused to have defective teeth removed or treated, and in general disregarded all the questions of slow eating, of not using water to wash down the unmasticated food, and remaining seated during the meal hour. The one thing which he has done is to increase the caloric intake. It is one of the cases where more food seemed to be the essential requirement; and having that greater amount of nourishment he was able to overcome all the handicaps of physical defects, bad habits, and bad environment.

The general condition cannot, however, be dealt with in this superficial manner. Too many children are underweight, and constantly so, for us to be satisfied with any special cases such as this. We must seek a reason for the failure of these children to increase in weight. The first condition which we may consider as an explanation for this failure is that of a possible biological variation which has not yet been completely understood. We have assumed that the maximum variation possible for a normal child is seven per cent. Certain individual cases lead us to suspect, however, that a normal variation of considerably more than this is possible. It may be that some children are biologically much lighter in weight for their height than other children.

Other considerations are those of emotional disturbances and the unusual stress of certain periods of the school life. We have information which leads us to believe that emotional disturbances influence the processes of nutrition. Cannon has shown that the emotions of fear and anger are attended by a cessation of the churning movement of the stomach and the cessation of flow of the gastric juice. In our classes we had children whose failure to gain in weight we thought might be due to the operation of these factors. We may also consider the stress of the promotion period. At the time when promotions were being considered in this group, the failure to gain was very marked. While the majority of the children had gained in the early weeks, during the week previous to promotion and the week of promotion, very few of the children showed any increase in weight.

Finally, we must consider the influence of physical defect or failure in physiological functioning. Concerning certain of the defects, we are fairly well convinced that they are important detrimental factors. The removal of diseased tonsils and adenoids has frequently been followed by marked increases in weight. The defect in physiological functioning may be the more important. We have cases where the ordinary physical defects have been removed and where the instruction in health habits seems to be followed but in which little progress is noted. These may be cases of biological variation. On the other hand, information as to the metabolism of nutrition is still meager and, in order to decide whether some of these children are functioning normally, prolonged and intense experimentation will be necessary.

Despite all these facts, I would strongly recommend the inauguration and the continuance of nutrition classes for health education. It may be that we are not able to solve the problem in this generation by this particular method, but certain results indicate the far-reaching effect of the procedure. The children who are thus being taught the desirability of regularity of habits and the necessity of eating proper food and the necessity of eliminating harmful stimulants, such as tea and coffee, will undoubtedly influence the nutrition of the next generation. How well they will do this may be indicated by the following illustration: One of the boys in the class came to the teacher with the remark that he had been trying to persuade his mother that "an ounce of prevention is worth a pound of cure." The teacher did not get the significance of the comment at first and asked the boy what he had been trying to do. His reply was that he had been interested in the class work. He had been reading about nutrition and had come across this statement. He concluded, " I tried for two hours to show my mother what that meant, and at the end of the time she did not know a thing about it." If attempts at the education of parents are made in this way, what may we not hope for in the education of children? We may not cure malnutrition by education, but we can develop habits and methods of living which will have a decided influence for good with our next generation.

Mrs. Andrew Wilson (State Chairman, West Virginia Child Welfare Committee): Dr. Lusk tells us that milk is essential. Dr. Emerson also had tea in his dietary lists, but Dr. Lusk, with some of the rest of us, thinks that tea and coffee are better left out. If we could correlate those facts I should like to hear the explanation.

Dr. Emerson: In the first breakfast was the list of food as brought by the child. in which he was having tea. My correction was to substitute cocoa. Tea and coffee are, I think, perhaps the most important single cause of malnutrition. In our group to which Dr. Mitchell has just referred, in New York, over 80 per cent were taking tea and coffee. It raises havoc with growth. That is the first thing to stop. And the children stop it when they see that it interferes with their gain.

The question of diet in the family, in the home, is a very difficult one. My idea is to work along lines of least resistance. If the father likes certain things and you upset him he resents it. So I do not make changes except when necessary. These children will usually gain if we bring the 24-hour amount of food above 2,000 calories. So that about the only suggestion I make is that they use cereal and milk, and make sure that they have the proper amount of milk. If we get their two-day list and make these changes, that seems to be enough to cover the question of diet so that we can go on with other things which are often of greater value.

I want to say in regard to Dr. Mitchell's problems—we have been working together—that in Public School 64 we have a group of children coming in without their mothers, whose presence is very essential. They are over 90 per cent Hebrew, and many of the mothers are at work in stores. The problem is most complicated when we have not the necessary control day and night. You can work your heart out during the day with the children, but when they are away from you, you can not tell what happens. On the question of going to bed, for instance, a little fellow said, "I have been better since I came to the class about going to bed." I said, "What time do you go?" He said, "I go at 10 o'clock." "What time did you go before?" "I used to go at 12." When neither parent is present at our classes to learn and then to carry out instructions at home, the element of overfatigue may upset all our calculations.

A Member: Is it safe to take cocoa each day? Is it not too stimulating?

Dr. Emerson: Cocoa is likely to be too sweet, especially if taken without other food. I try to limit cocoa to once or twice a day, and be careful to have them make their cocoa weak, simply using it as a flavoring for milk.

HEALTH EXAMINATIONS AND THE SCHOOL NURSE

By DR. THOMAS D. WOOD

Chairman, Committee on Health Problems in Education
National Council of Education

The conservation and the cultivation of the child's health are recognized today as fundamental and essential factors in the program of public education. Practice, however, lags far behind accepted principles in this as in other phases of education and of life. Enough experimentation and demonstration have been accomplished in the field of child health to convince sensitive, tender, and socially-minded citizens of the health needs of children and the responsibility of community, state, and nation regarding these crying needs.

The war has shown us with dramatic illumination the weakness of the nation's young manhood, dependent in vital measure upon the neglect of childhood and youth. A stunning indictment of our democracy is involved in the fact that the tragedy of a world war was needed to reveal such a vital source of national peril and weakness. The statistics of the draft showed that one-third of the young men at the age of the flower of manhood were unfit for first-class service in the defense of the country in time of war. But it has been known by some, for years, that three-fourths of the 22,000,000 school children in the United States have health defects which are actually or potentially injurious to them as prospective citizens of the republic. Efforts in this health program for school children have so far been desultory, spasmodic, and uncoordinated. National standards are needed today for genuine constructive progress in this branch of the great program of child welfare.

The health examination of school children involves two distinct phases of inspection and administration:

(a) The daily health inspection.

(b) The annual (or if required in individuals, more frequent) health examination.

The daily inspection and supervision are necessary to determine the child's fitness for attendance upon school, which fitness is dependent upon the absence of signs of health disturbance. Such signs may denote the pupil's personal unfitness for school that day, and such signs may also represent the preliminary symptoms of definite communicable disease. The possession of these signs may render the child a source and center of infection for his fellow pupils. For the best interests of himself and of his school companions he should be kept at home under such circumstances, and thus excluded from school before these indications of health disorders have developed into the recognizable and distinctive symptoms of disease. The school is by its very nature perfectly adapted to serve as an agency for assembling and distributing children's diseases throughout the community, and all too frequently this is just what occurs.

The best knowledge and skill of parents, teachers, nurses, physicians, and even of the children themselves are requisite for a satisfactory minimizing of these diseases of child life. If there is reasonably intelligent and conscientious cooperation of the individuals and agencies involved, there need be no epidemics in schools, and the school will be made in this vital respect a real health center.

No child should ever knowingly be exposed to contagious disease. The older the child is before being exposed by accident to contagious disease the less apt he is to catch it. The older a child is before having a contagious disease of childhood, the less severe, on the average, it is likely to be.

The following are indications of health disorders in children for which parents should keep children at home and notify the school:

Nausea or vomiting; chill; convulsions (fits); dizziness, faintness, or unusual pallor; eruption (rash) of any kind; fever; running nose; red or running eyes; sore or inflamed throat; acutely swollen glands; cough; failure to eat the usual breakfast; any distinct or disturbing change from usual appearance or conduct of the child.

The foregoing signs should be used also by teachers as a basis for excluding pupils from school for the day, or until the signs have disappeared, or until the proper health officer has authorized the return of the pupil to school. Children may be taught—without developing disturbing fears, or attempts to deceive—to notice the above-mentioned signs in themselves or in their companions, and thus help to protect the school from contagious disease. The detection of these first signs of health disturbance at home, by the parent or the child, before the child starts for school, is of especial importance in the country, where the longer trip to school with greater physical exertion, sometimes in bad weather, would be particularly injurious to a child at the beginning of an illness. In cases of contagious disease among school children, the length of time of exclusion from school must be determined by the health and the school authorities.

The second phase of the health examination of school children includes the investigation to ascertain the health status of the child, and the presence of the more permanent health defects and tendencies.

At least one per cent, or 200,000 of the 22,000,000 school children in the United States, are mentally defective.

Over one per cent, or 250,000, at least, are handicapped by organic heart disease.

At least five per cent, or 1,000,000, have now, or have had, tuberculosis, a danger often to others as well as to themselves.

Five per cent, or 1,000,000, have defective hearing which, unrecognized, gives many the undeserved reputation of being mentally defective.

Twenty-five per cent, or 5,000,000, have defective eyes. All but a small percentage of these can be corrected, and yet a majority of them have received no attention.

Twenty per cent at least, or 4,500,000, are suffering from malnutrition. Every child who is 10 per cent or more below weight for his height and age is suffering from malnutrition, and persistent efforts by cooperation of school, home, and community should be made to correct this. Poverty is not the most important cause of this serious barrier to health development.

From fifteen to twenty-five per cent, 3,000,000 to 5,000,000, have adenoids, diseased tonsils, or other glandular defects.

From ten to twenty per cent, or from 2,000,000 to 4,000,000, have weak foot arches, weak spines, or other joint defects.

From fifty to seventy-five per cent, or from 11,000,000 to 16,000,000, of our school children (and in many communities as high as 98 per cent) have defective teeth, and all defective teeth are more or less injurious to health. Some of these defective teeth are deadly menaces to their owners. This is the greatest problem, from the standpoint of its seriousness and from the standpoint of its enforcement, that we have. The teeth of the children of America can never be brought into proper shape without a social program to provide for the payment of tremendous bills. May I ask you to remember that Sir William Osler, our greatest living English-speaking medical authority, said ten years ago that more national physical deficiency in Great Britain was due to defective teeth than to alcohol.

Every school child should have a health examination once a year. More frequent examination should be provided for individual pupils who need special attention. All health examinations and health care in rural and in city schools should be under the supervision of regularly appointed school physicians thoroughly trained for their work. Every State should have a State health inspector of schools who should give special attention to the health work of the rural schools.

The routine tests of vision and hearing can best be made by the teachers, as these tests involve, to an unusual extent, mental and educational as well as health factors and require knowledge of the pupils,

HEALTH—THE SCHOOL CHILD

possessed by the teacher, as well as simple methods of examination which all capable teachers can easily learn. I am referring of course only to the routine tests of vision of all the children, not the examination of those found to be defective. In the rural schools the general health examinations can often be done most advantageously by the school nurse with the help of the teacher.

There should be for every child a health as well as a scholarship record which accompanies him through his school career. And this, let me say, should be a continuation of the record started when the child was born, which is handed down to the school when the child enters school. What has been said about the care of children during the preschool age will of course apply here. This should be a part of the record of the school which the child is attending. The following form or blank has been tested sufficiently in rural as well as city schools to prove its practical value:

HEALTH RECORD

Name................ Born in................ on (date)............
.... Nationality of Father.............. Mother..............
Number in family.......... Adults......... Children.......... Number of birth.................. History of Measles................. Scarlet fever.............. Diphtheria.............. Whooping cough.......
.... Pneumonia.................. Influenza................
Date of first examination.................. in school...............

	—— YEAR ——							
	1	2	3	4	5	6	7	8
1. Age and year..........	...	...	...	...	...	...	...	...
2. Grade	...	...	...	...	...	...	...	...
3. Class	...	...	...	...	...	...	...	...
4. Revaccinations	...	...	...	...	...	...	...	...
5. Diseases during year....	...	...	...	...	...	...	...	...
6. Date of examinations....	...	...	...	...	...	...	...	...
7. Height	...	...	...	...	...	...	...	...
8. Weight	...	...	...	...	...	...	...	...
9. Nutrition	...	...	...	...	...	...	...	...
10. Anemia	...	...	...	...	...	...	...	...
11. Enlarged glands	...	...	...	...	...	...	...	...
12. Nervous diseases	...	...	...	...	...	...	...	...
13. Cardiac diseases	...	...	...	...	...	...	...	...
14. Pulmonary diseases.....	...	...	...	...	...	...	...	...
15. Skin diseases	...	...	...	...	...	...	...	...
16. Orthopedic defect	...	...	...	...	...	...	...	...
17. Defect of vision........	...	...	...	...	...	...	...	...
18. Defect of hearing.......	...	...	...	...	...	...	...	...
19. Defect of nasal breathing	...	...	...	...	...	...	...	...
20. Defect of palate........	...	...	...	...	...	...	...	...
21. Defect of teeth.........	...	...	...	...	...	...	...	...
22. Hernia	...	...	...	...	...	...	...	...

23. Hypertrophied and diseased tonsils.......... ... ...
24. Adenoids ....
25. Mentality ....
26. Conduct ....
27. Effort ....
28. Proficiency ....
29. Treatment necessary..... ... ...

The eyes of children who wear glasses should be tested with the glasses, and if found normal should be so recorded. The following method should be used:

Hang the Snellen test letters in a good, clear light (side light preferred) on a level with the head, and so placed that the child does not face a strong light. Place the child 20 feet from the letters. Cover one eye with a card held firmly against the nose, without pressing on the covered eye, and have him read aloud, from left to right, the smallest letters he can see on the card. Make a record of the result.

Children who have not learned their letters, obviously, cannot be given this eyesight test until after they have learned them. Pupils who cannot read may, however, be tested by a chart with pictures of familiar objects designed for this purpose.

There is a number over each line of the test letters which shows the distance in feet at which these letters should be read by a normal eye. From top to bottom the lines on the card are numbered, respectively, 50, 40, 30, and 20. At a distance of 20 feet, the average normal eye should read the letters on the 20 foot line, and if this is done correctly, or with a mistake of one or two letters, the vision may be noted as 20/20 or normal. In this fraction the numerator is the distance in feet at which the letters are read, and the denominator is the number over the smallest line of letters read. If the smallest letters which can be read are on the 30 foot line, the vision will be noted as 20/30; if the letters on the 40 foot line are the smallest that can be read, the record will be 20/40. If the letters on the 50 foot line are the smallest that can be read, the record will be 20/50.

If the child can not see the largest letters (those on the 50 foot line), have him approach slowly until the distance is found from which they can be seen. If 5 is the nearest distance from which the 50 foot letters can be read, the record will be 5/50 (1/10 of normal).

Test the second eye, the first being covered with the card, and note the result as before. With the second eye, have the child read the letters from right to left to avoid memorizing. To prevent reading from memory, a hole 1½ inches square may be cut in a piece of cardboard, which may be held against the test letters so as to show only one letter at a time, and which may be moved about so as to show the letters in irregular order. A mistake of two letters on the 20 or 30 foot line and of one letter on the 40 or 50 foot line may be allowed.

Parents should be notified if:

(a) Vision in either eye is 20/40 or less;

(b) Child habitually holds head too near book (less than 12 inches);

(c) Child frequently complains of headache, especially in the latter portion of school hours;

(d) Either eye deviates even temporarily from normal position.

In testing hearing, if it is possible, one person should make the examination for an entire school in order to insure an even method. The person selected should be one possessed of normal hearing.

The examination should be made with the whispered voice; the child should repeat what he hears, and the distance at which words can be heard distinctly should be noted. The two ears should be tested separately. The test should consist of numbers, 1 to 100, and short sentences. To avoid imitation, it is best that but one pupil at a time be allowed in the room. For very young children a fair idea of the hearing may be obtained by picking out the backward or inattentive pupils and those that seem to watch the teacher's lips, placing them with their backs to the examiner and asking them to perform some unusual movement of the hand or other act.

Physical defects should be reported to the homes, and all possible efforts should be made by teachers, superintendents, school nurses and school doctors to persuade the parents to obtain for the child the care necessary for correction of all defects that it is possible to remedy. Facilities should be made available for the health reconstruction of all the school children.

It is vitally necessary that the best available efforts of official agencies, national, state, and local, shall be supplemented and reinforced by the cooperation of voluntary service of individuals and organizations enlisted for this essential form of social service, expressing results in the conservation and improvement of the nation's most vital and most neglected assets, the health and welfare of the children.

I would like to pay tribute to such organizations as the Child Health Organization, with headquarters in New York, which has given very striking support and cooperation to this movement for the correction of malnutrition, as a part of the general program for the health of the school children of America; to the Elizabeth McCormick Memorial Fund of Chicago, and to the Bureau of Educational Experiments in New York, as types of volunteer organizations necessary to insure these standards of health examination and health care.

Magnificent provisions have been made for the health care of our soldiers in war. Shall not the children, drafted by compulsory education into our schools, be assured of as skillful and satisfactory care as the soldiers in camp and trench? If health and physical efficiency are so important for the country as a whole, all of the necessary forces, both governmental and voluntary, must be marshaled for the task of protecting and developing the physical fitness of the young. The principle of universal training must, in a manner consonant with the spirit and methods of democracy, be interpreted and applied in the universal, compulsory health and physical care and training of all the children of the nation.

Physicians, surgeons, nurses, hospitals, dental and general clinics, and health centers of requisite type must be available to meet the needs of the defective children in the schools.

Health officers who supervise this program must have special and thorough training in modern educational principles and practice, in addition to medical education and experience, to qualify them for their work. Teachers and other school officials require adequate training in health principles and methods to enable them to cooperate most successfully. The curricula of training in all normal schools and in other institutions for the preparation of teachers must be broadened and modified to include the essential instruction in school health work before the structure of national education can be recognized as giving evidence of rational wholeness or soundness. Special teachers and supervisors of health and physical education, if properly trained, may render invaluable service in the health examinations, supervision, and health education of pupils.

Registered nurses employed as district and school nurses, or giving their time when necessary exclusively to the schools, have already demonstrated the extraordinary value of their professional services in this program of health examination and care of the school children. It is essential, however, that they should be firmly grounded in educational ideas and in special teaching methods, and possess the skill requisite for their highest usefulness.

It is apparent to careful students of this school health work that the teacher should have the benefit of the social and community methods of the best hospitals, clinics, and social workers; while it is equally necessary that school physicians and nurses should have the benefit of the best special training made available for teachers in universities, colleges, and normal schools.

There should be a school nurse for every 1,000 to 3,000 school children, according to geographical distribution and the presence or absence of cooperating agents for the health work.

The work of the school nurse may be briefly outlined as follows:

Routine class inspections to detect cases to be excluded from school and referred to physicians.

First aid in emergency cases.

Assisting in health examinations and keeping records.

Instructing pupils in various details of hygiene.

Advising parents of children found in health examinations to require remedial treatment.

Convincing parents of necessity of treatment.

Making adjustments for needed treatment.

Instructing children and parents in personal and home health.

Making arrangements for treatment of needy children.

Securing medicines, eye-glasses, etc., through philanthropic agencies.

Taking children to clinics and persuading them to accept the treatment advised; obtaining necessary data for the clinics.

The duties of the school nurse vary with the needs and resources of the community and may include in addition to the general activities here indicated special work with truants and with classes of physically handicapped children, such as the cripples, tuberculous, anemic, etc. Without the nurse, the statistics show that corrective work is done in 15 to 25 per cent of the cases reported and recommended. With the nurse, it is shown that from 75 to 90 per cent of the children receive the follow-up work and attention which has been urged.

The possibilities of vital accomplishment with a standardized national program of health examination and care of school children seem not only fundamental for national safety but limitless for national progress. The significance and necessity of the work to be done make the demand for constructive advancement imperative. No factor relating to essentials in public education or promotion of national welfare seems more important or more promising.

THE NUTRITION OF ADOLESCENCE

By DR. GRAHAM LUSK

Cornell University Medical College, New York City

An adequate food supply is the requisite of national existence. If too little food is available the first to suffer are the old people, and then the children, though these are often fed with the food designed for the mother, who sacrifices herself for the well-being of her offspring.

Before the war great numbers of people were habitually in a state of undernutrition. This reduces the working capacity and diminishes the resistance to diseases, especially to tuberculosis. Such a condition gradually undermining the welfare of a nation, may be exemplified by a description of the food conditions in Germany, a knowledge of which has lately become available.

It is stated by Rubner[1] that food difficulties first arose in the middle of 1916. One important article of food after another disappeared from the market or could be obtained only in homeopathic doses. Thus, the available amounts of meat, eggs, milk, and butter became less and less. During the winter of 1916-17, the failure of the potato crop of 1916 led to the substitution of turnips in the diet, both in the cities and in the industrial centers. From the effects of this diet the people never recovered. There was insufficient milk for the children. The censorship of the press prevented the true condition from being generally known, and people were taught to congratulate themselves upon their loss in weight.

A secret inquiry, made at the end of 1917, led Rubner to report to the Imperial Ministry of Health how widespread the evil effect of the war diet had been upon the welfare of the people. The psychology of the nation had changed. The only thought was to obtain a sufficient quantity of food, albeit devoid of flavor; there was no initiative, only unproductive depression. Children forgot how to laugh, to cry, or to play.

Information reached London early in 1918 that the insurance companies of Germany had secretly warned the government as to the failing health of the people, which was reported to be more disastrous in loss of life than were the military operations. This now appears as an undoubted reflection from the meeting described by Rubner.

---

[1] Rubner, M., Berliner klinische Wochenschrift (1919), LVI, 2.

The latter states that certain high-placed individuals forbade a further prosecution of the inquiry.

Kraus describes how hunger forms an excellent background for disease, and that anti-bodies are not produced as when adequate nutrition is possible. Hence, the tuberculosis death rate doubled during the war and is now at the height prevailing twenty-five years ago. He relates[1] that the food conditions affected women in such a way as to produce cessation of the menses, sterility, and a reduction in the quantity of milk of the nursing mothers, which milk was also poor in fat. The average weight of children at birth fell off. Cows' milk of inferior quality was given to children, for there was no longer any hygienic control. The evil effects of the one-sided diet on the older children became more pronounced the longer it was continued. A diet made up essentially of bread and potatoes proved injurious to children. There was a deficiency in protein, fat, and in vitamines, which led to scurvy, tuberculosis, rickets, and anemia. Nervous diseases were aggravated and constitutional anomalies intensified.

Reports have also come out of Germany showing how an absence of butter fat led to stunted growth and the affliction of xerophthalmia, a disease of the eye, both of which symptoms can be experimentally produced in young rats in the absence of the fat soluble vitamine contained in butter fat. These stories are not German propaganda. An American medical commission conducted an investigation into the condition of the children of Treves after its occupation by the American army and found a retardation in growth of two years, children of fourteen having the physical development of those of twelve.

In the Bohemian city of Prague a widespread presence of infantile scurvy as existing in the early summer of 1918 is bitterly described by Epstein.[2] Almost every preparation for the welfare of the sick child had disappeared from the market, the rich buying at high prices the "last bottle" of such material from the apothecary. Milk was very scarce at a time when the farmers were freely using half their milk, a food so necessary for sick children, in the preparation of butter. It is well known that this kind of profiteering had long been prevented in England.

These details are cited in order to emphasize the necessity of such an organization of agriculture or of food supply that the national welfare of a country be maintained. That such an organization is incompatible with industrial disorder is a self-evident proposition.

Both the quality and the quantity of food should be considered. Children should receive a diet containing a sufficient quantity of vitamines. Of fundamental importance for growth and good health

---

[1] Kraus, Berliner klinische Wochenschrift (1919), LVI, 3; Czerny, Ibid., p. 4.
[2] Epstein, Jahrbuch für Kinderheilkunde (1918), LXXXVIII, 237.

is the butter fat contained in milk or taken separately in the form of cream or butter. This has been set forth above. Stunted rats which have been long deprived of this substance grow to normal size when it is added to an otherwise adequate diet, so that it may be presumed that with the administration of butter fat to children whose growth has been retarded normal growth will be obtained. Vegetable oils, like olive oil, and pork fat do not contain the fat soluble vitamine and cannot take the place of milk. Beef fat, eggs, liver, and kidneys are, however, quite rich in this material, and it is present in spinach, lettuce, beet tops, and the like. Olive oil taken with lettuce or beet tops may take the place of milk in the diet of adults. Through eating the green substances of the field the cow gains for her milk this growth-promoting, life-preserving vitamine. It follows from this that the milk of a cow nourished on clover from the fields will be of higher nutritive value than that of one fed with corn ensilage. The cows in Great Britain have more vitamines in their milk than cows in America because pasturage is better there.

If a food be given which consists mainly of highly polished rice, or highly milled grains, beri-beri, a profound nervous disorder, results. Beri-beri can be cured by administering the aqueous extract of peas or of rice polishings or of the evaporated salts of milk. This disease has not appeared in war time in the European nations because wheat has been milled at about 85 per cent or more, so that a large proportion of the bran, which contains the water-soluble vitamine, has remained in the bread. When a child can receive an ordinary mixed diet there is no danger in partaking of white bread.

Scurvy appears when the diet contains no anti-scorbutic vitamines, such as are found in fruits, fresh vegetables, and tubers such as potatoes. The cure is found in lemon juice, orange juice, fresh vegetables, potatoes, germinated peas, beans, and lentils, and in canned tomatoes. Hess finds that the younger and more tender the green vegetable, the greater its vitamine content, hence an instinctive dietetic preference.

The question of vitamines for the welfare of the children is bound up in the development of dairy farming, fruit culture, and the production of fresh vegetables.

Furthermore, milk contains salts for the growth and repair of the bones, protein for the growth and repair of the muscles and other organs of the body, together with fat and sugar which give fuel for the maintenance of the human machine. Very few people realize that the cost of milk per 1,000 calories is usually only one-half the cost of beef. Thus, in Paris on September 1, 1918, 1,000 calories cost as milk 98 centimes (equal to 17 cents), as beef 175 centimes (equal to 31 cents); and in New York on January 1, 1919, as milk 24 cents and as beef 45 cents. In Paris beef was 82 per cent more costly than milk and in New York it was 87 per cent more costly. The controlled London market does not lend itself for comparison. On account of the great value and lesser cost of milk the writer has urged that a family of five should not buy meat until it has purchased three quarts of milk daily.

Milk is wanting in iron and hence children should be given green substances which contain this element, especially spinach, which contains a considerable quantity. The yolks of eggs also contain it, as do, of course, beef and beef juice.

The curse of the ignorant and poorer classes is the giving of tea and coffee to their children instead of milk. This is done in families in which meat is regularly purchased. There is not sufficient education for the parents to realize that milk is a cheap and well-nigh indispensable body-building food. It is not desirable to give to children or to adults the minimal quantity of protein compatible with existence, but it is safer to allow protein in a certain excess of the actual needs in order that the tissue cells be filled with it. Rubner has called such material an "improvement quota" of protein, and there is evidence that this descriptive terminology is justified. This, however, does not warrant the eating by any man of a pound or more of beef a day, meat which costs five times as much fodder to produce as does a similar food value in milk.

With regard to a sufficiency in the quantity of a diet the question becomes involved in the number of calories necessary for the maintenance of the living organism at various ages. Below are presented the relative physiological needs of food in the first column as estimated by Atwater, and in the second column as adopted by the Inter-Allied Scientific Food Commission of 1918.

	Age in years	Atwater	Inter-Allied Scientific Food Commission
Child	0 to 2	0.3	0.50
Child	2 to 6	0.4	0.50
Child	6 to 10	0.5	0.70
Boy	10 to 12	0.6	0.83
Girl	10 to 14	0.6	0.83
Boy	12 to 14	0.8	0.83
Boy	14 to 16	0.9	1.00
Girl	14 to 16	0.7	0.83
Men		1.0	1.00
Women		0.8	0.83

The British Food Committee of the Royal Society had computed that an average man doing an average day's work required 3,000 calories, as ingested, or 3,300 when the supply was considered from the national standpoint and allowed for waste. When later it computed the quantity of food available for their whole population in the five year prewar period, 1909-13, dividing it among the population in accordance with the relative values adopted by the Inter-Allied Scientific Food Commission, it was found that 3,410 calories had been available per man per day. With increased care in the use of food a national stock of 3,300 calories per "man" per day appears ample. The earlier statement that a nation could live on what it wasted before the war has been abundantly refuted.

The study of standards of metabolism has occupied much time during recent years. At the time of the establishment of the Russell Sage Institute respiration calorimeter in Bellevue Hospital satisfactory standards for the determination of what constituted normal metabolism were non-existent. From the work of Du Bois and his associates it has been firmly established that the well nourished, normal adult man, when resting in bed before breakfast, produces 40 calories per hour per square meter of surface within an error limit of about ± 10 per cent. This is known as the basal metabolism. Du Bois found that the metabolism of boys between 12 and 13 years old was 50 calories per square meter of surface, or 25 per cent higher than in adult men. At this time, before the onset of puberty, the intensification of the growth impulse is accompanied by a greatly increased metabolism when height and weight are regarded. Furthermore, Du Bois investigated the metabolism of these same boys two years later under identical experimental conditions. The metabolism per square meter of surface had fallen so that it was only 11 per cent above the average for adult men. In the three youngest boys the metabolism was actually greater in calories produced during the twelfth year than during the fourteenth year, although the boys showed gains in weight of between 35 and 50 per cent. It is well known that a normal boy is extremely active at this period of his life. Investigations by Gephart have shown that American boys in St. Paul's School partook of as much as 5,000 calories daily. Sir Henry Thompson, prior to his death on an Irish passenger steamer sunk by a German submarine in the summer of 1918, collected data which showed an average consumption of 3,500 calories daily by English school boys, even in the difficult days of the winter of 1918. At Eton and Harrow the spirit of patriotism at one time certainly caused too great a voluntary restriction upon the quantity of food taken and many boys lost in weight, often to the detriment of their health.

It has been reported from Berlin[1] that, in an asylum for foundlings in the third year of the war an attempt was made to nourish three boys between six and eight years old with food containing 1,000 calories, and four other boys between eleven and fourteen with 1,334 calories. This may be calculated as being less than the basal metabolism of the children and the result was what was to have been anticipated, a

---

[1] Fuhge, Jahrbuch fur Kinderheilkunde, (1918), LXXXVIII, 43.

loss in weight and in body protein of all these children, who were not only under height for their age but under weight for their height.

Five thousand calories daily certainly appears to be an extravagant quantity of food to furnish a boy. It is 20 per cent more than the amount consumed by a soldier at hard drill. It would be very interesting to investigate the economic efficiency of the muscles of the growing boy. Since his basal metabolism is higher than that of a man, it is not at all unlikely that his muscular efficiency is on a lower plane, that is to say, that he may require more energy to walk or to move a bicycle a given distance than would an adult of similar height and weight. This point has never been investigated.

The accompanying chart shows the food requirements of boys from birth to sixteen years of age, as calculated from all the material available a year ago.[1] To this have been added:

(1) The requirements prescribed by the Inter-Allied Scientific Food Commission (blue line).

(2) The requirements calculated by Atwater (green line).

(3) The actual consumption of food by rather inactive school boys, investigated by Carl Tigerstedt in 1912, reports of which have just reached this country (red dotted line).

(4) The reported food intake of American and English school boys and of English school girls (red solid lines).

In addition to this it may be noted that Pfaundler's[2] suggested corrections of the erratic, official dietary for the children of Munich, as of January 1, 1918, are in full accord with the recommendations of the Inter-Allied Scientific Food Commission from the end of the first year to the tenth year of age.

On reading the evidence it appears that much knowledge is lacking, much is needed to fill in the picture. There is now ample food in the country. Twelve thousand million dollars per annum, or one-quarter of the income of the working population, is paid for it by our people. Housewives are not organized politically, but the time is coming when the importance of a more thorough understanding of the science of nutrition will be realized in the land.

---

[1] Lusk, G., Journal of the American Medical Association, (1918), LXX, 821. The literature references are given here.
[2] Pfaundler, Münchener Medizinische Wochenschrift (1918), LXV, 173.

THE NEED FOR SEX EDUCATION

By ROBERT D. LEIGH
United States Public Health Service

The inclusion of the subject of sex education in a conference addressing itself to the task of fixing minimum standards for child welfare is something of a novelty. It may be an indication that to some extent this very important phase of child welfare is passing over from the period of unregulated, unorganized experimentation into that of partial standardization.

In dealing with either children or adults it is difficult to get away from the problems of sex education. The official agencies dealing with the health and morale of the soldiers and sailors during the war started out with the aim of reducing the incidence of venereal diseases. Before going far they arrived at sex education among civilians also, as one of the most important means to the attainment of the original, single-minded military aim. In organizing a comprehensive program for prevention and control of the venereal diseases among the civilian population of the United States the public health agencies of nation, state, and city have come to place emphasis on this same fundamental means of prevention.

We know that venereal diseases are spread largely through promiscuous sex intercourse. If these contacts could be eliminated syphilis and gonorrhea would rapidly diminish as a communicable disease problem. We know, too, that these contacts through irregular sex intercourse are not outside the control of the individual or personally unavoidable as are the contacts with germs of some other communicable diseases. We know that the individual exposes himself by a conscious act which serves no social purpose. It is, therefore, theoretically possible to eliminate these contacts by the proper education of the individual. Every rational anti-venereal-disease program must include the promotion of all kinds and types of training which will educate men and women to refrain from promiscuous sexual intercourse.

Let it be made clear that the term sex education as a preventive of venereal diseases is meant here in its broadest sense. It includes all influences, all types of training and habit forming, all kinds of instruction and activities which lead the individual to set up for himself a socially valuable sex life.

Much talk has been wasted at conferences in arguing that sex instruction—the imparting of facts concerning sex physiology, venereal diseases, etc.—cannot itself prevent venereal diseases or lead the individual into the right sort of sex life. This is setting up a straw man to knock it down. Those who are today advocating sex instruction are extremely humble in their claims. Their work is only an item of the large social program of sex education and prevention. There is practical agreement among them that sex instruction is only a small part of the set of influences which go to make up the education of the individual on matters of sex.

All of them would agree that moral training or character building in the home, by personal example, by religion, or by other agencies is of great importance in the individual prevention of venereal diseases and of sexual irregularity. All would agree that a rich recreational life with wholesome, out-door exercise and abundant motor activity is of the greatest importance in long-circuiting the sex impulse in adolescence and in promoting a normal sex life. All would agree that social intercourse between the young people of both sexes under favorable circumstances is a valuable means of sublimating the sex impulse and directing it into right channels. All would agree that the personal acquisition of absorbing interests or hobbies, compelling enthusiasms, and ambitions are of great value in directing those same impulses along socially useful channels.

All would agree that the reduction by all means possible of the stimuli leading to abnormal sex thoughts, and the elimination of direct temptations to commercialized vice are of value in promoting a sound sex life. Everything advocated at this conference, for instance, which will develop the recreational life of childhood and youth, or which will furnish better home life, is helping to meet the need for sex education. There is, however, a need for the giving of facts, for proper instruction in matters of sex. And its value is not inconsiderable.

One of the most extensive campaigns for sex instruction ever carried on anywhere was adopted in the army and navy during the war through the agency of the Surgeon Generals' offices, the Commissions on Training Camp Activities, the Y. M. C. A., and other cooperating agencies. This work was only part of a large scheme of prevention by various means and it was emergency work under the handicaps of limited time and rapidly changing locations of troops. But it was surprisingly successful. Although it is impossible to gauge statistically the results of army social hygiene education on the sex habits of the men, it is demonstrated statistically that the effects of law enforcement, instruction, and recreation employed simultaneously with specific groups of men materially reduced the prophylaxis rate. And the prophylaxis rate is quite an accurate gauge of the rate of irregular sexual relations.

But although statistics are not available for the effect of sex instruction alone, case histories obtained informally by the many social hygiene sergeants who had charge of the instruction work in the army camps gave unmistakable evidence of the value of this method of prevention of venereal diseases. In case after case the simple, scientific statements concerning sex hygiene or venereal diseases removed a load of worry which had been weighing a young man down for years and gave him ambition to lead a better sex life.

These personal testimonies reveal strikingly that sex education once undertaken has effects much more inclusive than the prevention of venereal disease. It has a direct bearing on the problem of illegitimacy and on the happiness rate of marriage relations. It also has a distinct and easily traceable relation to the happiness and mental normality of childhood and adolescence. From no other cause so much as ignorance of simple facts concerning sex do the fears, the worries, the broodings, the misunderstandings, so common in adolescence arise. Nothing, on the other hand, can make the period of youth so much a golden age of happiness and pleasure in life as accurate knowledge and normal attitude in matters of sex.

If there were no other matters involved, if it were possible to keep the child from proper instruction at the school ages and re-educate him or her later in college or adult life to normal habits and points of view, the worries and doubts and broodings imposed on boys and girls of the adolescent period as a result of lack of simple knowledge is a cruelty on the part of any society that is able to furnish that instruction. For the immediate happiness of the adolescent boy and girl, sex instruction is a clear duty. Modern psychological research, moreover, is revealing the destructive mental and physical consequences in adult life of the neglect to give the proper direction to the adolescent impulse.

Studies made of childhood and adolescent sex experiences bring out clearly this need of early and adequate sex instruction. A number of years ago Dr. M. J. Exner of the Y. M. C. A. obtained answers to questions concerning sex experience from 948 college men in the East, Central West, and Far West. These answers were obtained under circumstances favorable to accuracy and tending to understatement rather than to overstatement. The summary of the information obtained has been in print for some time. The only criticism made of its conclusions by those familiar with American boys at first hand is that they are too conservative. The conclusions are, in short, that the age at which most boys receive their first permanent sex impressions is $9\frac{1}{2}$ years and that these impressions, received from improper and unreliable sources, usually have a bad effect; that the age at which most boys are likely to begin some form of sexual practice is before puberty; that the age at which most boys receive sex instruction from well meaning sources is 15½ years; and that the effects of this instruction, however crude, are in almost every case good.

These answers show vividly that the recent generations of school boys coming from homes well above the average have been getting the wrong sort of sex education, that its effect is bad, and that the right sort of instruction comes six years too late.

No such extensive studies of the sex life of girls have been published. It is probable that within a short time similar studies of girls will be made available. More limited investigations, however, point to a situation fully as serious as among boys. Dr. Richards, of Philadelphia, questioning the 36 girls of one of her high school classes, found that most of them received their first sex information at the age of 11½ years from unreliable sources and that they received their first reliable information at the age of 15.

A study of 50 young women, 25 of whom were college graduates, reported in Social Hygiene, indicates that many girls of the more protected life received no adequate instruction regarding sex matters and venereal diseases until late adolescence and that the effect on those receiving at a late date information regarding the abnormal manifestations of sex was decidedly harmful. On the other hand, it indicates that those who received information on normal sex matters early in adolescence from mothers or teachers seemed not to have ill effects from hearing about prostitution and venereal diseases when it was given them at a later date.

From these studies as well as from the day-to-day experience of lecturers, teachers, and workers with boys and girls, it seems definitely established that sex instruction for boys and girls at the school ages is a crying need and that proper sex instruction has highly beneficial effects.

Various methods of meeting this need for sex instruction of the young are already developed and more are developing.

The methods and matter for the education of the child before puberty are fairly well established. The child at this period is interested in reproduction as in anything else going on about him and questions his parents for the satisfaction of his general curiosity. Sex instruction during these years consists mainly in giving truthful answers to these questions and in establishing confidence between parent and child. Aside from these questions and answers certain elementary instruction with regard to cleanliness of the sex organs is needed. These questions and this advice on hygiene belong to the home. No school method could be devised for taking over the task from the parents. There is practical agreement that all efforts should be directed toward encouraging the proper education of parents for this instruction.

The chief problem is just at this point. Mothers are not so easy to reach as school children. It is necessary to devise many ways of getting their attention and interest and of giving them the preparation for imparting proper instruction. Several private agencies in the past have done good work along this line. Recently the task has been taken up by the health officials of the States and by the Public Health Service. Pamphlets containing standard information for parents, issued in large quantities by these health agencies, are being widely advertised. Lectures, motion pictures, exhibits, newspaper notices, placards, all carry the publicity to parents. This year the Public Health Service has distributed hundreds of thousands of copies of its pamphlet entitled "The Parents' Part" in response to individual requests from parents.

The libraries have been enlisted in the work by the distribution of an official selected book list for the use of parents. The so-called Library Plan of the Public Health Service adopted by several libraries provides for the issuance of this book list to the addresses of all mothers available on school and library lists on the seventh and fourteenth birthday of their children. This is accompanied with a statement of the need for the instruction of their children, and the fact that the books can be obtained from the public library. It is possible that, later, advisers on this subject will be supplied and teaching clinics developed in connection with libraries.

It is important that all groups and organizations dealing with mothers carry this information to them along with their other work. The cooperation of all health centers, and of all persons in personal contact with parents, is needed to extend this simple, valuable instruction through mothers to children.

Although the home can do much in the later education of the adolescent boy or girl on sex matters, there comes at this period a new method and shift of emphasis. The life of the youth is centered more in the school. Its many activities take most of his time. He turns to his teachers for the answers to his questions about life. At this period also the sex impulse appears to confuse and bewilder him. The problem of instruction becomes more properly a part of the task of the school.

The necessary sex instruction during these years belongs in the curriculum. It is only by running away from the facts concerning human reproduction, sex hygiene, and venereal diseases normally rising in connection with physiology, hygiene, biology, domestic science, and physical education that teachers fail to give the proper information. The problem of putting sex instruction into the high-school curriculum is not one of adding another course or another teacher. It consists in removing deletions in several subjects.

Realizing the need for reorganization of the high-school course to include the sex facts in their proper places, the Bureau of Education and the Public Health Service have for the last year been cooperating in work among high-school teachers. A series of ten conferences of high-school teachers has been held in various eastern states. They will be extended in the course of another year to all parts of the country. In these conferences it has become evident that there is general agreement among teachers and experts that sex instruction should be given and given in connection with the courses mentioned above. It has also become known that such instruction is being given successfully in several high schools.

There are many variations of method and arrangement of such courses. But always the facts with regard to reproduction, the hygiene of sex organs, the venereal diseases, and prostitution are given in their proper and natural setting as a part of all life, of general hygiene, and of communicable diseases. It is not so important to have these matters presented in any one of the three or four suitable courses as it is to have the course giving the instruction compulsory.

The training of teachers is also being taken up by these cooperating governmental agencies. Through the Interdepartmental Social Hygiene Board colleges are being encouraged to train teachers in physical education and other subjects who will have the background and personality for giving the necessary instruction. The Bureau of Education and the Public Health Service, through their joint organization, are trying to centralize information covering experiments in teaching these subjects and are now issuing a series of monographs to thousands of high school teachers, presenting reports of successful experiments. Teachers themselves do not need to be convinced of the need of this sex instruction; they are too close to individual boys and girls. They do need training, however, and they ask for guidance and methods.

The fact that many students are graduating from high schools without this necessary instruction, together with the ignorance of many more who are not in school, constitutes an educational emergency. Fortunately sex instruction can be brought to boys concisely and attractively as a part of a personal physical-fitness program. The Public Health Service, in cooperation with the Bureau of Education, has prepared exhibits, lantern slides, and pamphlets presenting the material arranged in this form. This year in more than thirty States the high school boys of the two upper years are being reached systematically with this material. Several groups are presenting the same material to out-of-school boys. Much work is yet to be done in bringing these facts to the boy who cannot be reached through the normal groupings of school, club, or industry. This instruction to out-of-school adolescents, therefore, as well as to parents, needs for its success the full cooperation of all public and private agencies touching such groups.

The education of a draft army reaching all groups and kinds of young men has given us a new conception for the extension of sex instruction. We have come to see such instruction as the right of every young man and every young woman in America. We have come to set standards. We have come to insist that every parent shall answer his child's questions truthfully and that every growing boy and girl be prepared with the necessary facts, at least, to help in meeting the problems that arise from the existence of the sex impulse in its many manifestations.

EUROPEAN EXPERIENCE

BRITISH ORGANIZATION

By SIR ARTHUR NEWSHOLME, K.C.B., M.D.
Late Principal Medical Officer, Local Government Board, England

In the following pages an attempt is made to summarize the history and present extent of official and organized voluntary work directed to secure the welfare of mothers and their infants. For fuller particulars it will be necessary to consult the reports of medical officers of health of our chief towns during the last thirty years, and the official reports issued by the Medical Departments of the Local Government Board and of the Board of Education.

The subject of child welfare, in its chief developments, cannot be separated from that of public health, of which it forms a constituent part. I do not ignore the fact that child welfare is largely dependent also on the extent to which child labor is exploited, and to which expectant and nursing mothers—as also other mothers—obtain extra-domestic employment, or employment for gain within the home itself, which involves neglect of young children.

Improvement in child welfare has occurred as the sanitary progress of the country has advanced. This is not the time for writing the history of sanitation in England, but its effect—and the effect of the concurrent improvement in social conditions generally—is shown in the fact that whereas in the decade 1871-80, when money began to be spent more freely on elementary sanitary reform, the expectation of life or mean after-lifetime at birth of males was 41.4 years and of females was 44.6 years; in the years 1910-12 these had increased to 51.5 and 55.4 years respectively. The greater part of the saving of life implied in this addition of ten years to the average duration of life was the result of reduced mortality in children under 5 years of age.

The special influence of sanitation may be further illustrated by the statement that in 1871, 12,709 deaths from enteric fever were registered in a population of 22 4/5 millions, while in 1916, in a population of 34½ millions, the deaths from this disease only numbered 1,137.

The first direct steps towards the reduction of infant mortality were probably directed against epidemic or summer diarrhea. Medical officers of health have always been required in their annual reports to summarize the vital statistics of their districts; and since 1905 a more detailed statement of infant mortality during each part of infancy has been required. Annually, therefore, as well as when they received the weekly returns of deaths from the local registrars, there was forced upon their attention the fact that deaths of infants under one year of age formed a high proportion of total deaths at all ages (12.9 per cent in 1917), and that of these infantile deaths a large proportion were caused by diarrhea, the number varying with the temperature and the deficiency of rainfall in the summer months. In 1912, a year of relatively small mortality from diarrhea, it caused 8.1 per cent of all deaths under one year of age.

For many years past it has been customary for medical officers of health to issue warnings as to summer diarrhea, to arrange for the distribution of leaflets of advice concerning this disease, and to urge the necessity of more thorough cleanliness, both municipal and domestic, during the summer months. Even before the early notification of births became obligatory, in many areas the addresses of infants were obtained from the registrars of births and special visits were made to the mothers of infants during the months of June and July and especially to the mothers of those infants known to be artificially fed.

The reports of medical officers of health of many of the large towns from 1890 onward show that much valuable work was being accomplished, and the way was being prepared for more general measures against infant mortality.

The importance of municipal sanitation in the elimination of diarrheal mortality is shown in the experience of many towns, and strikingly by the comparative experience of Leicester and Nottingham. The chief difference between the sanitary condition of the two towns was that in Nottingham in 1909 pail closets still served more than half the houses, while Leicester had abandoned this system entirely, substituting water-closets. Between 1889-93 and 1909 the diarrheal mortality in Leicester had declined 52 per cent; in Nottingham it had declined only 4 per cent.

Diarrhea is not the only disease of infancy which can be greatly diminished by improved public health administration. Tuberculosis and whooping cough and measles figure largely in the infantile death returns. Over 21 per cent of the total deaths in infancy are due to these three diseases and to diarrhea. The amount of syphilis appearing in the death-returns is small; but its actual amount is much greater than this. If pneumonia and bronchitis, which account for 19 per cent of the deaths in infancy be regarded—as they should be—as infective diseases, then it may be said that the problem of saving child life and of securing the correlative improvement in the standard of health of survivors to higher ages, consists very largely in the prevention of infectious, including diarrheal, diseases and acute respiratory diseases.

It follows from this that even if the limited and erroneous view be taken that sanitary authorities are concerned only with the prevention of infectious disease, the reduction of infant mortality is a duty devolving on these authorities, and cannot be effectively carried out failing their cooperation. Voluntary effort must therefore always, in large measure, be directed towards stimulating local authorities to perform their duties.

The influence of diarrheal summer mortality on the progress of child-welfare work is further shown by the fact that among the earliest efforts were those to provide pure cows' milk to infants. In England, official milk depots for this purpose never were numerous; and but little voluntary effort went in this direction. There now remain very few such milk depots, but many local authorities provide milk, more particularly dried milk, to infants for whom it is specially prescribed at infant consultations. Early investigations at Brighton and elsewhere showed that the mortality of infants fed on condensed milk—chiefly of the sweetened variety—was even greater than that of infants fed on fresh cows' milk; and directed attention to the supreme importance of domestic cleanliness in the prevention of summer diarrhea. The milk depots and the concurrent agitation for purer cows' milk served a useful purpose; though it cannot yet be said that the cows' milk ordinarily supplied in England is satisfactorily clean.

It became evident ere long that the broadcast distribution of instructions as to how cows' milk might safely be stored and prepared for infants was liable to be misinterpreted by mothers, as an encouragement to abandon breast-feeding; and there is reason to believe that these instructions did sometimes have this effect. Hence the importance of the work initiated by the late Dr. Sykes at the St. Pancras School for Mothers, which brought into relief the importance of encouraging breast-feeding by every possible means. In towns in which the aided supply of milk was continued, advice as to its use was also initiated; and thus gradually infant consultations—in which the main element was the giving of individual advice and treatment as required—superseded milk depots, and were established in very large numbers where milk depots had never been started. These had educational value as well as medical and hygienic activities; and there need be no dispute as to the relative value of these two aspects of the work of infant consultations (also known as schools for mothers, child-welfare centres, baby weighings, mothers' welcomes, etc.); for whether advice and instruction are given to the individual mother or to mothers collectively—or as is advisable, in both ways—it should be exactly the advice which a physician skilled in the hygiene of infancy as well as in the treatment of infantile complaints would give to his individual patient. In this sense it remains true, as Professor Budin, the distinguished founder of infant consultations, said: "An infant consultation is worth precisely as much as the presiding physician." This is true whether it is possible to arrange for a physician to be present at each meeting of a child-welfare centre; or whether, as has happened during the Great War in England, nurses or health visitors trained under such a physician have given hygienic advice in his absence.

Notification of Births

For many years before the Notification of Births Act was passed, it had been customary, especially in towns, to arrange for inquiry by a sanitary inspector or female visitor into deaths occurring under one year of age, and in many instances for the giving of systematic advice to mothers concerning their infants. More than 20 years ago the Manchester and Salford Sanitary Association had initiated a system of home visitation by volunteer ladies and by women workers paid by the association, who went from house to house, gave elementary sanitary advice, and reported serious defects to the sanitary authority. The city council, at an early stage, showed its appreciation of the importance of this work by giving grants towards the expenditure incurred.

In order to enable early visits to be made, the town council of Salford had begun as early as 1899 a system of voluntary notification of births by midwives.

It should be mentioned at this stage that prior to the period when early notifications of births were obtained, the medical officer of health was dependent for his information on the registration of births, for which an interval of six weeks after birth was permitted before it became compulsory. During this interval a large proportion of the total mortality of infancy had occurred—approximately one-fifth of the total deaths in the first year after birth occur in the first week, and one-third in the first month after birth—and the possibility of successfully influencing the mother to continue breast-feeding had gone. The action of the town of Huddersfield in 1906 in obtaining Parliamentary power to secure the compulsory notification of births within 36 hours of birth, represented a rapid growth of opinion based on experience in that and other towns to the effect that, in the absence of early information of birth, the necessary sanitary precautions and counsel as to personal hygiene could not be given with the greatest prospect of success. This local pioneer work doubtless facilitated the passing of the Notification of Births Act in 1907.

This act was "adoptive," each local authority deciding whether it wished to obtain early information as to births or not. At the middle of 1914, the act had been adopted or put into operation in each metropolitan borough; in 75 out of 80 county boroughs, representing 97.0

per cent of their total population; in 104 out of 243 other boroughs, representing 67.0 per cent of their population; and for 35.7 per cent of the rest of the population of England and Wales.

Much important work followed the notification of births. Home visits to the mother were regarded and continue to be regarded as the most important part of this work; but there also grew up rapidly the present system of Infant Consultations and similar organizations.

As the Notification of Births Acts form the basis of child-welfare work, it is convenient to give here the purport of the Notification of Births (Extension) Act, 1915, which made the enforcement of this act universal, and empowered each local authority administering the act to exercise any powers which a sanitary authority possesses under the Public Health Acts "for the purpose of the care of expectant mothers, nursing mothers, and young children." In drawing the attention of local authorities to the terms of the act the Local Government Board, as earlier in the war, deprecated false economy. They said:

"At a time like the present the urgent need for taking all possible steps to secure the health of mothers and children and to diminish ante-natal and post-natal infant mortality is obvious, and the Board are confident that they can rely upon local authorities making the fullest use of the powers conferred on them."

The Board in the same circular laid stress on "the importance of linking up this work with the other medical and sanitary services provided by local authorities under the Public Health and other Acts."

The act enjoined that the powers of the act should be exercised by a committee which shall include women and may comprise, if it is thought fit, persons who are not members of the authority. The passing of this act has been followed, as will be shown shortly, by an increasingly rapid development of maternity and child-welfare work. For England the Notification of Births Act had only empowered local authorities to undertake such work as is authorized by the Public Health Acts; whereas, in Scotland, more general power had been given to carry out any work necessary for the welfare of young children. The technical doubt as to their legal powers had been an excuse for inaction on the part of some local authorities; and to remove this doubt the Maternity and Child Welfare Act was passed in August, 1918. This act made it obligatory on each council exercising powers under the act to appoint a maternity and child welfare committee, which must include at least two women, and may include persons specially qualified by training or experience in subjects relating to health and maternity who are not members of the council. In the circular letter sent out to local authorities explaining the new act, the Local Government Board reemphasized its previously stated views that child welfare work was second only in importance to direct war work, and was really a "measure of war emergency," and added:

"Although we have enjoined upon local authorities the necessity of the strictest economy in public expenditure, we have urged increased activity in work which has for its object the preservation of infant life and health. We are glad to note that the great majority of local authorities have realized the value of continuing and extending their efforts for child welfare at the present time."

The Course of Child Mortality

It is convenient at this point to give a brief outline of the course of infant mortality in England and Wales and to discuss how far the experienced reduction in this mortality is ascribable to the special work undertaken by voluntary agencies and by official authorities.

The general course of mortality in the first five years of life during a series of years is shown in the following figures: Comparing the period 1911-15 with the period 1871-75, the death rate in infants under one year declined 39 per cent; in the second year of life the death rate declined 41 per cent; in the third year, 50 per cent; in the fourth year, 53 per cent; and in the fifth year, 50 per cent.

No consistent and continuous decline had taken place in infant mortality prior to 1900, although there had already been marked reduction of mortality in each of the next four years of life. This difference corresponds in the main with the fact that greater success had been achieved in the general measures of sanitation and in the reduction of the prevalence of and mortality from such infectious diseases as scarlet fever, diphtheria, and enteric fever, than in respect of the special causes of mortality in infancy. These causes may be placed under three headings: First, infections—acute respiratory diseases, measles, whooping cough, syphilis, tuberculosis, and diarrhea; second, errors of nutrition, due largely to poverty, to mismanagement, and to imperfect provision of facilities for healthy family life; and third, developmental conditions present at the birth of the infant. Under none of these headings had marked success been achieved prior to 1900, though the steady work devoted to the subject of diarrhea had already begun to bear fruit.

The statistics of infant mortality may be stated as follows:

Period	Deaths of Infants Under 1 Year Per 1,000 Births
1896-1900	156
1901-1905	138
1906-1910	117
1911	130
1912	95
1913	108
1914	105
1915	110
1916	91
1917	96
1918	97

HEALTH—EUROPEAN EXPERIENCE

The foregoing are the crude rates, when the infantile death rate is stated by the usual method per 1,000 births during the same year. Owing to the great decline of births during the war, this method overstates the infant mortality in recent years. In a table given in the Registrar General's annual report for 1917, this unusual source of error is corrected. When this is done, and the infantile deaths are stated "per 1,000 of population aged 0-1," the rates for the years 1912-17, inclusive, in successive years become respectively 104, 117, 113, 111, 98, and 94. In other words, there has been a steady and uninterrupted decline in the death rate of infants during the war.

This decline has followed similar declines in preceding years, and it is to be noted that these declines occurred in part during the period when the hygienic work affecting child welfare was confined to general public-health measures, and that the declines anticipated the more direct and active measures adopted by voluntary societies and by local authorities for the prevention of infant mortality. Comparing the five-year periods 1896-1900 and 1901-05, a decrease in the infantile death rate of 12 per cent is seen; comparing 1901-05 with 1906-10 a decline of 15 per cent occurred; comparing 1906-10 with the average experience of the three years 1911-13 infantile mortality declined 5 per cent; comparing these three years with the average experience of the five years 1914-18, during which war conditions prevailed more or less, a reduction of 9 per cent was experienced. The actual reduction during war time is greater than is indicated by these percentages, when allowance is made for the statistical error indicated above. The experience of the year 1911 illustrates one of the chief sources of error in forming conclusions on the experience of a single year. In this year the summer was excessively hot, and summer diarrhea prevailed to an exceptional extent. The illustration is important, as serving to remind us of the limitations of the value of statistical tests and of the fact that increase of good work tending to improve child life may be associated temporarily with increase of total infant mortality.

School Medical Inspection

In the development of child-welfare work in England important place must be given to the system of medical inspection of school children initiated in 1907. The numerous physical defects found in school children have led to the beginning of measures for remedial action, confined in some areas (in addition to advice given to consult private doctors or to resort to hospitals) to measures for securing greater cleanliness and the treatment of minor skin diseases; but extending in other areas to such measures as the remedial treatment of adenoids, the cure of ringworm, the correction of errors of refraction, and the provision of dental treatment. Perhaps the chief value of the system of medical inspection of school children has been the fact that it has demonstrated the extent to which children, when they first come to school, are already suffering from physical disease which might have been prevented or minimized by attention in the preschool period. The information thus accumulated has had much influence in encouraging the institution of infant consultations, with a view to the early discovery of disease or of tendency to disease.

Statistical Studies

The intensive study of our national and of local vital statistics has also had a most important bearing on the further development of maternity and child-welfare work. In successive official reports it has been shown that infant mortality varies greatly in different parts of the country, irrespective of climatic conditions; that it varies greatly in different parts of the same town, in accordance with variations in respect of industrial and housing conditions, of local sanitation, of poverty, and of alcoholism; that the variations extend to different portions of infant life, the death-rate in infants under a week, or under a month in age, for instance, being two or three times as high in some areas as in others; and that the distribution of special diseases in infancy similarly varies greatly. Intensive studies of infant mortality on these and other lines have pointed plainly the direction in which preventive work is especially called for, and have incidentally demonstrated the fundamental value of accurate statistics of births and of deaths in the child welfare campaign. Surveys of local conditions, both statistical and based on actual local observations form an indispensable preliminary to and concomitant of good child-welfare work, and it is such work which has rendered possible the improvement of recent years. To act helpfully we must know thoroughly the summation of conditions which form the evil to be attacked.

One important result of investigations such as those already mentioned has been to bring more clearly into relief the fact—in the past partially neglected—that child-welfare work can only succeed in so far as the welfare of the mother is also maintained. This may imply extensions of work in which serious economic considerations are involved; but apart from such possibilities and apart from questions of housing, and of provision of additional domestic facilities for assisting the overworked mother, there is ample evidence that medical and hygienic measures by themselves can do much to relieve the excessive strain on the mother which childbearing under present conditions often involves.

The Course of Mortality from Childbearing

The general course of mortality from childbearing (including deaths ascribable to pregnancy) in England and Wales is shown in the following table:

Average Annual Death Rates Per 100,000 Births From

Period	Puerperal Septic Diseases	Other Diseases of Pregnancy and Childbirth
5 years, 1902-06	185	228
5 years, 1907-11	152	215
3 years, 1912-14	148	233
2 years, 1915-16	151	239

It will be noted that although there has been a marked decline of deaths from puerperal sepsis, the death rate from other complications of childbearing has not declined. The decline in puerperal sepsis is general throughout the country, and evidences of greater care in midwifery both on the part of doctors and of midwives. The administration of the Midwives Act 1902, has doubtless done much to secure this. The death rate from conditions other than puerperal fever continues to differ greatly throughout the country. It is highest in Welsh counties, Westmoreland, Lancashire, and Cheshire coming next in order of unfavorable portion; in many industrial, including textile, towns it is also excessive. The general conclusion reached by the writer in an elaborate official report on the subject is that "the quality and availability of skilled assistance before, during, and after childbirth are probably the most important factors in determining the remarkable and serious differences in respect of mortality from childbearing shown in the report. The differences are caused in the main by differences in availability of skilled assistance when needed in pregnancy, and at and after childbirth."

The Midwives Act, 1902

This act forbade any woman after April 1st, 1905, who was not certified under the act, from using the title of midwife or any similar description of herself. It forbade after April 1st, 1910, any such woman from "habitually and for gain attending women in childbirth, except under the direction of a qualified medical practitioner"; and it forbade any certified midwife to use an uncertified person as her substitute. The act defined the limits of function of the midwife by stating that it did not confer upon her any title to give certificates of death or of stillbirth, or to take charge of any abnormality or disease in connection with parturition.

The act set up the Central Midwives Board, giving it special disciplinary powers over midwives. It also imposed on county councils and the councils of county boroughs the duty of supervising the work of midwives. For further details the act itself and the rules of the Central Midwives Board made under the act should be consulted.

The Midwives Act, 1918, gave further powers to the Central Midwives Board and to local supervising authorities, and made it the duty of the latter to pay the fee of a doctor called in by a midwife in any of the emergencies for which rules are made by the Central Midwives Board. The fee paid is to be in accordance with a scale prescribed by the Local Government Board.

As at least three-fourths of the total births in England and Wales are attended by midwives with or without the assistance of doctors, their work is of great importance in relation to the reduction of maternal disablement and mortality and to the prevention of early infant mortality, and it is of happy augury that they are being enlisted more and more in official work for safeguarding the health of the mother and of her unborn or recently delivered infant. An important recent addition has been made to the rules of the Central Midwives Board, which makes it obligatory on the midwife to notify the medical officer of health of any instance, while the patient is under her charge, in which for any reason breast feeding has been discontinued.

Largely through the machinery provided by the Midwives Act and the Notification of Births Act a system of supervision of maternity and child welfare has been organized in every county and county borough, which has been responsible for a large share of the improvement experienced in recent years. The character and extent of development of the work varies greatly in different centres; and as a rule the work is more fully developed in county boroughs than in counties. In county districts it has been found possible and often desirable to unite the offices of assistant inspector of midwives, infant visitor, and tuberculosis visitor in one adequately trained health visitor, thus saving time in travelling, by enabling the visitor to have a smaller district allotted to her than if she undertook only one branch of work. In some counties the school nurse's work is also undertaken by the health visitor. In some country areas arrangements have been made for infant visiting to be carried out by district nurses who are also midwives.

Much of the success so far achieved in improving the health conditions of infancy and childhood has been secured by cooperation between voluntary and official health visitors. Excellent work has been done by local and other societies, particularly during the last ten years, in educating public opinion and in direct assistance to mothers and their infants. It is essential that such voluntary work should have a nucleus of highly trained and well-paid workers; but given this condition, a large amount of good work can be accomplished by voluntary aid.

The main work has been that of health visiting. The details of this work, the conditions of qualification of workers, the number of visits which it is desirable to make, and the character of the advice intended to be given at these visits, are set out in an official memorandum of the Medical Officer of the Local Government Board, and it is unnecessary to repeat this information in these pages.

A similar remark applies to the next most important development of work, the institution of maternity and child-welfare centres. The conditions of work of these institutions are set out in the same document.

The following additional facts are taken from my annual report to the Local Government Board for 1917-18 and will serve to supplement the information already given.

Up to the end of 1917, 542 centres for maternity and infant welfare work had been established by local authorities, and 551 by voluntary societies. At the end of June, 1918, the numbers were 700 and 578, respectively.

On June 1st, 1918, there were 751 whole-time health visitors, 760 part-time health visitors, and 1,044 district nurses, engaged by local authorities in maternal and child welfare work, in addition to 320 health visitors in the employment of voluntary societies. The district nurses employed as health visitors are almost entirely engaged under county schemes. An increasing number of voluntary societies suffer from deficiency of funds, and in many instances help has been given to them by local authorities, either financial or in the form of staff. The Board repay half the approved expenditure for assistance granted in this way.

It is important that the same persons should act as health visitors and as inspectors under the Children Act, 1908, and advice to this effect has been given to boards of guardians and sanitary authorities.

In many areas the work of inspection of midwives continues to be relatively unsatisfactory. This is the more regrettable as in some of the most populous counties and urban districts half or more than half of the midwives are bona fide practitioners, having been placed on the roll because they were practising before 1901. The best inspector of midwives is a medical practitioner, but under present circumstances this is seldom practicable. The appointment of the superintendent of the county nursing association to act under the control of the county medical officer has proved satisfactory when she is qualified and experienced. This arrangement is economical of traveling expenses and time, as she can also supervise district nurse midwives, the number of which, who are also acting as health visitors, is 1,044 at present.

Very satisfactory progress has been made during the year in the provision of midwives in districts in which there were none or the number was insufficient. The urgency of this provision has increased, owing to the demands on the time of medical practitioners, many of whom cannot afford time to attend normal confinements. This provision has usually been made by county councils working through the medium of county nursing associations.

The provision of additional trained midwives is a pressing problem. The increased cost of living, longer training required, and the rapid development of less laborious and more lucrative occupations, have made it difficult to secure women to train as midwives, or to continue to practise in this capacity after qualification. In many industrial areas the older bona fide midwife is preferred, although it is the almost universal experience that the trained midwife more quickly detects conditions endangering the life of the mother or infant, and sends for medical help. In order to encourage further the supply of practising midwives, the Board are allowing to rank for grant increased remuneration given to midwives newly appointed by local authorities, sufficient to recoup them in the course of a few years' service for the cost of their training. The Board have also allowed the cost of providing outfits for midwives subsidized by local authorities to rank for grant.

It remains the fact that at a recent date, of some 30,543 trained midwives on the Roll, only 6,754 were returned as being in actual practise as such.

In order to make midwives available for all women needing them, the Board repay to local authorities and voluntary associations half the cost of the provision of a midwife for necessitous women. In various forms a woman may receive considerable assistance in her confinement; for in addition to the above—

(1) If she is the wife of an insured person, or if she herself is insured, she received under the conditions of the National (Health) Insurance Act 30s. in cash, or if she is insured and the wife of an insured person, 60s. in cash.

(2) If she is the wife of a soldier or sailor and not entitled to maternity benefit she receives from 10s. per week up to £2 from the Local Pensions Committee.

(3) If she is a munition worker she may be aided under a scheme provided under the Ministry of Munitions.

(4) She also may obtain priority for the supply of milk, or obtain free milk, or milk at cost price under the Board's Food Control Order, No. 1, 1918, empowering local authorities to supply milk and food and an extra ration under the Food Controller's Order. In addition, after confinement she has available the ration apportioned to the infant and its allowance of milk under the priority scheme.

There is evidently need for simplification and unification of effort in the above cases.

In many instances maternity nursing is required. The midwife may have too many patients to be able to give this during the ten days in which she is in charge of the patient; and even when she carries out her duty in this respect in accordance with the rules of the Central Midwives Board, additional help is required in the feeding and care of the mother and infant and in the care of the household. Often nursing is also required for both mother and infant for a considerable period beyond the ten days. For these reasons the Board are now prepared to give grants for maternity nursing and for "home helps."

Even when all the above requirements are or can be fulfilled, there remain a large number of cases of pregnant and parturient women, and especially of unmarried women, who cannot be satisfactorily confined at home, either because of social or sanitary circumstances, or because abnormal or complicated childbirth is expected. For such cases hospital provision is needed. This is one of the most urgent requirements of the present time. Most local authorities have not yet appreciated the great need for institutional provision for complicated midwifery and for a certain number of normal cases, though some are already taking steps to meet it. Other local authorities have been deterred by the doubtful position of the law as to their powers to provide institutions for normal midwifery. This doubt is now removed.

Present provision, as I pointed out in my last annual report, is much more adequate in the metropolis than in the rest of the country; and I connected with this fact the exceptionally low mortality in childbearing in London due to causes other than puerperal sepsis.

Under present conditions, institutional lying-in provision is chiefly voluntary in character; and the Board are advising local authorities to contract for its use, rather than wait for the erection of special hospitals. In other instances houses are being taken and adapted as maternity homes.

For some years hospital provision for complicated midwifery has been made by the local sanitary authority in Birmingham, St. Helens, and Bradford; and at the present time similar provision is being arranged at Batley, Bournemouth, Burnley, Blackpool, Croydon, Dudley, Hull, Leeds, Nottingham, Rochdale, Smethwick, Southend-on-Sea, Stockton-on-Tees, Swindon, York, and other towns. In nearly all these instances it is proposed to utilize existing hospitals or to convert existing premises into hospitals.

Official assistance for the provision of medical assistance has been greatly developed during 1917, many county councils and county and metropolitan boroughs having made arrangements for this purpose. The Board have expressed their willingness to approve a scale of fees recommended by the British Medical Association in 1915. It is hoped that ere long the payment of such fees to medical practitioners called in by midwives will be made obligatory on local authorities.

The progress made in the organization of antenatal work is slow for reasons which are fairly obvious. There is difficulty in securing assistance from doctors and midwives, and medical practitioners have no time for the work at the centres. There is the well-known difficulty as to notification of pregnancy, which the Board have not encouraged, except when the definite consent of the mother has been previously obtained. The facilities for help provided at the centre have in some areas succeeded in attracting patients; and health visitors and midwives have done much in other areas to persuade mothers of the advisability of safeguarding themselves against possible complications, as well as of securing adequate preparation for the lying-in period.

This subject is closely associated with that of abortions, stillbirths, and deaths in the first two weeks after birth. One of the most promising methods for securing the sound development of antenatal work consists in the investigation of stillbirths and early infant mortality. At these inquiries mothers can be induced to obtain medical advice not only at the time, but also in the event of a subsequent pregnancy. The investigation at the patient's home of all such cases and assistance in prevention of recurrence of unnecessary antenatal, natal, and early postnatal deaths have as great an importance as the building up of a successful antenatal clinic. The anti-syphilis work now being carried on will help greatly in this direction.

There has been a large extension of dental assistance at centres, for expectant and for nursing mothers, and for children, especially in the metropolis and its vicinity. The Board has lately extended its grant to cover dentures for mothers who are nursing or pregnant, if the medical officer of the centre is satisfied that the woman's health will be materially improved by the denture, and that she is unable to provide it for herself.

The increased calling up of doctors for the Army and Navy has caused increasing difficulty in obtaining medical advice at maternity and infant welfare centres, and without this the utility and popularity of the centre must necessarily suffer. The assistance of judicious voluntary workers, the promotion of social clubs, the development of self-constituted and self-regulated clubs or guilds, with a social propaganda for the improvement of themselves and their fellow workers, friends, and neighbors, in some instances are having marked effect. It is noteworthy that at many centres the poorest women and those for whom help is most needed are those least often in attendance, and these women are also the most skilled in avoiding visits of health visitors. The formation of guilds and institutes will do much to increase the scope of present work.

Creches and day nurseries may be expected to exercise influence in educating mothers in the care of their children. For this purpose it is very desirable to have the creche attached to or near an infant welfare centre. The Local Government Board, as well as the Ministry of Munitions, are empowered to assist creches by grants.

These creches, unless managed with the most rigid standard of medical and general cleanliness, are very apt to spread infectious diseases; not merely such diseases as whooping cough, measles, and chicken pox, but also catarrhal and diarrheal diseases. In the prevention of all of these the enforcement of the strictest cleanliness is essential, especially during the summer months for the last named diseases. For the prevention of catarrhal infections, it is essential that the creche should be conducted, so far as practicable, on strict open-air lines. Open-air creches give admirable occasional relief to mothers, even when these do not go out to work. The "toddler's playground" is a blessing to all concerned, but the indoor creche may be, and often is, mischievous. The risks are greatly reduced by insisting on open-air conditions and by not allowing large groups of children to come together. Smaller groups mean greatly decreased possibility of cross-infection.

At infant welfare centres infants are not infrequently seen who fail to make progress while living at home, and who yet are not ill enough to be sent to a hospital. This especially applies to cases of defective nutrition. For these cases beds in connection with centres have been found to be necessary for observation purposes and to initiate further treatment. In some instances, especially for failure of breast feeding, it is advisable to admit the mother with the infant. During the year, representatives of the chief children's hospitals in London, of general hospitals having children's departments, and of infant welfare centres, conferred with the officers of the Board, and it was generally agreed that there was need for further accommodation in hospital beds as indicated above. There is no doubt that after the war such accommodation will be provided to a greater extent in the larger hospitals; meanwhile, both in London and the provinces, such beds are now being provided almost entirely at voluntary centres. The Board have drawn up the following rules for the guidance of those providing such beds:

1. Acute cases of illness, such as would ordinarily be admitted to existing hospitals, and cases of infectious disease should not be treated in cots at a centre. The centre should, if practicable, be associated with a general hospital or a children's hospital, with a view to prompt admission of acute or serious cases of illness.

2. The experiment of providing cots at centres should be on a small scale, with not more than two wards with four cots in each, and the fittings and furniture should be as simple and inexpensive as possible.

3. A whole-time nurse should be in charge by day and one by night, and the nursing staff should, as a rule, be distinct from the staff engaged in the ordinary work of the centre.

4. If a medical officer is not resident on the premises, there should be arrangements for securing his prompt attendance when required. The Board would welcome arrangements of the treatment of mothers, with their infants, when breast feeding fails.

Nursing

An increasing number of local authorities are now providing or arranging to provide nurses at the patient's home for cases of measles, whooping cough, ophthalmia neonatorum, and acute diarrhea in children under five years of age; also for women after confinement, and for cases of puerperal fever, especially where hospital accommodation is unavailable.

New Work

The Board have recently been authorized to assist by grants new work comprised under the following headings:

Hospital treatment for children up to five years of age;
Lying-in homes;
Home helps;
Creches and day nurseries.

Also,

For the provision of food for expectant and nursing mothers and for children under five years of age;

For convalescent homes for nursing mothers and for children under five years of age;

For homes for children of widowed and deserted mothers and for illegitimate children; and

For experimental work for the health of expectant and nursing mothers and for children under five years of age.

Government Aid for Child Welfare Work

A beginning in grants for child welfare work was made by the Board of Education for the establishment of schools for mothers and similar institutions in which collective instruction to mothers was given and some degree of regularity of attendance of the mothers was secured.

On July 30th, 1914, the Local Government Board sent a circular letter and covering memorandum by their Medical Officer which may be claimed to have initiated maternity and child welfare work on a larger scale, more generally distributed throughout the country, and more completely covering the whole sphere of medical and hygienic work for this purpose than had previously been envisaged. Although the country at that time might be said to be already under the shadow of war, these documents had been previously prepared, and their appearance four days before the declaration of war was a coincidence. The chief burden of the additional work to which local authorities were urged was that there should be continuity in dealing with the whole period from before birth until the time when the child is entered upon a school register; and the memorandum contemplated that "medical advice and, where necessary, treatment should be continuously and systematically available for expectant mothers and for children till they are entered on a school register, and that arrangements should be made for home visitation throughout this period."

It was added that "the work of home visitation is one to which the Board attach very great importance and in promoting schemes laid down in the accompanying memorandum the first step should be the appointment of an adequate staff of health visitors."

The memorandum was as follows:

Maternity and Child Welfare

A complete scheme would comprise the following elements, each of which will, in this connection, be organized in its direct bearing on infantile health.

1. Arrangements for the local supervision of midwives.
2. Arrangements for:

    ANTENATAL
    - (1) An antenatal clinic for expectant mothers.
    - (2) The home visiting of expectant mothers.
    - (3) A maternity hospital or beds at a hospital, in which complicated cases of pregnancy can receive treatment.

3. Arrangements for:

    NATAL
    - (1) Such assistance as may be needed to ensure the mother having skilled and prompt attendance during confinement at home.
    - (2) The confinement of sick women, including women having contracted pelvis or suffering from any other condition involving danger to the mother or infant, at a hospital.

4. Arrangements for:

    POSTNATAL
    - (1) The treatment in a hospital of complications arising after parturition, whether in the mother or in the infant.
    - (2) The provision of systematic advice and treatment for infants at a baby clinic or infant dispensary.
    - (3) The continuance of these clinics and dispensaries, so as to be available for children up to the age when they are entered on a school register, i. e., the register of a public elementary school, nursery school, creche, day nursery, school for mothers, or other school.
    - (4) The systematic home visitation of infants and of children not on a school register as above defined.

Grants were promised to local authorities or to voluntary agencies for work done under the scheme set out amounting to one-half of the total approved expenditure. About the same time a circular was sent out by the Board of Education promising similar grants for schools for mothers. The grants to voluntary agencies were made conditional on the work being coordinated so far as practicable with the public health work of the local sanitary authority and the school medical service of the local education authority.

The increased work since that date may be gathered from the following table, which shows the increase each year in the grants given on the 50 per cent basis by the Local Government Board and the Board of Education.

AMOUNT OF GRANTS IN EACH FINANCIAL YEAR TO LOCAL AUTHORITIES AND VOLUNTARY AGENCIES, ON THE BASIS OF 50 PER CENT OF TOTAL APPROVED LOCAL EXPENDITURE

Financial Year	Grants of Local Government Board (Pounds Sterling)	Grants of Board of Education (Pounds Sterling)
1914-15	11,488	10,830
1915-16	41,466	15,334
1916-17	67,961	19,023
1917-18	122,285	24,110
1918-19 (estimated)	209,000	44,000

These grants do not cover the entire scope of child-welfare work carried out throughout the country, and their amount must not be taken as a complete indication of the extent of this work.

The increase during the war period has been very great, and this can be attributed to the desire to do everything practicable for mothers and children, especially for those belonging to soldiers and sailors who were risking their lives for the country; and to the increased realization of the importance of preserving and improving our chief national asset, which consists in a healthy population. During this period there was a great increase in the industrial employment of women, including married women, in factories, including munitions and other works. This increase it is believed amounted to a million and a half workers. The Ministry of Munitions took an active part in arranging for welfare work in the establishments for which it was responsible; and this work included, in some instances, special care for pregnant women and for nursing mothers.

Notwithstanding the many adverse influences, to which must be added great overcrowding in many industrial areas, especially those in which new industries were hurriedly started, and the increasing cost of food and especially of milk with a scarcity of supply, it has been seen that infant mortality remained low and on the whole declined during the entire period of the war.

To what circumstances can this be ascribed?

It is unnecessary to assume that this result was entirely due to the active measures favorable to maternity and child welfare which were taken, on an unexampled scale, though these measures can claim an important share in the result.

A number of contributory factors were at work:

(1) In none of the years in question did the summer weather favor an excess of diarrheal mortality. When this factor, however, is eliminated the infant mortality was lower each year than in previous years.

(2) Although so many husbands were away from home, in a large proportion of cases the wife, in virtue of her separation

allowance, was financially in a more favorable position than when she was dependent on her husband's wage or such portion of it as he allowed her for the support of the household.

(3) In addition, every soldier became an insured person, and his wife was therefore entitled to the maternity benefit of 30 shillings on the birth of a child, and an additional 30 shillings if she was herself an employed person.

(4) There can be no reasonable doubt that the restrictions on the consumption of alcoholic drinks and the limitations of hours for opening public houses constituted a factor in improving domestic welfare.

But, attaching full value to these and other similar factors which undoubtedly were at work, chief place must, I think, be given to the awakening of the public conscience on the subject, and to the concentration on the mother and her child which had been urged in season and out of season, and which now became a fact. An indication of the public mind is given by the advice issued by the Local Government Board in August, 1918, which is quoted on page 274.

The special measures carried out during the war for which the grants are payable to local authorities or local voluntary agencies to the extent of half the total approved expenditure are enumerated in the following extract from the regulations issued by the Local Government Board in August, 1918.

Regulations under which grants not exceeding one-half of approved net expenditure will be payable by the Local Government Board to local authorities and to voluntary agencies in respect of arrangements for attending to the health of expectant mothers and nursing mothers and of children under five years of age.

1. The Local Government Board will pay grants during each financial year, commencing on April 1st, in respect to the following services:

(1) The salaries and expenses of inspectors of midwives.

(2) The salaries and expenses of health visitors and nurses engaged in maternity and child welfare work.

(3) The provision of a midwife for necessitous women in confinement and for areas which are insufficienctly supplied with this service.

(4) The provision, for necessitous women, of a doctor for illness connected with pregnancy and for aid during the period of confinement for mother and child.

(5) The expenses of a centre, i. e., an institution providing any or all of the following activities: Medical supervision and advice for expectant and nursing mothers, and for children under five years of age, and medical treatment at the centre for cases needing it.

(6) Arrangements for instruction in the general hygiene of maternity and childhood.

(7) Hospital treatment provided or contracted for by local authorities for complicated cases of confinement or complications arising after parturition, or for cases in which a woman to be confined suffers from illness

or deformity, or for cases of women who, in the opinion of the medical officer of health, cannot with safety be confined in their homes, or such other provision for securing proper conditions for the confinement of necessitous women as may be approved by the medical officer of health.

(8) Hospital treatment provided or contracted for by local authorities for children under five years of age found to need in-patient treatment.

(9) The cost of food provided for expectant mothers and nursing mothers and for children under five years of age, where such provision is certified by the medical officer of the centre or by the medical officer of health to be necessary and where the case is necessitous.

(10) Expenses of creches and day nurseries and of other arrangements for attending to the health of children under five years of age whose mothers go out to work.

(11) The provision of accommodation in convalescent homes for nursing mothers and for children under five years of age.

(12) The provision of homes and other arrangements for attending to the health of children of widowed, deserted, and unmarried mothers, under five years of age.

(13) Experimental work for the health of expectant and nursing mothers and of infants and children under five years of age carried out by local authorities or voluntary agencies with the approval of the Board.

(14) Contributions by the local authority to voluntary institutions and agencies approved under the scheme.

2. Grants will be paid to voluntary agencies aided by the Board on condition:

(1) That the work of the agency is approved by the Board and coordinated as far as practicable with the public health work of the local authority and the school medical service of the local education authority.

(2) That the premises and work of the institution are subject to inspection by any of the Board's officers of inspection.

(3) That records of the work done by the agency are kept to the satisfaction of the Board.

3. An application for a grant must be made on a form supplied by the Board.

4. The Board may exclude any items of expenditure which in their opinion should be deducted for the purpose of assessing the grant, and if any question arises as to the interpretation of these regulations the decision of the Board shall be final.

5. The grant paid in each financial year will be assessed on the basis of the expenditure incurred on the service referred to in Article I in the preceding financial year, and will be, as a rule, at the rate of one-half of that expenditure where the services have been provided with the Board's approval and are carried on to their satisfaction. The Board may, at their discretion, reduce or withhold the grant.

These regulations widen the provisions made for the giving of grants for maternity and child-welfare work which have been in operation since July, 1914, the chief additional services for which the grant was made available being:

Hospital treatment for children up to five years of age.
Lying-in homes.
Home helps.

The provision of food for expectant and nursing mothers and for children under five years of age.

Creches and day nurseries.

Convalescent homes.

Homes for children of widowed and deserted mothers and for illegitimate children.

Experimental work for the health of expectant and nursing mothers and of infants and children under five years of age.

The circular published by the Local Government Board on August 9th, 1918 (M. & C. W. 4), should be consulted for fuller details.

The Board of Education has during the war encouraged the further teaching of mothercraft to girls over twelve years of age in elementary schools, as well as the establishment of day nurseries or creches for which grants were payable as for institutions subsidized by the Local Government Board.

The provision of milk for infants and young children became more difficult during the war, and a priority scheme was eventually put forward which gave priority to expectant and nursing mothers and to children under five. The order made in February, 1918, under the Defence of the Realm Act, enabled any local authority to arrange for the supply of food and milk for expectant mothers and nursing mothers and of milk for children under five years of age, and required them to provide such a supply when instructed to do so by the Local Government Board. In necessitous cases on the certificate of a medical officer the provision of food or milk free or below cost price was authorized. These provisions were utilized to a considerable extent; but there was no evidence of widespread suffering of infants or of their mothers through lack of milk or other food. In a large number of instances dried milk was utilized to supplement local deficiencies of supply, and the Ministry of Food made itself responsible for the distribution of a large quantity of full cream dried milk. A considerable number of authorities supplied free dinners for expectant and nursing mothers; but as the war progressed the additional earnings of the main mass of the population diminished the need for these. The need was still further diminished by the separation allowances for each soldier's or sailor's wife. Thus a wife with four children drew in October, 1914, 22 shillings a week; in March, 1915, this was raised to 25 shillings; in January, 1917, to 31 shillings, and in October, 1918, to 35 shillings a week.

BELGIAN ORGANIZATION

By DR. RENE SAND
University of Brussels, Belgium

You may be a little puzzled to see a medical man who a few months ago was at a hospital in the front, stand before you and attempt to speak upon child welfare, but it is perhaps not as preposterous as it seems at first sight.

It is quite true that I was in a big hospital at the Belgian front a few months ago, but near that hospital was a civilian population of about 10,000 people. The military authorities had wanted them to go because we were only eight miles from the German trenches, but they refused to go. The civilian authorities had also wanted them to go, and probably the Germans wanted them to go also—at least they bombarded them, which was equal to manifesting their desire—but the people did not want to go. And so as there were mothers among them, and as babies were born, the military hospital started a maternity and babies' clinic. We considered it quite an unusual thing to do, but war has done away with many prejudices.

Well, then, it has been shown what a good teacher is adversity. When the Belgian government had to leave the country the need for some unofficial organization was felt. So a few business men and political men of high standing came together and formed a national committee. This committee had no judges, no police, and no army to enforce its decisions. Nevertheless they were obeyed as the decisions of any regular government had never been. This committee had to care for every need which could be helped, and had of course at first to distribute the food and supplies which you so generously sent to us. But it started a benefit relief organization, and in doing so it developed a plan of which every government could have been proud. It included many things.

First of all there were so many unemployed in Belgium. Almost everyone was unemployed because to have worked would have been to work for the Germans. So the national committee decided that courses would be open not only for general education but also for vocational training of all unemployed, but that they could not enforce because the Germans flatly opposed it. The Germans did not want us to emerge from the war more or less prepared.

So they started another scheme, a medical scheme. Of course a great majority of the population was more or less ruined—it is now almost completely; and they could no more pay for their doctors or for their medicines. So the national committee decided that every citizen with a limited income would be entitled to free medical service. Specialists and maternity and hospital care were provided in the same way, and for the first time a national medical service was instituted. Everyone had a right to choose his own doctor, and the doctor was paid at the per capita rate by the national commission.

The national committee started also a war-orphan scheme and a crippled-soldier scheme, and finally a child-welfare scheme.

We had before the war a child-welfare league in Belgium. It was under the presidency of our Queen whom you are always sure to find wherever there is a need to placate or a sufferer to help. But the activity of that league was like a drop in the cup of infantile mortality. Now, war breaks out. The future of the race is imperilled. The necessity of caring for the children becomes evident, and there springs up a child-welfare organization which almost at once reaches the tiniest villages in the country. Before the war we had only 60 babies' clinics in Belgium. There are now more than 700, and they have distributed over one billion gallons of milk—mostly your milk.

In 1914 two cities only had dinners for mothers; there are now 600 municipalities which have followed this example. The result came very quickly. Infantile mortality, instead of increasing, decreased in Belgium during the war.

We have not been and we could not be as happy in our results with the older children. Very precise figures have been communicated to the Belgian Academy of Medicine, and they show that the average Belgian child is, on account of the war, one full year behind his normal development. The average Brussels schoolboy has lost three pounds in four years, and the average Brussels school girl seven pounds, and this applies to almost all classes of the population.

However, many means were employed in order that this evil should not be greater. Every day two ounces of special bread made with the best available wheat was distributed to every school child, and this bread which was baked in individual lumps was such a treat compared to war bread that it became very soon known as school cakes. One million two hundred thousand of such cakes were distributed daily in the whole of Belgium, together with cocoa or milk. Those lunches had to be taken in the schools under the supervision of the teachers, because experience showed that many children were so self-sacrificing that they took the cakes home in order to share them with older brothers and sisters who were not entitled to receive them. Special dinners were provided for anemic children, and day camps and colonies were started for them. The children remained there for three weeks, and under the influence of fresh air and good diet they generally gained four pounds and sometimes as much as ten or twelve pounds in that very short time.

Besides this official work, girls and women organized through the whole of Belgium dinners and luncheons for the children between the ages of 3 and 18. Those girls and mothers were quickly known under the charming name of "Little Bees."

Now, all those activities, which are really due to the war, will be maintained and developed. A bill has been passed through the Belgian Parliament in order to create a national children's bureau, which will take care of the whole work of child welfare in Belgium. It will be a semi-official organization. It will work under the patronage and supervision of the State, but it will be free from too much red tape and from political intervention. It will have to see to it that in every city, in every village, there will be organized at least one babies' clinic under the care of a local committee, to which will also be entrusted the care of the babies and of the children boarded out by their parents and guardians. Besides this compulsory work the national children's bureau will have also to provide for every kind of volunteer work.

This organization cannot stand quite alone. We cannot in the hygiene, or in any social work, maintain a policy of enclosed fields. Child welfare has to go hand in hand with mothers' welfare and fathers' welfare and everybody's welfare. This we must yet plan and develop. We have yet no program for that work, but we have a slogan, and the slogan has been given to us this afternoon by Miss Lathrop. She said "cooperation and education." It sounds quite American, does it not? It is given under your guidance, and I feel certain it will lead us to success.

A PHYSICAL CLASSIFICATION OF CHILDREN

By PROFESSOR FABIO FRASSETTO, D. S., M. D.

Director, Anthropological Institute, University of Bologna, Italy

The preservation of the child in perfect health and in equilibrium with the natural and social environment during its growth is the supreme purpose toward which should be directed all the efforts of child-welfare workers.

The essential requirement for perfect health is perfect balance of functions (whether direct or primary balance depending on perfect proportion among the organs and the parts of the body, or secondary or indirect balance, depending on the mutual reaction by which those functions may be compensated for a longer or shorter period for modifications in related functions). But this ideal condition of equilibrium is rarely found in the human body. Most of the individuals present an unstable lack of proportion in the development of their organs, resulting in disturbances of functions, permanent, continuous, or temporary, which disturbances are the first step toward disease.

The lack of proportion among the organs which is called in medical language predisposition has its natural origin in that combination of organic and functional characteristics termed in medical language constitution. The less the functions, in their anomalies, are susceptible to disturbances, the smaller is the predisposition and the greater the resistance of the body to disease; and, vice versa, the more the functions are susceptible to disturbances, the greater is the predisposition and the lower the resistance of the body. In the first case it is said that the constitution is strong; in the second case that it is weak; and these adjectives strong and weak do not refer to muscular force, as it is generally thought, but to the harmony among the organs and to equilibrium among the functions. It is necessary to clarify these conceptions of predisposition and constitution because of the uncertainty in regard to this matter prevailing even among medical men. To this should also be added that a good or bad constitution of an organ or of a body is the main foundation for its health or its illness.

Our next step will be the discussion of the methods to follow in the study of the constitution. According to the brilliant anatomical investigations by Morgagni in Italy, continued by Theophile Borden and Bishât in France, the conception of constitution was based on anatomy, while at present its bases are considered anatomy and physiology combined; that is, morphology. The study of constitutions on the basis of morphology was first introduced by De Giovanni in Italy, whose writings on the subject were first published about 1880, and who founded the School of Italian Clinical Morphology. This school has shown very clearly on the basis of the biological law of correlations of development that the exterior constitution of the body reflects its inner constitution; and that any defect in the morphology of the body, whether external or internal, will result in a functional defect; the school has also shown that the degree of this defect represents the degree of the predisposition to disease.[1]

Let us see now what kinds of constitutions there are in existence. Even a very superficial and hasty examination allows us to distinguish in the apparent kaleidoscope of varieties of size and form two types of constitutions, well defined, with distinct contrasting characteristics, the heavy physique and the slender constitution present in all times and among all races, as illustrated by the accompanying plates.[2]

If we examine carefully these two extreme types shown in figures 1 and 2, Plate I, we can easily see that they are in complete contrast to each other, not only anthropometrically, but also functionally and pathologically, since, as we stated previously, there usually exists a constant relation between the external morphology of the individual and his internal visceral organs and between the condition of these latter and disease.

The principal anthropological, physiological, and pathological characteristics of these two types are listed below:

I. HEAVY PHYSIQUE (with predisposition to apoplexy)[3]

Habitus apoplecticus (macrosplanchnia)

A. Principal Anthropological Characteristics

1. Body (soma). Larger than normal (macrosomia).
2. Morphological type. Brevilinear (brachymorphous) with the proportion of the parts of the body like those of an infant.

---

[1]Achille De Giovanni, for instance, has shown that when the handle of the breast-bone is considerably too long in proportion to the body, it is accompanied by congenital atrophy of the left ventricle and of the aorta. Giacinto Viola has shown by clinical experiments and anatomical observations that a considerably insufficient development of the whole medullary system and a very great shortening of that system after its removal from the vertebral canal are always accompanied by considerable nervous sufferings in the spinal region, and the stretch of the arms is in such cases shorter than the length of the body. Dr. Messedaglia has shown a direct relation between the external size of the abdomen and the development of the liver, the stomach, and the intestine. The localization of Pott's disease is confined to those places where there is a lack of proportion among the parts of the vertebral column; and similarly many other diseases are caused by the lack of proportion between the abdominal cavity and that of the thorax, between the heart and the vascular system, between the extent of the surface of the arteries and that of the veins, between the size of the trunk and that of the limbs. (Cf. A. De Giovanni, Lavori dell' Istituto di Clinica medica di Padova, Milano, Hoepli, 1907–1914.)

[2]See pp. 299-302.

[3]See figure 1, Plate I, p. 299.

3. **Height.** Less or equal to the stretch of arms.

4. **Trunk.** Larger with sagittal diameters exceeding the transverse diameters; abdomen larger and rounder than the thorax; thorax relatively deficient, having the shape of the inspiratory thorax, as in children, with slight inclination of the ribs in relation to the vertebral column, and the shoulder line horizontal.

5. **Limbs.** Short in relation to the trunk (brachyscelia). Upper limb longer than lower one.

6. **Skull.** Short antero-posterior diameter, with tendency to the brachycephalia (large skull).

7. **Neck.** Short, with circumference, both absolute and relative, exceeding the normal.

8. **Thyroid cartilage** (pomum Adami) slightly prominent.

B. Principal Physiological and Pathological Characteristics

The system of vegetative life, represented by the organs of the trunk, prevails over the system of life of relation, represented by the limbs; which fact is expressed by less agility and action (velocity) of the organism; hence the tendency to sedentary life.

The heart is in a very oblique position, almost horizontal. Generally there is an excess of development of the right heart and a deficient development of the left heart, which is frequently accompanied by a greater development of veins and a relatively deficient development of arteries. As a result there is a permanent state of slow circulation, and a tendency to venous stasis, and generally to diseases of the circulatory system and especially to apoplexy.

The excessive development of the abdominal organs requires abundant nutrition, but, because of relative deficiency of the thorax and relatively small size of the lungs and heart, there is less power of oxidation and less heart action. Because of these characteristics, and of the tendency to sedentary life, there is a reduction of the metabolism of carbohydrates, and hence the predisposition of the organism to polysarcia (corpulency) when there is a deficient burning up of fats, and to glycosuria in case of deficient metabolism, or combustion of sugar. Moreover, such disproportion between the storing up of the energy and its expenditure explains morphologically the constitutional abnormalities of metabolism and the pathology of arthritism (gout, diabetes, urinary calculi).

Because of the excessive development of the lymphatic system and of the lessened heart action due to the underdevelopment of the left heart, there is a lack of equilibrium which produces stagnation of lymphatic secretions followed by glandular tumors, the formation of which is also aided by the tendency to venous stasis.

The skin is oily, that is, rich in sebaceous secretions with tendency to seborrhea, and such condition causes premature baldness. The subcutaneous fat is abundant.

The nervous system is inactive, with torpor of physical and psychic life.

II. SLENDER CONSTITUTION (with predisposition to tuberculosis)[1]

Habitus phthisicus (microsplanchnia)

A. Principal Anthropological Characteristics

1. **Body (soma).** Smaller than normal (microsomia).

2. **Morphological type.** Longilinear (dolichomorphous) with the proportion of the parts of the body far different from those of an infant.

---

[1] See figure 2, Plate I, p. 299.

3. Height. Greater in length than the stretch of arms.

4. Trunk. Small with transverse diameters exceeding the sagittal diameters; abdomen poor and flat; thorax relatively larger, having the shape of the expiratory thorax, with marked inclination of the ribs in relation to the vertebral column, and the shoulder line drooping.

5. Limbs. Long in relation to the trunk (macroscelia). Lower limb longer than the upper one.

6. Skull. Long antero-posterior diameter, with tendency to the dolichocephalis (narrow skull).

7. Neck. Long, with circumference, both absolute and relative, less than normal.

8. Larynx (pomum Adami) very prominent.

B. Principal Physiological and Pathological Characteristics

The system of life of relation, represented by the limbs, prevails over the system of vegetative life, represented by the organs of the trunk, which fact is expressed by great agility and action (velocity) of the organism, hence the tendency to active life.

The heart is in a more vertical position and altogether small.

The lungs are relatively large.

The stomach has a tendency to a vertical position.

Because of the deficient development of the abdominal organs, which causes a poor general nutrition, and of relatively large metabolic forces, these characteristics, with a tendency to an active life, produce a lack of equilibrium between the ingestion and elimination, with prevalence of the latter. As a result there is a tendency of the organism to be of a delicate build, often very extreme organic poverty, with very poor disease resistance.

The lymphatic system is chronically undernourished, therefore, for this reason also there is an insufficient nutrition of tissues, with inflammation and marked vulnerability toward pathogenic agents of whatever nature, such as chlorosis, neurasthenia, derangement of female genitals. Generally there is a marked predisposition to diseases of lymphatic type, or to diseases which very easily develop owing to such lymphatic substratum, for instance, scrofulosis, pulmonary tuberculosis, lupus, cold abscesses, tumor albus of the joints, etc.

The skin is thin, transparent, and dry, with poor subcutaneous fat.

The nervous system shows morbid excitability, physical and psychic, and is easily exhaustible.

In order to avoid incorrect ideas about these two types I must state that not all the characteristics specified belong to the two types exclusively and constantly, as none of the diseases specified are limited to one or the other constitution. We are merely speaking of the majority of cases. In reality factors of heredity and crossbreeding often modify these two types in such a way that the number of the kinds of constitutions is considerably increased, but not indefinitely, because the laws of interorganic correlations produce a limiting effect on that number. After having combined among themselves the three kinds, small, medium, and large size of head, trunk, and limbs, I was able to ascertain through mathematical calculations the possibility of twenty-seven morphological types distinctly different from each other.[1]

To return now to our two fundamental types, we must add that they can be recognized not only among men as shown on Plate II, but also among women (Plate III), and not only among adults, but in all ages; for instance, according to Viola, they have been recognized among children eight and five years old (Plate IV); and I maintain that they can be recognized also among the newly born. It would be of the highest scientific interest and the greatest practical use to follow the course of the various developments which may take place in the cases of the individuals of the two types during the period of growth, and which are connected with the particular phases of growth. For example, it is not infrequent to find individuals of the slender type who in their early childhood had slow dentition combined with symptoms of rickets; in their second period of childhood symptoms of scrofula combined with irritability of the respiratory passages (bronchial catarrh); during puberty hemorrhages from the nose, blood expectoration, and palpitation of the heart, and finally later pulmonary tuberculosis.

Having then established the possibility of classifying morphologically the child and of tracing through the period of its growth various kinds of predisposition to definite morbid conditions, the Italian School of Clinical Morphology proposes through appropriate artificial means to restore the proper balance of functions in the body. Modifying more or less, through food and exercise prescribed in accordance with individual preventive hygiene—and not general, as is now commonly done—those functions which are in close relation with the organs and parts threatened by disturbances in their development, we will be able to check, or at least to retard the beginning disturbance, which if left to itself, would inevitably lead to disease. This program applied to a growing body tends to re-establish the proportion among the parts so that they may regain their balance in the course of time. When the efforts exerted on an individual, first in his childhood and then in his adolescence, do not succeed in removing the danger and do not restore the morphologic equilibrium of the body, and the tendencies toward disease increase with maturity, preventive individual hygiene should be advised to the person; he should be warned to take good care of those organs of his body which are especially vulnerable.

CONCLUSIONS AND PROPOSITION

But in order to obtain these results, the organizations available, although very useful, are not sufficient. The work now done by them must be combined and coordinated in one harmonic whole by a new

---

[1] See Appendix, p. 297.

office, which I would name the International Child Survey, because of the presence in America of many children belonging to different nationalities and because of the scientific and practical necessity of adopting an international plan of work, which would facilitate the collection, coordination, and comparison of data collected in the various countries of America, Europe, and Asia. These data would allow us to determine the general laws governing the normal and pathological growth. This new office must have as its main purposes to study the child morphologically, to distinguish the normal children from those that are defective or delinquent, to watch their health during the principal phases of their growth, and to order their physical and mental work in such a way as to enable them in their maturity to use their powers in the best way for their own benefit and that of society. This office must contain a staff able to compute with the greatest accuracy those measurements of the body which, as we believe we have demonstrated, are indispensable for a good morphological classification of individuals.

APPENDIX

Achille De Giovanni, on the basis of relative proportion among the principal parts of the body, distinguishes three types of constitutions which he calls "morphologic combinations."

Giacinto Viola, besides the data furnished by relative proportions, considers, as does De Giovanni, his teacher, in addition also the total bodily size of the individual; he has established a relation between the volume of the trunk and the length of the extremities and on the basis of this distinguishes five types.

In the following table [1] we give the two classifications:

TABLE I

DE GIOVANNI	VIOLA
1. Morphologic combination.	1. Microsplanchnic individuals (small trunk, long limbs).
2. Normal type.	2. Normosplanchnic individuals (well proportioned).
3. Morphologic combination.	3. Megalosplanchnic individuals (large trunk and short limbs).
4. Morphologic combination.	4. Microsplanchnic individuals (well proportioned).
5. Not given in De Giovanni's classification.	5. Megalosplanchnic individuals (well proportioned).

But in this classification we notice the absence of an element of primary anthropological importance—the head. Considering the sizes of the head, small, medium, and large, and the corresponding sizes of the trunk and limbs, we succeed by means of mathematical calculations in establishing twenty-seven morphological types, as given in the

---

[1] Prof. F. Frassetto, "Di una nuova classificazione antropometrica delle individualità." Der anatomische Anzeiger, XXXV Band, 1910, p. 468.

table below, clearly distinct from each other, all equally probable, but not all equally frequent.

TABLE II [1]

The Greek letters in the table indicate small sizes: α for a microcephalous head; β for a microsplanchnic trunk; μ for micromelous limbs.

The small letters designate medium sizes: a for a normocephalous head; b for a normosplanchnic trunk; m for normomelous limbs.

Large letters indicate large sizes: A for a macrocephalous head; B for a macrosplanchnic trunk; M for micromelous limbs.

β	α {μ, m, M}	Microsplanchnic	microcephalous		micromelic / normomelic / macromelic
	a {μ, m, M}		normocephalous		micromelic / normomelic / macromelic
	A {μ, m, M}		macrophalous		micromelic / normomelic / macromelic
b	α {μ, m, M}	Normosplanchnic	microcephalous		micromelic / normomelic / macromelic
	a {μ, m, M}		normocephalous		micromelic / normomelic / macromelic
	A {μ, m, M}		macrocephalous		micromelic / normomelic / macromelic
B	α {μ, m, M}	Macrosplanchnic	microphalous		micromelic / normomelic / macromelic
	a {μ, m, M}		normocephalous		micromelic / normomelic / macromelic
	A {μ, m, M}		macrocephalous		micromelic / no-momelic / macromelic

[1] F. Frassetto, "Di una nuova classificazione antropometrica delle individualità." Der anatomische Anzeiger, XXXV Band, 1910, p. 472.

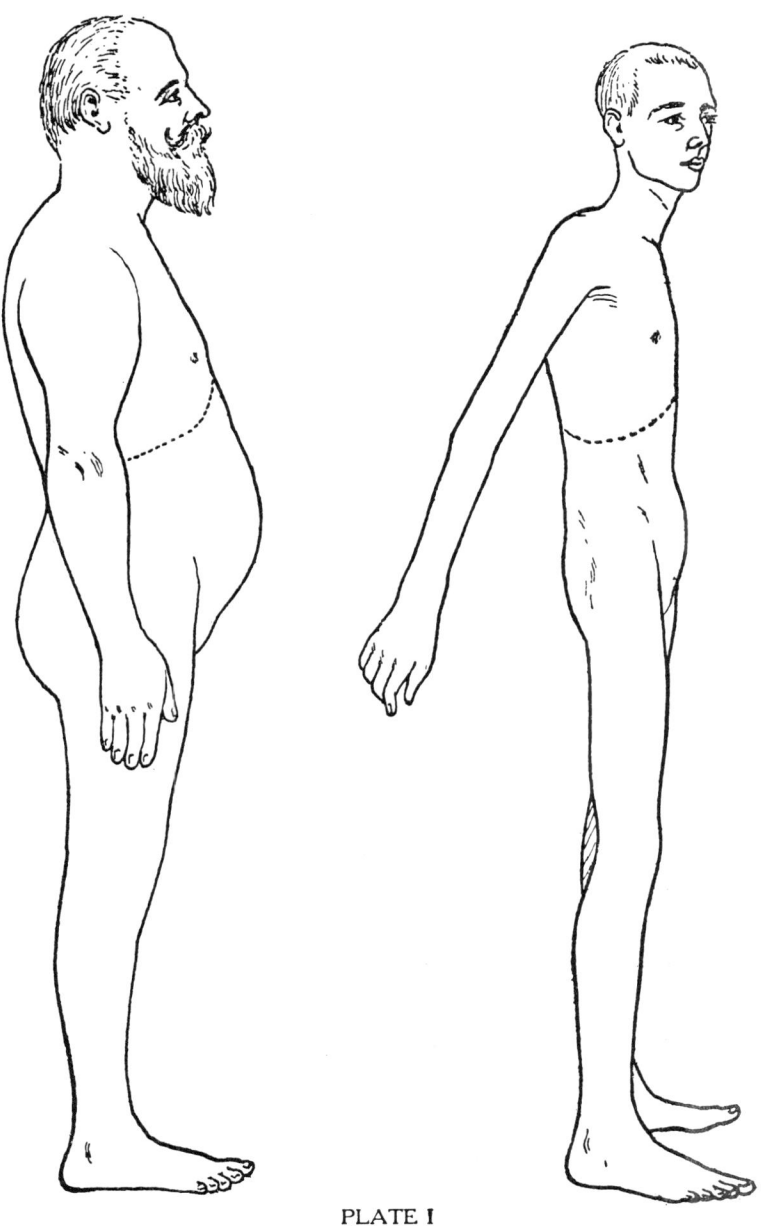

PLATE I

FIGURE 1
Heavy physique, with
predisposition to apoplexy
(Macrosplanchnia)

FIGURE 2
Slender physique, with
predisposition to tuberculosis
(Microsplanchnia)

Figure imitate da Viola e Fici (cf. A. De Giovanni, Lavori dell' Istituto di Clinica Medica di Padova, Milano, Hoepli, 1914).

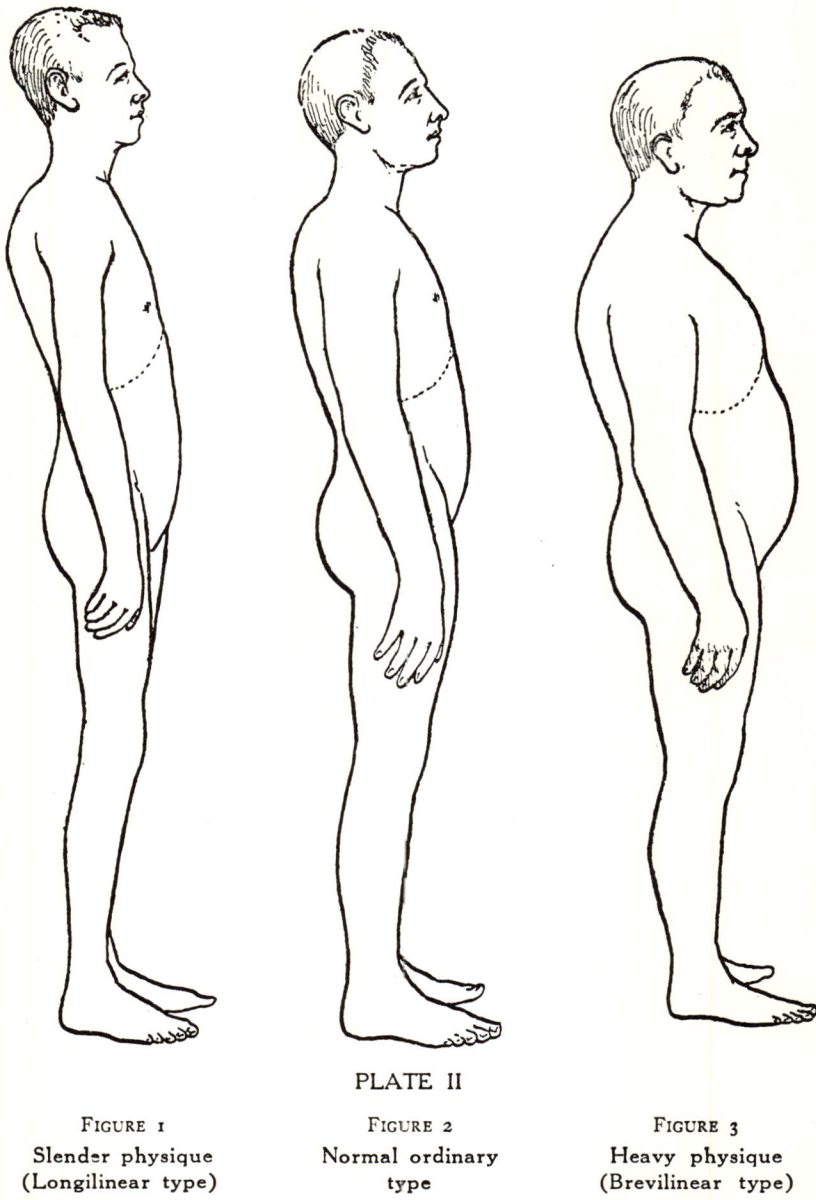

PLATE II

FIGURE 1
Slender physique
(Longilinear type)

FIGURE 2
Normal ordinary
type

FIGURE 3
Heavy physique
(Brevilinear type)

Figure imitate da Viola (cf. A. De Giovanni, Lavori dell' Istituto di Clinica Medica di Padova, Milano, Hoepli, 1914).

HEALTH—EUROPEAN EXPERIENCE 301

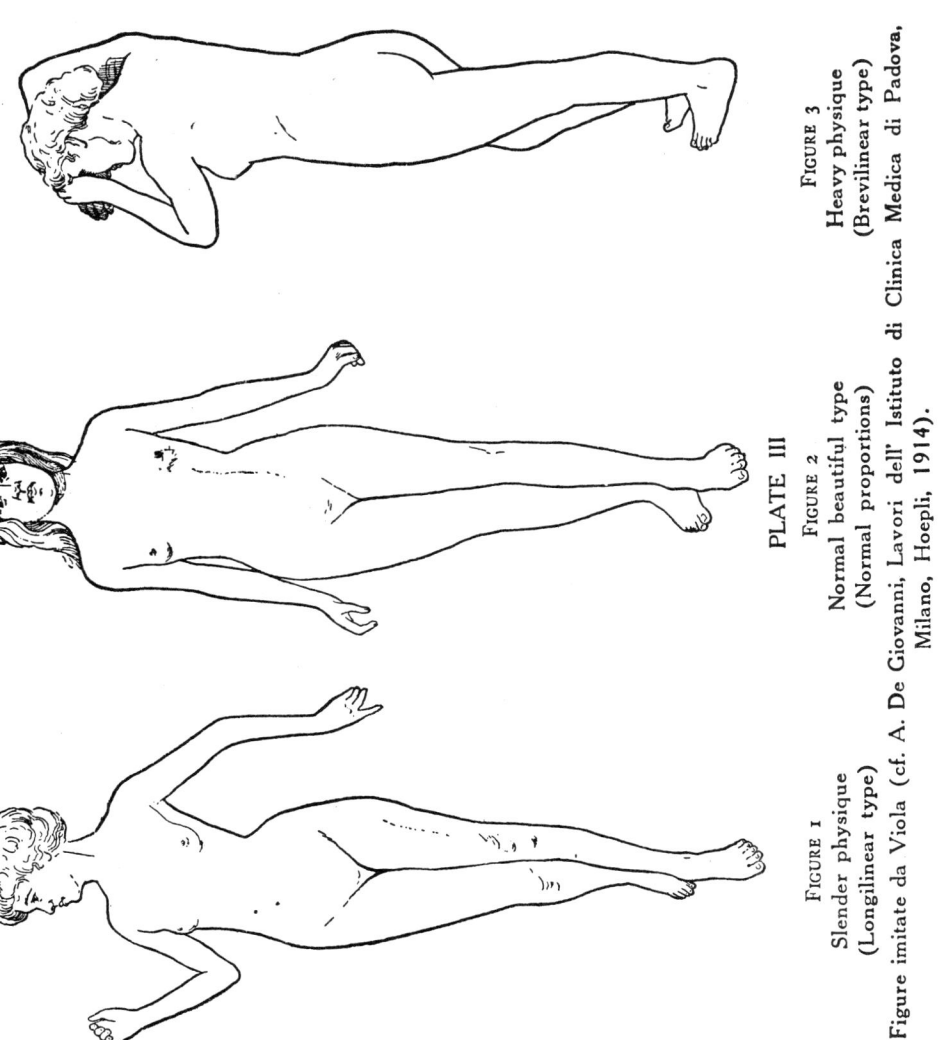

PLATE III

FIGURE 1
Slender physique
(Longilinear type)

FIGURE 2
Normal beautiful type
(Normal proportions)

FIGURE 3
Heavy physique
(Brevilinear type)

Figure imitate da Viola (cf. A. De Giovanni, Lavori dell' Istituto di Clinica Medica di Padova, Milano, Hoepli, 1914).

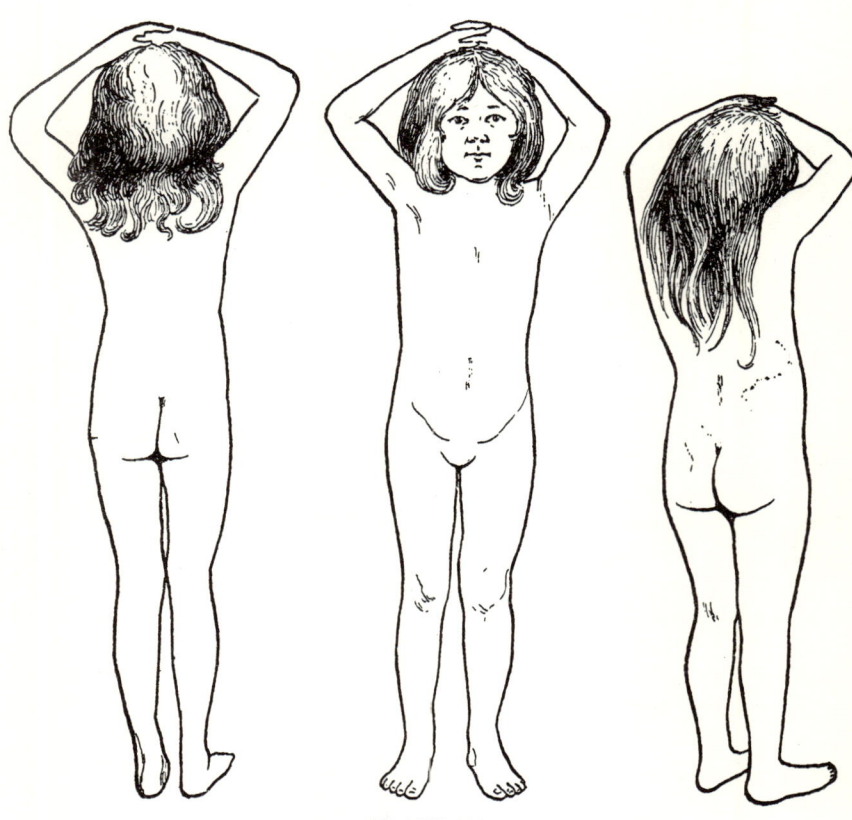

PLATE IV

GIRLS EIGHT YEARS OLD

Figure 1	Figure 2	Figure 3
Slender physique (Longilinear type)	Normal type (Normal proportions)	Heavy physique (Brevilinear type)

Figure imitate da Viola (cf. A. De Giovanni, Lavori dell' Istituto di Clinica Medica di Padova, Milano, Hoepli, 1914).

THE INTERNATIONAL RED CROSS AND CHILD WELFARE

By LIVINGSTON FARRAND

Chairman of the Central Committee of the American Red Cross

One thing particularly impressed me at the conference at Cannes, where medical experts from the five great allied nations were brought together to formulate the broad principles upon which an international organization of the Red Cross might be based and to advise the Red Cross organizations of the world as to what particular fields of preventive medicine and public health such an organization might advantageously undertake. This was the fact that after the tuberculosis experts and the malaria experts and the venereal disease experts and the general public health experts and the infant mortality experts had held their conferences and had reached unanimity upon certain general principles, and had begun to unite upon general recommendations to make as to the International Red Cross, they all agreed that the first and most important field to be attacked and the one which offered the greatest promise of immediately successful results, was the field of the child and child welfare; that we could well afford to postpone if necessary action in the other fields in order to attack promptly this great problem of infant mortality and to increase the welfare of childhood throughout the world. Now that is exactly the history of every public health movement in the world. Those of us who have had years of experience in this field, who have been interested personally in this or that particular phase, always come back to the child as the essential feature.

Another conclusion which all those of us who have worked in public health have reached very soon is that the responsibility for public health, the responsibility for the welfare of mankind, is an official responsibility. It is not a matter for private philanthropy. Private philanthropy only takes it up because it has to. It must sometimes take the first step and make the first demonstration. It must educate the people. It must create a public sentiment. But the responsibility after all is a public and an official responsibility. And consequently we are demanding that State and municipal health departments shall concern themselves not only with certain obvious things, but shall accept the entire responsibility for the protection of the public health. In order that they may accept it and carry it through we must provide for them the support of a public sentiment. Here, as I conceive it, is one of the chief functions of a great organization like the Red Cross.

We are faced in the Red Cross today with a very grave responsibility. We have to effect the transition from a time of war to a time of peace. We have to make certain very far-reaching decisions. So far as I am concerned some of those decisions were not difficult to make. I am certain that the Red Cross is to be an active organization in time of peace. It seems obvious to me that this great sentiment which has been built up in time of war for the welfare of mankind, for the relief of suffering and distress, for the improvement of conditions generally, should be preserved so far as possible to solve the great problems of peace, which after all are much more serious than the problems of war. How much of it can be preserved depends, of course, upon the wisdom and effectiveness of the peace program adopted and carried out.

The beginnings of that transition have already taken place. The international movement that I have spoken of has given the stamp of approval to such activity not only for America but for the entire world, and the plan is now included among the covenants of the League of Nations and will have the force which that League will have, whatever that may be.

There is no difference of opinion as to the fact that the great factor in the peace program of the Red Cross is going to be public health. But I do not see the American Red Cross as a great operating concern to take the responsibility for carrying through the child welfare program of the United States, or the tuberculosis program, or the venereal disease program, or any other. I do see it as the great cooperating body in the United States that will enable you, the child welfare workers, to get the results which you know are legitimate, and which can be obtained if you have the proper audience and the proper aid.

We will give you that audience, but we will not attempt to absorb you and attempt to operate your different activities. And what is true in the field of child welfare will be true in the field of tuberculosis and in the field of the other public health questions. We shall demand that the responsibility for all of these problems shall be assumed by the public authorities; we shall endeavor to cooperate with the public authorities and with all other legitimate agencies in furthering their particular aims. And thus we shall be able in various ways to bring about certain very necessary coordinations, and to give an impetus toward this great end of the prevention of disease and the protection of public health, in which field nothing rivals the problem of the child in importance.

Section IV

Children in Need of Special Care

(The minimum standards for the protection of children in need of special care adopted by the Washington Conference will be found on pages 440-444.)

THE FUNCTION OF THE STATE

THE RESPONSIBILITY OF THE STATE

By ROBERT W. KELSO

Executive Director, Massachusetts State Board of Charity

I wish at the outset to offer three fundamental points regarding the nature of human society; and to follow them by some considerations touching the responsibility of the State for children who stand in need of special care.

First: It is necessary to the advancement of any community that the forthcoming generation be superior physically and mentally to the generation out of which it springs.

Second: Consequently, organized society owes to the growing child who is in need of special care sufficient protection to render reasonably probable his upgrowth to the age of self-support with physical health and intellectual attainment equal to that of the average child in the community.

Third: The history of mankind shows that the monogamous union of one man and one woman for the purpose of procreation and the rearing of their offspring is a natural evolution extending over a geologic age; that it stands, under the short name of the "family," as the vehicle and the basis of our social order. Hence it is the proper channel through which the average opportunity for development which I have just mentioned is to be sought.

The various course of history—the growth of early communities, the rise and fall of empires, the up-spring and decline of communistic experiments—shows these three fundamentals to be sound.

What then, in specific form, is the responsibility of organized society—the state—toward those of its children who need special care,—the dependent, the neglected, the delinquent, and the defective.

Successful community life presupposes that the individual will support himself after reaching the age when he is physically able to do so; and that parents will support their offspring through infancy and childhood until they can become self-supporting. The first boundary mark of this responsibility of the state, then, is negative; namely, that no policy should be inaugurated or practice carried out which deprives the child of the care, comfort, and affection of his parents; or which tends unnecessarily to relieve the parent of the natural burden of supporting and fostering his child.

With these points in mind, I wish to discuss this state responsibility in the light of the experience of Massachusetts. The primary unit of government in that State is the Town, with its selectmen and its town meeting. City government is an elaboration of this ancient town system, subject to the principles of town law. County government exists, but its functions are so far circumscribed that it may be termed for the most part a judicial unit merely. All poor relief is administered locally, in the first instance, always by cities and towns. The overseer of the poor, a local officer, is the agency through which the government takes notice of dependency. The State treasury is called upon for reimbursement of aid rendered where the child is without legal settlement. The State has an elaborate and complicated settlement law.

THE DEPENDENT CHILD

In Massachusetts, public aid to children whose only handicap is a failure of support is given almost exclusively in the child's own home. Since September 1, 1913, when the Mothers' Aid Law became operative, assistance in the home, given mostly in cash and totalling $3,886,678.58, exclusive of administrative expenses, has been given to 7,651 mothers, in order, as the law states, to enable them to bring up their 24,464 dependent children under 14 years of age in their own homes. Under other relief laws, overseers of the poor render temporary aid in the home to many children where sickness, accident, or other cause has cut off natural support. According to law, the State board of charity may receive dependent children for support, but they are not now taken where dependency is the only cause. The dependent children now in the board's custody are those who have been orphaned, neglected, abandoned, or abused.

The illegitimate child falls within the group of dependents. For him the family has failed. It is the obligation of the State to guarantee to the illegitimate as much of its family rights as can be preserved. Thus, it has a right to its mother's affection and personal care. Hence, mother and child should not be separated in cases where the mother has a passable degree of intelligence. The illegitimacy statute of Massachusetts makes illegitimate paternity a crime. It protects the man by requiring proof beyond a reasonable doubt, as in any other crime. It imposes upon the father as much responsibility for the support of his offspring as is required of the legitimate parent. The parties in interest are the public and the child.

Considering the responsibility of the State for the dependent child, I submit that when the normal child, through the loss of parents or for other reason not due to its own conduct, is deprived of its natural home and the support necessary to its growth, the State owes the positive obligation of transplanting it to a foster family home as the best substitute for the home that has been lost. Experience shows that such homes are readily found.

THE NEGLECTED CHILD

The neglected child is dependent and should be treated according to that standard. But the family, of which it is the most valuable part, is an offender against society. The parents are delinquent. The State, obliged as it is to safeguard the institution of the family, owes a positive duty to punish and to correct parental neglect of children.

Only as a last resort should the family be broken up. Compulsion under non-support and desertion laws can do much. The 155 probation officers of our 88 Massachusetts courts of first instance collected in 1918 from non-supporting husbands and fathers and from persons who failed to support their aged parents a total of over $485,000 and turned it over to the dependents of those backsliders. The item for the support of aged parents is probably less than ten per cent of the whole. The State board of charity collected $25,936.02 in the same period from parents of children who by court order or through other provisions of the law had been placed in the custody of that board.

When the child is removed because of neglect, that act of severance should be accompanied by all practicable compulsion of the parental responsibility for support. The Uniform Desertions Act should be in force in every State in the Union. It declares wilful failure to support to be an offense. It makes that offense extraditable. It makes it possible to commit the offending parent to hard labor, the government repaying to the dependents a sum per day for his labor. A charge of neglect should lie against the offending parties only. It should not, as in Massachusetts, be brought as though it were a charge against the child. The little fellow, innocent as your child or mine, stands wide-eyed before the court wondering why he is so accused. Seen through his eyes, poverty is a great sorrow, but neglect is tragedy.

THE DELINQUENT CHILD

Delinquency among children arises, as I apprehend, from two chief sources: (a) bad environment; and (b) abnormal mental development or mental defect. Its treatment must follow widely divergent channels in accordance with the one cause or the other. If the cause is environment, the child should not be removed from the family until the full possibilities of court probation have been exhausted and every effort made to correct the home conditions. This effort may take the form of moving the family bodily to another district. In these environmental problems, the child is found often to do well when placed in a foster family home. Very many wayward children coming out of wrong home conditions do well after probation when placed out in families. The State Board in Massachusetts has 304 such children in family homes under the supervision of field visitors. All of them came to the board as delinquents and none of them has been in an institution for delinquents.

Where the child's conduct is such as to demand custodial care, he should be sent to an industrial training school which is developed on the cottage plan and to which is attached an effective parole system—so that the child may be placed out as soon as his conduct appears to warrant so much confidence. There are three such schools in Massachusetts, two for boys and one for girls. They contain 1,145 inmates, and there are 2,831 other children who have been in these schools and who are now placed out in family homes or who are with their parents on parole. These remain still under the custody of the trustees of the schools.

THE DEFECTIVE CHILD

The defective child is almost always a dependent. He is often neglected, and he is in very many cases a delinquent. His defective mind indicates at the outset small likelihood that he will be able to adjust himself to his surroundings to the satisfaction of society. The insane and the feeble-minded in Massachusetts are cared for by the State Government. A feeble-minded person is committed to institutional care in much the same manner that an insane person is committed. There are two schools for the feeble-minded, now housing 2,806. A third has been authorized, but is not yet ready. There are over 1,000 persons on the waiting list for admittance to these schools. Over 100 of these remain constantly at the State Infirmary, which is the State's almshouse, where they do not belong.

The defective child does not necessarily need institutional care in all cases. Estimating approximately 15,000 feeble-minded persons in Massachusetts, there is a strong likelihood that almost half of these will not need restraint in an institution. This proportion will readily obtain among the children. Either they are found to have watchful and helpful relatives; or they are of such low grade that they do not come within the dangerous class of breeders. For whatever reason may appear, they are not a menace to the public welfare. All these should be supervised in their own homes by the State Government.

Research discovers that feeble-mindedness is transmitted by inheritance in about three-fourths of all cases. Consequently, the great menace caused by this group is that of procreation. The State owes the positive obligation of protecting itself against the transmission of demonstrated hereditary mental defect. This duty it will carry out in the way that is most humane. Our present method is segregation of the sexes.

For the defective child who is not feeble-minded, institutional training can do much, and so long as there is reasonable hope of returning him to the community with enough capacity or sufficient mental habit to get along without endangering society, his care in the institution should include vocational training.

The condition of feeble-mindedness is not curable, though it is improvable, within narrow limits, in the direction of self-support. It must follow that institutional care of feeble-minded children should seek to fit them for such occupation as their capacity will admit; and for the rest, should make them as nearly self-supporting in the institution as humane treatment will permit. Where facilities for care are inadequate to meet the need, preference should be given in the admittance of cases to the institution to the feeble-minded girl with sex tendencies, as she represents the greatest threat to society.

Research discovers another vital fact about feeble-mindedness, namely, that it never develops in adult life. Where present, it must have existed either from birth or from early childhood. This fact, together with that other finding on heredity, should point the line of responsibility for the State. American childhood has a right to be protected in adolescence. More than this, it has a right to be well born. The State will not have protected itself in any true sense until it shall have approached its child problems with a view to preventing them—until in the case of the feeble-minded, it shall have sought out the defective in the days of his childhood, at the outset of his career, and before he has created problems of illegitimacy, of venereal disease, of crime, and of tragedy for every heart along his trail of anti-social conduct.

I have mentioned here and there the experience of Massachusetts in these problems. Last year the Government, State and local, exclusive of the maintenance of the 5 county training schools, expended approximately $3,230,289 in the care, custody, and treatment of the children of these several classifications. Yet that was not the only contribution. Large sums were expended by private incorporated child-caring agencies. There are 110 of these corporations in Massachusetts. Forty-five are congregate homes for children, some of them with placing-out systems attached. Fourteen do only placing-out. Twenty-seven are day nurseries, and nine are special hospitals for sick children. The total capital funds of the 90 of these societies that reported are $15,906,882. Last year they rendered child care in 106,717 instances at a total expenditure of $1,833,170. They received from or on account of beneficiaries $428,455 and from investments and all other sources $1,496,121, making a grand total of $1,924,576 received. The State board of charity has 6,440 children in its custody, and of these 5,531 are in foster family homes. The total expenditure last year for the care of these children, including administration and tuition in the public schools, was $925,010.

One may rightly inquire in view of my insistence upon a positive responsibility in Government itself, what is the function and the responsibility of the private charitable agency in child care. That true relationship I take to be this: The primary obligation rests upon organized society—the state itself. The care of children needing special care is therefore a function of the State. The private agency, in fact as well as in law, is a public trust, performing a function of Government. To borrow the words of our greatest judicial definition of charity, the private agency in its operation is "relieving the burdens of Government."[1] Hence the process of child care, whether it be public or private, is based upon those same fundamental elements of responsibility which rest upon organized society, and must therefore conform to identical standards.

---

[1] Gray, J., in Jackson vs. Phillips, 14 Allen, 539, at p. 556.

STATE SUPERVISION OF AGENCIES AND INSTITUTIONS

By C. V. WILLIAMS

Director, Children's Welfare Department, Board of State Charities, Ohio

The humanitarian impulses manifested by the majority of the people of the country have been responsible to a large degree for the commercializing of physically handicapped or unfortunate children by unscrupulous individuals. In States where there is no regulation of child-caring agencies, persons utterly unfit are permitted to exploit these defenseless children for their own gain. In some such States a fearful traffic in infants is carried on through so-called maternity hospitals or lying-in homes where adoptions or abortions may be had for a consideration.

Everybody recognizes the necessity of securing the elimination of these human parasites from the community, but I am of the opinion that of even greater harm is the operation of institutions by well-meaning but incompetent men and women who retain the standards of a generation ago. Some of these institutions are well supported, and are tolerated in the community because nobody wants to hurt the manager's feelings. The health and happiness of thousands of children is sacrificed because of the failure of the State to secure the protection of these children through a system of State regulation which will demand minimum standards of efficiency from every child-caring agency.

To be specific I will cite a few conditions common to States where there is no provision for the supervision of child-caring agencies. Only the greatest care will prevent the best-managed institutions in the land from becoming a "dumping ground" for parents who do not care to support their children or for agencies that summarily and unnecessarily separate children from their parents. A large number of so-called dependent or delinquent children have been separated from parents because of their delinquency which has been due to conditions for which the community is responsible. With the development of a program of service for the family, a large number of these homes can be reclaimed and the children returned to their parents. Only constructive State supervision can prevent the needless detention of children in institutions.

A practice common today in many institutions smacks of conditions existing a generation ago. Respectable and worthy mothers are compelled to relinquish all right, and claim, and title to their children in order that they may receive the care of some of our public and private child-caring institutions. The social crime of this procedure is overlooked by the enterprising, ambitious agent of the Home, who is more interested in finding an attractive child for a prospective foster parent than in recognizing the God-given rights of an unfortunate woman who at the moment is neither physically nor mentally responsible for her conduct.

State regulation is necessary to humanize some institutions to which these children are committed and where children are practically buried for many of the most important years of their lives. Their timidity, their rat-like faces, their undernourished bodies, their closely cropped heads, their frightened though eager and hungry look, reveal something of that great though unsatisfied longing for parental care, which of course institutions cannot give. They become a part of a system; their individuality is consequently dwarfed, and though maintained at great expense, a large number of these children can never overcome the baneful influences incident to this early training.

Many of these children still eat their meals while sitting upon backless benches. The use of the oilcloth table cover, of ironware or tin dishes, and of spoons instead of knives and forks, does not contribute to their training in proper table manners.

Tooth brushes in some of these institutions are unknown. Infectious diseases are communicated through the use of a common towel. Three or four children frequently sleep together in one bed. Much immorality prevails, as dormitory supervision is lacking and the mingling of the sexes is frequent. In many well-supported children's institutions, that invention of the devil, the "silent regime," still prevails. Here the children eat their meals in silence, march from one room to another in silence with hands behind their backs, and sit in their playrooms in silence, doing nothing. In many institutions there is no attention whatever given to remediable physical defects of children who remain wards for long periods of time. Some institutions boast that the physician rarely comes—that it is not necessary.

One of the greatest problems requiring standardization is the system employed by agencies engaged in the placing of children in foster families. I have personal knowledge of the ease with which persons physically and morally unfit have secured even from so-called substantial organizations the custody of homeless children. I know that many of these children have not only been placed in unfit homes, but that they have subsequently been literally abandoned by the officials who were entrusted with their care and guardianship. I also know that the lives of great numbers of these children have been irreparably blighted because of the failure of the State to secure their protection through a competent system of State supervision.

In many of these institutions the records concerning the children and their antecedents have been mislaid or lost; nor is there information available concerning the manner in which some of the children have been disposed of. Nobody knows where they have been placed, and supervision is rendered impossible. The futile efforts of children who have reached their majority, who seek to ascertain something concerning their family history or their relatives, is sufficient commentary on the seriousness of this neglect.

It is highly significant that nearly every State has developed some system for the protection of neglected children. Provision has been made for courts of certain jurisdiction to remove neglected children from the custody of their own parents and to award their guardianship either to public or to private child-caring agencies during their minority. However, it so happens that sometimes the children thus legally and properly removed from their own parents are legally placed in the care of an institution or agency even less competent to care for them than are their parents.

In outlining the scope of supervision, I would consider that the responsibility of the State for the standardizing of child-caring agencies should apply to the same extent to private as to public institutions. The State is more interested in the nature of the treatment afforded these unfortunate children than in the auditing of financial accounts to ascertain whether or not the funds of public agencies have been wisely expended.

The Ohio law provides for the supervision by the Board of State Charities of all institutions or associations, public or private, incorporated or otherwise, that receive children or that place children in foster homes. All of these institutions are subject to inspection and endorsement by the State department and a penalty is provided for the non-observance of this statute. The Board of State Charities is required to pass upon the manner in which the wards of these institutions are cared for and also to examine into the systems employed in the admission and discharge of children and their placement in foster homes. It is required to visit such children as have been placed out in foster homes by the agencies under supervision as, in the judgment of the board, may be necessary to determine the actual character of the work accomplished by the agency.

The present legislature has also provided for the licensing of all boarding homes in the State where private families care for children not related by blood or marriage for "hire, gain or reward." This law will make it possible not only to reach the "baby farms," but also to regulate the activities of individuals, who in the past, without any board of managers, have been exploiting children. The Ohio law also provides that the Board of State Charities shall pass upon the merits of all institutions or associations desiring to incorporate, whose objects may include the care of children or their placement in foster homes. This provision has enabled the board to prevent the incorporation of useless and even vicious organizations.

The Ohio law is weak, however, in that it makes no provision for the supervision of children who are placed out in foster homes by juvenile court judges. Nor has it jurisdiction over the operation of the humane societies which engage exclusively in the enforcement of the anti-cruelty laws. These agencies are just as greatly in need of standardization and regulation as the recognized child-caring associations, and should be included in the development of a State supervisory program.

State supervision, to be constructive, must be sympathetically exercised. Any investigator can find abundant opportunity for criticism in the best ordered institutions. It becomes therefore a task necessitating unusual tact and discretion to secure needful corrections without dissipating the altruistic activities of the trustees. The State is as greatly concerned in the conservation and the development of the initiative of managers and trustees as it is in the correction of the abuses of their institutions. It is therefore necessary to employ in this service only such persons as are able to maintain a properly balanced perspective, who have an understanding of children, and who understand the technique of case work and family rehabilitation and at least the fundamentals of institutional administration. The investigators must have a profound sympathy for the children concerned, and a vision as to the possibilities of their future. Such investigators will readily impress the officials in charge of the institutions of their desire to be of real service in the solving of the institution's problems. They will be able to advise with the superintendent sensibly concerning the creating of a normal atmosphere in the institution. They will be able to secure for the children the recreational, the vocational, the physical, the social, the educational, and the religious opportunities so frequently denied. If the low standards of the institution have been due to ignorance, the investigator should remain in the institution long enough to work out a program consistent with available resources. If the institution's standards are sacrificed because of the necessity of keeping within a low per capita, it becomes the privilege of the investigator, through the development of educational propaganda, to secure for the institution needful financial support. The State will make a serious mistake if in the exercise of its police function, in the elimination of bad agencies, it forgets its greater opportunity in rendering helpful and constructive service to the weaker agencies under its supervision.

The State should establish a uniform record and blank system, and when desired, should assist in its installation. It should secure the registration of all of the wards of the public and private child-caring institutions in the State. This can be readily accomplished through a system of monthly reporting on the movements of children, which can be readily posted on a card index. The supervision by the State of children who are placed in foster homes by child-caring institutions, is a task necessitating the exercise of unusual tact. The State is primarily interested in determining the fitness of the endorsed agency to engage in this work, and unnecessary duplication of effort should be avoided. Irreparable harm can come through the unnecessary visit of a tactless field agent. It is of far greater importance to the State that it secure the maintenance of the necessary standards incident to investigations, supervision, and records, from the supervised agencies, than it is to perform that function itself. When there is any indication of the failure of the agency adequately to perform this function, each of its wards should be visited, such as are found in improper homes removed, and a definite program created by the State which must be accepted by the institution as a minimum which will justify subsequent endorsement. Each institution should be required to develop a record system sufficiently intensive to satisfy the State investigator as to the type of work accomplished. This record kept on file in the office of the institution and available to properly accredited agents of the State supervisory board, should ordinarily furnish sufficient data for a determination as to the agency's fitness for endorsement.

The exercise of a supervisory prerogative unaccompanied by a penalty for violation is without great value. The Ohio law provides that any person who receives a child or solicits money on behalf of an unendorsed institution or association, upon conviction thereof, is subject to a fine. It has been the experience of the Ohio board that the civic pride of a community is in itself generally sufficient to accomplish certain reforms when the official family refuse to maintain proper standards. And I am of the opinion that better results are ultimately accomplished by confining the power of the State to its function of licensing or refusing to license than in actually giving to the State the control over the wards of the institution except where it is impossible otherwise to secure them proper care. The Ohio Board of State Charities has met with certain difficulties which are local in their nature, in securing the protection of the wards of unendorsed agencies who have been placed out in unfit homes. The State, having refused or revoked the license of an institution, can go no further, and the indifferent trustees permit the continuance of the neglect of these children. A remedy for this condition may ordinarily be found through the juvenile court judges or the courts exercising that jurisdiction in the counties where the children are neglected. The strongest possible pressure that can be brought to bear upon the officials is through local public opinion, and wisely directed sympathetic and constructive State propaganda locally directed will in most instances accomplish the necessary reforms. It is a primary duty of the State to make the community see its problems, and then to treat them.

A supervisory board will early make a survey of the children's needs of the entire State. It will inform itself concerning the conditions prevailing in localities where there is a preponderance of child dependency and child delinquency and will develop community initiative to the end that the conditions producing these conditions will be changed. It will not only standardize and intensify the activities of the existing organizations under its supervision, but will assist in bringing into existence necessary agencies to meet the needs of children in neglected communities, and it will undertake to secure a coordination of all the agencies interested in human welfare. It will operate as a clearing house to which all problems concerning children may be referred. It will conduct community conferences, circulate educational literature, and take the initiative in the development of legislative programs. It will be a tremendous factor in the development of the thought that in the care of neglected children the State needs the service of every individual. It will undertake to dissipate the complacency of individuals based upon accomplishments for some of the children of the State, by directing their attention to the unfinished task; to the great multitude of children who, surrounded by vicious influences, will be driven into lives of delinquency unless protected, and to that large group of children found in every State who, because of physical or mental handicaps, are in special and imperative need. The State has an unquestioned responsibility not only in securing the protection of those who are cared for by existing agencies, but also in the development of a State-wide program which will recognize as its minimum of responsibility, the adequate protection of every child.

How long will the State remain indifferent to the needs of these defenseless children who deserve at least a chance to become useful citizens?

DISCUSSION

Miss H. Ida Curry (State Charities Aid Association, New York City): I am greatly interested in some of the suggestions Mr. Williams has made in regard to State supervision and State licensing, which is something in which I strongly believe, and which I should like to see extended very greatly in all of the States.

We have everything in New York, from the very best institution to the very backward institution; and I think that, in some of the towns where the backward organizations exist, we are sometimes in the position of waiting for somebody to die. As Mr. Williams has suggested, we fail to improve our methods because we do not want to hurt somebody's feelings—some person that helped to organize the institution.

And yet it was only a few years ago, that one little institution in New York State had a punishment closet built for the children, and had it painted black inside.

When the State Board of Charities objected to this, the board of the institution held a meeting and solemnly decided that they could not do away with the punishment closet, because they could think of no other mode of punishment for disobedient children. That was only about five years ago. But the other day a young woman, a member of that board of managers, came to our office and talked over a plan for selling that old-fashioned little building, in which they kept almost as prisoners about forty little children, and doing away with it in its present form. She discussed with us a plan for organizing a receiving home, which would receive the children accepted as public charges, find out what they really needed, and pass them on to a boarding home or to a special institution if they needed special care —in fact give each child what each needed.

Progress is being made, even in the more backward institutions. Certainly we do need, in most of the States, much more careful inspection of the placing-out work. The better organized placing-out agencies are probably doing as good work as can be done. But there are very many unsupervised agencies.

In a little maternity home of which I know, the physician is placing out children all the time. In one instance—we laid the facts before the authorities in this case—he placed out a child giving a false date of birth, making a false statement of the circumstances of the birth; the only name recorded on the adoption papers is the name of the foster parents; there are no names at all of the real parents of the child. Such instances still prevail in our old Eastern States, and I suppose in other States as well. We need more State supervision; we need State supervision in all work done for the children, both by private and by public agencies.

Mr. C. C. Carstens (General Secretary, Massachusetts Society for the Prevention of Cruelty to Children): There is a question which, it seems to me, is coming into the social work for children and needs our very careful consideration during the next few years. There are States of the Union where the private agencies are practically doing all, or at least 75 per cent of the work. There are other States in the Union where public agencies are practically doing all, or, we will say, 75 per cent of the work. I know of State agencies that are in every way discouraging private agencies to get under way and to assist in doing the work. I know States where there are private agencies that in a good many ways are blocking the public work. I think it is time for us to find out where we stand on that question. What shall be the relation of the private agency to the public agency? There is a fundamental service that both can render. I do not mean that at this moment I am ready to give any outline of what it shall be. But I believe that we have got to do some thinking about it, and have some considerable discussion of it, so that we may have both, for I do not believe the development of any State, whether it is in the Middle West, the Far West, or the East, will be right unless there is a relationship growing up between public and private services so that they may supplement each other, and that neither shall think it its duty to kill off the other.

Mrs. Ada E. Sheffield (Director, Bureau on Illegitimacy, Boston, Massachusetts): I have worked on a public board, and I have had connections with quite a few private agencies. It has impressed me that boards of private agencies are, with few exceptions, looking for the promising cases; they like to see results; and of course, as the judge of the court of special sessions in New York once said to me, one can make work 100 per cent successful by taking up only the best cases.

It has been my opinion that, as between the two kinds of work, work for promising children and work for children that do not show promise on the face of things, the public agency is fairly well equipped to take care of the promising child.

It is not well equipped to take care of the difficult child, who needs close intensive study and experimenting—trying-out of methods that the State has not yet taken over. That seems to me to be the only excuse for having private agencies. At present, the boards of private agencies are not interested in that kind of work; but it is my own opinion that they could be brought to be interested in it. That would give the excuse for having private agencies. The latter are going to be asked, before a great while, what their function is. Why should we give money to those agencies, when we pay taxes to maintain the public agencies? Under such a division of functions, private agencies would fill a genuine need.

Dr. Hastings H. Hart (Russell Sage Foundation, New York City): I am convinced not only that we need public supervision, but that we need supervision of some of our supervisors. The truth is that a good many people who have that responsibility laid upon them have not yet got a conception of what is meant. What we need is to get supervisors in these institutions to study their jobs.

CHILD WELFARE WORK IN JAPAN

By TAKAYUKI NAMAYE

Department of Interior, Japan

Ellen Key said that the twentieth century was the century of the child. It is well said, for the world is beginning to realize the importance of children's welfare as never before. The protection of children is demanded not only from the consideration of humanity, but also from the self-evident truth that the future welfare of society and nation at large depends upon the healthy minds and bodies of the present children. It is the realization of this fact that has made the question of children's welfare a social and national problem from the latter half of the nineteenth century up to the present time. The fact that a bureau for children's welfare was organized in the American Labor Department about six years ago, although many States at that time had highly efficient organizations for children's welfare work, must have been due to the same consideration.

Japan is not behind other nations in appreciating the importance of children's welfare; but our means for promoting it are far inferior to those of America and the nations of Europe. Various circumstances, customs, and habits are responsible for the poor accommodations; but it is beyond the scope of this paper to discuss them. I shall confine myself chiefly to stating what regulations and provisions different departments have in regard to child welfare, and give explanations and personal views only occasionally. The departments that supervise children's welfare are the Department of Interior and the Departments of Education, of Justice, and of Agriculture and Commerce. In discussing children's welfare work, it is convenient, therefore, to divide it as it is divided by the departments.

THE DEPARTMENT OF INTERIOR

Children's welfare work under the Department of Interior may be divided into two classes; namely, that which is regulated by law and that which is not.

Under the first class we have (1) the provisions of the Poor Law concerning the children of the poor, (2) the Foundling Act, and (3) the Reformatory Act.

(1) The Poor Law was enacted in Japan in 1874, and the provision in question states that the forlorn children under thirteen years of age

shall be given rice at the rate of three bushels and a half per year, and states also that the children who, although not strictly forlorn, have no relatives under seventy and above fifteen years of age, and are in distressing condition, shall receive the same amount of rice as that allowed to the forlorn children. It is hardly necessary to say that this method of relief is very primitive and the recipients necessarily very few. The expenses are to be paid by the national treasury; but as a matter of fact the local public corporations supply the deficiency, which amounts to a considerable sum, although their legal responsibility in the matter ends with the actual carrying out of the relief measures.

The latest statistics, which are those of 1917, will give a general idea about the amount of expenses and the number of recipients, as they have not increased or decreased to any great extent in late years.

Government expense	[1]Y 3,070
Local expense supplementary to the government expense	Y 8,452
Local expense	Y23,630
Total	Y35,152

The total number of children cared for was 1,203, of whom 213 were cared for at government expense and 990 at local expense or at local expense supplementary to government expense.

It should be noticed that, although the local public corporations are not required by law to provide money for the relief of the poor children, the actual financial assistance given by them to the relief work is comparatively large, as the government allowance is insufficient, its policy being to let them take the matter as much as possible into their own hands.

(2) The Foundling Act was passed in 1871, and is the oldest of the relief enactments now in force in Japan. The original act enjoined that three bushels and a half of rice per year should be given to each foundling until he reached his fifteenth year; but in 1873 the age limit was reduced from fifteen to thirteen, and has remained so ever since.

The number of foundlings found in Japan in a year is very small compared to those found in any of the European countries within the same length of time,—a fact of which Japan can be proud. For illustration the number of foundlings for several recent years may be given:

Year	Foundlings
1911	225
1912	274
1913	242
1914	188
1915	301
Average for the five years	246

[1]A yen is worth approximately fifty cents.

In a country possessing a population of more than sixty millions, only two hundred and forty-six foundlings a year is indeed a very small proportion. One might suspect that this scarcity of foundlings may be due to the strangling of infants or to abortion; but now such crimes are seldom perpetrated in Japan, though in the past they seem to have been quite frequent. In 1916, the total number of the foundlings under the protection of this law was 1,733, and the total expense for them Y 66,826. The foundlings being so few, it is scarcely necessary to have separate asylums for them; so the public corporations put them under the care of orphan asylums.

It will be seen that the total number of the children under the protection of the Poor Law and the Foundling Act is about 2,930 for a year, and the aggregate sum of expenses for them only about Y 101,970. European and American specialists may, no doubt, wonder at these small figures; but I believe that the chief causes are the following facts:

(a) The Japanese Poor Law is extremely retrenching.

(b) Social consciousness of the necessity of supporting the poor has not yet dawned.

(c) The spirit of mutual help is quite strong.

(d) The strong solidarity of the family system.

(e) The strictness of legal responsibility of parents to take care of their children.

(f) The natural kindness of Japanese people towards children.

(g) The comparatively small disparity between the rich and the poor.

(3) The Reformatory Act was first enacted in 1900 and was amended in 1908. The act requires each prefecture to establish reform schools to take in delinquent children under eighteen years of age, the upper age-limit of the inmate being twenty. The bulk of the expense is to be paid by the prefecture; but one-half of the expenses required in founding reform schools and one-sixth of running expenses are to be granted from the National treasury.

There are 54 local reform schools in Japan at present. They are divided into two kinds, public and private. The public reform schools are 28 in number, the private ones 26. The total number of inmates of all these reform schools at the end of 1917 was about 2,100, of which about 500 were taken in during that same year. They are mostly treated under the family system or under a system which is a combination of the family system and the dormitory system. One hundred and fifty is the largest number of inmates that a reform school has at present, and 9 or 10 is the smallest. Under the family system, about 10 inmates are taken in as a rule and the master and mistress or nurses look after them. They are given some elementary school lessons in the morning and some practical lessons in the afternoon, mostly in agriculture and manual labor. We have no accurate statistics as yet on the results of these efforts; but we can say that 70 per cent of the inmates come out of the reform schools much improved. The total expense in 1917 was Y 246,886, of which Y 44,000 was Government subsidy.

Besides the local reform schools, there is one national reform school which was opened in March of this year. The number of inmates is limited to 100. A training school for officers and staffs for reform schools in general is to be established in this institution.

The special feature of our Reformatory Act is that the executive department, and not the judicial, is the one that places the delinquent children in the reform schools. This is because we believe that the purpose of placing delinquent children in reform schools is not to punish or imprison them, but to educate and improve them, and to make them decent members of society. It is, therefore, the prefectural governor who issues the orders to be served upon those whom he thinks it to be advisable to put under the care of a reform school. This is a procedure which is seldom seen in other countries.

The reasons why there are only about 2,000 delinquent children in more than 50 reform schools are (1) the scarcity of delinquent children in Japan, and (2) the inadequacy of the Reformatory Act. The Government is contemplating a revision of the act to make it more effective.

Under the welfare work not regulated by the law, we have (1) orphan asylums, (2) day nurseries, (3) the Committee on Social Affairs for work on the Bureau of Local Affairs, (4) the Committee on Investigation of Health and Sanitation, and (5) the Lectures on Sanitation for Women.

(1) Orphan Asylums.—The origin of orphanages in Japan was more than ten centuries ago; but it is unnecessary to dwell upon its long and obscure history. I shall speak only of the orphanage work since the Restoration of 1868. The first orphan asylum built in Japan in the Meiji era was started by a French Catholic nun in 1874. This orphanage has been making great efforts for poor and orphan girls for the past 45 years and takes the first rank among the orphan asylums in Japan in the number of children taken in, which is over 4,100. Besides this, one of the best known asylums in Japan is the Okayama Orphan Asylum, which was started by the late Juji Ishii, who had been greatly inspired by George Muller. This is widely known as the model orphanage in Japan.

There are at present 138 orphan asylums with 6,500 inmates. Their aggregate expense for a year is about Y 420,000. Their properties are estimated at more than Y 2,000,000. They are, with very few exceptions, private enterprises founded by some benevolent person; and in financial matters they are always hard pressed because there are not enough of public orphan asylums to relieve the private ones of their burdens. It is true that the Department of Interior subsidizes, to some extent, such institutions as are doing excellent work, and each prefecture gives some financial aid to those that are within its jurisdiction, out of the interest on the common fund of Y 5,000,000, which was granted by the Imperial Household; and the money that comes from public corporations when they give the charge of foundlings to orphan asylums is of some help. But all these aids are far from being sufficient to enable orphanage workers to carry on their work as they wish.

There are now about 700 charitable institutions in Japan, and there are indications that they will increase year after year. It seems that Christianity is responsible for this stirring up of the public conscience. There are more than 70 charitable institutions under the management of Christians, and 30 of these are for orphan children. But charitable institutions are not monopolized by Christians by any means. In fact, Buddhists have more than 80 of them under their management, and their institutions for orphan children also outnumber those conducted by Christians. It should be mentioned here as a tribute of praise to both Christians and Buddhists that, though they differ in their religion, they are working hand in hand for the cause of charity.

The unweaned orphans are mostly placed under the care of farmers' families and when they reach school age they are, as a rule, taken into the regular orphanage. In Japan the farming population is very large as compared with the city population, and there is not much difficulty, therefore, in finding suitable families among farmers to whom to entrust these children, and the result has been excellent. Those who can not be placed in families are taken into the regular orphan asylums where they are now mostly treated under the family system, though in the past they used to be treated under the dormitory system. The orphan asylums conducted under the family system have from ten to fifteen inmates with a nurse or a master and mistress to look after them.

(2) Day Nurseries.—The first day nursery in Japan was established by the Kobe Women's Public Service Association during the Russo-Japanese war. At that time when it was necessary to support the poor families of soldiers who went to the front by giving them some work, and to enable mothers with small children to work they hit upon the idea of the day nursery and immediately some hundred day nurseries sprang up in different parts of Japan; but soon after the war all except one or two closed. Lately, however, their necessity was felt again owing to the demands of the times, and as a matter of fact they are increasing rapidly in number compared with other charitable institutions. Almost all the day nurseries in Japan are private establish-

ments. They are divided into creche and infant schools. The former take both the unweaned and infants, the latter the infants only. The four day nurseries managed by the War Memorial Day Nursery Association of Kobe, and the Samegahashi Infant School of Tokyo are among the best known in Japan. There are over fifty day nurseries now and over three thousand infants taken care of by them. The total expense is more than Y 50,000. In every day nursery great care is taken about the health of the children.

In Japan there is very little settlement work; but in the day nurseries they have family meetings from time to time, and they even visit the poor families and encourage them to save money and give other advice. In this way they are doing a sort of settlement work to the great benefit of the poor. Though the day nurseries have been only recently organized, their good work is already appreciated by the public.

(3) Committee on Social Affairs.—The Japanese Government, in view of the tendency of the times, deemed it advisable to make investigations about the social conditions, both at home and abroad, with the purpose of availing itself of the suggestions obtained from the investigations in coping with problems that may arise in the future, and organized a committee on social affairs, consisting of twenty members, partly selected high officials of the Government and partly experts who have special knowledge and experience on such matters. The committee makes investigations about such matters as are requested by the Minister of the Department of Interior, and makes reports giving its views on them. The scope of investigation is quite extensive. At the last year's meeting the subjects brought for discussion were the public market, the housing problem, the employment bureau, the adjustment of capital and labor, and others. The committee is to make a thorough investigation of children's welfare work in the near future with the purpose of aiding those institutions already in existence and of establishing new ones.

From time immemorial the Japanese have had the custom of ancestor worship and even now they attach a peculiar importance to the notion of "family," and children as future successors to the "family" are treated with great care. They are regarded literally as family treasures. A well-known old Japanese poem says:

> Silver, gold and precious stone,
> What are they in comparison
> With a daughter and son?

Traveling through any part of Japan you will see images of Gods and Goddesses which are regarded as protectors of children. From this superstition also you can see how solicitous they are for children's welfare. At any rate, the birth rate is always on the increase, and Japan does not have to resort to a premium system for the encouragement of

SPECIAL CARE—THE STATE

childbirth as in other countries. The following statistics show that not only does the birth rate exceed the death rate, but it is also steadily increasing every year—a phenomenon seldom seen in any other country.

Year	Birth Rate	Death Rate	Rate of Increase of Population per 1,000
1885	1,058,137	753,456	7.8
1895	1,335,125	876,837	10.9
1905	1,614,472	1,016,798	12.8
1910	1,737,674	1,037,016	13.4

The statistics for 1910 show that the number of births exceeded that of deaths by over 700,000.

But though we are very optimistic about the birth rate we are somewhat alarmed about the death rate of babes and infants, for it has been increasing in the past except in very recent years, as can be seen in the following statistics on the death rate of the unweaned less than one year old.

The following figures show the yearly average ratio of these deaths for every hundred births:

1886-1890	11.7
1891-1895	14.7
1896-1900	15.3
1901-1905	15.4
1906-1910	15.7
1912	15.4
1913	15.2

The slight decrease in the death rate as shown in the last two figures may be due to the efforts which the Government has been making of late years.

The average death rate per hundred children over one year and below five years of age is as follows:

Period	Age 1-2 Years	Age 2-5 Years	Age 0-5 Years
1889-1893	4.51	2.24	5.82
1894-1898	4.29	2.07	5.92
1899-1903	3.38	1.70	5.65
1904-1908	4.37	1.98	6.13

The above figures show that the death rate of children under five years of age has not materially decreased, but is still about twice as high as that of some European countries. It is a regrettable fact that notwithstanding this enormous death rate of children there are very few private enterprises to combat this problem. At present there is only one mothers' consultation society in Tokyo and another in Osaka. There are hospitals for children, the circuit hospitals, visiting nurses, and such organizations, which may be available in giving medical treatment to sick children, but these accommodations are but a few drops in a bucket. This state of things may look strange in a country which has been called by some "the paradise for children," but the fact is that the social consciousness has not been awakened to the actual state of affairs, the public at large having no knowledge of it.

(4) *The Committee on Investigation of Health and Sanitation.*—Two very promising organizations have been started lately to probe this problem—namely, the Committee on Investigation of Health and Sanitation and the Lectures on Sanitation for Women. The former, which was started by Imperial Decree in 1916, is under the supervision of the Department of Interior and at present has thirty-six members, part government officials, part non-official experts. The Vice Minister of the Department of Interior is the president of the committee. The work of the committee is divided into eight divisions, and one of them is the investigation of the health of infants, school children, and youth. The matter which has already been investigated and published is the death rate of children under five years for the last ten years. Other matters now under investigation are the sickness of school children, physical development of babies, the health conditions in the day nurseries and orphan asylums, and the condition of about 20,000 sick infants in the pediatric departments of the medical school. The completion of statistics on those matters will facilitate in ascertaining the causes, whether this higher death rate is due to poor nutrition or to the mother's lack of knowledge in rearing children or to endemics. Then the committee will be in a position to devise some suitable means to check the widespread deaths and diseases.

(5) *The Lectures on Sanitation for Women.*—In prefectures and public corporations in our country, lectures on sanitation are held for women. Although these were first started scarcely ten years ago they are now held throughout most of the country. The aim of these lectures is to diffuse among women knowledge in the rearing and care of children. The regular meetings continue several days at a place and sometimes they have exhibitions of things which are of interest to the work, something like the Baby Week Movement.

It is possible that by these means, the death rate of infants in Japan will be reduced as low as in other countries.

THE DEPARTMENT OF EDUCATION
The Primary School Education

(1) *History.*—Compulsory education is the most important means of building up a healthy nation by inculcating a wholesome national spirit and diffusing general knowledge among the children of school age. All nations of Europe and America have adopted it long ago. In Japan it was in 1886 that compulsory education was adopted. The present school regulation requires six years' course of instruction and as a rule does not charge any school fee.

(2) *Matriculation and Attendance.*—Though it is only thirty years

since school education became compulsory, school houses have been built all over the country. The following table shows the percentages of matriculations and attendance from 1911 to 1915:

Year	Percentage of Matriculation	Percentage of Attendance
1911	98.23	92.47
1912	98.16	92.78
1913	98.26	93.36
1914	98.47	93.69
1915	98.61	94.25

(3) The Number of Schools and School Children.—The number of schools in 1914 was: public, 20,440; private, 136. In 1915 it was: public, 20,518; private, 150. The number of school children in 1914, 6,700,000; 1915, 6,900,000.

(4) Finances.—Expenses are paid by public corporations. They amounted in 1914 to Y 56,720,000 and in 1915 to Y 60,000,000. This rapid increase of expenditure is due to the fact that the population of Japan increases by 600,000 or 700,000 every year and consequently many new school houses must be built. Such being the case, the burden of the self-governing communities becomes heavier yearly, and in some towns and villages the school expenses amount to one-half of their whole expenditure. Last year the Government decided to grant ten million yen annually to relieve the self-governing communities to some extent.

(5) Exemptions.—Children of school age afflicted with lunacy, idiocy, or serious illness may be excused from matriculation. Guardians too poor to send their children to school may postpone their matriculation. It is to be regretted that the nation and self-governing communities have no legal responsibility for educating these poor children. But the Government is contemplating making their education compulsory, though it is not known yet when this provision will be put in force. There are some public and private schools, however, which take in these poor children. So, in fact, this defect in our school regulations is not so bad as it appears. As those special schools have the double aspect of being institutions of education and of relief, they are under the joint supervision of the Department of Interior and the Department of Education.

(6) Institutions of Relief for the Defective and Destitute Children.—In 1917 there were twenty-nine schools for the blind and dumb (both private and public); three schools for the deaf, and thirty-eight schools for the blind. The number of children taken in by these institutions was 3,326. They are given four or six years of common education and practical training, in most cases free of charge. Some of these special schools have dormitories where the students can board with little expense. Most of the blind students be-

come masseurs after their graduation; but as the deaf and dumb cannot easily earn a living, employment offices are established especially for their benefit. The total expense of these 70 institutions was Y 176,000 in 1916. The National treasury, the self-governing communities, the educational associations, and some individual volunteers contribute to defray the expense.

In 1916 the number of the blind children of school age was 3,240; that of the dumb children of the same age, 6,039. These numbers are rather large in proportion to the number of the children taken in by these institutions for defective children. But as they are building new schools and enlarging some of the old ones, they will be able to take in a larger percentage in the future.

To come back to the education of the poor children, although the self-governing communities are not legally responsible for the education of the poor children whose matriculation is delayed for reasons stated before, some of them have voluntarily established schools for the poor children. Besides these there are some conducted by individual benefactors. In 1915 there were 67 schools of this kind, of which 52 were day schools and 15 were night schools. The total number of the pupils in these schools was 14,176. The expenses for the same year amounted to about Y 142,000. Moreover, almost every town and village has societies for the protection of the children of school age. Textbooks and lunches are distributed by them among the poor children. In this way, the inadequacy of the school regulations is supplemented to some extent.

(7) The School Physicians.—In 1898 an Imperial Decree was issued to the effect that all primary schools except those in small towns and villages having less than 5,000 inhabitants should hire physicians to improve their sanitary conditions, the physicians to be appointed by the local magistrates. Now most schools are too poor to hire private physicians exclusively attached to them—only those in large cities can do that. Consequently they hire ordinary practitioners. Thus, nearly 57 per cent of the entire primary schools, that is, 15,300 out of 27,000, have their physicians. Those physicians inspect the sanitary conditions of the schools from time to time, and once a year they make physical examinations of all the pupils and report to the Department of Education and also to the guardian of the students.

The results of the physical examinations of the school children for ten years (1906-1915) show that their height, weight, and lung capacity are getting more satisfactory.

Although considerable efforts are thus being made for the improvement of the sanitary condition of schools, sometimes the improvement does not come up to the expectation, because most of the school physicians, being poorly paid, cannot give sufficient attention to the schools. Therefore, in the large cities the schools are trying to have their own physicians if possible. Under the present regulation the school physician does not examine the mental condition of the children, but something will have to be done to remedy this defect.

(8) The Central Organ.—For better supervision of the sanitation of schools, the Department of Education established the School Sanitary Office in the Department in 1915, and in addition to this organized the School Sanitary Association as the consulting organ of the Minister of Education, and also holds a lecture class in the department for the benefit of the school physicians from all over the country. Apart from this supervision of the Department of Education some prefectures have their own supervisors.

The Supplementary Industrial Schools

In Japan as elsewhere there are many graduates of primary schools who desire to engage in some industry. To meet this demand the Japanese Government issued the Industrial School Order, encouraging the establishment of such institutions as are necessary to give proper training to these graduates. Those institutions are technical, agricultural, commercial, mercantile, marine, and supplementary industrial schools. I shall speak here only of the last.

The supplementary schools are divided into technical, agricultural, fisheries, commercial, and other schools. They matriculate primary-school graduates and those who have an equivalent education. The length of the course and the number of study hours vary according to the season, locality, and the like; for instance, the supplementary agricultural schools are opened during the winter season when there is little agricultural work to be done. The supplementary schools are of very recent origin in Japan, but they are making rapid progress. Of these, the agricultural schools are most numerous, which is quite natural, Japan being essentially an agricultural country. The lessons taught in common throughout the various kinds of supplementary schools are morality, the vernacular, and arithmetic. Other lessons vary according to the kind of school.

In 1916 the number of the public and private supplementary schools was 7,063 and that of the students 369,000. The following are the statistics for all kinds of supplementary schools for the same year:

	Public	Private	Total
Number of Schools..	9,344	3,021	3,697
Number of Pupils...	565,899	11,868	577,747
Expenditure	Y931,134	Unknown	Unknown

The supplementary school education is not yet compulsory, but the wonderful growth of this kind of school in a short period shows that it is almost as good as compulsory, and it is believed that the Government will extend this course of instruction by two years and then require those who do not receive high-school education to attend one of the supplementary schools.

The Religious Education

Catholicism was introduced into Japan several hundred years ago; but Protestantism came in only at the beginning of the Meiji era (1868). In the fifth year of Meiji, that is in 1872, the first Sunday School was opened, but for some time the growth was very slow. About twelve years ago, however, Mr. Brown, general secretary of the World Sunday School Association, came to Japan and organized the National Sunday School Association of Japan, and from that time the Sunday School work has made a rapid progress, until in 1917 the number of Sunday Schools reached 2,473 and that of the Sunday School children 160,000.

The following table will show how rapidly the Sunday School work is growing:

Year	No. of Schools	No. of Attendants
1907	857	64,910
1912	1,588	106,599
1917	2,773	156,245

Prominent men like Marquis Okuma, Baron Shibusawa, and others were appointed as the promoting committee of the World Sunday School Association Convention, to be held in Japan in October of next year, and preparation for it is already on foot. The expenditure, it is said, will be Y 150,000. It is believed that the coming convention will bring a new epoch to the Sunday School work in Japan and will make a great contribution to the general education of the Japanese children.

Sunday schools were at first all Christian institutions, but of late Buddhists also began to feel the need of them and established their own, and it should not be overlooked that they have made a remarkable progress with them.

The Young Men's Association is an institution wherein the boys, who, though graduates of primary schools, can not receive higher education, get together and learn about supplementary studies, industrial work, and citizenship. The management of the institution is left to the self-governing communities, the government only giving instructions on proper occasions. Most of these associations were organized after the Chino-Japanese War and again after the Russo-Japanese War. They had already done much good for social improvement, and in 1915, in view of the Great European War and for the future welfare of Japan, the Ministers of the Education and the Interior Departments gave joint instruction to the prefectural Governors for the improvement of the Young Men's Associations, which brought them under a system and made them doubly efficient.

In most cases each city, town, and village constitutes a Y. M. A. district and has its headquarters; but within a district branches are established to facilitate the work and to bring the members into close touch. In some counties and prefectures they have headquarters to supervise Y. M. A. work within their districts. The age limit is not quite uniform throughout the country, but in most places twenty, and in some, twenty-five years of age is the limit. According to the last year's report of the Department of Interior there are 18,482 associations and 2,932,113 members.

Among the various works carried on by the Y. M. A., the most general are the supplementary education, circulating library, keiro kai (veneration of aged people), temperance work, physical training, improvement of amusement, popular education, and the moral training of young men. Instruction is mostly given from time to time by lectures by school teachers, local officials, religious leaders and sometimes by business men.

The expenses of the associations are paid: (1) out of money earned and contributed by the members of the associations; (2) by subsidies from the cities, towns, and villages; (3) by individual subscriptions; (4) by income from the capital; (5) the proceeds from cooperative enterprises of the associations. The total expenditure of all the associations in the country for 1916 was Y 736,750. Their property in the same year was estimated at Y 1,000,000.

The aim of the Young Women's Association is practically the same as that of the Young Men's Association, namely, to make more efficient those girls and young women who are graduates of primary schools, but who cannot get higher education. The work of this association is naturally different from that of the Y. M. A. It includes domestic work, hygiene, rearing of children, cooking, sewing, family nursing, morality, and so on. The instruction is given by lectures of experts in these lines. These associations are all of very recent origin; but they already number 8,852 and have 1,049,652 members. The age limit of the membership varies from twenty to thirty years.

One very noteworthy feature of these two organizations is that they sometimes have joint meetings. The occasions for these joint meetings are when they have school exhibits, pictures, lectures on moral culture, charitable work, and so forth. I say it is noteworthy because in Japan commingling of young men and women in this way is very rare, and those joint meetings, though humbly started, may if wisely conducted on a large scale have a great significance for the social welfare of Japan.

THE DEPARTMENT OF JUSTICE

Treatment of Juvenile Criminals

The treatment of criminals, especially young criminals, is an important question for criminology. In 1907 the criminal code of Japan was revised and the age of discretion was fixed at 14. The act says "the acts of persons under 14 years of age are not punishable." Young offenders above that age are punished by ordinary criminal law, there being no special laws for them.

When a police officer apprehends a young offender, he takes him into a police station and there and then they examine him. If the offense is only slight they let him off with an admonition; and if it is not so slight or so serious they keep him in the house of detention for not more than 30 days; if it is serious they send him to the public procurator's office and the procurator examines the case and decides whether the offender should be prosecuted or not. The average number of young offenders who were subjected to judicial examination in five recent years was about 30,000; of these only 10,000 were prosecuted according to the regular law—some of them were fined, some put in jail, and others imprisoned. The average number of those who were imprisoned during the period of the five years 1913-1917 was 2,248. The statistics, however, reveal an annual decrease in the number of juvenile offenders in prison beginning with the year 1914, as shown in the accompanying table:

Year	Male	Female	Total
1913	2,156	183	2,339
1914	2,684	189	2,873
1915	2,092	172	2,264
1916	2,021	163	2,184
1917	1,828	148	1,976

The form of trial of young offenders is not uniform throughout the country, but in large cities like Tokyo, Osaka, and others, the courts have a juvenile department with a special judge. They usually segregate the young offenders from adult criminals and have a separate room for them. The trials are not open to the public. In these matters the spirit and the method closely resemble those of the juvenile courts in America and Europe. But as there are no special laws for children they are judged according to ordinary criminal law.

The prison regulations provide that the offenders under 18 years of age who are subjected to more than two months of penal servitude may be put into special prisons or special departments of regular prisons, and that they be kept in them until they reach their twentieth year. Thus the juvenile offenders are treated in a different way from that in which ordinary criminals are treated, the object being their protection and reformation more than punishment. Moreover, they are obliged to attend school a given number of hours every day, and even the labor they are required to do is rather for their training than for supplementing the funds by which the prisons are maintained. At present there are nine such juvenile prisons in principal places of Japan, and several more will be established in the near future. In the treatment of juvenile offenders both the grade system and the mark system have been adopted and the choice between them is left to each prison. Whether they use the grade system or the mark system, they keep each prisoner in a separate cell for the first three or four months of his imprisonment in entire seclusion from the outside world, and if he shows signs of improvement he is promoted to a higher grade and treatment becomes more lenient.

The result of this treatment is shown in the accompanying table:

Year	First Offenses	Second and Later Offenses
1913	2,220	585
1914	1,903	470
1915	1,851	413
1916	1,787	397

Thus it may be seen that the number of offenses is decreasing every year, but the number of second and later offenses has not materially changed. The latter fact may be due partly to not imposing an indefinite sentence and partly to the lack of social sympathy with the discharged prisoner.

It can easily be imagined that many of those who are set free without trial will repeat the offense if adequate protection is not given to them. Therefore whether the juvenile offenders are homeless or not, some further means of protection is absolutely necessary. In this regard we regret there is no probation system in Japan as yet. Not that there is nothing done in the way of their protection, for there are two homes for boys and one for girls in Tokyo. In those two places for boys they look after more than a thousand boys every year, and their work in seven cases out of ten is successful. There are more of these societies outside of Tokyo, but they are not so active in their work as those in Tokyo. It is to be hoped that many more such societies will be organized in the future to give adequate protection to the misguided youth.

The Children's Act

Though various attempts have been made at devising means of prevention of juvenile crimes, they have not accomplished the desired results; but it has been thought that the establishment of juvenile courts would be best suited for the accomplishment of this object. The law investigating committee have been working at a bill for some years, and the bill is nearly completed. It is not time yet for its publication; but—generally speaking—it seeks to apply a sort of probation system to those under 18 years of age who have committed some criminal offense or are inclined to do so. What the bill seeks to accomplish is as follows:

(1) To give admonitions from the court.
(2) To obtain admonitions from the principal of the school.
(3) To demand a written promise for repentance.
(4) To hand delinquents over to some protector on certain conditions.
(5) To place them under the care of some religious organization or protective society.
(6) To place them under probation officers' care.
(7) To send them to industrial schools.
(8) To send them to reform schools.

There are also features not seen in the laws of other countries, but on the whole the provisions are practically the same as the juvenile court regulations of America and of Europe. If the bill passes, after some amendments, it will do a great deal of good in the way of rectifying the defects of the present law.

THE DEPARTMENT OF AGRICULTURE AND COMMERCE

The development of factories in Japan is of very recent origin. In fact it is not fifty years old yet. Therefore the capitalists and factory owners of Japan have not had experience in the management of such enterprises. Before the introduction of the factory system, the various industries of Japan carried on their business by means of handicraft and home industry. In those days, when international trade was forbidden and the principal of "self-supply" had to be enforced, no great inconvenience was felt from those old-fashioned methods, and the handicraftsmen and those who were engaged in home industries dragged along in their work from morning till late at night in a most lax manner without any definite restriction of time. The relation of the employer and employee was, of course, that of master and servant. But when Commodore Perry came and broke the spell of a long dream, all of a sudden the policy of isolation was abandoned; international commerce was allowed, and in fact everything changed in a very short time. The social, political, and business conditions underwent a complete change and left no trace to remind us of former conditions. In the industrial circle also the factory work took the place of home industry and a great many operatives began to work with wonderful machinery and to have definite hours of work. But even when such violent change had been accomplished, the relation of the capitalist and the factory workers remained that of master and servant. As to the long hours of labor, too, employers, employees, and the public at large, being accustomed to it, never thought anything was amiss.

The Factory Act

Such being the conditions under which the factory system had developed, the Government perceived the necessity of taking some protective measures and in 1882 organized a committee to investigate the actual conditions and customs of the factories throughout the country. In 1897 a bill was drafted based on the results of the investigation by this committee. But very unfortunately the Parliament dissolved at that time and the bill was not even presented. After many years of hard labor in overcoming obstacles thrown in its way, the bill finally passed through both Houses in 1911 for the first time; but it was not until 1916 that it became operative, owing to the fact that deciding on the rules of enforcing the law took a long time.

As a result of this law, an Imperial Decree was issued ordering the Department of Agriculture and Commerce to establish a factory section in the Department. In pursuance of this decree the Department appointed the Vice Minister as the sectional chief with four factory supervisors and five sub-supervisors to assist him. Moreover it has been decided to have local supervisors placed in several important places, and in fact there are now about two hundred of them distributed in various parts of the country. The expenditure required in this work is about Y 200,000. Although we have now this Factory Law for the protection of child laborers, no special law has been enacted as to the restriction of the work hours of adult laborers, it being left entirely to the agreement between the employers and the employes.

The restrictions placed upon child labor are as follows:

(1) THE AGE OF THE CHILD LABORER. "The factory owners (employers) are not allowed to hire children under twelve years of age except under special administrative permission."

(2) THE PROHIBITION OF NIGHT WORK. "All children under fifteen years of age are not allowed to be employed in any work after 10 P. M. and before 4 A. M. But for fifteen years after the enforcement of this law, those special industries which require night work or continual day-and-night work may be exempted from the application of this law by the permission of the Minister of the Department."

(3) HOLIDAYS AND RECESS PERIODS. "To children under fifteen years of age, two holidays should be allowed in a month and to children of the same age who are employed in a business requiring day-and-night work, four holidays should be allowed in a month, and if the working time should exceed six hours a day, a recess of at least half an hour should be given to them, if ten hours, a recess of at least one hour."

(4) CASES WHERE ASSISTANCE IS TO BE GIVEN. "When a factory operative meets accident, falls sick, or dies without any serious fault of his own, the employer is required to give financial assistance to him or to his surviving family."

The Number of Child Laborers in Japan

The number of child workers in factories in 1916 is shown in the accompanying table:

Age	Total	Boys	Girls
10-12	10,914	1,938	8,976
12-15	133,570	29,853	103,717
All ages	144,484	31,791	112,693

The total number of the adult operatives and the child laborers in factories being about a million, children form nearly fifteen per cent.

Welfare Work

Special arrangements made for the promotion of the laborer's welfare are not few. Since the operation of the Factory Law, they have rapidly increased, although their exact number is not yet ascertained. In the Prefecture of Tokyo there are about 1,600 factories of all sizes and about 230,000 operatives. There are about 500 factories that employ more than 50 workers. Sixty-three out of these 500 factories have mutual aid societies, some of which, in case of sickness or retirement of the members, give financial aid out of the fund paid up by operatives exclusively, and others of which give aid out of the fund contributed to by the operatives and the employers. The latter usually contribute as much as or half as much as the total sum of the contribution by the employees. There are also day nurseries, rent-free houses, dormitories, bath-houses, places of amusement and so on, altogether numbering 210. And for the education of the employees there are fifty-six institutions where they train apprentices and give supplementary instruction or primary school education, and the prospect is that these institutions will gradually increase.

I must confess that what has been said above is a very imperfect presentation of the subject. And time does not allow me to discuss fully the advisability or inadvisability of the long hours of labor to which Japanese children are subjected. I should only say that labor in Japan has a peculiar history and circumstances, and now to adopt the American or European system bodily in entire disregard of that history and circumstances would be only to bring on unnecessary disturbance if not disaster. As principles, the propositions made by the Committee on the International Labor Alliance meet our approval, but Japan is under the necessity of steering her course in this matter with due regard to her peculiar internal conditions as well as external circumstances, and for this reason Japan may have to be treated as an exception. We are not, of course, satisfied with the present condition of the Factory Act; but we must be patient. Perseverance has accomplished wonders. Rome was not built in a day. Japan, though not very slow in making progress, requires time to bring about such fundamental changes as suggested by the committee now meeting in Paris.

CARE OF DEPENDENT CHILDREN

THE CONCLUSIONS OF THE WHITE HOUSE CONFERENCE—TEN YEARS AFTER

By DR. HASTINGS H. HART

Director, Department of Child Helping, Russell Sage Foundation
New York City

One of the last official acts of President Theodore Roosevelt was the calling of the White House Conference which met at Washington January 25 and 26, 1909. The idea of this very remarkable conference was conceived and its details were executed by James E. West, now Chief Scout Executive of the national organization of the American Boy Scouts. About 200 delegates were invited, representing every State in the Union, and every kind of agency for dependent and neglected children: State boards of charities, boards of children's guardians, charity organization societies, associated charities, children's home societies, children's aid societies, societies for the prevention of cruelty to children, juvenile protective associations, juvenile reformatories, orphanages, children's homes, and institutions for mothers and children. The delegates represented all forms of religious belief, including Catholics, Protestants, Jews, and the Salvation Army.

It was felt that the conference ought to formulate some kind of a statement embodying those principles upon which these delegates could agree, which might contribute to a better understanding between them, pave the way for a greater degree of cooperation and serve as a point of departure for future progress and for the standardization of child-welfare work. On the night before the opening of the conference, a small representative group of about 30 people met in the New Willard Hotel to consider the possibility of agreeing upon such a statement. There appeared such a wide diversity of opinion, especially between the representatives of the child-placing societies and those of the orphanages, that it seemed as if it would be impossible to agree upon any comprehensive platform; but the subject was amicably discussed, and it was agreed that the attempt should be made.

On the following day the conference convened at the White House, with President Roosevelt in the chair. A committee on resolutions was appointed, of which I had the honor to be chairman. The other members were Edmond J. Butler, Homer Folks, Julian W. Mack, and James E. West. All of the members of the committee worked earnestly and harmoniously. It is only fair to say, however, that the credit for the great report of that committee belongs chiefly to Col. Homer Folks, who was its author, together with the late Thomas M. Mulry and Judge Julian W. Mack, through whose wise and farseeing cooperation a surprising and happy result was attained.

The conference sat for two days, during which the committee on resolutions was hard at work. At times they sat in the conference to catch the spirit of its deliberations; at other times they consulted with members of the body as to what should be included in or omitted from the document.

The report of the committee on resolutions contained fourteen articles, covering home care, preventive work, home-finding, the cottage system, incorporation, State inspection, inspection of educational work, facts and records, physical care, cooperation, undesirable legislation, permanent organization, a Federal Children's Bureau, and a summary. It is impossible, in 15 minutes, to discuss in detail this great platform of 3,000 words. It included such vital propositions as the following:

1. The creation of a National Children's Bureau, accomplished by the prompt action of President Roosevelt and seconded by his successor President Taft, which resulted in the splendid bureau whose guests we are today.

2. The conservation of family home life as "the highest and finest product of civilization," "not to be broken for reasons of poverty, but only for considerations of inefficiency or immorality," and to be preserved by "such aid . . . as may be necessary to maintain suitable homes for the rearing of the children . . . to be given by such methods and from such sources as may be determined by the general relief policy of each community." This proposition has been realized: first, through an increasing recognition of the importance of preserving home life, by the courts, by children's aid societies and children's home societies, and by the constructive work of such agencies as the societies for the prevention of cruelty to children in Boston, Brooklyn, and Philadelphia, and the Cleveland Humane Society; second, by the development in most of the States of the Union of the plan of "mothers' pensions," "mothers' assistance," and so forth. This plan has developed with such rapidity that it has not had time to crystallize into fixed and definite policies. It is clear, however, that it has come to stay, and that it involves a new realization of the value of home life and the community's responsibility therefor.

3. An emphatic endorsement of the doctrine that "the carefully selected foster home is for the normal child the best substitute for the natural home," with the proviso that "such homes should be selected by a most careful process of investigation, carried on by skilled agents through personal investigation and with due regard to the religious

faith of the child," and that, even for temporary care, "contact with family life is preferable for these children, as well as for other normal children." The use of boarding homes was suggested, but the difficulty of finding such homes was recognized by the statement: "unless and until such homes are found the use of institutions is necessary."

4. Recognizing a legitimate field for some institutional care of dependent children, it was declared that "these institutions should be conducted on the cottage plan, in order that routine and impersonal care may not unduly suppress individuality and initiative. The cottage unit should not be larger than will permit personal relations between the adult caretaker . . . and each child therein. Twenty-five is suggested as a desirable cottage unit, subject to revision in the light of further experience."

5. It was urged that "child-caring agencies, whether supported by public or private funds, should by all legitimate means press for adequate financial support," and that "cheap care of children is ultimately enormously expensive and is unworthy of a strong community."

6. It was proposed that only incorporated institutions should be allowed to assume the duty of child-caring, and that incorporation should be permitted only after careful investigation and certification by a responsible State board; that "all agencies which care for dependent children, whether by institutional or by home-finding methods, and whether supported by public or private funds" should be subject to thorough inspection by trained agents of the State; and that the State inspection should extend to their educational work as well. Since 1909 there has been a gradual increase in the number of States adopting such legislation.

7. "The establishment of a joint bureau of investigation and information by all the child-caring agencies of each locality" was "highly commended, in the absence of any other suitable central agency."

8. The declaration was made that "we greatly deprecate the tendency of legislation in some States to place unnecessary obstacles in the way of placing children in family homes in such States by agencies whose headquarters are outside the State, in view of the fact that we favor the care of destitute children, normal in mind and body, in families whenever practicable."

9. A proposition was offered for "the establishment of a permanent organization to undertake in this field, work comparable to work carried on by the National Playground and Recreation Association, . . . the National Child Labor Committee, and other similar organizations." A movement is now on foot for the development of such an organization through the expansion of the "Bureau for Exchange of Information," an association of about 50 of the leading child-welfare agencies of the United States.

10. The spirit and essence of the "Conclusions" was expressed in the following summary: "That the particular condition and needs of each destitute child should be carefully studied and that he should receive that care and treatment which his individual needs require, and which should be as nearly as possible like the life of the other children in the community."

In view of the diverse interests represented in the conference, and in view of the advanced and in some respects radical declarations contained in the conclusions, it was anticipated that this platform would arouse a vigorous discussion and that it would be necessary to amend it at various points in order to secure anything like harmonious action. And indeed it seemed almost too much to expect that, even with such discussion and amendment, unanimous agreement could be secured. In order to give opportunity for free discussion and amendment, the report was presented at four o'clock on Tuesday, January 26, and two hours were allotted for its consideration.

The report of the committee was read to the conference. Its adoption was moved by Mr. Edmond J. Butler of the Society of St. Vincent de Paul, and seconded by Mr. Sherman C. Kingsley, of the United Charities of Chicago. Then Mr. M. V. Crouse, Superintendent of the Cincinnati Children's Home, arose and said: "I favor the report of the committee most heartily throughout, with the exception of one single word. In speaking of the frequent visitation of children placed out, it says that in some cases it would be greatly to the advantage of the child in the family to be frequently visited. I suggest to the committee 'adequate visitation.'" This important and far-reaching amendment was solemnly considered by the members of the committee who were present on the platform, and was accepted by them. Favorable remarks were made by Dr. W. P. Spratling of Baltimore, Dr. Edward T. Devine of New York, Mr. J. P. Dysart of Milwaukee, and Mr. Charles W. Birtwell of Boston. The question was then called for. The Chairman said: "If there is no further discussion I will put the question." A rising vote was called for, and the entire conference rose to their feet. The negative was called for, but there was not a single adverse vote.

Thus this great platform of 3,000 words was unanimously adopted, with the change of only a single word, by as representative a body as could be convened in the United States.

I have been asked to indicate what portion of the program thus adopted "has been outgrown or proved undesirable." To the best of my knowledge, only two of these fourteen articles have been seriously questioned during the ten years since they were adopted.

There are some who still believe that the transfer of dependent children from State to State should be prohibited. This belief takes two forms. Some oppose such transfers on the ground that the immigration of dependent children imposes an unjust burden upon the community into which they come; but a very little investigation will demonstrate that healthy children, not vicious, are an asset to every community, especially in these days of declining birth rate and deficient man power. Others oppose the transfer of children from State to State because they believe that dependent children should be the wards of the court within whose jurisdiction they are found, and ought not to be taken beyond that jurisdiction.

The other article which has been challenged is the proposition that the carefully selected foster home is for the normal child the best substitute for the natural home." In view of the long-continued prejudice in favor of the orphanage as against home-placing, it has been surprising to see the general acceptance of this idea, even among the people who maintain orphan asylums; but there are still a limited number of people who advocate the commitment of all dependent children to orphanages.

In the City of New York, under the administration of John Purroy Mitchel as Mayor, and John A. Kingsbury as Commissioner of Charities, there was inaugurated an enterprise for placing children in family homes, which was the largest in the United States except that of the Massachusetts State Board of Charity. This work was developed under the immediate management of Mr. William J. Doherty, Deputy Commissioner. A trained and efficient corps of social workers was organized, and the work was put on a practical and modern basis. Homes were selected with great care, and thorough supervision was undertaken. The placing-out method was adopted only for children under the age of seven years, while older children continued to be boarded out in institutions.

Upon the election of a new mayor and the appointment of a new commissioner, this valuable agency which had been created with so much labor and at great expense was discarded. It was announced that experts were not wanted; and while a limited amount of placing-out was continued, vigilance was relaxed, and the careful standards which had been established were lowered. Recently, however, the Commissioner of Charities has taken steps to make arrangements with a number of private accredited child-placing agencies to find boarding places for children who are wards of the city, the expense to be borne by the city.

I believe that it is fair to say that, after ten years, the conclusions of the White House Conference stand as a permanent and authoritative declaration of the principles which should direct the treatment and care of dependent and neglected children, and that they have the indorsement and approval of the great body of intelligent students of children's work.

DISCUSSION

Mr. S. C. Kingsley (The Welfare Federation, Cleveland, Ohio): It seems to me in general that this program has had a profound effect on the thought and practice of the whole country. As far as I have sampled the attitude of my own and the practice of the different communities, I can say that one can trace the effect of that notable meeting.

As I have listened to the speakers this morning, knowing as I do something about the plans and hopes for this meeting, it seems a happy augury that such a gathering should have been called together now on not only a national scale, but an international scale. Since that meeting ten years ago, the world has moved along very fast. We are thinking now in terms of countries as well as in terms of States and communities. All of these countries which were quite strange to us then, now seem neighbors. The matter of taking painstaking and discriminating care of the child has not gone as far as I wish it had and hope it will. We have not, in my opinion, outgrown these recommendations.

I am interested in the child-caring agencies in Cleveland as a group of people responsible for one section of the field. We have not begun to catch up with this program. I think what we need today in the way of information is the interpretation of experiences gained and facts gathered in the prosecution of the work. We are not getting enough of that sort of thing. We are all individualistic, each holding some little sector of the child-betterment front, but without enough of orderly procedure and mobilization of the child forces to go warring against the various causes that are producing trouble in the field. I do not feel that in many places the information which those who are doing the work on these definite fields have obtained is positive enough and well enough interpreted to give a community the guidance and leadership it should have. I think the community has a right to ask the workers of the child-welfare field for that necessary information.

We have not gone far enough in this matter of giving to the child the kind of a real home it ought to have. We are still under the spell of bricks and mortar—something we can look at and touch. There are many of us who have our faces toward the bricks and mortar while our backs are toward the world from which the children came. We are too much interested in seeing little people stand up on the platform and sing. So I would say: Be more alert now in this day, when it seems to me we are calling for leadership; we want to know where we are going; we are more interested in the solution of these problems than in the maintenance of a given number of organizations.

WHAT CONSTITUTES SUFFICIENT GROUNDS FOR THE REMOVAL OF A CHILD FROM HIS HOME

By JUDGE VICTOR P. ARNOLD
Cook County Juvenile Court, Chicago

If a twelve-year-old boy smokes cigarettes, should he be taken away from his home? If his father habitually brutally mistreats him, should he be taken from his home? Should he be removed if he has committed a burglary? Should the State take him in its arms if he is feeble-minded?

The very serious responsibility is laid on me to tell you what constitutes sufficient grounds for the removal of a child from his home. It is my daily duty in the Juvenile Court in Chicago to make decisions which remove children from their homes. In the year 1918, I found it necessary to enter 1,448 such decisions in the cases of dependent or neglected children, and 989 decisions in the cases of delinquent children.

The authority for taking children away from their homes is generally to be looked for in the juvenile court laws which are now on the statute books of a great proportion of the States. These laws also define under what circumstances a child is dependent, or neglected, or delinquent, and their inclusion of circumstances under these terms is usually very broad. In the short time allowed me I cannot review the situations covered by these laws, nor is that necessary, as I shall draw upon my experience which is governed by the laws of Illinois. It is enough to say in general at this point that the juvenile court laws are usually so broad that the State, in its capacity as parens patriae, through the juvenile court, will take jurisdiction over practically every significant situation where it appears it should do so in the interest of the child or the State, whether that situation be caused by the nature, bad training, or conduct of the child, the unsuitability of the home, or the controlling bad influence of environment.

Yet this jurisdiction should be exercised with grave caution. The integrity of the family circle is a relation so fundamental and held in such high respect that the law, both legal and ecclesiastic, has clothed it with a special sanctity. It will be apparent that the court, under these laws, exercises a discretion in a responsibility so great that under its order the sacred bond of the family can be broken. These laws, however, intend that this drastic action shall only be used as a last resort when it appears that any course less drastic has failed or will fail of remedy. Juvenile court laws are laws of mercy and not vindictiveness, and should be mercifully and sympathetically administered, always throwing the advantage of the doubt, if there is one, in favor of the child. Of the juvenile court is expected also an unusual patience and hopefulness, and faith in the capacity of human beings to improve. The result of all this will be, in the hands of the enlightened juvenile court judge, that the court will to the utmost try to influence the child or his family to the proper mode of life, and probation and supervision will be tried generously as a remedy. Decisive firmness must, however, be used when it appears that the child must be taken from his home, whether to be placed under guardianship or to be committed to an institution.

In my administration of the Juvenile Court Act of Illinois in Chicago, I do not hesitate to take from his home a child, neglected or dependent, where it is clear from the evidence that the immediate prospects of the home are hopeless, whether this is due to immorality or depravity on the part of the parents or guardian, or to cruelty or positive neglect of the child, or to some other unfitness.

In cases where the mother of young children is leading an immoral life, if it appears that the mother's conduct is due to ignorance and lack of standard rather than depravity, and if it also appears that there is still a basis of good in her and if she is otherwise a good mother, she should be permitted to keep her child or children under supervision of a probation officer of the court and under the strict warning that her immoral or compromising conduct must cease. If the mother appears depraved and callous to any moral improvement, the child should be placed under the care of a guardian. If the home is depraved by habitual drunkenness of the parents or guardian, or by habitual furious or violent quarreling, or by habitual indecent, vulgar and profane language, then I have no scruples about taking the children from them. If the evidence shows that the parents have until recently maintained a suitable and fit home, but by reason of drink have made their home a rendezvous for disreputable characters, the children may remain with them only if I can be sufficiently satisfied that the cause of complaint will be removed or the dangers lessened, and then only on probation under supervision to an officer of the court.

In cases of cruelty, if the cruelty is such as to indicate a depraved mind on the part of the parents, the child should be rescued from that menace by taking him away from the home. If the cruelty is due to ungoverned temper on an exceptional occasion, or to a mistaken idea of parental authority and what parental control ought to be, I may give the parents an opportunity to correct their conduct and allow the child to return to the home on probation to the officer of the court. I heard the case of one little girl, a child of about twelve, whose father in his inhuman treatment of her fractured her arm and threw her out. The poor frightened child hid under the house until found some days later by neighbors who notified officers of the court, who in turn took her in charge and had first aid given her. In this case it was clear that the child should be taken from her home, the father being subsequently dealt with in another jurisdiction.

Cases of neglect are of great variety. In a large group of cases of this type I invariably try probation if the parents show a disposition to cooperate, and resort to taking the child from the home only after I have found that probationary supervision has failed. In this group I class such cases as follows: where the neglect has been due to the ignorance of the parents in properly caring for or supervising the children; where the parents have refused to give the child adequate clothing and nurture; where the mother has been shiftless, has neglected her children, has failed to supervise their conduct; where both parents have worked outside the home, leaving the children without supervision during the day to the detriment of their behavior or the neglect of their school attendance, but an agreement is made that the mother shall remain at home and give the necessary supervision; where the father has been spending his money on drink, failing to provide clothes and food for his children; where one of the parents is a step-parent and has assumed an obstinate attitude resulting in the neglect of the child, but promises to improve according to the suggestion of the court; where the child has been allowed by the parents to beg or gather alms, but the parents assure control; where the parents have kept the child from school to work. In cases such as these I am not likely to take the child away until after a probationary trial with failure. Of course, in cases of homeless or abandoned children there is no alternative for the court but to make a final disposition.

In cases of delinquency of children I never order the child taken away from home on the first time in court, unless the delinquency with the circumstances attendant is so gross as to show a depraved, vicious, or recklessly destructive spirit with respect to life and property, or unless the delinquency, while very obviously reprehensible, has been done with the approval or active encouragement of the parents; or unless the home of the parents or guardian is so bad that it cannot be a factor in a plan for correcting the child. In such cases as these I must immediately be drastic to protect the community and to save the child. In these extremes are included such cases as those where boys break into a store at night and wantonly destroy the contents; or where they steal an automobile and race down the streets endangering human life; or commit a robbery and deliberately shoot a person; or assault a girl; or where a boy strikes and injures his mother; or where he teaches small children bad habits or criminality. These are merely suggestive of what I mean by extreme cases.

In the great majority of cases of delinquent boys in court for the first time, I try probation. In many cases I try probation repeatedly when the boys come into court for subsequent delinquencies. A decision should never be made hastily. Such a complex and vari-colored community as Chicago has its currents of degradation and vice that flow through hidden channels and find the congested poor districts especially non-resistant and easy of penetration. It is not easy for a child or his family to correct the fault in such unlikely circumstances, and great patience is necessary. I take the child from the home only as a last resort.

The cases of delinquent girls who come before the court are in a great majority of instances for immoral conduct. Such cases present a distinct, special problem, and involve so much for the sake of the girl that they require a more final disposition by the court than cases involving depredations on property or many types of other delinquent conduct. This is brought out by the statistics of the Chicago Juvenile Court, which show that for the past three years from 45 to 55 girls are placed on probation at home per year as against 100 taken from the home and committed to institutions or placed under guardianship or in some home other than their own. During the same period, from 110 to 200 boys were placed on probation at home as against 100 taken from their homes. The girls frequently come from homes where they receive little, if any, supervision, where the relations between the members of the family are infelicitous and unsympathetic, or where the parents are ignorant of our language and customs, and are easily imposed upon by their precocious daughters. A great number of girls are incorrigible, and their appearance in court is due to their refusal to recognize parental control.

We are in need of further legislation, which should render subject to the jurisdiction of the State children who have remediable marked physical abnormalities which greatly handicap them, whether caused by accident, injury, malnutrition, or heredity. In cases where parent or guardian neglects or refuses to permit medical attention to remedy the above condition, the court could on a proper showing order that such conditions be remedied. As with juvenile court legislation and legislation on feeble-mindedness and insanity and epilepsy, such legislation would be for the mutual good of the child and the State; however, it should be conservative and drawn with the utmost caution. Hand in hand with this should go legislation by which children suffering from curable diseases or from serious ailments, who have not been given proper attention by their parents or guardian, should come under the jurisdiction of the State to the extent of requiring remedy upon a proper finding by a competent court.

After a careful investigation of the home and the social environment has been made, and all family facts available preliminary to the hearing have been secured, together with full information concerning the specific offense, the tendency should be to permit the child to remain in the home if the home can be made a proper place for the child. In other words, if the judge hearing the case can be given a fair guaranty that the child will no longer be menaced by former conditions in the home, a supervision or probation order should be entered. In delinquent cases, probation is desirable where the child indicates a corrected attitude toward society and shows a willingness to submit to court supervision, and that of the natural guardians.

Great caution should be exercised by officers investigating complaints of dependent, neglected, and delinquent children, to the end that no child should become a court case where it is possible to reconstruct conditions in the home so that the home can be made fit, or where the causes of delinquency can be corrected without court action. In Cook County, during the year 1918 over 16,000 complaints of juvenile delinquency were adjusted out of court under the direction of the judge and chief probation offcer and about 3,000 became court cases in a total of 19,000 cases. In dependency and neglect, 2,350 family adjustments were made out of court, while but 660 families were brought into court.

All honor to the family, its high meaning, its great function; yet to idealize it does not give it any immunity from ignorance, or the sad train of consequences that go with ignorance. Enlightenment is the very foundation of civilization and any advance in civilization. Can the State have any greater responsibility than to throw the focus of enlightenment into the dark places of ignorance and maladjustment, and to counteract the unhappy results of these by the beneficial ministrations of the agencies of enlightenment?

It is essential for the proper administration of the law and for constructive and effective work by the Juvenile Court that the officers be competent and efficient. The judge enters the order or decree but does not carry it into effect. If the officers of the court are not specially trained, if they are lacking in devotion to their duty and are not capable in every way, the court order or decree will not accomplish that which is desired. The probation officer is, in reality, an extension of the court.

I cannot approve the policy in some jurisdictions of assigning judges to juvenile court work for short periods. My own experience would indicate that it takes approximately a year for the judge to become accustomed to and understand the administration of the law in the juvenile court. Judges experienced and trained in the administration of the juvenile laws are as essential as trained probation officers.

DISCUSSION

Judge James Hoge Ricks (Juvenile Court, Richmond, Va.): I feel especially keenly the force of the points that Judge Arnold has made. This question of taking children from their homes is indeed of most vital importance. It must be an absolutely last step. Within the past six months I have had to take children from families which we had been holding together for a period of a year or even several years. In one instance recently I took three of the younger children of a family which we began to deal with in 1912. I admit that it does seem that the court should have learned in shorter time than seven years just whether the children should be taken from that home or not; but I do feel that if our social agencies had really been on the job in that particular case it might not have been necessary to remove those children at all. This is the point that I want to bring out: that if the social agencies of the community will stand solidly behind the court, and particularly if the churches and religious influences will cooperate with the court in helping to build up the standards and the ideals of the home, then fewer children will have to be taken from the home; and that is the ideal which I believe every right-minded judge seeks to attain.

Mr. Arthur W. Towne (Superintendent, Brooklyn Society for the Prevention of Cruelty to Children, Brooklyn, New York): I think we can all agree to three points without any discussion: First, no child should be removed from his home on account of poverty; second, many judges of juvenile courts need to be educated as to child psychology and social points of view; third, each case must be looked into on its own merits.

No law can minutely define what constitutes neglect or cruelty. What applies to one family will not apply to another family, because of a difference in age, or grade of intelligence, or some other factor.

Now, the degree of neglect formerly considered insufficient to remove children from home is in many cases today considered sufficient to cause removal. Moreover, the field of neglect is extending in scope and the rights of children are multiplying; things formerly not recognized as being sufficient ground for removal are often considered sufficient today. For example, years ago children having hereditary syphilis and wilfully deprived of treatment were not thought of as subjects for court action; now they are subjects for court action. So, with moral influences in the home—those intangible subtle suggestions that influence the minds of children.

Two or three questions should be asked in all cases before we decide to take them into court. First, is the child in jeopardy? It does not mean that we are going to remove children simply because one bad act has been done on the part of the parent. Is it going to continue? Second, we want to know whether the condition is remediable, and we want to give the benefit of the doubt to the child and the parent, and to the preservation of the home. If through friendly influence we can build up the home, and can get the parents to take an interest in the children, then we do not want to consider removing the children. If that does not work there is another possibility—to take the parents into court, and put them on probation, and make them mend their ways. Only as a third resort should we remove the children. Social workers, in general, do not know the necessity of legal evidence in such cases. I think our schools of philanthropy should train social workers more in the principles of evidence. Moreover, we want to be assured when we remove a child it will be better off than under its present conditions.

Mr. Bernard J. Fagan (Chief Probation Officer, Children's Court, New York City): I do find that a great deal of the burden is upon the social workers who bring many of the cases to court without having a knowledge of what constitutes evidence. The court is a court of law, call it by what other name you like, and it must be governed by the rules of evidence. It is not a psychopathic laboratory. When it comes to a question of breaking up a home, the responsibility rests where the people have placed it—upon the shoulders of the judge. I find few who even after they have had a supposedly adequate training know what our courts can do. A great many do not even know the functions and powers of the juvenile court in their community.

Mr. C. C. Carstens (General Secretary, Massachusetts Society for the Prevention of Cruelty to Children): One thing that Judge Arnold said leads me to call attention to the fact that the doubt should be in favor of the child. I am inclined to think that judges even in our better juvenile courts have less hesitation about resolving the doubt in favor of the child in the case of the first action, but are inclined to resolve the doubt in favor of the family when it comes to returning the child to the home. Some of us who are active in work for the protection of children feel that judges usually interpret the evidence presented in the same way as those who are presenting it, in the first instance, but when it comes to the question of the return of the child one month, two months, or six months, or even several years later, there are a number of other things that have to be taken into consideration besides evidence. We must continue to favor the child, rather than say "Now, this home has straightened out and this child must return," when, as a matter of fact, the cleavage that existed in the first place has grown greater during the time while the child has been away. There arises a nice question as to whether the child should be returned even though the home may have gotten somewhat straightened out.

I hope also the time will come when the child will not be brought into court in cases where the question is whether he is being properly cared for. I do not think that it is a good thing for the child to get familiar with courthouses and court procedure. We ought to recognize the fact that the child should be taken care of somewhere else while the parent is brought in to be disciplined. As a rule the child has no evidence of any particular value.

The work of the children's protective agencies is of two sorts—the prevention of the breaking up of homes and the helping of their breaking up. Helping to break up is easy; it is the prevention that is the hard work; and it is towards this that we should direct our greatest energy. Let us see that the numerous agencies working for the protection of children devote themselves definitely towards reshaping the home long before breaking up is possible. That, I think, is the function of the State, though it may not be the function of the juvenile court. That, it seems to me, is the work to be done in the protection of the child, so that the break-up does not need to come. How soon will the State undertake that job?

Mr. Fagan: What is the procedure in courts throughout the country as to having the child appear?

Judge Ricks: In the Richmond court, in cases of dependency and neglect, the children are always sent out of the court room.

Judge Arnold: In Chicago, in cases involving facts and circumstances which children should not hear, the parents remain and the children step out.

Mr. Fagan: In New York the children are arraigned and the names certified to, and they are then sent out and hear nothing of the testimony given by the parents.

Mr. Carstens: I plead for an arrangement by which the children will be left miles away from the court.

Mr. Fagan: Would you still have the judge commit them without having him see the children in court?

Mr. Carstens: That is a perfectly fair question when it is a case of the removal of the child, but you will notice that I spoke of the procedure against the parent when the child would be only a witness. If it is necessary to have a child committed away from the parents, I believe the court should see the child, but we should not require that a child be brought into court unless it is absolutely necessary.

Dr. Hastings H. Hart (Russell Sage Foundation, New York): There is one point that has been overlooked in this discussion which seems to be a necessary corollary of what has been said. The sacredness of the home and the care that should be taken in separating parent from child, or child from parent, has been emphasized here this morning, but nevertheless such separation is constantly accomplished without having the court say anything about it. A poor mother is advised that she can have relief if she parts with one of her children. She simply signs a paper and the child is gone. The thing is not adjudicated by a competent court. A poor girl lies in a hospital with a baby. While she is lying there, a man persuades her to sign a paper and the child is separated from her forever. Before I left the city of Chicago the Children's Home and Aid Society adopted a rule that under no circumstances would it be a party to a transfer of guardianship of a child without taking the matter into court. In every case the judge is to determine the question whether the guardianship should be changed. I think that is an essential question for every one interested. It should be understood that in no case shall it be possible for a parent to be divested of guardianship unless the case is passed upon by the court. That does not necessarily imply that the parents shall appear personally in the court. Under the Illinois law an unmarried mother may sign an appearance and consent, and the judge, if he sees fit, need not have that mother present, but the guardianship is not accomplished until the court has passed upon it.

STANDARDS OF CHILD PLACING AND SUPERVISION

By EDMOND J. BUTLER
Executive Secretary, Catholic Home Bureau
for Dependent Children, New York City

In order to keep within the limits of the time and outline of subject allotted me, I shall have to present these standards in somewhat brief outline. I realize the necessity for these limitations in view of the many divisions of child-welfare activity scheduled for the conference and the possibility of duplication of treatment of particular phases of the work which have a direct relation to all, but I nevertheless feel that these limitations deprive me of the opportunity to furnish adequate reasons or explanations for the standards offered.

The plan I have adopted for the presentation of the subject is as follows: (1) Definition of terms; (2) the child; (3) the foster parents; (4) home finding and investigation; (5) supervision; (6) discharge from supervision; (7) after-care; (8) records.

DEFINITION OF TERMS

Placing-Out.—The term "placing-out" has acquired, during the past fifteen or twenty years, a distinctive meaning which should be generally known, especially to charity workers, in order that the confusion which has resulted from its improper use may be avoided. It does not mean boarding-out, indenturing, baby-farming, the securing of employment or the mere transfering of the custody of a child from one person to another or to an institution without regard to the object of such transfer. It means placing a placeable child in a free family home for the purpose of making it a member of the family with whom it is placed.

The New York State Law defines the subject as follows:—"The term place-out . . . means the placing of a destitute child in a family, other than that of a relative within the second degree, (parent, grandparent, brother or sister), for the purpose of providing a home for such child." This definition, with the qualifying of the home as a free home, offers a complete definition of the term.

Boarding-Out.—This term qualifies the act of placing a dependent child in a family home, where payment is made to the boarding-home mother for the care of the child.

Adoption.—The law of New York State, which is probably

similar to those of other States, defines this subject in the following terms:

"Adoption is the legal act whereby an adult takes a minor into the relation of child and thereby acquires the right and incurs the responsibility of parent in respect to such minor."

As the future development and welfare of the children concerned in these activities depend for success upon a proper recognition of the needs and rights of the child, all persons or organizations engaged in conducting such work should be required to secure a license from the State for that purpose and should be subject to inspection by the State board of charities.

THE CHILD

As a general proposition, any normal healthy child is a placeable child, but aside from this subjective qualification there are many conditions which would render placing-out undesirable.

The age of placeable children may be briefly stated as follows: Boys to and including the age of fourteen; girls to and including the age of ten. The placing of girls over ten years of age, particularly where there are other children in the family, does not give promise of good results. The most flagrant exploitation of child labor and neglect of scholastic training occurs in the cases of girls between the ages of ten and fifteen. The experience of placing-out agencies will show that the most successful results occur in the cases of children placed at or below the age of five years. No child should be placed out who is suffering from any physical or mental defect. All such children should receive the attention necessary to bring them up to normal standards before placement.

No child should be placed without a sufficient guarantee that it will be kept at school until it reaches the age of sixteen.

Parent and child should not be separated because of temporary disability. If poverty, illness or even improper guardianship make it necessary to give a child temporary care, nothing should be done to cause a definite and continuous separation, if there is hope of rehabilitating the parent and again restoring the normal relation. As the natural order provides for parental care, based upon love and affection, for the support and training of the child, it also demands a reciprocal service for the aged based upon filial love and duty. When, therefore, there is possibility of reuniting parent and child, such a child is not placeable, but should receive temporary care in a boarding home or institution.

Careful investigation should be made as to the cause of death or any present probable incurable condition, mental or physical, of the parents of the child to ascertain what, if any, inherited tendencies are likely to develop in the child. If there is any danger from this source, the child is not placeable. Such a child should be cared for in a boarding home or institution until in the opinion of experts all danger from such a source has disappeared, when the child should receive, if possible, the advantages of a normal home.

The placing of a child with a family for the purpose of legal adoption, without investigation as to whether all of the requirements for that procedure can be complied with, is a matter likely to create serious consequences. Courts cannot abolish by any legal process the parental rights recognized by all civilized governments, and many instances may be cited of the reversal of legal adoptions. When one or both parents of a child are living, such a child is not placeable for adoption, unless the parental consent is provided or the legal conditions favorable for such action exist.

Consent to legal adoption should depend upon a favorable probation period—of at least one year. It is absolutely necessary, before undertaking to place out any child, to secure definite information as to its family history and the possibility of subsequent difficulties which might result from ignorance with regard to the matter. For the children who are not placeable, there is the boarding home and the institution, either of which may be used to meet the temporary or permanent care needful for them.

THE FOSTER PARENTS

In view of the fact that the vast majority of the families of our country consist of persons having a limited amount of wealth, an ordinary education, and little or no distinction of a social character, it would be unwise, if not futile, to set up standards for foster parents of so high a character as to limit our possibilities for success.

We should realize that most, if not all, of the children we aim to help, do not come from homes where at any time unusual conditions of wealth or distinction prevailed. If we can secure homes and foster parents among the wealthy or well-to-do, we shall be pleased to have the opportunity to contribute uncommon means for future welfare to some poor children. It does not however necessarily follow, that children so placed have greater futures in store for them than those placed with families who have been accustomed to making personal sacrifice to maintain their positions in life; in fact, that willingness to make such personal sacrifice may contribute more to the child's welfare by securing greater personal attention, consideration, and allowance for the trials incidental to child life than could be expected from those who delegate such care and attention to a hireling.

We should aim to secure for foster parents, persons who desire a child for the child's sake. They should have an income, with a reasonable prospect of its continuance, sufficient to ensure proper care and support of the child. They should not be advanced in years, as otherwise the child might lack the continuous care necessary to enable it to reach manhood under their training and supervision. They should be persons of good physical and mental health, industrious and thrifty, should possess at least average education and intelligence, and should enjoy the respect and endorsement of their pastors and neighbors as law-abiding and respectable citizens of their communities. They should be of the same religion as that of the child to be placed with them, and should be vouched for by their pastors as persons who are practical in the performance of their religious duties and as persons who will provide religious training for the child assigned to them.

The foregoing standards, except as to the financial requirements, apply also to the parent or parents of the boarding-home. In this matter, however, it should be distinctly understood that the parents should not be dependent solely upon the sum received for the board of the child to enable them to supply the care and attention necessary for its support and training.

HOME FINDING AND INVESTIGATION

Home Finding.—The methods to be adopted for developing homes will vary according to the experience obtained by those engaged in the work. My own indicates that advertising is not worth the cost. "Sob stories" may develop a large number of appeals for children but many of them will be from persons who demand impossibilities. Some publicity, however, is necessary and the interesting and appealing press items and stories will play an important part in preparing the way for other methods.

We have found that the efforts of a careful, conscientious agent can produce more satisfactory results than may be secured by any other method. In making his appeal to prospective parents, he has the opportunity to eliminate much waste of time and money needed for investigation, by selecting approved sections and neighborhoods, and desirable families. He will also learn of the local opportunities which may offer helpful assistance to the family in matters of education, religious training, recreation, companions for the child, etc. The securing of homes by such a method will, I am sure, be found the most satisfactory means employed in this phase of the work.

Investigation.—Following the receipt of an application for a child, the most thorough investigation should be made concerning the applicants, their home, the members of the family, and the locality of the home. This investigation to be complete should be made by an agent duly qualified for the purpose, and the report of the agent should include definite information on the following lines:

SPECIAL CARE—DEPENDENTS

1. Character of house, location and surroundings.
2. Personality of (a) husband, (b) wife, (c) children, (d) other members of household, (e) possible companions or neighbors.
3. Religion and general character of parents.
4. Business, occupation or earning power.
5. Remarks of pastor or reliable neighbors.
6. Has family ever had a child before? How treated?
7. Proposed occupation and arrangements for care of child.
8. Such additional facts as may tend to give a complete survey of all conditions affecting the character of the foster parents and their home.

SUPERVISION

Within a month after a child has been placed it should be visited by an agent of the placing-out society with a view to learning whether the home fits the child and whether the child fits the home and is a welcome member of it. Thereafter the child should be regularly visited by the agent, not less than twice each year and as much oftener as the necessities of the case demand. No person or society should engage in doing placing-out work unless prepared to follow this initial feature by providing adequate supervision continued for the period necessary to ensure good results. To place out without such supervision is a crime and should be treated accordingly.

Agents when visiting the children should ascertain and make complete reports as to the child's physical and mental condition; conduct and attitude towards family; attendance and progress in school; attention to religious duties; the kind of work, if any, performed in the home or elsewhere; if working, the compensation given, savings and bank account and amount of same; sleeping accommodations; clothing and bodily comfort; recreation facilities and companions; and such other matters affecting the interests of the child as may be necessary for a comprehensive knowledge of the situation by the administration of the placing-out agency. They should also note any change of address and, where same occurs, give complete details of the new home and its location, and should state what changes or additions have occurred in the make-up of the family since the last visit, the attitude of the foster parents toward the child, their attention to their religious duties, and such other matters as may indicate whether they are continuing their qualifications as desirable foster parents for the child. Where adverse conditions occur which justify the removal of the child, the agent should transfer the child at once to such approved home as may be available or return it to the placing-out agency.

Placing-out and supervision are not and cannot be looked upon as separate pieces of work. From the time we begin our search for a free foster home, procure it, and place the child in it, whether it remains there or is transferred to another home or homes, up to the time when we may be able reasonably to declare that the child no longer needs supervision, all of the work done in connection with the care of that child is a continuing act, which is not completely or well done if we should discontinue supervision, except in the cases mentioned hereafter, at any time prior to the age of twenty. Proper supervision in the cases of children placed in boarding homes requires that the visits should be more frequent. Due to the fact that the relation of the child with the boarding-home mother is based primarily upon a money consideration, it is necessary that the minimum requirements for this service should be those established by the Board of Minor Wards of Massachusetts. The knowledge gained by the years of experience of this board should prove a valuable guide as to all details concerning the boarding-out system.

DISCHARGE FROM SUPERVISION

The position taken by the Catholic Home Bureau, with an experience of twenty-one years in dealing with the problems arising from the care and supervision of more than four thousand children placed by the bureau in free family homes, is that such supervision should not cease until the wards of the bureau, both boys and girls, have attained the age of twenty years.

This standard does not apply to such cases as are disposed of by adoption, as all such cases automatically leave our jurisdiction upon completion of the legal formalities of adoption. Nor does it apply to such exceptional cases as may arise from time to time where it becomes desirable, because of unusual and justifiable conditions, to cease visitation in the interest of the future welfare of a child; as where the latter has been living for a number of years in an ideal home, under the most favorable conditions, believing that its foster parents are its real parents, and a strong bond of affection exists, and the necessary publicity of visitation by our agent might result in breaking up existing relations. These cases however will always be small in number as compared to the whole, and cannot be used as fixing the period for necessary supervision.

We have found by experience in dealing with children who are not in the homes intended for them by the natural order, those of their parents, that the most critical period in the lives of such children lies between the ages of sixteen and twenty in the case of boys and between fourteen and twenty in the case of girls. It is during this period that the child begins definitely to manifest that spirit of youthful independence and disregard for authority which results so disastrously in some foster homes which lack the complete tempering affection of the fatherhood and motherhood of a normal home. In such cases the aid and advice of our interested agents are needful to adjust the difficulties and restore harmony. It is during this same period that the boy and girl develop an earning capacity which should be properly directed and for which due recognition should be provided by procuring for them a wage commensurate with their service and home conditions, to the end that they may have an opportunity to put something aside for the possible break in home conditions or other phase of adversity. Where such recognition is denied them they should be removed and placed in other homes where they will receive adequate recognition and compensation for their labor.

Foster homes are subject to the same fatalities that befall those of the normal type. Death, sickness, adversity, or other causes may lead to the breaking up of the home, and as a result the child placed therein may be forced out into the battle for existence at an age when a boy or girl is unable to make the struggle unaided. Again, intemperance or other adverse influences may enter the home and cause it to be so disorganized and unsafe as a shelter for the young as to make it desirable to remove a child from such conditions. It surely cannot be claimed that a boy or girl of immature age is competent to meet these adverse conditions and make proper provision, unaided, for the adjustment of them. It should be and is our duty to anticipate such results by a continuous supervision up to a time in the life of the child when we may feel certain that we have completed the work undertaken by us in placing the child in the home of strangers; and we feel, as the result of our experience, that as a general proposition supervision should not cease before the age of twenty for both boys and girls.

AFTER CARE

Complete service in placing-out work requires that when discharging a child from supervision he should be informed that the placing-out agency is not bidding him farewell, but wishes to continue as his friend and to be one indeed should he need one at any time. Hundreds of instances could be cited of wards of our bureau who have visited us when grown to manhood and womanhood seeking advice, aid to employment, adjustment of family or other difficulties, etc., and many consoling results have followed such visits.

RECORDS

The records of child-placing agencies should be most complete in all details. They should include a record of the child; its physical and mental condition, scholastic training, family history, birth certificate, etc., at time of placement; all reports concerning the child and its home subsequent to placement, details as to discharge from supervision, legal adoption, and after-care. All records should be kept in such form as to make it possible to secure prompt and complete information concerning the case.

DISCUSSION

Mr. Edwin D. Solenberger (Pennsylvania Children's Aid Society, Philadelphia): There is a group of children presenting problems that are special to themselves, so that it seems wise to relate the discussion of standards of care for dependent children to the standards of care for children of illegitimate birth. Now, I am going to ask Dr. Sheffield, Director of the Bureau on Illegitimacy, of Boston, to continue this topic by taking up that particular division of the subject.

Mrs. Ada E. Sheffield (Director, Bureau on Illegitimacy, Boston, Massachusetts): There are two questions related to placing-out work that appear again and again in connection with unmarried mothers. They are both questions of method, and questions to which I myself can offer no answer. The first is this: Is it better that pregnant girls should be placed in maternity homes up to the period of confinement, or is it better that they should be boarded out or placed out? We have found in Boston that the maternity homes hold the one view, and certain of the child-placing agencies hold the other. So far as I know, it is a matter of opinion, and not a matter of adequate evidence on either side. The second question is: Should the mother and child be placed together—dual placement—or should they be supervised separately, the mother at her work and the child in a foster home?

I suppose we all agree that the mother and child should be kept together through the nursing period. But how is that to be done? It is frequently done by keeping the two in a maternity home, the home giving them care and protection over a period of several months. It is sometimes accomplished by placing the mother and infant together at domestic service. It might also be done by giving the mother a pension. There are those, however, who feel that the mother should not be kept in a maternity home for a long time. There are also those who believe that the placement at domestic service will not do; that it is asking too much of the mother that she support herself and her infant at the same time.

For the sake of argument, we will assume that we are talking about fit mothers. When the mother and child have been kept together through the nursing period, then arises the question, how much longer ought we to urge that they be kept together? There is considerable evidence showing that many unmarried mothers give up their children at anywhere from one-half year to three years of age. Now, ought we to urge that they should keep them longer than that? If on the other hand we are going to encourage the separation, ought we to aim to bring it about at the end of the nursing period rather than try to have them stay together for a matter of months or of two or three years? Of course, we all hope in this work with the mother and baby that we may get some support from the father. Thus far, however, in most organizations that hope has been rather a vain one. The organization which has done most in that direction in Massachusetts is the State board of charity. They have had the services of a special lawyer, who for several years has prosecuted all the cases on which they had sufficient evidence to warrant prosecution. I have not the figures as to the proportion of cases which they have taken into court, but it is not large—which means that in many instances it is difficult to get the necessary evidence. The head worker of the department of the State board of charity told me a few days ago that in her experience the excellent law which we have for the prosecuting of the man in the case is not a success from a financial point of view; that the mothers are not getting much money to help with the support of the children. Undoubtedly we can improve the enforcement of that law, but much as we would like to get adequate support from the man, it would seem to me from present indications that we must regard help from these fathers as supplementary rather than as sufficient.

I venture to present these questions to which I can offer no answers because the inspiring part of our work lies in its unsolved problems.

Mr. Solenberger: There arises in this connection, of course, the question of whether or not the child should remain in the home. Mr. Butler has said that his agency has taken the child of the unmarried mother in certain instances. That is true, I suppose, of practically all child-placing agencies. It is probably also true that the removal of the child of the unmarried mothers from the mother is in most States often a matter of chance.

Miss Mabelle B. Blake (Boston, Massachusetts): I want to refer to two points in Mr. Butler's paper. If I understood him correctly, he said it was almost impossible to place girls over ten years of age. I would not want to go that far. Although it is difficult to place older girls, it is possible; the whole importance of the matter is in selecting the right family for the girl. I happen to know of forty-two girls who are placed out, earning their own way and attending high school. Thirty-two have had sex experience. Three are preparing for college. One will enter normal school next year.

There is one other point, namely, the selection of the boarding home. One of the most important ways to get the right kind of boarding homes for the children is through the education of the foster mothers and foster fathers that we already have. I mean the successful foster mothers. In this way sometimes we have been able to get together the foster mothers and tell them what our work is and how we expect them to help.

Furthermore, I do not believe we ought to accept a family as satisfactory when it is dependent upon the amount which we pay for the board of the child. The board ought to be absolutely an additional amount.

Mr. W. W. Hodson (Director, Children's Bureau, Minnesota State Board of Control, St. Paul): The Minnesota law provides that the father of an illegitimate child shall be subject to the same responsibility for the care of that child as though the child had been born in lawful marriage. The statute also places upon the State board of control responsibility for seeing that the child is given a fair chance, and more particularly to see that the proceedings to establish paternity are begun, and that having been begun and properly concluded, the natural responsibility is thereby assumed. The activity of the board of control has been centralized in getting the evidence necessary to establish paternity in any given case and then in overcoming the out-worn prejudice against bringing proceedings under the bastardy law. I am very glad to say that Minnesota no longer talks about the bastardy law, but has stricken that word from the law entirely.

The point upon which the board of control has laid specific emphasis has been that when this responsibility on the part of the father is established, the mother also shall assume the natural responsibility of nursing her own infant; and to that end the State board of control and the State board of health have joined in a resolution providing that every hospital licensed by either board shall require the patients to nurse their babies so long as they remain in the hospital.

Mr. John P. Sanderson (Executive Secretary, Connecticut Children's Aid Society, Hartford): I have been interested in Mr. Butler's paper because he laid before us certain definite standards in child-placing work. To my mind the critics of child placing have criticised principally not the family care for children but the mechanism we have used in placing the children.

To my mind the standards for child placing are identical in any type of home we use, whether it be a boarding home, a free home, a wage home, where the children are working for so much a week, or a home for adoption. Perhaps the latter types require more thorough work, but the fundamental principle, I think, which we should work out is to set up a code of case-work standards. The child is our responsibility.

CHILD CARING WORK IN RURAL COMMUNITIES

By MISS H. IDA CURRY

Superintendent, Children's Agencies, State Charities Aid Association, New York

The need of social work in cities has long been recognized, and recently there has been an increasing recognition of an equal need in rural communities. In any large city will be found a long list of social agencies, each dealing with a particular social problem: charity organization societies and associations for improving the condition of the poor, that deal with family problems in the home; hospitals, dispensaries, visiting nurses, and milk stations, endeavoring to cure and to prevent sickness; institutions, child-caring societies, child-rescue societies, home-finding societies, child-labor associations, day nurseries, kindergartens, special industrial schools, and fresh-air movements for children; probation and prison associations dealing with delinquents; lodging houses and temporary shelters for the homeless man and the wandering woman; social settlements, organized recreation facilities, saving and loan societies, committees on housing and sanitation; and scores of other agencies that seek to better living conditions in the city. The name of each of these organizations presents to our mind a recognized city condition demanding organized social service.

Let us now look at a family living in the country, one mile from a small town. The house is a two-room shack on the hillside. In one room live an old woman, her son, and from time to time anywhere from one to four or five relatives. This room is almost devoid of furniture, but is always clean. In the other room lives the old woman's unmarried daughter with two children and the man who is the father of a coming baby. This room contains a bed, a broken stove, and a chair, and is dirty beyond description. At noon on a warm day of early summer the woman and children were found on the filthy bed of rags. The one window two by three feet was tightly shut, as was the door. The air within was suffocatingly hot and heavy with unwholesome odors. The water supply for this dwelling is a nearby brook, and the only toilet facilities are those provided by nature on the hillside.

The group abiding in this place pick up a living by doing odd jobs in winter, the old woman acting as a midwife, and frequently using her one room as a maternity hospital. In summer the men, women, and children pick fruit on a nearby farm. School attendance is irregular at all times, and during fruit season it ceases. These people are all of old, if degenerate, American stock.

The situation described can be duplicated over and over in the rural parts of the country, and it presents problems of over-crowding, unsanitary conditions, irregular employment, lack of nursing care—especially maternity care—child labor, non-attendance at school, general neglect of the children, and many other antisocial situations.

Social problems are, after all, problems of people rather than problems of place, and are to be found wherever people live. In the rural communities, no less than in cities, do we find immediate need for some social agency to deal with all of these problems. Even more than the city does the rural community, with its high death rate, need improved care for the sick. Intelligent child care is also more urgently needed, possibly, than in the city, and a need at least equal to that of cities is found for social effort on behalf of the delinquent, for organized recreation, for better housing, and for improved sanitation.

In all rural communities we find the destitute child or the child belonging to a destitute family. When destitution is the only problem, there should be readjustment within the home. Successful experiments in various places are being made in improving the existing machinery or creating new machinery for public relief to needy families—notably through widows' pensions or mothers' allowances—so that the same adequate and intelligent care may be given through public agencies as is now being given by the best private relief societies. But usually the relief to the destitute is but poorly administered, and there is urgent need for it to be guided aright.

The neglected child is found everywhere. Possibly more gross forms of neglect can be found in isolated rural communities than in a city where the proximity of neighbors tends to control individual action. For the neglected child, some agency is essential to improve conditions in the home if possible, to remove children from unsuitable homes when necessary, and to prosecute wilfully neglectful parents. After children are removed from unsuitable homes, it is of greatest importance that an intensive study be made of the personality of each child and of its future needs. Bearing in mind the principle that family life is essential for the normal development of the normal individual, care suited to each child should be planned—in a boarding or free home or in an institution, as circumstances demand.

Delinquent children, too, abound in all communities. To deal with these in rural communities is needed a development of the juvenile court and probation system. An improvement in dealing with truants is also essential. By the consolidation of school districts it should be possible to employ a well-trained visiting teacher instead of a low-paid truant officer, who not infrequently in rural schools at present, is also the janitor, and who generally is more competent as janitor than as truant officer.

Defective children are found everywhere, both those who have some physical disability and those mentally handicapped. The social wellbeing of the community as well as that of the individual demands that the blind and the deaf shall have specialized education; that the crippled shall not be excluded from schools because of physical handicap, and that they shall have the most expert orthopedic advice available to prevent deformities or to correct them as far as possible. The mentally defective require even more careful attention, as they are apt to be a greater menace in a community. Protection and oversight in the home, or custodial care in institutions, must be provided.

Medical care in rural communities is of prime importance. Outside of cities there is at present little or no facility for dispensary or hospital care or for expert medical service. Great progress is being made in developing the nursing service in rural communities throughout the United States. In certain States—notably in Vermont, New York, Massachusetts, and Minnesota—highly specialized aftercare of poliomyelitis has been organized by State departments of health with traveling clinics which have carried expert orthopedic advice to the most isolated neighborhoods. Recently similar traveling tuberculosis clinics have been tried in New York State. The success of these clinics seems to point to a method whereby other specialized medical advice might be made available in regions where it is now so sadly lacking.

How all of these varying social needs of childhood in rural communities can be met, becomes a very practical question. Probably in most of the United States the county is the most practicable geographical and political unit for general child care, although in certain phases of children's work the State is the smallest practicable unit. Particularly is this the case in the finding of free homes for children, as it is always desirable that there be a wide range of homes from which to select the one most appropriate for a particular child. It is also generally essential that a child's foster home be at a distance from undesirable relatives as well as from neighbors who have known of the family disability which has cast the child upon the community for care.

A rural social program may be organized by public or private initiative, or by a combination of the two, but it must be accepted by the community as a local community endeavor. To be effective it must recognize the natural and inevitable variety of local conditions; it must be elastic enough to meet local needs, and it must be a growing program to meet changing needs. It should function along lines most natural to the particular community, and it should, to the greatest extent possible, use the forces already existing therein.

Experience has led me to believe that one central-directing organization for the social work of a county is highly desirable, except possibly where a city of considerable size is located in the county. It is sometimes desirable in such counties to have one organization for the city and another for the county outside of the city, as the problems of the two sections may be quite dissimilar. It is desirable that local organizations should be closely associated with some outside agency of at least State-wide interest, equipped to stimulate development and to standardize methods; and whether under public or private control, they should always be subject to State supervision.

It is obviously impracticable to have separate organizations to deal with all the different problems found in the rural field, but any rural program, to be adequate, must include at least a nursing service and a social service. Success will depend more upon the human element—upon the expertness and the adaptability of the persons selected to carry through the program—than it will upon the program itself. It is important that the nurse should be a general public-health nurse, rather than one dealing only with tuberculosis, with baby welfare, or with any other one phase of public health. It is equally important that the social agent should be a general practitioner in the social field, sufficiently familiar with all welfare effort to deal intelligently with maladjustments of whatever nature. There should be, however, as has been suggested, some opportunity to call into consultation outside experts when particular difficulties arise, just as the general medical practitioner will call a specialist into consultation when necessary. In New York State the appointment of public-health nurses in the counties and the appointment of county children's agents has been furthered by a State-wide private organization, the State Charities Aid Association, which has furnished such consulting advice. But I am inclined to think that such functions, when carried by a private association, should be turned over to a State department of charities and to a State department of health as soon as these departments can safely assume the responsibility.

To sum up:

(1) The county is probably the best administrative unit for rural organization, but a State-wide agency should be used for the placing-out of children and possibly for other specialized work.

(2) Every rural community should have a nursing and a social service, which may be organized under private or public control, or a combination of the two, but which should invariably be under the public supervision of the State.

(3) The nursing and the social service should be under the same general direction or under closely affiliated direction.

(4) The nursing service should be in the hands of broadly educated public-health nurses, to further public and private health programs,

including the establishment of adequate home nursing and of suitable clinics and hospitals. The social service should be rendered by broadly trained investigators to deal with social maladjustments and to further public and private programs for rural betterment.

(5) Success will depend primarily upon the personal and professional qualities of the field workers.

CARE OF JUVENILE DELINQUENTS

STANDARDS OF ORGANIZATION IN CHILDREN'S COURTS

By JUDGE JAMES HOGE RICKS

Juvenile and Domestic Relations Court, Richmond, Virginia

I am going to paraphrase my subject as a discussion of the machinery of the juvenile court. I think it was Andrew Carnegie who startled the industrial world by scrapping practically new machinery whenever newer and better machinery could be found to take its place. This has been true also in the educational world. Wherever teachers have found a new way of teaching or a new text-book better than the one in use they have cast the old one aside, although it may have been scarcely used. That is even true in the medical world, although I must confess that a doctor is almost as slow to learn as a lawyer. It remains for the lawyer to be guided by precedent and tradition.

In the Eastern States we have inherited our laws from England. The English law came from three sources—the statute law, the decisions of courts, and customs which the courts after a certain number of years treated as having the effect of law. In other words, the very antiquity of a custom or a way of doing things gave it the force and effect of law. In the eyes of the courts, what is so must continue to be so. I think we have no clearer illustration of how hidebound courts are than in this particular subject which we are now discussing.

At a very early date in England the courts of chancery began to administer the property of children. Wherever a man died leaving small children and it became necessary to dispose of their property, the court of chancery, representing the Crown itself as ultimate guardian of the child, took charge of the property and administered it. That proceeding is a very careful and a very thorough one. First, a bill stating all the facts in the case has to be filed with the judge, who refers it to the commissioner in chancery. The commissioner calls in witnesses and inquires whether it is to the best interest of the child that the property should be sold, and, if so, what disposition should be made of the proceeds. He makes a report and a recommendation which is returned to the judge; the judge reviews that report and then makes such final disposition of the case as the welfare of the child demands. What a careful and wise provision for the protection of the property of the child!

Suppose, however, that a child is the son of a laboring man who has been able to accumulate (we will say) enough to buy a small lot costing probably $500. If it becomes necessary to sell that property the interests of the child will be safeguarded. But if, because that child is half orphan, his mother has to work in the factory all day, and the child is left to run in the streets at will; if, because he wants a baseball mitt or glove such as the other fellows have, he breaks into a store and gets it; then he is haled before a magistrate and his case is heard, sometimes in three minutes or even less. No question is asked as to why he is there or what can be done for him. He has violated a law, has offended against the peace and dignity of the commonwealth, and he must be punished for his offense. In the shortest space of time his whole life may be made or marred with no thought of his moral and spiritual development or even of his education.

There are in America today three ways of dealing with children. One is the old one I have been describing, and it is still far too prevalent. Even in those States where we have laws that provide for special procedure in children's cases, we often still have this old way of treating the child, of sending him to jail, or even to the penitentiary. That is the first method which has been handed down to us through the ages.

The second method, a modification of the first, is the one generally used in the courts of the Eastern States of the Union today—the handling of children under quasi-criminal proceedings, in which the child is still treated as an offender against the law but in which the harshness of the ancient criminal law is modified as far as possible.

The third method is that of the chancery proceeding. There is plenty of law to sustain the handling of the child through the chancery courts, as the following quotations show:

"The custody of a child is always a proper subject of chancery jurisdiction, and courts of chancery generally exercise a wide jurisdiction over the persons and property of infants as 'wards of court,' exercising the right of the Crown as parens patriae to protect and care for incompetent persons. The benefit of the infant is the foundation of the jurisdiction, and the institution of any proceedings affecting his person is sufficient to make him a ward of court."[1]

Lord Eldon in Wellesley's case said:[2]

"It is not from any want of jurisdiction that it (the court of chancery) does not act, but from a want of means to exercise its jurisdiction, because the court cannot take upon itself the maintenance of all the children in the kingdom. It can exercise this jurisdiction fully and practically only where it has the means of applying property for the maintenance of the infant."[2]

Nevertheless, in most States we still find our lawyers will not let us institute the chancery method of procedure in dealing with delin-

---

[1] 22 Cyc. 519.
[2] 2 Russ. 1 (1827).

quent children. At the last session of the Virginia legislature a bill was introduced providing for dealing with delinquent and dependent children through chancery proceedings. The city attorney, when he read that bill, said that it was a "monstrosity." He said: "It is something we have never heard of before." My friends, the "monstrosity" that had been imposed upon the legislature of Virginia was a bill prepared by a special committee appointed by the Attorney General of the United States to draft a juvenile court law for the District of Columbia, which had been revised so as to make it as nearly as possible fit the conditions in Virginia.

The proceeding in chancery is the ideal and surely the proper manner in which to deal with a delinquent as well as with a dependent child, treating the child and his future as of more consequence than the offense and the penalty to be exacted therefor. In such a proceeding the paramount questions, once it has been determined that the child is wayward, are: Why is this child here? What are the underlying causes of his delinquency? What can the court do to set him straight—to mould him into a decent, self-respecting citizen?

Most of the statutes relating to the trial of children provide for a hearing "in chambers" (that is, in the judge's office), or at least at a "special session" of the court with no one present except the officers of the court, the witnesses in the case, the child, and his parents. Surely this is a reasonable provision and one which can be observed by every court whether it has the complete machinery of a juvenile court or not. Let us insist upon the strict observance of this rule in every court, however small, so that the child may at least be spared the humiliation of a public trial.

There is no greater blot upon the fair name of the American States than the wrong which they have perpetrated upon their wayward boys and girls in confining them in station houses, jails, and even penitentiaries, which to them have proven veritable schools of crime. Think what must be the effect upon the plastic mind of a young child of associating day after day, week after week, and month after month, with adult offenders many of whom have become vicious and depraved!

The Virginia statute expressly provides that:

"No court or justice, unless the offense is aggravated or the ends of justice demand otherwise, shall sentence or commit a child under 18 years of age, charged with or proven to have been guilty of any crime, to a jail, workhouse, or police station, or send such a child on to the grand jury, nor sentence such child to the penitentiary."

Pending trial and disposition, the delinquent child should be held, where that is necessary, in a detention home established and maintained for that purpose. In the smaller cities and rural communities where such an institution cannot be maintained, private homes should be secured in which juvenile offenders can be boarded temporarily until their cases are disposed of. The city of Boston, I believe, still uses this method of detention, considering it best. If Boston can work such a plan successfully, there is no excuse for any smaller community to confine its erring children in jail on the plea that "we only have a few children in court each year." If it were only one child, is not that child as much entitled to protection and a decent chance in life as the hundreds who pass through the portals of the large city court?

Further carrying out the spirit of the new procedure in children's cases, it is essential that not merely the evidence in the particular case at bar be laid before the court, but also the surrounding facts and circumstances, including the previous history of the child, his present social environment, and his physical and mental condition. These facts should be secured accurately and impartially by the probation officer of the court. In making such an inquiry the probation officer should first talk with the child himself, seeking to win his confidence and his friendship. This is the most important step in the investigation, for after all it is the child whom we must know and understand thoroughly if any definite reformation is to be effected. Next the probation officer should visit the child's home and talk with his parents, explaining to them that his mission is entirely friendly and in the interest of the child. He should communicate with the school, or, if the child has been working, with some of his former employers. Every available source of information should be consulted. Wherever it is possible, and especially in serious cases, or where physical or mental defect is apparent, the probation officer should arrange for the physical and mental examination of the child. His purpose should be to discover all facts about the child which will throw any light upon the causes of his delinquency or which may be helpful to the court in deciding upon the wisest disposition of the case.

I like to compare the modern juvenile court proceeding to a medical clinic. When a child is ailing physically, the parent consults a physician. The physician, either personally or through his assistants, first seeks the symptoms of the ailments, and gets his physical findings. When he knows what these are he proceeds to make a diagnosis, and then to prescribe a remedy. Just so, the judge of the juvenile court should view each delinquent as one who is morally sick. The investigation of the probation officer, and the physical and mental examination should disclose the underlying causes of the delinquency. In the light of these facts the judge should then proceed to deal with the child with an eye single to his welfare and reformation.

There are three general methods of disposition open to the courts today, namely: probation, commitment to an institution or a child-placing organization, and commitment to an industrial training school. Whenever possible, first offenders and those charged with minor offenses for even the second or third time should be released under the friendly supervision of a probation officer and allowed to return to their own homes. It then becomes the duty of the probation officer to throw around the child every available influence for good, inducing him to join a boy scout troop or some similar club and to go to Sunday school, in every way encouraging him to seek clean amusements and companions of the right sort. If, however, the child's parents are hopelessly weak or morally bad, or if he has no home, he should then be given a chance in a good institution or foster home. If his delinquency has become so confirmed that neither of these remedies will effect a cure, then the child should be sent to an industrial school, where he will receive discipline and training.

What should be done with the information obtained by the probation officer in his investigation? In my opinion, any information that is worthy of the consideration of the court is worth recording in writing and preserving for future reference. The child may again appear in court; if no record be kept of the facts learned when he made his first appearance, the work done by the probation officer in his initial investigation will have gone for naught. Furthermore, information obtained then may not be available later. It is, therefore, essential that a clear and concise statement of the legal and social facts of the case should be prepared by the probation officer, and that this report, together with the physical and mental diagnosis, should be filed away among the permanent records of the court.

It is in keeping with the spirit of the new era, however, that the child should be protected against an improper use of the record in his case. There is even some sentiment in favor of the destruction of such records entirely. A few years ago the speaker of the Virginia House of Delegates introduced a bill providing that all records in juvenile cases should be destroyed after a certain time had elapsed. This bill was too drastic and it failed of enactment.

The special committee appointed by the Attorney General of the United States in March, 1914, for the purpose of preparing a model juvenile court law for the District of Columbia, in its report, called attention to the fact that in the District alone upward of 4,000 children had had judgments of conviction entered against them, and were in consequence disqualified under the law from voting, performing jury duty, holding public office, etc. The committee recommended the enactment of a law which would emancipate all children who had appeared before the juvenile court from the disabilities which had thus been imposed upon them. Its Juvenile Court Bill provided also for a proceeding in chancery instead of the old quasi-criminal procedure, and further provided that the records of all cases be withheld from indiscriminate public inspection in the discretion of the court.

These recommendations of the Attorney General's special committee would seem to be the reasonable solution. Under such a statute, the important social facts of a child's life could be preserved and used as a source of information in later years should the occasion arise. On the other hand, the fact that the child had appeared in the juvenile court in his youthful days could not be used against him in the criminal court as a "previous conviction," nor could it be used as a Banquo's ghost to haunt him in his public or private life.

The best opinion today is that the same tribunal which hears the cases of delinquent children should also have jurisdiction of the proceedings against those who have offended against children or caused them to offend. Under this general principle the enforcement of such laws as compulsory school attendance, child labor, contributory delinquency, and domestic relations statutes is brought within the jurisdiction of the juvenile court. It would seem most appropriate that this class of cases should be heard by the judge who deals with the child. He knows the effect upon the child when these laws are violated. He sees most clearly the necessity for their rigid enforcement. He knows that the child who is neglected by his parents today is the potential delinquent of tomorrow. He knows that the child who is permitted to go to the factory too early in life is apt to show a reaction that is detrimental not only to his physical and mental development, but oftentimes to his moral character as well. Furthermore, it is in the interest of efficiency that the same tribunal which gathers the facts in the child's case should handle the other matters naturally arising out of those facts. For instance, the hearing in a child's case frequently develops the fact that the cause of delinquency lies in the neglect of an indifferent parent or in the malicious influence of a vicious adult companion. Thereupon the court can hale before it the offending party and deal with all phases of the case, rendering it unnecessary to refer a part of the matter to another tribunal which must consider the case with no knowledge of what has already transpired in the juvenile court, and perhaps with no appreciation of the tremendous issues involved.

The child of today is the citizen of tomorrow. He will be precisely what we make him. Wise and merciful treatment will be rewarded with good citizenship—indifference and injustice with crime.

DISCUSSION

Robert W. Kelso (Executive Director, Massachusetts State Board of Charity): I think we should take note of Judge Ricks' thought that the juvenile court should be developed along chancery lines. To me that does not mean that we should make the juvenile court an administrative agency. After all, the juvenile court is a tribunal of justice. It is a tribunal to administer the law on a modern basis; and the place to socialize is not there in the first instance; it is in the law. Your court will administer whatever law there may be, and in general it will administer it according to an absolute set of rules. Now, it is for us as a community to develop and to socialize the law for the court to apply, and to eliminate from that tribunal of justice the obligation of going out into the community and running an administrative business for the Government. There is a distinction, and we must observe it. A tribunal of justice with chancery powers is that instrument which, when properly allied with the social agency in the community, can effect genuine social justice. The bar has not yet seen it. They think you are trying to make a white blackbird out of a court of law. I think we should win them back by showing them we do not mean that at all.

Dr. Hastings H. Hart (Russell Sage Foundation, New York): Judge Ricks has referred to a matter which seems of vital importance, that is, the case of the children awaiting the action of the juvenile court. I have had occasion frequently to recommend, especially to rural counties, the adoption of the Boston plan of making an arrangement for the care of these children in private families. One of the great difficulties is the lack of a social agency such as the Boston Children's Aid Society to administer it. It requires good judgment in the selection of the homes and in looking out for the children. It cannot always be done through the ordinary country judge who has comparatively few cases in a year. I believe that in many counties some kind of a detention home must be provided. I have had recently three applications for advice with reference to such a home. I do not know of a single detention home in any of the smaller communities which can be referred to as a reasonable model. I am working to accomplish the establishment of a home that can be used as such a model.

I was interested recently to discover that the representatives of children's welfare work in Massachusetts were recommending the establishment of three or four homes for different classes of children, especially for the older boys that cannot be handled by the method of placing in private families. I was startled to learn that in the State of Massachusetts last year there had been 100 children detained in jail awaiting trial. We ought to solve that problem in such a way that people who want advice will know where to get it. I have not yet heard of a satisfactory plan. As a rule, an old dwelling house is taken for the detention home. But the boys and the girls and the delinquent children have to be separated, and when the proper separations are made you have not less than six classes. It is difficult, therefore, to devise a plan whereby you can erect a building at a moderate expense which will provide for these six classes of children.

Mr. J. Prentice Murphy (Boston Children's Aid Society): Dr. Hart is right in saying that the Boston plan is not perfect. There are two or three aspects to which I would like to refer. We do not have dependent children in the courts of Massachusetts, and the courts do not have the administration of mothers' aid. This relieves the judge of an enormous burden. There are no detention homes in the State, but I think we need three or four.

The important part of the Boston plan—or the Massachusetts plan, as it should be properly called—is that a very determined effort is made with each particular child before the juvenile court to avoid removing him from his own home for placement in even a family temporary "detention home" unless it is absolutely necessary that he should be removed. I think I am right in saying that in the country at large there is too general a tendency to make the separation of a child from its own home always a first rather than a last consideration. A movement is under way for the erection of a few small detention homes throughout the State, the same to be under the control of the State board of charity. The latter body already has ample family detention homes to meet its needs. In the city of Boston a large part of the detention service necessary for the Boston juvenile court and some other courts in the city is given by the Boston Children's Aid Society through a number of subsidized and highly trained and carefully supervised private families in the city proper. The success of this special work deserves wider mention. It might easily cover all of Boston but for a lack of funds. There is needed for Boston one of the special institutional detention homes referred to above, to be located within the city limits, to which could be referred the small number of older children, both boys and girls, who are not suitable for temporary care in a family home. On a rough estimate about 150 older boys throughout the State spent from one day to three weeks in various jails while under juvenile court supervision during continuance or awaiting admittance to one of the State schools. Some of these boys were almost eighteen and there is a question whether they have suffered much if at all from being in jail, but the protection of those children liable to injury should be complete, and a small detention home offers a certain measure of this protection. The Massachusetts courts need a few non-jail places to which they can refer a very small number of children of a type almost certainly bound for disciplinary or correctional institutions.

A few of us are questioning the extensive detention home movement that is under way throughout the country. Some reaction to these large congregate affairs is inevitable. The larger the type of detention home the more complicated and involved are its social problems, and the greater is the danger that it will be used in lieu of the determined effort that each child should be kept in his own home unless great and sufficient reasons exist for a different procedure.

STANDARDS OF PROBATION WORK

By DR. LOUIS N. ROBINSON

Chief Probation Officer, Municipal Court, Philadelphia

I am the chief probation officer of the Municipal Court of Philadelphia, which has jurisdiction not only over the juvenile cases, but also over a great variety of other cases. I say this, in order that you may understand that my position does not give me the intimate knowledge of details in the administration of juvenile work that I perhaps might have if I did only that work.

It has not seemed to me advisable to discuss the problems involved in dealing with actual cases. I shall confine my attention to some of the broader principles of probation work which determine very definitely the success or failure of such work.

The general public, as a rule, does not have a clear conception of probation work and is therefore unwilling to give it the necessary financial support. Last fall I visited a court in one of our Middle Western States having jurisdiction over misdemeanants. This court had nearly eighteen hundred persons on probation and had three probation officers to handle the entire number. Under such circumstances, probation could be nothing but a farce. It meant merely the setting at liberty of eighteen hundred people found guilty of some petty crime. The general public can easily understand that it costs money to run an institution for the detention of prisoners, but they have not been educated to perceive that the somewhat intangible probation work costs money also. Buildings, land, walls, food, clothing, guards, are easily visualized, but it is not so easy to see the cost involved in securing reliable information on which the court may base a wise decision, or to appreciate the fact that men and women fitted to act as discerning friends to the unfortunate cannot be expected to render their services free of cost to society.

Every day that goes by makes it clearer to all who are in the work that the investigation side of probation work is bound to broaden greatly. Take for example the problem of juvenile delinquency that is discussed in Dr. Healy's book entitled "Mental Conflicts." It can mean only that there are a rather large number of cases of normal intelligence which will yield to neither ordinary probation nor institutional treatment, and that to effect any cure whatsoever, it will be necessary to probe deep into the content of the mind and to find out what has taken place there perhaps years ago. Our knowledge of social causation, of heredity, of the relation of physical condition to conduct, and of the springs of human action is increasing constantly, and wherever science leads the way the probation officer must follow. As we get further and further away from the idea of punishment for an act inimical to society, and direct our attention more and more to the problem of restoring to society an individual sound in mind, in body, and in conduct, the task of rendering justice becomes ever more complicated and baffling; and yet this is the task which we took upon ourselves when we set up probation systems.

The broadening of the work of investigation means additional demands upon probation officers. The investigation becomes in fact the work of specialists. When we can have skilled physicians, psychologists, and social workers who are trained to pick out the significant features of the social environment, all cooperating in the common task of diagnosing each case, we may feel that we are at least starting our task in the right way.

But if the newer type of investigation demands a newer type of probation officer to conduct the investigation, it is no less true that the work of supervision is certain to increase in complexity. If it takes specialists to make the diagnosis, must we not also expect that the cure will require expert attention? It seems to me that we will unquestionably get away little by little from the practice of assigning probationers to probation officers by districts, or by sex, by race, or by religion, and assign them according to the function for which a probation officer has been trained.

The point which I want especially to make is that the old time probation officer, supposedly capable of handling any and every kind of a case, will probably disappear; or if not, he will have to be trained to carry out the orders of those who have thoroughly studied the case. The child needs something more than a good-natured friend; he needs skilled direction. We can get this in part from those who make the diagnosis, and we can get it also from a wise use of agencies, organizations, and individuals lying outside of the probation machinery, who can usually be persuaded to render their services if tactfully approached. In my opinion, we have not yet exhausted the possibilities of the volunteer. In the past, the volunteer has been the kindly disposed but untrained citizen from whom we have no more right to expect success in handling a case than if he had been a paid probation officer of the same stamp. But is it not possible to make a far greater use of the men and women who have been trained to do some special thing for the human animal? I believe that there are many such in most communities who would gladly do a special task for which they are particularly fitted by their skill or training.

Placing on probation is often looked upon as a substitute for commitment to an institution. Historically this is correct, but the statement gives a wrong impression of what should be the relation between probation and institutional care. Unfortunately this dilemma often confronts a judge sitting on a case with the record spread before him—a choice between sending a child to an institution which is not suitable for him and placing him on probation, which is also the wrong thing to do. Probation, he feels, will probably be more beneficial, or stated negatively, will probably be less injurious, and he therefore places the child on probation. The information which we are slowly accumulating as a result of more scientific investigations, does not show us that there will be no need for institutions in the future, but rather that there is great need for institutions of a new and better type. In a city or State well equipped to handle delinquents, probation will not be regarded as a substitute for commitment; but both probation and commitment will be considered as separate, distinct tools, each fitted for a given task, and the record of the case will automatically determine which will be used. Probation officers and judges who must decide what is to be done with a given case are today fully aware that we cannot successfully handle the problem of delinquency without a great improvement in the character, an increase in the number, and a differentiation in the type of institutions for delinquents.

If the character of probation is to be such as I have indicated in the preceding paragraphs, then there must be the utmost freedom to experiment with new methods and new ideas and to adjust our machinery of probation accordingly. Let us not, for example, tie ourselves down legally to time limits in the handling of cases. Prison reformers have never been entirely satisfied with the indeterminate sentence which in practice is never wholly indeterminate. So in fixing the conditions of probation, let us of course see that the rights of probationers are fully safeguarded, but let us also realize that permanent probation of certain individuals, which is now undoubtedly a necessity, may be a possibility in the future.

I cannot in closing fail to add a word about the relation between a public agency like a court and the various private agencies which are at work on the same or allied problems in the community. Very often one finds surrounding the relation of the two an atmosphere charged with hostility, contempt, or indifference. The attitude of private agencies is very often similar to that held by the early economists who believed that a public agency was by its very nature unfitted to perform any but the most mechanical of tasks. Case work, many social workers feel, requires too much initiative, too much freedom of action, ever to be carried on successfully by a public agency, and they are therefore prone to feel that whatever is done by a public agency must of necessity be slipshod and indifferent. Public officials can view the work of private agencies from another angle than that from which they view themselves. Officials know ofttimes that they themselves are accomplishing a great deal of good in spite of their defects, and they rather resent being looked upon as people living in a Nazareth out of which no good can come. Personally, I do not believe that we can settle in any *a priori* fashion this question of whether social work should be done by public or private agencies. However, I am sure that the success of our future civilization lies in governments adding to their responsibilities and taking on work which people have not hitherto been willing to intrust to them. At any rate, the social work which we have inherited from the ages is so vast that public and private agencies should cast aside petty jealousies and distrusts and should delay falling out with each other as long as the whole field is so imperfectly covered.

DISCUSSION

Mr. Bernard J. Fagan (Chief Probation Officer, Children's Court, New York City): I wish to express my sincere gratification at the about-face movement in some communities which now recognize that the juvenile court is not a cure for all the ailments of the juvenile population. I remember several years ago standing practically alone on the proposition that we deal with only two classes of children—delinquent and neglected. We in New York have always felt that it was not the duty of the juvenile court to correct any other conditions in the community than those responsible for delinquencies and neglect.

I must say that I disagree with Judge Ricks on the proposition of not having the child brought into court. It reminds me somewhat of bringing an empty stretcher to a hospital and telling the physician to look it over and prescribe treatment, while the injured patient is down somewhere in the railroad yards. It seems to me that the judge in delinquent cases and in neglect cases must see the children. He must have in mind a picture of the child. It may be a case of malnutrition, or one where the children have been cruelly treated, or a mental examination may be necessary. I do not see how a judge can proceed intelligently without having the child before him.

I am in accord with the proposition of extending chancery powers to juvenile courts. We are aiming for that in New York and I am certain we will attain it eventually.

I do not think it practicable for juvenile courts whose territory is confined to large and congested localities to assign probationers to probation officers according to types. I believe, however, that the special abilities displayed by probation officers should be more generally recognized and utilized in investigations and probation work.

In conclusion, permit me to state, that while legislatures throughout the country have declared that juvenile delinquency is not a crime, the Laws of God still hold these acts to be sinful, and I believe that the religious forces in our community are the strongest bulwarks that the juvenile courts have at hand in preventing and reducing juvenile delinquency. The strongest possible use of the existing cooperative agencies in the field should be made. The churches of all denominations are beginning to recognize the work of the probation officer, and we must, in turn, recognize the helpfulness of the churches.

Judge James Hoge Ricks (Juvenile Court, Richmond, Virginia): May I be permitted to say that Mr. Fagan misunderstood me. I do not believe in bringing an empty stretcher into court. I believe that the child should be in court in delinquency cases. In cases of dependency and neglect, however, I do not think he should be. It may be necessary under certain conditions to bring the dependent child in, but he should not remain through the entire hearing. I thought that I made that distinction clear; I certainly intended to do so.

I want to say this in connection with the discussion of the paper that has just been read. I know, of course, that Dr. Robinson could not cover every point fully in this short time at his disposal, and I want to emphasize the importance of personality in the selection of probation officers. If you train a man and make him a perfect machine, he will probably be the worst probation officer you can find. Unless a man has personality and can get a grip on the child, he is not fit to be a probation officer.

Mrs. Joseph P. Mumford (National Congress of Mothers): I am glad to see that it has been agreed here this morning that it is possible to scrap even a new institution if it is not doing all the work it should be doing.

I want to make one suggestion, that perhaps the public school might take over a part of the work now done by the juvenile court, which comes properly within its survey. Where there is a compulsory education system, there is practically a little court for children, with officers who visit the homes of the children. The difficulty begins with truancy; I think there is no probation officer here who would not acknowledge that. It is my thought that truant children should be dealt with within the school, and never have to carry the stigma of having been arrested or seen in a court of law.

Dr. Helen T. Woolley (Director, Vocation Bureau, Cincinnati Public Schools): I have been most interested and was very glad to hear Mrs. Mumford mention the public schools. Hers was the first mention of the schools as an agency to be counted upon in helping to solve the problem of delinquency. We are making a beginning in that direction in Cincinnati. Most of the children that come to the juvenile court have, we find, already been problems in the public schools. Corrective measures are being introduced in two directions. We are keeping full and complete records of the children who pass through the schools, in the form of a cumulative record card on which four kinds of information are recorded—academic records, medical examinations, fundamental family facts, and teacher's estimates of personality. In addition, we have a psychological laboratory which examines about 1,000 children a year, and those are, of course, the problem children of the schools.

The system has been in operation long enough to show that many of the cases which come to the court are those of children for whom we have already a fairly adequate and accurate record, in terms of mental tests. A part of the investigation is therefore already made for the court.

We are now beginning a movement by which delinquent school children are to be taken care of along the lines suggested by Mrs. Mumford; that is, the lesser cases of delinquency in children who are still under the compulsory education age will be handled by the school. A few years ago our attendance department used to send many truancy cases to court, while now it sends almost none. Judge Hoffman is thoroughly in sympathy with the idea, and we are trying to work out a plan of cooperation.

Miss Mabelle B. Blake (Boston, Massachusetts): In connection with Judge Ricks' remarks with respect to the personality of the probation officer, it seems to me that one of the great factors to be considered is that the probation officer must not give up too easily. Boys and girls are put on probation, and perhaps they do not do just as well as the probation officer thinks they ought to. Often in a few weeks' time—certainly within a month's time—he has gone back to court and said, "Probation is a failure; this child is not doing well," and consequently the child is surrendered to the court. That is a very serious situation. We must give children time to make good, and for that reason we need probation officers who are not going to give up quickly. We need those who are not too far away from children themselves, so that they will not forget the ordinary and natural things that children do.

In regard to volunteers, if we do use them, they should if possible be especially trained, and they should be carefully supervised and under the direction of a probation officer who knows his job.

Miss Anna B. Pratt (Director, White-Williams Foundation for Girls, Philadelphia): We began in a very small way in Philadelphia with some delinquent girls whose difficult problems were brought to us by the bureau of education. We have gone into one school with the idea of trying the experiment with all the children in the school, beginning with the fifth grade, and taking up the health problem. We have made a special study of each child in order that its peculiar problems might be understood, and we have endeavored to bring an understanding to the teacher. Next year it is our intention to begin in the primary grades.

Major Bird T. Baldwin (Walter Reed General Hospital, Washington, D. C.): There is one phase of the problem which has not been touched upon. After every great war we have found the country flooded with derelicts, dependent men who have been unable to find themselves again. We are at the close of a great war. For the past year and a half I have had charge of the reconstruction work at the Walter Reed Hospital. Our object has been to take the wounded men—the same will hold true of the enlisted men in general—and prepare them to go back into society as normal men, physically, socially, and economically. We want each man to be a social asset rather than a liability in his particular community. It is not an easy job. We started in one room and for six months we have averaged 1,200 young men. These are largely boys, and most of them are untrained. A great many of them have had only meager education. Of the first thousand, 90 per cent had not passed beyond the seventh grade. If you will go to the Walter Reed Hospital today, you will find 40 or 50 men learning to read and write.

Now, what is the problem? To get the boys back into society as normal men. It is a very difficult problem, and I think the probation officer can be of direct assistance in studying society rather than the men for a little while. These men are face to face with very difficult situations, for society encourages mendicancy. We started to have the boys sell newspapers—"The Come Back"—and people would give them 50 cents and $1.00 for a 5 cent newspaper. We had to stop it. In other words, society is, in a way, the wounded boy's worst enemy, and we must teach society not to misdirect its sympathy toward these young boys, whose greatest assets are their independence, their self-reliance, and their self-respect.

MEDICOPSYCHOLOGICAL STUDY OF DELINQUENTS

By WILLIAM HEALY, M. D., and AUGUSTA F. BRONNER, Ph. D.

Judge Baker Foundation, Boston, Massachusetts

The most fundamental need of courts which deal specifically with human problems is knowledge of the qualities of the human beings concerning whom a decision is to be made and knowledge of the causes of the behavior which is the affair at issue. Why should there be the slightest expectation of doing anything like the best that can be done in court work without following the guiding principles of science and common sense which have led to all improvement and success in other fields? These principles involve, primarily, scientific acquaintance with material handled, and with the relation of adequately ascertained causes to ascertained effects, including the effects of court action. The application of such principles requires, here as elsewhere, the development of a technique of studying causes—which, as we can readily show, are frequently not at all superficial or easy of discernment—and requires, as well, the building up of a rational system of observing effects.

It is certainly not impertinent to the dignity of the law—in this day of aiming at progress—to ask why this particular department of human effort, this deciding of human affairs under the provisions of legal procedure, should in any way be exempt from investigations of efficiencies and of the reasons for the failures which we know exist in such large measure. Indeed it is no small matter for wonderment that there has never been any keen necessity felt by the legal profession for at least the sort of critical and interpretative statistical treatment of success and failure that is considered an absolutely necessary periodical procedure in other human activities. It is plain, however, that the special study of fundamental causes has lagged behind because it is only recently that a science of behavior has been even projected.

In this brief discussion of the part that medicopsychology can and should play in aiding solution of the problems of delinquents, we especially desire to make clear its function in gathering, differentiating, and interpreting the facts of the background and of the possibilities in the given case. This may perhaps best be done by centering about a concrete case; the last one seen before this paper was written is typical enough in many ways.

A boy, 11 years old, is in court as a night vagrant; repeatedly during the last few months he has been staying away from home all night, and sometimes even two nights. The police have several times found him after midnight. His parents appear with the officers to substantiate the complaint. The lad, Jim, is a very ordinary-looking boy, with nothing in any way remarkable about his appearance. What basis has the judge for decision in this case?

There is, of course, the lad's offense. Anyone with experience or imagination can apprehend that this is a very important case because of danger for the boy's future, danger to him and to society. His night habit of wandering about and sleeping here and there, will probably lead him straight into a thieving career, perhaps into burglary; he is likely to become acquainted with sexual misdemeanors and acquire bad sex habits; to say nothing of a general lowering of his moral standards and conditions of health. The repetition of his misbehavior, of course, has greater weight than a single escapade, but any wise judge knows that the bare fact of repetitions of offense or of previous court record offers no criterion for safe judgment. The fact is that the day has long gone by when a decision concerning the juvenile offender can be regarded as good procedure if it is made merely on the basis of offenses, even when they are as serious as the above.

The boy's age signifies little; many a long career of crime has begun as early. His nativity—he was born in Boston, and his parents in Italy—denotes nothing in itself; similar misconduct is found equally among other nationalities, even our native stock. His physical appearance, his size and signs of normal health, offer no help for adjudication. The other facts presented to the judge—that the lad is normally advanced in school for his age and social group, being in the fifth grade, that the parents seem to be decent people and partake in the complaint, that he lives in one of the most crowded districts—likewise suggest no solution.

The judge proceeds further, giving as much time as the press of other cases allows. He learns that the parents are intelligent above the average immigrants. According to the officers, they bear a good reputation and are not alcoholic. They are concerned about their boy, and have searched for him at night. They say that until five or six months ago he gave no trouble, and that since then they have punished and scolded and begged him to do better. He has made many promises, but very soon stays out again. They know nothing of his companions or of his night doings, and he does not answer when they ask him about this. He is a healthy boy, of good habits otherwise, and not peculiar in any way, as far as they can tell. The officers state that Jim engages in no other delinquencies; the boy bears a good reputation in school, except for occasional truancy. Then it comes out that he often attends school after he has been out all night. The boy himself insists that he always stays out alone and that he merely wanders about looking at things. Jim's attitude towards his parents is normal in the court room, and he says that they treat him well and that he loves them. Finally, he states in ordinary boyish fashion that he does not know why he prefers wandering on the streets to sleeping in his own bed.

The judge has taken nearly an hour, skilfully obtaining a clear statement of these essential facts to supplement the investigation already begun by an officer of the court. Here is a case without obvious intricacies; but what are the real guides to rational adjustment? The parents in genuine solicitude say they are willing that Jim be sent to an institution; that they have tried hard with him and have failed. The boy does not want to go, and renews his promises to remain at home. At this point the judge, without pretending to know the real personality of the boy or the causation of his misbehavior, may make the shrewdest decision he can. (Of course, sometimes there is pretense from the bench of ability from vast experience, and so on, that makes it possible to diagnose mentality, causation, and what not from an interrogation lasting even a few minutes—but then from other judges comes the more ingenuous assertion that a judge is paid to make a guess in these matters, to be sure, the best guess that he can make.)

On behalf of probation in this case the judge may think of the possibility of modifying behavior through fear of the court, or through friendly supervision of the probation officer. But if we may judge by other careers which have begun with this type of offense these general measures are not particularly likely to prove effective, since they cannot meet special needs which are really not known. The probation officer without specific knowledge has no specific remedy to offer. The other usual alternative, an institution for delinquents, is the easiest solution. But would this, either, meet the boy's individual problem? Everyone knows what an institution for such a case means; artificial conditions of home life, repression of many normal activities and interests of boyhood, companionship with other older and worse delinquents, costliness to the State, and so on. Puzzled, the judge may continue the case for further information. This ordinarily means nothing but gathering more facts about the objective features of the home life and neighborhood.

The point of view of medicopsychological study and diagnosis may now be considered. First, what can be known through ordinary courtroom observation of the physical makeup of this boy? He may have some significant defect or irritative condition, not at all suggested by his normal appearance. He may have astigmatism and headaches in the evening, or even a heart lesion of which his parents do not know or a hernia, or definite symptoms of some nervous disorder. Such physical findings may have significant relationship to causation, prognosis, and treatment of his delinquent tendencies.

The developmental history has not been ascertained; evaluated in the light of a careful professional inquiry, this history may in some cases be largely explanatory and show the limitations and possibilities of treatment for delinquency. For example, Jim may be subject to the slighter forms of epilepsy, readily overlooked, which in certain cases are so clearly associated with the impulse to wander. Or some fact of earlier disease or injury may throw light upon the present tendencies. The possible variations of antecedent causation are many.

Many facts told straightway in professional consultation, but rarely revealed in the court room, often include very significant data concerning the heredity, family life, habits, and behavior reactions of the young offender. And specially do we note that, naturally, this account of the boy's character and conduct often much more nearly approaches the truth than the picture given to the judge.

Most important of all, however, is what may be learned through medicopsychological study of the mental aspects of the boy's life. And we must insist, first and last, that by psychological inquiry we mean study of the functioning of ordinary normal mental processes and laws as well as possible abnormal phases of mental life. Mental habits, ideations, imageries, repressions, commanding interests, special abilities, particularized disabilities, form a field of greater importance for understanding if one is really to know the total range of problems presented by delinquents, than does the discovery of mental defect and psychotic conditions which all recognize as one of the big single factors in the production of delinquency. In the dynamic features of mental life and in the mental content itself we have material for explanation and for redirection and reeducation that is invaluable. This is true even of some of the cases where there is abnormality of slight degree.

To come back to Jim; the fact that he answers fairly well the judge's questions and that he is reported to be in the fifth grade, means little concerning his mentality. He may be mentally defective in important ways and still be a fair conversationalist; he may possess the good memory powers characteristic of many of the feeble-minded, and so have progressed to the fifth grade; or, on the other hand, he may be above average or even be a genius in some particular ability or in general, and yet be no further advanced in school. We are acquainted with just such irrational school advancements and retardations, and have seen many individuals whose mentality it would have been quite impossible to estimate as they appeared in the court room. To what extent the offender may or may not be psychopathic, or what peculiar personality traits he may have, is also not in the least revealed without special psychological examination.

Moreover, without this study what can be known of his inner life in the aspects mentioned above? Who knows what he is thinking about or repressing, or what moods, or grudges, or feelings of limitation and conflict in his own household he may be harboring? The exciting cause or the underlying motive of such behavior, the force of which the experienced psychologist knows, ranges from such a general fact as feelings of distaste for old country standards in his home on the part of a young American, to some secret subtle revulsion against some one experience. Or what about an unknown hold of a bad companion upon the boy, or some obsessive ideation concerning hidden knowledge, usually of sex affairs, one of the strongest driving forces towards delinquency?

It is perfectly clear, then, that to understand even the minor essentials of Jim's case he must be looked over physically (perhaps some special physiological tests being made), and be given a full round of psychological tests, not alone grading him according to a mental age-level, but also looking for specialized features of the mental functioning, strong or weak; and that then by the most skilful methods his inner mental life and mood and attitude must be explained in its relationship to his misbehavior.

Accepting, as always, the challenge of the practical issue, we may meet the fair question: What is ascertained through this study that the judge did not know, what facts that bear upon the really proper treatment of the case? Our answer is: The contributions are both positive and negative; the latter quite as valuable as the former. It is as essential in Jim's case, for instance, to rule out epilepsy, chorea, hysteria, syphilis, psychosis, mental defect, and various other possibilities which we have found active factors in other cases of delinquency, as it is to discover that he is physically healthy and particularly energetic, and that he is highly supernormal in general mental ability and possesses dynamic qualities that demand much in the way of interests, activities, and new material to satisfy them. Likewise careful summation of data shows that there are probably no very significant facts of heredity and development bearing upon the boy's tendency to delinquency.

Analysis of the boy's reactions as exhibited in his own account of them show no indication in this first study of him that there is clash of ideals in the household, or that bad attitudes and grudges have been formed. For the more positive side, it stands out clearly that though the household is well-managed and favorable in many ways for the development of a boy of the most mediocre capacities, and though there is quite normal affection displayed, there has been no understanding whatever of Jim's peculiar needs (perhaps this has led to a certain reserve which Jim shows towards his parents but has not exhibited elsewhere) and there is very little at home to hold the interest or provide outlets for such an active-minded and capable lad.

The necessary careful psychological analysis of effects of influences outside the home shows early acquaintance with bad companions, rejection of their modes of conduct, the dwelling on ideas of adventure in city life received from them, a first taste of it alone; and then, following the laws of repetition of pleasurable effect and of mental habit, frequent renewal of adventures in which much that was new and of great interest was experienced. Always alone, Jim found in his night wanderings satisfaction not obtained elsewhere. In the early morning hours, for instance, he would be held by the romance of huge printing presses turning off newspapers for the day.

The essence of such study is the focussing and intepretation of sufficient data, negative and positive, for the purposes of treatment. Brought together and evaluated are many more facts and even types of facts than the judge in court can ascertain. The way to a better adjustment of the situation concerning Jim is now obvious. It cannot be doubted that an institution would probably be his undoing; it is equally clear that there are special measures which very likely will prove reconstructive, even if he remains at home.

Summing up, we know on the basis of long experience that such medicopsychological study frequently brings out points that are absolutely essential to knowledge of causation, which, in turn, is the only rational and immediately effective approach to treatment. Short cuts to such knowledge are not possible; why should one expect to find them, considering the complexities of human behavior and mental life? And what are hours of diagnostic study compared to months of treatment which may be unnecessary, as in institutional life, or to efforts ineffectively directed during probation?

Without desiring in the least to usurp the functions of the law, and without the least argument against punishment in appropriate cases as a good therapeutic agent, and holding no brief for any theory of either causation or treatment, we may insist on medicopsychological study as representing a minimum standard of welfare in the treatment of delinquency.

A rational method of meeting the needs of the youthful offender, which indirectly affords, of course, the greatest protection to society by thwarting his prospective career, is only to be developed by utilizing the facts acquired through a good technique of medicopsychology. This procedure, carried out with sympathy and thoroughness, will contribute greatly to the effectiveness of courts and of other human agencies which attempt some solution of the problems of delinquency. Many of the huge number of failures which occur under the ordinary system it will be possible to avoid. Moreover, concerning any method or régime, the only legitimate conclusions, as judged even by successes and failures, are possible when the essential facts that deal with the potentialities of the human material handled and with causation form the basis of judgment.

DISCUSSION

A Member: I would like to ask, What is the matter with "Jim"?

Dr. Healy: The time is too short to say much about "Jim" himself. I want to mention one thing, however. Suppose the judge had thought, here is a case where fear of the court will improve the boy's conduct, and on the basis of this had sent him home. In reality, after his appearance in court Jim stayed at home just two nights and then went out again for three nights, showing that the idea or the impulse towards wandering was not inhibited in the least by fear of the court. He now is of course, what is known as a "repeater". He is an individual on whom the law has laid hands, and in spite of this he continues in his delinquency.

A striking fact about treatment under the law, which has not been impressed upon us enough in this country, because we have no national statistics on the point, is that individuals coming before the court in a large share of the cases go right out and commit the same offense again. In connection with this matter I remember reading in the English Blue Book the fact that in one year—I think 1907—there were 187,000 convictions in England, of which 10,000 were of persons who had been convicted upwards of twenty times before. Your "Jims" handled by the courts in the ordinary way, without an understanding of their condition, as to whether they are feeble-minded or supernormal, or, indeed, without any knowledge of their characteristics or the causations of their behavior, in a large share of the cases become recidivists. Would we in any other line of human effort proceed in such an unscientific way as to continue a system that in a large share of cases gets us nowhere? These are actual facts to be considered in connection with this situation.

You ask me: What can one do with "Jim"? I say that you know as well as I do what to do with "Jim". It is a matter of using your common sense. What do you think should be done for a very bright boy who comes from an unlettered family, exceedingly poor, who have no books and things of interest at home? Someone just said to me that the boy had the making of a poet in him. That may be perfectly true. He is a most charming individual who sees romance in life, who wants experience, who has not mental pabulum enough to satisfy him; and he finds in the joys of night wandering and street experience things that are more satisfying.

How do such problems turn out? In general I can say this: Take the cases that have been failures as handled by the court and under probation, attempt to study them, and then do the thing that really needs to be done, and you will get the most marvelous returns you have ever seen in any line of effort. Just as this particular individual needs all sorts of properly provided mental food, instead of being allowed to find it in the streets at night, another individual may require segregation from bad companionship, or may need hard work, or friendly conferences, or commitment to an institution for the feeble-minded, or any one of a thousand things which may meet his special needs.

A Member: May I give one incident that illustrates this principle?

My "Jim" was a boy of sixteen who was in a good home. He was about the average boy. He became very tired of his studies in school. He wandered at night, though he did not stay out all night. He loved his parents, but he came to the point where he thought he could not stand home any longer; he felt bound. I got the permission of "Jim's" parents to help "Jim" run away. "Jim" ran away from home under chaperonage. He went to work in a mill, and he worked out some of his love of adventure and desire for excursion in the world. Then he came back and completed his education. He is now a desirable citizen.

Mr. Bernard J. Fagan (Chief Probation Officer, Children's Court, New York City): The New York statistics show that 20 per cent of the children brought into court have previous records. Eight per cent had previously been on probation, 7 per cent had previously had institutional treatment, and 2 per cent were on probation at the time of the new arrest. I find that what we lack is enough psychiatrists and physicians with whom the probationary staff can consult constantly during the probationary period. We do get a report from a psychopathic clinic, and we may or we may not understand all that it contains. We would like frequent consultations. This should be made as much a part of the treatment as any other phase. Where we have but one psychologist in a city or town, I feel that the probation officer cannot go very far in following out the excellent suggestions as to what to do with "Jim."

Mr. J. Prentice Murphy (Boston Children's Aid Society, Boston, Massachusetts): Dr. Healy has opened the eyes of a number of children's workers in Boston to the possibility of a new kind of case work for children. He has brought out the idea of the necessity for more emphasis on the subjective and for less emphasis— or not too much emphasis—on the objective, in each social inquiry. It has been very interesting to watch the trend within the last eighteen months since he came to Boston—a place which has talked a lot about its case work—and to see how much the work of the children's organizations has been changed and how much more often the emphasis is placed upon the contents of the child's mind, where it should be. The usual procedure in most social work is to spend a short period with the individual who is most vitally concerned with whatever plan is made and then to chase all over the earth for people who do not really know him. We have been bringing to Dr. Healy children presenting new difficulties or recurring old ones whom we have had in our care for five, six, or more years, and he tells us things that we should have known when the children first came to us. He reveals mental contents which account for or explain many delinquencies and poor social adjustments—the understanding of which is the very basis of helping the individual. This new power of understanding makes the job of dealing with a difficult child a thing of promise.

Dr. David Mitchell (Bureau of Educational Experiments, New York City): I would like to emphasize one point which Dr. Healy has made—the necessity of studying the individual. I greatly fear that too much of our work has been concerned with establishing a mental rating, and deciding that because the child fails to do a particular thing he is feeble-minded and therefore should be committed to an institution. The fundamental part of the study of the child in the court is the study of his emotional disturbances. Undoubtedly a great many of the children are in the juvenile courts largely because of these emotional factors, factors which so far we have almost invariably neglected to study.

I should like to suggest further that such studies be carried on long before the children reach the stage where they enter the juvenile court. The suggestion was made this morning that the work might be done in the public schools. It seems to me that this would be a much better way than to wait until the child reaches the juvenile court.

Dr. Frankwood E. Williams (The National Committee for Mental Hygiene, New York City): Of course the medicopsychological clinic is a comparatively new thing, and it is not surprising, therefore, that a good many probation officers and some medical workers have a tendency to feel that the object of these clinics is primarily to classify the individuals who come before them. The matter is not so simple. I want to emphasize the fact that there is a particularly large group of delinquent children and of difficult children in the schools who do not fall into any classifiable group, and, further, that among those who are classifiable there are frequently such marked individual differences that the classification can be considered as but the first step in the understanding of the child. The problem is complex, and we must recognize it as such if we are to make headway at all. We must study, as Dr. Healy has so well suggested, the personality and the character traits of the particular individual; only in this way can we handle the larger part of the defective and special children. We must get away from the notion that classification is sufficient, or that diagnosis (in the sense of diagnosing a disease) is sufficient, or that we can find a short cut.

CARE OF MENTALLY HANDICAPPED CHILDREN

THE PLACE OF MENTAL HYGIENE IN THE CHILD WELFARE MOVEMENT

By DR. C. MACFIE CAMPBELL

Associate Professor of Psychiatry, Phipps Psychiatric Clinic, Johns Hopkins Hospital, Baltimore, Maryland

Mental hygiene is a term with a cold and formal sound; it seems somewhat remotely connected with the ideas which arise when the topic of health is mentioned. To those, however, whose daily work brings them into contact with the sick, the term represents a body of simple common-sense principles, dealing with factors in life, which are most intimately connected with human health, happiness, and efficiency. Mental hygiene deals with real life in its actual complexity, it deals with real human beings in their concrete enviroment, not merely with their component organs isolated in a laboratory; it deals with men and women who crave, and strive, and suffer, who are driven by deep-seated forces, only partly controlled by reason. When these men and women fail in their adjustments, whether the symptom of the failure be palpitation, headache, indigestion, or irritability, misinterpretation, delusion, mental hygiene comes to the situation willing in an unbiased way to give weight to factors which laboratory medicine is wont to ignore.

In these factors the key to many disorders is found; conflicts in the instinctive life, emotional tension with its bodily expression (cardiac, gastrointestinal, muscular, etc.), earlier experiences and situations, which have sensitized the individual to special topics, the true inwardness of the family and social environment, the fictitious gain to the patient from the invalidism, may all contribute something to an apparently simple case of sickness.

The physician has to be sensitive to the presence of such factors, and must be willing to ask frank questions about them, even although he may seem to intrude on private matters; he must not be embarrassed by the necessity of a personal analysis, as the "Straightener" in Erewhon by the patient's reference to physical ailments.[1]

---

[1] In the drawing-rooms of Samuel Butler's Erewhon indigestion could only be referred to under the decent euphemism of kleptomania or dipsomania, and even in the consulting room of the "Straightener" any reference to physical ailments was considered very embarrassing.

These factors, to a large extent neglected by modern medicine, are the complex or personal or so-called mental factors, to which mental hygiene tries to do justice. It is unfortunate that the term "mental," with its medieval associations, should be such a stumbling block; mental hygiene is merely hygiene adequately conceived, hygiene which does justice not merely to the individual organs and systems of the body, but to the more complex factors involved in instinct, emotion, and personality. It is dawning on the medical profession that these factors cannot be ignored in dealing with the wide problem of health, as it is dawning on the economist that labor unrest is a malady, which may require for its explanation not merely the abstract economic data of the past, but consideration of the real living working individual with his cravings, his repressions, his tensions, and his dissatisfactions.

In scientific work, medical as well as economic, one has periodically to return to the fullness of reality in order to get a deeper insight into causal relations. One of the outstanding results of this recognition of the importance of complex or personal (to avoid the use of the misleading term "mental") factors in health problems, is the realization of the fact that the efficiency and health of the adult adjustment to the tests of life is profoundly modified by the experiences and situations and influences of childhood. In this connection there passes at once before the mind's eye a procession of adults, the fundamental basis of whose maladjustments can be traced to sources in childhood; some are suffering from obscure and elusive invalidism (gastric, cardiac, etc.), others from futile and ill-balanced enthusiasms; others are disillusioned, critical, unproductive; others in revolt against all authority; others with unexplained estrangement from those who should be nearest and dearest. In how many cases is a profound marital maladjustment due to the influences of the childhood period! How often the adult is still subconsciously harking back to a paradise that can never return, and therefore is embittered by a reality in which he has not been trained to find true satisfaction! How often is a distorted career with odd enthusiasms and fads to be traced to the fact that the individual was not trained to face at the start some of the crude difficulties of human nature! How much adult invalidism is to be traced to childhood training and influences!

Whoever has to deal with these adult maladjustments is profoundly impressed with the importance of the period of childhood, as determining the later health and efficiency of the individual. He would have these facts known to the community at large and become more than data of scientific record; he would have them assimilated by all those who have a positive influence in promoting the welfare of the child. Such is the motive of this paper.

To show how real, solid, and concrete are the facts with which mental hygiene deals, how close they are to the actual problems of workaday life, a few cases may be cited, taken practically at random.

A little girl of 5 is carried into the dispensary by an over-solicitous mother, who states that the child is unable to walk; the child is a little fidgety, but is found to be capable of walking with normal gait. At home the child has been kept in bed or has been carried around by the mother; in order to avoid tantrums the mother gives the child her own way; the diet is regulated by the child's own whims—she will take neither milk nor eggs. One of the reasons for the solicitude of the mother is that an older child had well-marked chorea and his care had entailed a great deal of hardship on her.

With a nervous child of this type it is important that the régime should be regular and determined by objective considerations; the child should be trained to adapt itself to this régime, and not find that it can dominate the environment by playing on the emotions of the mother. The mother must be encouraged to carry through a healthy régime with regard to food, sleep, and toilet habits; there must be no evidence of alarm over trifling symptoms; the child must not find invalidism a potent weapon.

Advice of this nature is apt to leave a mother rather bewildered, she needs help to carry it out; it is not so simple as to give a teaspoonful of medicine three times a day. In this case a social-service worker visited the house, to organize the daily program for the child and to show the mother that the advice could be translated into action; a dietitian also visited the home to show the mother how to prepare suitable food for the child.

In some cases mother and child react upon each other too strongly for the former to be able to control the situation, to break up the domination of the nervous child; a brief stay in a children's hospital or in a better home environment may be very helpful; in the hospital there is an objective atmosphere, and the group influence, which is very important. "It does not matter in the hospital whether you cry or not," said a disillusioned child, who at home had given her mother the greatest difficulty with regard to food; in a few days she was devouring the regular hospital diet with avidity.

A girl of 9 has always vomited food which she dislikes; her aunt had the same trick. Needless to say her mother has been at the mercy of the child's demands; at home the child has tantrums, but it is interesting to note that in the more objective atmosphere of the school there are no tantrums. As to the ability of the mother to regulate the child's life one may judge from the fact that the child has had coffee since she was 3 years old. In this case the possibility of infection from the aunt has to be considered; what is due to bad example and training is likely to be put down to heredity.

A boy of 9 would vomit if forced to take food which he disliked; he had other evidences of a nervous constitution. The mother was encouraged by a social-service worker to carry out a well organized program and the vomiting was eliminated.

A boy of 17 had for many years vomited if forced to face any uncongenial task; he had thus avoided going to school, for the tender-hearted mother kept him at home when the anticipation of school made him vomit. Under this regime the boy had remained uneducated, was living in the closest emotional dependence on his mother, and making no steps in the direction of adult independence. Here too heredity might be wrongly blamed for the result of faulty training. The mother had been likewise dependent on her parents, and was fostering the dependence of her child; she liked to have a 17 year old baby, but the pleasure meant a distorted mental life for the boy. Here again intensive social-service work was of great help to mother and child.

A girl of 12 vomited on school days; she complained "of feeling a chunk of blood in her throat;" she was a bed-wetter and suffered from night terrors. In this case the factors which determine the vomiting are not on the surface, but require a detailed study of the complex life of the child.

The above cases have been chosen on account of their simplicity, with the prominence of an apparently bodily ailment, viz., vomiting; a symptom, however, which could only adequately be explained when one took into account not merely the diet and its chemical constitution, not merely the gastric function with the degree of acidity, etc., but also the reaction of the whole child to the actual environment, its emotional life, its self-assertiveness, the formation of its associations, in other words, took into account the mental factors.

The physician is in danger of dealing with the situation in a much more abstract way; he may treat the symptom, or the stomach, instead of treating the child. He can give sedatives or tonics or alter the diet; but to give the most help he has to treat the situation in a concrete way; he has to deal with child, mother, home and school atmosphere, and must help to organize the necessary factors required for the welfare of the child. Prejudices have to be overcome; mothers have to be convinced and given practical demonstrations. It is interesting to note the answer of mothers to the question, "Did you ever make the child eat anything it did not want to?" For example: "No, thank Heaven, there has always been enough for the child to have what it wanted" (proudly); "I consider it criminal to make a child eat what it does not want" (indignantly). The mother does not recognize that, while a few drops of coffee in the child's milk may not have serious toxic consequences, they may be a bribe which has an unfortunate influence on the formation of habits of the child.

At an early age the child may develop poor habits of adjustment of a different type, exaggerated emotional reactions which will be fostered or eliminated according to the injudicious or judicious behavior of the mother. It is not necessary to give a description of all the forms which these tantrums may assume.

One may mention a child of 11, who, if displeased, throws himself back in a condition which alarms the mother; a judicious punishment may eliminate this, while weak yielding fosters it and other reactions. With one child of $2\frac{1}{2}$ years, who had such tantrums, the injudicious régime was illustrated by the fact that he still got a bottle, would go to the movies, and bought candy. The later development of the spoiled child is illustrated by a boy of 14, spoiled at home, at school unable to adapt himself and therefore teased, withdrawing from hard reality into an imaginative world of his own, and frequently evading school on account of headache.

The fundamental principle to emphasize is that the child should be encouraged to form good habits of adapting himself to the reasonable requirements of the environment and to make progress to independence at a good rate; the child should not be allowed to tarry at any stage in order either to give the mother a sentimental pleasure, or to avoid the trying but temporary incidents that go with good discipline. So it is undesirable to allow the child to continue to use the bottle indefinitely, undesirable to have the child dominate food and sleep conditions, undesirable to have the child accustomed to demand and receive an unwise amount of caressing and personal attention.

Not only does an unwise regime tend to produce, even during childhood, such symptoms as have been illustrated in the above cases; it is a poor preparation for the tests of adult life, it does not enable the individual to meet efficiently the tests of a world, which is no respecter of persons, which refuses to be moved by tantrums and expressions of ill humor. Unless he overcomes the handicap of the earlier attitude, the spoiled child is liable to demand too much, to blame the environment for its scanty display of affection, to adapt himself by either withdrawing from it and consoling himself with phantasies of his own worth and of the world's defects, or by physical invalidism with its protean manifestations. So does he wring from the medical profession and the environment an attention and an interest, which is the substitute for the tender affection of the fostering mother.

As an unwise régime fosters such symptoms as tantrums and vomiting, so it may be at the basis of, or foster, other manifestations—night terrors, poor sleep habits, headache, fidgety movements (choreiform conditions), fainting attacks, etc. But quite apart from these simpler conditions we have to recognize that in childhood we find already the same types of neuroses which are so familiar in adults.

Thus a little boy of 5 with a stiff right leg, who said, "I want to be a cripple," is the naive prototype of the adult hysteric. Frequently one meets epileptiform attacks on an hysterical basis, an emotional reaction to certain situations, fostered by the gain accruing from an environment without insight.

A little colored boy of 3 for two years had been afraid some one would bite him; corrected for masturbation, he showed obsessive cleanliness. At 3 he was still taking milk from the bottle.

A girl of 12 had for some time suffered from morbid ideas and scruples; she scrutinized carefully every glass of water or milk to make sure that it was clean; she washed her hands constantly and was afraid to eat if her hands had touched anything. At night she carried on an interminable discussion as to whether she had been disobedient, etc.; she was preoccupied with thoughts of falling sick; she had always to have her mother within ear shot. She made great demands on her mother's affections; she had been accustomed for a long period to sleep in her mother's arms. These cases of neuroses are important because they show in an extreme form forces at work which have to be reckoned with in general.

There are also cases where the disorder of adjustment takes the form of wandering episodes, moods, pilfering, lying, outbreaks of violence, sexual activities or interests of unusual degree or nature, which demand the attention of the physician.

The great problem with regard to these children is how to be sure that in a community there are fair opportunities for help for those who need it. First of all it is important that physicians in general should become sensitive to the issues referred to above. It has to be recognized that, although in the medical profession preventive medicine or hygiene is much in vogue at present, it is hygiene inadequately conceived, the hygiene of organs and systems, rather than the hygiene of persons. To the average physician the term mental has an embarrassing and unscientific sound; the people he deals with are thinly clad versions of the abstract entities of the laboratory; medievalism is firmly entrenched in medical laboratories. In the interests of child welfare we have to see that a sound grasp of mental hygiene becomes part of the equipment of every medical graduate. The great number of war neuroses has done much to bring the actual situation before the medical profession and to show that mental hygiene deals with real and vital factors of practical importance, open to scientific study and management.

The nursing profession, the valuable auxiliary of the medical profession, must have the same opportunity; especially is this part of the curriculum necessary for the visiting nurse, who enters the home of the poorly educated, and meets situations which are so important for the health of the individual child. The cases cited above have shown that the environmental influences of the child must be made as much a subject of accurate study as its pulse and temperature; the visiting nurse must be sensitive to these problems.

But how can we disseminate in a more universal way throughout the country the important gospel, bring to the majority of homes the needed outlook? To the newspaper-reading public, appeals may ·be made by propaganda, but this method is obviously insufficient.

There is one social apparatus already in existence, of which every child is forced by statute for many years to be a member, the school system. In this system he is under supervision by trained workers, whose special problem is to educate him. The idea that education consists merely of furnishing children a stock amount of information is yielding to a nobler conception, the conception that education is preparation of the child for the adult tasks of life.

Then we must know for what the child is constitutionally equipped; we must not assume that all can be prepared for the same later activities. We shall give children the opportunity of developing each one his own talents. We shall lay less stress upon the amount of information acquired; that is not what determines adult health, efficiency, and happiness; the latter depend upon the harmonious adjustment of the conflicting demands of human nature; they depend upon being able to adapt one's self happily and productively to the mutual restrictions of community life, upon the ability to grasp situations objectively and not through the distorting influence of passion and prejudice; they depend upon pertinacity of purpose, adequate output of energy, responsiveness to the deeper issues of life.

If such be the goal of education, the teacher will need to be as sensitive to moody periods on the child's part as to bad spelling; will pay attention to day-dreaming as well as to faulty declensions; will take truancy not as a statutory crime, but as a personal problem, the roots of which have to be traced; will regard pilfering and lying as problems of equal interest; will note any sexual aberrations not as awkward incidents disturbing one's own prudish repressions, but as indications that one of the most important biological forces is causing difficulty, and that help may be needed.

The teacher imbued with these principles and taking seriously the task of training the child, will seek to make the atmosphere of the school tonic, character-building as well as instructive; and will be forced to recognize that the school and the home cannot be treated independently, that there should be a continuity of influence over the child, that home training and school training should be guided by the same principles.

The teacher, therefore, will feel it obligatory to have some knowledge of the total situation and to help in the home situation if help be required. The teacher with her special training can come to the assistance of the parent, and the interest in the child will give the teacher an entrée and an influence which otherwise might be denied. This work may be done largely by means of special school nurses.

Already we have gone part of the way; the school sees that teaching grammar to an empty stomach is poor policy, and that a child learns slowly who cannot see the blackboard nor hear the teacher; teeth, nose, and throat are being attended to, and the school has accepted partial responsibility for these organs. The next step is to accept responsibility for the child, and to realize that beside the impersonal factors influencing childhood conduct, there are other more complex factors—instinct, emotion, personality, and environment—equally deserving of attention.

Summary

The welfare of the individual child will be better safeguarded, when parents, nurses, and physicians realize that simple symptoms are not always an indication of simple bodily ailments, but are frequently due to the complex action of instincts and emotions, to the reaction of the whole personality of the child to definite situations.

It is important that physicians and nurses directly engaged in childhood welfare work, should have some personal experience with these facts, and should be sensitive to these problems.

The broadening of medical work to include preventive medicine or hygiene, and to give effect to the principle that hygiene adequately conceived is not hygiene of one organ or group of organs but includes the hygiene of the personality, is an important problem in medical education.

It is especially important that visiting nurses, who are brought continually face to face with family situations, should recognize this aspect of the health problems of the home.

The most complete apparatus for the survey and supervision of childhood material is the school system, backed by compulsory school attendance laws; this comprehensive machinery is beginning to be used for more than imparting information, it is now utilized to make children more healthy, as well as more literate; it has begun to pay attention to the hungry stomach, the diseased teeth and tonsils, the faulty eyes and ears of the children; the next step is to take an interest in the carrier of these organs, the child himself, with his instinctive and emotional problems and his individual environmental problems.

In order that the welfare of the school child may be adequately safeguarded and guaranteed, teachers, school nurses and physicians, and truant and probation officers, must learn to appreciate the important problems of health which are involved in the personality of the child.

A STATE PROGRAM FOR THE CARE OF THE MENTALLY DEFECTIVE

By DR. WALTER E. FERNALD
Massachusetts School for the Feeble-Minded

It is now generally understood that the feeble-minded and the progeny of the feeble-minded constitute one of the great social and economic burdens of our modern civilization. We have much accurate knowledge as to the prevalence, causation, social significance, prevention and treatment of feeble-mindedness, its influence as a source of unhappiness to the defective himself and to his family, and its bearing as a causative factor in the production of crime, prostitution, pauperism, and other complex social diseases. The literature on the subject has developed to enormous proportions. An intelligent democracy cannot consistently ignore a condition involving such a vast number of persons and families and communities, so large an aggregate of suffering and misery, and so great economic cost and waste.

Nearly every State in the Union has already made a beginning in the way of a program for dealing with the mentally defective, either directly or indirectly. The development of this program in the different States varies greatly in degree and method. Even the most advanced States have not yet formulated a plan for reaching all of the feeble-minded of the State. It is safe to say that no State has yet officially taken cognizance of ten per cent of the mentally defective persons in that State. No State has even ascertained the number of feeble-minded in the State, their location, or the nature and expression of their defect. The great majority of these defectives receive no education or training, and no adequate protection and supervision. We know that feeble-mindedness is highly hereditary, but in most States there is no legal obstacle to the marriage of the moron, the most numerous class of the feeble-minded.

There are many reasons for the lack of a formal accepted program. The problem can not be solved by a simple formula, which can be expressed in one definite piece of legislation. It is an infinitely complex problem, varied according to the age, sex, degree and kind of defect, presence or absence of hereditary traits or criminal and antisocial proclivities, home conditions, etc. The idiot, imbecile, and moron present different needs and dangers. Each of these groups has different troubles, according to age and sex. Rural, sparsely-settled communities, with homogenous racial population, have conditions pertaining to the defective which differ from those of urban industrial centers, with cosmopolitan racial complications.

The first step in a rational program would be the beginning of a complete and continuing census of the uncared-for feeble-minded of the whole State—this would state and define the problem. Many privately conducted surveys show the feasibility of such a census. The data for this census would be furnished by physicians, clinics, court and jail officials, social workers, town officials, teachers, etc. No doubtful case should be registered. Only those persons whose mental defect has been scientifically diagnosed should be registered. The register should be highly confidential and accessible only to properly accredited persons.

This coordination of existing records would be available for social workers, school authorities, and other agencies, and would be of enormous service in the solution of the individual problems which the feeble-minded constantly present. This alone would mean a great saving in time, effort, and money. This official census would give a logical basis for intelligent management of the mental defectives of the State.

A census of the feeble-minded would make possible and desirable some provision for a central governmental authority responsible for the general supervision and assistance and control of the uncared-for feeble-minded of the State, who do not need immediate institutional commitment. This State supervision of the feeble-minded should be directed by a State commission for the feeble-minded, or a properly constituted State board of health, or other similar body. Its responsible officer should be a psychiatrist, with special knowledge of mental deficiency and its many social expressions.

The local administration of this supervision could be carried out by the use of existing local public organizations, existing local private organizations and societies, or by properly qualified volunteers in each community. These peripheral workers could be made efficient by the use of suitable manuals, etc. This systematic supervision of the feeble-minded could easily be made to cover the entire State, with a local representative in each community, but all under the direction of the central authority.

Each defective could be regularly visited and kept under observation by the local visitor. The reports of these visitors, covering the life histories and the family histories of many cases, would soon constitute an invaluable treasury of information as a basis for scientific research and study in the search for practical methods of prevention. The official visitor would advise the parents as to the care and management of the defective, and would have opportunity to inform the family, the local officials, and the community generally as to the hereditary nature and the peculiar dangers of feeble-mindedness.

The registration of every feeble-minded person, and the regular visitations, especially of children of school age, would make it possible to inform the parents of the condition of the child, of the probable necessity of life-long supervision, and of the possible need for future segregation. Suitable, tactful literature should be prepared, which could be gradually presented to the parents in a way that would have great educational value. Sooner or later, the parents will probably be willing to allow their child to be cared for and trained in an institution if he needs such care. In suitable cases parents should be allowed to have the custody of their child, with the understanding that he shall be properly cared for and protected during his life, that he shall not be allowed to become immoral or criminal, and that he shall be prevented from parenthood. Whenever the parents or friends are unwilling or incapable of performing these duties, the law should provide that he shall be forcibly placed in an institution, or otherwise safeguarded. The local representatives of the central bureau would officially serve as advisors and sponsors for pupils graduated from the special school classes, for court cases under probation and observation, and for institutional inmates at home on visit or on trial.

Under this plan there would be a person in every locality familiar with the opportunities for mental examination and methods of permanent commitment. The extra-institutional supervision and observation of cases in their homes would do away with the necessity of institutional care of many persons who would otherwise have to go to an institution, thus reducing the expense of buildings and maintenance.

There should be legal provision for the commitment of uncared-for defective persons to the permanent custody of the central authority. This commitment should formally recognize the actual mental age and degree of responsibility of the defective person so committed. The legal status of a defective should be that of a normal child with a mental age of 8, 9, or 10 years. The permanent 8 or 9 or 10 year mentality of the defective should be legally acknowledged.

The extra-institutional supervision should include cases dismissed from institutions, so that the defective who has spent many years in an institution would not be thrown out into the world with a freedom which he does not know how to utilize. In these cases, the supervision would constitute a permanent parole which would be most effective. This provision would enable the defective to be returned to the institution if he did not properly conduct himself in the community. Such provision for registration of the feeble-minded and for extra-institutional supervision would ensure that those defectives who most need institutional training and protection would be sent to the institutions, and that those who can live safely and happily in the community would be allowed to do so.

The keynote of a practical program for the management of mental defectiveness is to be found in the fact, which seems to have been proved, that those defectives whose defects are recognized while they are young children, and who receive proper care and training during their childhood, are, as a rule, not especially troublesome after they have been safely guided through the period of early adolescence.

Every child automatically comes under the control of the school authorities between the ages of 6 and 14. Every case of mental defect can be easily recognized during this period. Present methods of health examination of school children could easily be extended so as to ensure and require a mental examination of every child obviously retarded in school accomplishment. It would not be necessary to give a mental examination to all the school children. It would be sufficient to examine only those children who are 3 or 4 or more years retarded in school work, perhaps 2 or 3 per cent of the primary-school population.

In the large cities, the mental examinations could be made by special examiners and at mental clinics. The rapid development of out-patient mental clinics all over the country will soon furnish facilities for such examinations in all the large cities. Rural communities and small towns could be served by a traveling mental clinic, as a part of the State government. This clinical group, or even a single clinician, could examine the presumably defective children over a very large area. A visit to each small town once each year would be sufficient. Every institutional school for the feeble-minded should conduct out-patient mental clinics at the institution, and in the various cities and towns served by the school. At the time of the mental examination, the parents should be informed as to the mental condition of the child, and of his need for special training and protection.

Suitable manuals should be prepared by the State board of education, which could be placed in the hands of every teacher, especially in the rural schools, describing the methods of training and management which should be applied to these cases. It should be recognized that the defective child is entitled, even more than a normal child, to education according to his needs and capacity. The defective children who can not be taught in the regular schools should be referred to the special classes or the institutional schools.

Cities and towns of over five thousand population are likely to have groups of at least ten or more defective children. Such communities should be required to establish special classes for defective children. The proper authorities should decide upon the courses of study and the equipment of school materials which are necessary for these special school classes. Provision should be made in the normal schools for training teachers of defective children. Every normal training school for teachers should be required to give suitable instruction to teachers, to enable them to recognize the probable cases of mental defect, and to give them a general idea as to the training and discipline of such children. The State board of education or some other branch of the State government should prepare simple manuals of facts for the use of the parents of feeble-minded children. This literature should be prepared in series with special articles for young boys, for young girls, for older boys, for older girls, and for other groups, and should kindly and tactfully instruct the parents as to the limitations of these children in the way of scholastic acquirements, and emphasize the importance of the development of habits of obedience and industry, and the necessity of protection against evil influences and companions during the formative period and of the possible need of institutional care in the future.

The great majority of mental defectives are of the moron group. If the plan suggested for the early recognition and the intelligent education and training of the moron in public schools and at home is carried out, many of this class can be safely cared for at home. We have begun to recognize the fact that there are good morons and bad morons, and that it is often possible in early life to recognize the moron with antisocial and criminalistic tendencies, who will probably need institutional care. Morons from families unable properly to protect and control their children will need institutional training and care. The fact should be emphasized that the neglected moron is the defective who makes trouble later in life, and that during the formative period of his life he should receive proper care and training either at home, with the special help of the regular teacher, or the special class, or in an institutional school.

The special public-school classes also serve as clearing-houses for the recognition of defective children who are markedly antisocial and immoral, and who need permanent institutional care. It is an easy step from the special class to the institution. The children who graduate from the special school classes should have the benefit of follow-up or after-care assistance and help.

In the majority of States, the only provision for mental defectives is furnished by an institutional school for the feeble-minded, providing care and protection for a limited number of idiots and imbeciles, education and industrial training for the morons, with permanent segregation for a certain number of defectives, and with special emphasis upon the life-long segregation of feeble-minded women of the hereditary group. It was formerly believed that it was possible and desirable to provide institutional care for practically all the mental defectives of the State. This was before the actual extent of the problem was known, and its cost computed, and before the difficulty of securing the commitment to an institution of many of these cases was realized. In practice it has been found very difficult to ensure the life-long segregation of the average moron. The courts are as ready to release the defective as they are to commit him in the first place. However proper and desirable it may be in theory to ensure the life-long institutional segregation of large numbers of the moron class, it is a fact that there is a deep-seated prejudice on the part of lawyers, judges, and legislators towards assuming in advance that every moron will necessarily and certainly misbehave to an extent that he should be deprived of his liberty. That such misgivings are well-founded is apparently shown by the studies made of discharged patients at Rome and Waverley. At Waverley, a careful study of the discharges for 25 years showed that a very small proportion of the discharged male morons had committed crimes, or had married or had become parents, or had failed to support themselves, or had been bad citizens.

It has been fairly well demonstrated that the average male moron, without naturally vicious tendencies, who has been properly trained in habits of obedience and industry, and who is protected from temptation and evil associations during his childhood, can be safely returned to the community when he has passed early adolescence, if his family are able to look after him and give him proper supervision. A very much larger proportion of these trained male defectives would be suitable for community life if the above-described extra-institutional control and supervision could be provided.

The average citizen is not yet convinced that he should be taxed to support permanently an individual who is capable of 30 or 50 or 70 per cent of normal economic efficiency, on the mere theory that he is more likely than a normal individual to become a social problem. Thousands of morons never give any trouble in the community.

The after-care studies of the female morons who have received training in the institutions were not so favorable, but many of these too led moral and harmless and useful lives after their return to the community. The study of discharged female cases at Waverley showed a surprisingly small number who became mothers or who married. While it is true that the defectives with undesirable habits and tendencies are not easily controlled, it is equally true that defectives who are obedient and moral and industrious are apt to continue these traits permanently. It is as difficult for them to unlearn as it was to learn. Those defectives whose tendencies are such as to make them undesirable members of the community should not be allowed their liberty, but should be permanently segregated in the institutions. No other class of human beings so surely avenge neglect in their childhood, socially, morally, economically, and eugenically.

The defectives who develop markedly immoral or criminalistic tendencies in the institutional schools for the feeble-minded should not be retained permanently in the institutions devoted to the care and training of the average defective, for the feeble-minded are most suggestible and easily influenced, and should be protected from the companionship and influence of the defective with criminalistic tendencies. These "bad" defectives should be committed to and cared for in an institution especially for that type, where the discipline could be made more rigid, and permanent detention more certain.

If 25 per cent or more of the inmates of our penal and correctional institutions are feeble-minded, as has been shown, it should be required that a mental examination should be made of all inmates of such institutions, and that those criminals who are found to be mentally defective should not be automatically discharged to return to the community, but should be committed to a special institution for defective delinquents, and should be permanently segregated, and discharged only under the strictest sort of supervised parole. Provision should be made for the mental examination of all persons accused of crime when there is any suspicion as to the mentality of the accused.

There is no doubt that every State in the union needs greatly increased institutional facilities for the care of the feeble-minded, not only as a matter of justice and fairness to the feeble-minded themselves and to their families, but as an investment which would repay the cost many times over.

There is no panacea for feeble-mindedness. There will always be mentally defective persons in the population of every State and country. All of our experience in dealing with the feeble-minded indicates that if we are adequately to manage the individual defective we must recognize his condition while he is a child, and protect him from evil influences, train and educate him according to his capacity, make him industrially efficient, teach him to acquire correct habits of living, and, when he has reached adult life, continue to give him the friendly help and guidance he needs. These advantages should be accessible to every feeble-minded person in the State. Most important of all, so far as possible, the hereditary class of defectives must not be allowed to perpetuate their decadent stock. The program for meeting the needs of these highly varied and heterogeneous groups must be as flexible and complex as the problem itself. It will be modified and developed as our knowledge and experience increases.

To sum up, the program now possible includes the mental examination of backward school children; the mental clinic; the travelling clinic; the special class; directed training of individual defectives in country schools; instruction of parents of defective children; aftercare of special-class pupils; special training of teachers in normal schools; census and registration of the feeble-minded; extra-institutional supervision of all uncared-for defectives in the community; selection of the defectives who most need segregation for institutional care; increased institutional facilities; parole for suitable institutionally-trained adult defectives; permanent segregation for those who need segregation; mental examinations of persons accused of crime and of all inmates of penal institutions; and long-continued segregation of defective delinquents in special institutions.

The above program would require team work on the part of psychiatrists, psychologists, teachers, normal schools, parents, social workers, institution officials, parole officers, court officials, prison officers, etc. There would be highly centralized formulation of plans and methods and of authority, but much of the real work would be done in the local community. The degree of development of the program in a given State would depend upon existing knowledge and public sentiment on the subject in that State and this in turn would be measured by the wisdom and experience of the responsible officials. Nearly every suggestion in the proposed program is already being followed in some State. No one State has anything like a complete program.

DISCUSSION

Sir Cyril Jackson (Board of Education, England): The question of the feeble-minded has been studied for quite a long time, as you know. As early as 1881 we had the question of the mentally defective child brought before us in London. We started classes then. Dr. Fernald has told me that he has investigated some of our London classes, and I was very glad to hear that he thought well of them. I believe that we now have day classes for practically all mentally defective children. We have tried to work out a scheme for treating them differently from the treatment given those in the ordinary schools. I may say that so far as defective children are concerned we quickly discovered that it was not of the least use to attempt to put them upon the ordinary curriculum. We have put a great many of them on hand work and thus have made them utilize their fingers, and by that means utilize what brains they possess. We have been successful in that method.

Our difficulties have been the same as yours. There is, in the first place, the difficulty of knowing when the child is defective. I remember that one of my club boys came to me a short time ago because a son of his had been taken into the mentally defective class. As you well know, children are not always in the defective classes because they should be there, but because teachers are sometimes anxious to get rid of them. This father said that he discovered no signs of the child being mentally defective. The teacher had taken him to the doctor and the doctor had sent him to the mentally defective class. The child, perhaps, had refused to answer the questions which the doctor asked. As all of us know, if we do not tell the doctor our symptoms we cannot expect to be cured. This father said to me that if I would get his child out of the defective class he would teach him at home. I managed to do that and the father did teach his child. It was clear that that child should not have gone into a mentally defective class.

Some teachers are very kind, indeed, in these matters. I remember one teacher who produced a child who the doctor said should go into the defective class. She took particular pains to make this child come forward, and succeeded in improving him until she had him in the class of backward children instead of among the mentally defective.

There was a new act passed just before the war, which was to help us to deal with this problem better than ever before. But it has not yet had a fair chance. This new act is interesting because for the first time it really makes it the duty of the special authority, which is to be called the Public Control Board, to ascertain all mentally defective children and to supervise them in their homes, and, where necessary, to provide institutions for them. In the past we have ascertained these children through our ordinary school method, and I think probably, with tolerable success, have gotten most of them into special day schools, but the new act is going to see that everybody is supervised and that everybody who is neglected or uncared for is to be looked after either in the home or in an institution. It also gives new authority to provide a permanent institution for classes of cases which we have up to the present been unable to provide for and for which we have had to rely upon voluntary effort.

Just as in the States, so in England, in the rural districts there has been great difficulty in getting centers even for the ordinary mentally defective children which would take them away from the school and put them into proper classes. Where a teacher has been able to give personal attention no doubt the child has been as well off in the village school as in the special school. We have been gradually arriving at a scheme by which children in the country districts may be sent into the towns which have good schools under the guardianship of foster parents selected with extreme care so that the children may be in a position to attend day school and yet live in home surroundings.

We have in England, as you no doubt have here, a controversy between people who believe in the institution and people who hate the institution and who say the only thing to do is to place out the child with foster parents. I think the foster parents of defective children must be more carefully selected than those of any other child. Defective children are not pleasant company. They want both a mother and a specially trained teacher; and to find a foster mother able to fulfill those requirements is a difficult task.

A Member: Will Dr. Fernald tell us about the "Jim" whom he mentioned after closing his address?

Dr. Fernald: I can state "Jim's" case in one minute. "Jim" was a man 40 years of age. He had spent 30 years in an institution for the feeble-minded. At the beginning of the war when the young morons began to go out and get employment at good wages, Jim said, "I have been a good boy; I have been here for many years; why shouldn't I go out and earn my living?" We sent him out. Six months later his employer called me up on the telephone and said, "Jim wants to talk to you a little." He also said, "I want to tell you he is one of the best teamsters I have in my employ. He has only one fault; he will go to bed at 7:30 every night." You see the point? It is difficult for the feeble-minded to learn. Our psychological friends have told us it is equally difficult for them to forget. If we get the defective at an early age and bring him to manhood with good habits and keep him from bad associations, he will, in all probability, settle down and continue those good habits for the rest of his life. If, on the contrary, we allow that defective to roam about and to be influenced—and he is very easily influenced because he is suggestible—if we allow him to have bad associations and to get into bad habits, it is impossible for us to remove those bad habits.

Section V
Standardization of Child Welfare Laws

GENERAL STATEMENT

By THE REV. WILLIAM J. KERBY

Secretary, National Conference of Catholic Charities

I am very fond of a remark of Ruskin to the effect that the important thing in this world is to know, not details, but the way things are going Details are symptoms. The drift of things reveals the great formative forces that shape institutions and adapt them to new vision of ideals.

The world is moving in a way to show increasing solicitude for the welfare of children. Scholarship, as well as sympathy; insight into the future, as well as understanding of the present; respect for the natural and divine rights of childhood, rather than for worn-out social philosophy and fallacious property rights; these are conspicuous in the drift of the world to-day. This Child Welfare Conference is significant as an expression of new idealism and proof of new determination to cause the beneficent sun of justice to brighten the days of our children and secure to them the fuller life to which they have a right.

Rights are formulated usually after menaces present themselves. Rights are protective. We recognize that actual social conditions and ignorance are increasingly sources of danger to children. Definitions of children's rights are expanding in their content to meet these dangers with a force that is irresistible, and in obedience to the touch of an idealism which honors this epoch in the history of the world. I have in mind not only legal definitions of rights, but also the clearer expression of the moral sense of society and the finer conscience that is shaping itself under the stress of modern life.

The state is, however, showing an increasing interest in legal protection of childhood, because moral forces do not operate with a sanction sufficient to overcome the dangers which threaten it. The state is the highest form of physical power that we know. It is the most representative of society, since all the separate social interests that divide our life merge in it. It has power to make and to enforce definitions. Hence, we turn to it with increasing frequency for such action as may safeguard the endangered rights of childhood. We would be nobler were this not necessary. We would be more democratic were this accomplished by the moral and social forces of society, and not by the lower coercion of law. But this is not our happy lot, and hence we invoke the law, determined to do the best that is possible for our children.

One of the many dangers of this process is that of drifting into the habit of legislating for social interests, instead of for human persons. An analogy may make the thought more clear. Division of labor promoted invention, by simplifying operations, and inventing mechanical devices to perform them. Synthesis then combined many mechanical devices into single, wonderful, complex machines that defy description, such is their ingenuity. Similarly, we are dividing the complex life of society, particularly of children, into great simple interests, such as those of health, recreation, economic efficiency, and education, and we legislate for the protection of these separate interests, while losing sight, perhaps, of the more delicate note of personality and individuality which is, or should be, the mark of real democracy. We tend, then, to synthesize these separate lines of legislation into codes, such as children's codes—in the hope of coming back to the real, whole, human view of life which we should ever have in mind.

This conference is to be given over to the serious study of standards of child care, to a review of what we are attempting, and a formulation of our larger purposes and ideals. Our work will be wisely done in proportion as we keep a whole view of life before us, and aim to coordinate all social forces in the protection of childhood. If democracy is primarily moral and social, and only secondarily political, as I believe it to be, we must count to the fullest on the power of all moral and social forces in safeguarding childhood. We must, in fact, have more laws, more adequate enforcement of laws, and more faithful understanding of their spirit. But we must not cease to endeavor to arouse all moral, religious, and social forces to the fullest realization of their concomitant or (perhaps better) prior duties, toward the childhood of the nation. If democracy means a maximum of order with a minimum of coercion, the ideal toward which we ought to work is that of doing the most for childhood with the least resort to law, and with supreme appeal to the higher sources of order and justice.

THE NEED FOR STANDARDIZATION [1]

By FRANKLIN CHASE HOYT
Presiding Justice, Children's Court, New York City

The experience of all of us who are engaged in any form of social work has demonstrated beyond any argument, the vital necessity for the maintenance of certain minimum standards in the various fields connected with the training and protection of children. We have found too, that it is not enough to safeguard these standards in one direction, only to neglect them in another. They are all interdependent, and a break in the weakest link of the chain will cause disaster to the rest. If, for example, precautions for the health of our children and the barriers against their employment are swept away, what will become of their educational standards? If proper forms of recreation are to be denied them, what is the use of troubling any further about their health or their moral training?

In this connection, I quote from our annual report, which has not yet come out of the printer's hands:

"In our general satisfaction over the fact that New York City exhibited a definite decrease in juvenile delinquency during 1918, there is one interesting point that should not be overlooked. It may or may not be significant, but nevertheless it is disquieting. While delinquency decreased for the year as a whole, it increased in rather alarming proportions after the middle of November. In other words, it decreased during the war, but immediately increased after the signing of the armistice. In December, 1918, the arrests for delinquency jumped to 648 as compared with 371 in the same month in 1917. This increase may be due to the constant change which is normally to be expected from one month to another. Indeed it is customary for our monthly arraignments to show varying totals when compared with the same months in previous years. If so, it is without any special meaning, and can be dismissed from our consideration. I believe, however, that it may possess a very real significance and that it emphasizes a situation which deserves serious thought and attention. Since the summer of 1918 there has been a great drift among children away from school. The authorization of vacation working certificates made employment possible for those who could not obtain regular working papers. The wages were extremely high and out of all proportion to the real earning capacity of the children. Then too, the schools were greatly demoralized by the epidemic of influenza this past autumn, and many of the classes were suspended because of the illness of both teachers and pupils. As a consequence of these conditions many have refused to return to school, and being unable to continue to find legal employment have resorted to truancy and comparative vagrancy. The number of truants reported to the court during the past few months has been extremely large, and it is almost

---

[1] Delivered at the New York Child Welfare Regional Conference, May 8, 1919.

impossible to cope with the situation as the truant schools are filled to overflowing. (It is not at all surprising that there should be a great increase of delinquency among this class, and that this economic unrest should result in ultimate social disorder.)

"There is but one way to meet this situation, and that is to cooperate in the 'back to the school' drive which is being organized on a national scale. If the children and their parents can be shown the desirability of continuing in school, and the child-labor laws raised and vigorously enforced, much of this threatened danger may be successfully averted."

Thus we find that the increase of juvenile delinquency during the past few months, can be definitely traced to the relaxation of child-labor laws a year ago, and the inability of the school authorities to deal adequately with the truancy situation. Our problems and those of education and child labor are closely related, and we are dependent upon the authorities in those fields for support and protection in meeting our own problems.

Cooperation is after all perhaps the most important feature in the maintenance of proper standards. Indeed the Children's Bureau has stated that cooperation may be called the keynote of the Children's Year. We are all aware of the lack of coordination now existing among the various social agencies dealing with child welfare. It is quite possible for one case alone to have received the attention of a great number of organizations and yet for these agencies never to compare or to harmonize their efforts. We have found families whose troubles have been known to the church, the school, the relief societies, the settlements, the hospitals, the courts, the institutions, the city departments, and yet except by fortunate accident their knowledge has never been brought together nor their activities coordinated. It has been said, "Each has groped oblivious of the others. Sometimes they have collided, but even this has not happened often, for the problem is vast. Each of these elements of social aid, of human hope and worth are moving, as it were, in avoid. The solitude of the desert surrounds them."

If we had a set of proper standards, such a state of affairs could not occur. If we could count upon the existence of minimum standards in the various fields of child-welfare work, and could feel sure that these standards would be observed and enforced, many of our problems could be simplified and in every case the children of the community would be the gainers.

The question of cooperation naturally suggests a kindred subject, and that is our crying need for a comprehensive Children's Code in New York State. We must have a thorough revision of existing laws relative to the protection and training of children.

There is a great need at present for a codification of these statutes, which as has been said, "are scattered about without systematic arrangement, a condition which could hardly be avoided owing to sporadic amendment and spasmodic constructive legislation." The corner stone for our proposed Children's Code is to be found in the constitutional amendment now before the legislature, granting equity powers to children's courts and courts of domestic relations. I have not the time to discuss this amendment in detail, but I can say that until the Constitution permits the creation of courts with proper powers to administer social justice, the formulation of a satisfactory children's code will be impossible. To enforce the standards as provided by the code we must have as our first requisite a court of competent jurisdiction. I trust that every one interested in the cause of child welfare will do his utmost during the coming year to see that this amendment shall receive favorable action at the hands of the legislature in 1920.

The day of casual and indefinite methods in provisions for the protection and training of children is drawing to a close. Too long have we been satisfied with a sort of hit-or-miss system, which is pitifully suggestive of wasted effort, and indicative of wholesale demoralization. President Wilson said: "Attention is now being given to education and labor conditions for children by the legislatures of both France and England, showing that the conviction among the Allies is that the protection of childhood is essential to winning the war." Is it not our duty now that the strife is over to give our attention to these self-same problems, and to look upon the protection of childhood as essential to the finer development of the nation in the new era which lies before us? I am not a believer in the multiplication of laws and statutes which will deprive a man, or a child for that matter, of independent action or thought. I do not believe in making an individual a mere automaton in the operation of a super-socialistic State, but I do believe in comprehensive effort and planning for the protection and proper development of the children of our nation.

THE METHOD OF PROCEDURE

By C. C. CARSTENS

General Secretary, Massachusetts Society for the
Prevention of Cruelty to Children

During the early years of the war, from 1914 to 1917, one of the most striking facts in connection with public sentiment on all matters relating to the Great War and to our American attitude towards it was the lack of a strong public opinion, either for or against. This lack exists in many other matters relating to American civilization, and is particularly noticeable in the plans for social legislation which are being shaped by municipalities, by counties, or by States. When the United States finally cast in its lot with the Allies, it was because there had come into our thinking an expression of national ideals which had crystallized our thoughts and directed all our energies toward the accomplishment of one definite purpose.

There is more than a slight analogy between that situation and the one to which we are to give our attention.

Diversities of race, of language, and of political development in our various States have led to a complicated divergence in children's laws and in the organizations which care for the various groups that are the subject of our interest. In Michigan, Minnesota, Massachusetts, and certain other States a clear recognition that the State has a central responsibility for its wards is shown in the development of its institutions. In Pennsylvania, Connecticut, and many other States the State as a unit of administration gives little if any indication of the assumption of such responsibility, while New York, Ohio, and Indiana seem to lie between the two extremes. The fact of such diversity, which is recognized by all of us, is not to be lamented so much in itself as in the fact that it connotes a lack of clear thinking, of the proper adaptation of our institutions to our needs, and of such a minimum uniformity as is after all needed between States.

The Federal Government is giving increasing recognition to the social welfare of the people of this country. This has been evidenced in various ways, and in children's work particularly by the establishment of the Federal Children's Bureau and by the passage of a Federal law protecting children from exploitation through labor. But for the proper development of child-welfare standards and child-welfare institutions, the United States is still very largely in the position of a group of forty-eight little republics each of which may learn from its neighbor but none of which needs modify its plans because of the existence of a better procedure in a neighboring State.

The task before any group who are urging the standardization of children's laws throughout the Nation resolves itself in large part into an effort to inspire groups in the various States to study good methods in children's work, to learn the weaknesses of the plans of their own State, and to work for the adoption of a new children's code, or to discover the next logical steps to take in the development of the State's child-welfare institutions. The method which has been pursued by several States with the greatest success has consisted in obtaining the appointment of State commissions by the governor, either with or without legislative sanction. Such commissions generally consist of a group of citizens interested in various forms of child welfare. An executive secretary is appointed to undertake the secretarial work and the direction of the various investigations that are needed. The Federal Children's Bureau has given great aid by providing not only an index of child-welfare legislation in the particular State, but also digests of certain types of laws in force in the various States. If a State cannot convince its governor or its legislature that a commission to revise and codify children's laws is desirable, a group of citizens who have become convinced of this need can make at least a preliminary investigation and can generally bring about the appointment of a commission at a later date, or can draft laws to submit to the legislature without the assistance of a commission.

The procedure of any such State commission may be outlined as follows: At the beginning it should determine how broad its field of work shall be. For instance, shall it deal with the needs of the various classes of handicapped children only? Or shall it concern itself with all children, and so include for instance the welfare responsibilities of the school, such as medical inspection, physical education, vocational guidance, continuation schools, and various other subjects that have such a large part in the life of the child and his training for the world's work? Then the field chosen must be carefully studied. There are in all our States at the present time colleges and universities, members of whose staffs are ready to take their share in making and directing investigations. Civic leagues; bureaus of research and child welfare; and family, neighborhood, and industrial agencies are also ready to help The coordination of these various resources provides a means for making field and library investigations of great value. The Federal Children's Bureau has made important investigations, enunciated important principles and standards, and is becoming increasingly valuable in child-welfare work. In the gathering together of facts many different agencies can contribute, but in studying the results of the investigation and making recommendations for changes, the commission must become a well-organized body in order to coordinate these recommendations with each other and with the body of child-welfare law already in existence in its State. When the law recommendations have been decided upon, there comes the important procedure of drafting the code or the separate bills. This is a service which law schools like to share with drafting departments of the universities of our various States.

There are certain clearly marked tendencies in the development of child-welfare legislation in our various States. While there are now but few States in the Union where a central board, such as a board of charity or a board of children's guardians, has assumed responsibility for the care of the children of that State, sentiment is growing in favor of legislation to establish such a body. Under whatever name such powers may be administered, it is essential that States should have such a board with State-wide power and responsibility. This body should be charged not only with the State's responsibility for the handicapped groups, but should consider also the welfare of the hundred per cent of children, and should be required to investigate untoward conditions and propose to the legislature needed changes in legislation without waiting to be specifically asked to do so.

Along with the development of such a central body there grows increasingly a sense of the need of a well-organized local public-service unit. In most parts of the United States this unit should cover the area of the county in which it would perform the various social functions in connection with probation, parole, recreation, protective, and other child-caring work. Although the county shows here and there a backward development, it offers the largest opportunities of usefulness. Some of our States have begun to organize county boards of public welfare. Missouri, Kansas, and North Carolina will shortly have lessons to teach us in this field, and Dutchess County, New York, has been carrying on an interesting experiment in developing a county social welfare unit.

The importance of these two, the State and local units of service, and their interrelation, will become increasingly appreciated as we come to add varying forms of social service. The lack of them has already led to the development of unrelated boards or the addition of administrative functions to juvenile courts in many States and cities.

Much of the impetus for new boards to administer mothers' pensions, industrial schools, probation, and such activities, has come because of the revolt against the word "charity" and the bald facts of charitable administration. A board of children's guardians avoids this objection and may easily undertake a variety of functions that are at foundation closely interrelated.

The scheme of having forty-eight individual republics independent as far as State and local legislation is concerned, has some very decided advantages when once we have grasped certain national ideals in social service and education. In the different States it is possible to experiment with various forms of administration while the subject is still in the experimental stage.

Mothers' pensions a few years ago became a national ideal, to the development of which social workers had unconsciously contributed but in the shaping of which they had taken very little part. The administration of such laws was still in the experimental stage when the drive began. The administrative body was generally made a new kind of relief agency without any tying-up to agencies dealing with the same families. The sum total of mothers' pension legislation will be beneficial without doubt, but the procedure of our States in putting these laws on their statute books is largely a lesson in how not to do it.

Juvenile court legislation is another subject requiring constant study and revision. It is now twenty years since the first juvenile court law was passed. A well-developed State plan of service needs to be presented for criticism, adoption, and trial.

The interrelation of public and private child-welfare service is not one of the least important questions to be determined by a children's code commission, especially in all the eastern States. Upon the expression of that relationship will depend, on the one hand, the progressive development of the State's functions in child welfare, and, on the other hand, the encouragement of private effort and association in such a way that it will never hamper the public as it does now in certain States, but will remain as a friendly critic, a guide for greater public effort, and an anchor for good public service.

These are but a few of the many subjects that must have the consideration of a child-welfare commission. The drive is on. Minnesota has set the pace; Kansas and Missouri have gained part of their programs and are making another attempt; Indiana sends word that a commission has been authorized; in Pennsylvania a bill for a commission has been presented; what new State is sufficiently interested in its children's problems to be the next? Uniformity we shall probably never have. That is not our goal. But we would that certain national ideals in child welfare might be clearly enunciated and become the warp and woof of our child-welfare legislation in the various States.

THE MINNESOTA CHILD WELFARE COMMISSION

By W. W. HODSON

Director, Children's Bureau, State Board of Control, St. Paul, Minnesota

The Minnesota Child Welfare Commission was the result of five years agitation for a revision of laws relating to children. In 1911 our State Legislature was asked to appoint a commission for that purpose, but no action was taken. Two years later a bill providing for the appointment of a commission by the Governor passed the lower house but was defeated in the senate, probably because a small appropriation was included.

Meanwhile the State of Missouri had pointed a way out of preliminary legislative difficulties by inducing its Governor to appoint a commission without express statutory warrant. In 1916 various civic and philanthropic bodies in the State joined with a large number of social workers and interested persons in asking Governor Burnquist to name members of a group which should study our laws and make recommendations for general revision and codification. The request was granted in August, 1916.

Careful consideration had been given to the personnel of the commission, and the Governor approved many of the suggestions made by those interested. Twelve persons were appointed, nine men and three women. Of the men three were judges—two members of the district bench, assigned to the juvenile court, and the third a former justice of the supreme court; two were members of the legislature, one from each house; and the remaining four were an assistant secretary of a civic and commerce association of long professional training in philanthropic work, a member of the State board of control, which manages the institutions of the State, the superintendent of the State school for dependent children, and a Jewish rabbi who had taken an active interest in civic affairs. Of the women, one was active in the management of a social settlement in the largest city of the State, another was the director of the bureau of women and children of the State labor department; and the third was a woman of broad civic interests, long active in the advancement of suffrage.

While all the members of the commission displayed a keen interest in its work, a smaller group of six were mainly responsible for the results achieved.

Shortly after its appointment the commission organized by electing

Edward F. Waite, Juvenile Court Judge of Minneapolis and member of the Hennepin County District Court bench, chairman, and Otto Davis, Assistant Secretary of the Minneapolis Civic and Commerce Association, secretary. The writer had the privilege of serving as executive secretary, and devoted his full time to the work. An office was established in the State Capitol, with stenographic assistance; the expenses of the commission, approximating in all about $2,500, were met by voluntary subscription throughout the State, though the cities of Minneapolis and St. Paul gave the great bulk of the amount raised. The money was given largely as the result of letters of appeal. The State board of control and the State labor department contributed considerable service, and a small deficit was finally paid out of the Governor's contingent fund.

Our study was undertaken on the basis of four general subdivisions, suggested by the Federal Children's Bureau:

1. Defective children, with reference to the blind, the deaf, the crippled, and deformed, the feeble-minded and epileptic, and—as related matter—the protection of children from transmissible disease and the regulation of marriage.

2. Dependent and neglected children, touching upon courts, and procedure, illegitimacy, adoption, public relief at home, maternity hospitals, lying-in places, baby farms, placing-out agencies, institutional homes, abandonment, and desertion.

3. Delinquent children, including courts and procedure, correctional institutions, moral safeguards, and adults contributing to delinquency.

4. General child welfare, including birth registration, vital statistics, regulation of midwives, school attendance, regulation of employment, and crimes against children.

Four committees were appointed to study the field as outlined, and to report findings to the general body. Six months after its appointment, the commission transmitted its report, with forty-three proposed laws, to the Governor. The findings of the commission were adopted in almost every instance by a unanimous vote of that body. Where there was a division, a substantial majority had approved. As the legislature was then in session, the Governor promptly sent the report to the legislature, with his approval, and asked favorable consideration for the program as a whole, since it was closely interrelated as to details.

Persons friendly to the proposed legislation secured the consent of the speaker of the house and the president of the senate to the appointment of a joint committee on child welfare, with five members of the senate and seven members of the house. The writer, because of his connection with the commission, was made clerk of this joint committee, which gave the commission important strategic advantages both in committee and on the floor of the houses when the bills were under discussion.

The joint committee reported favorably to the legislature thirty-five of the forty-three measures submitted. Eight were withdrawn, not because of the opposition of the committee, but because it was regarded as impossible to pass the entire program if these eight highly controversial measures were to be thrashed out in the short time remaining before adjournment. The measures withdrawn were not essential to the general scheme proposed, though they were in themselves of considerable importance. The thirty-five bills, bearing the double indorsement of the joint committees from both houses, were enacted into law by the legislature with but few and unimportant changes. This was accomplished by the skillful work of two members of the joint committee, one in each house, who led the fight and succeeded, in the face of a late introduction of the bills and the inevitable crush and confusion of the closing days of the session. The bills were made a special order of business in each house at intervals on four different days, and final action was taken within seven days of adjournment.

RESEARCH AND EXPERT ASSISTANCE

A careful survey of the laws of the State relating to children was undertaken by the commission as the first order of business. An index of Minnesota Laws prepared by the Federal Children's Bureau served as a basis for the inquiry, and the chairman of the commission made an intensive analysis of the various statutory provisions as they affected minors. The study of the laws of other States was facilitated by the large number of comparative studies already in existence on various subjects such as marriage, so-called mothers' pensions, child labor, recreation, dependent classes, etc. Whenever, in the course of investigation, it became necessary to study special points in greater detail, the executive secretary prepared summaries of the laws of other States, which were put at the disposal of the committees in need of them.

A considerable library was collected, consisting of reports from Federal, State and local agencies, and from the private agencies of the country doing children's work. Magazine articles, reprints of addresses, the proceedings of the National Conference, and of State conferences, (notably New York and Massachusetts), and other sources of a like character, proved of great assistance. Advice was sought from such authorities as Dr. H. H. Hart, Mr. C. C. Carstens, Mr. J. Prentice Murphy, Mr. Alexander Johnson, the Federal Children's Bureau, and others, on particular points as the various problems presented themselves. A lively correspondence was conducted with juvenile court judges and experienced child-welfare workers and institutional heads in our own State in an effort to get local reaction as to needed legislation.

No special expert assistance was employed. Three members of the commission and the executive secretary were lawyers. Occasionally mooted legal points were submitted to outside attorneys, who rendered opinions without remuneration. The problems were only incidentally legal; the inquiry was rather one of social facts, involving matters of policy and administration. In this regard the commission kept its objectives constantly free of confusion. It recognized that a legalistic conception was not the true one. Five members of the commission were of professional training in social fields, three were especially qualified in child welfare and administration. The problem was to discover and make proper use of the wealth of expert opinion available, both inside and outside the State.

EDUCATIONAL PROPAGANDA

The commission found that frequent public hearings served two purposes: opinions and criticisms were voiced and the discussion served as a means of propaganda. No less than twelve public hearings were held on the various issues raised, and these hearings were well attended by social workers, secretaries and boards of directors of children's homes, hospitals, and child-placing agencies, juvenile court judges, and professional men. Special invitations were sent to those most vitally affected by any proposed legislation, and a general invitation to others was extended through the press. As a result of the public hearings, sound objections could be met and future opposition in the legislature avoided. In addition the discussion of issues served to exploit the proposed legislation at the same time.

I have already spoken of the voluminous correspondence carried on for the purpose of seeking opinions and explaining the measures advocated by the commission. As rapidly as the various bills assumed their tentative final form, they were printed and sent over the State broadcast. The services of an expert press representative were obtained for special articles on the more fundamental changes proposed. This reporter was regularly stationed at the Capitol and was more or less familiar with the commission's work for that reason. His stories were written in the so-called feature style and were distinctly popular in their character, though conveying, to a marked degree, the essential points involved. This material was sent to all the newspapers of the State and was used quite freely, as our clipping service later disclosed.

When the work of the commission was completed, careful attention was paid to the character of its printed report. It contained, first, a general summary of its investigation and conclusions, written briefly and with no attempt at details. The basic principles upon which the legislation was founded were explained and the scheme of administration outlined. Every proposed measure was printed in full, but each with a short preliminary paragraph of explanation and summary. The casual reader could thus get the gist of the measures with slight effort. The measures themselves were drawn in simple and non-technical language, so far as was consistent with accuracy and clarity.

The report was sent to an extensive mailing list, together with a letter requesting the addressee to write to his representatives in the legislature, urging the passage of the laws recommended. The report was placed in the hands of all the legislators, and hundreds of extra copies were left with the clerks of both houses. People who had not previously received a copy were then urged to write their representatives for copies, and over five hundred were thus disposed of by the legislature through its members. The various women's clubs of the State were enthusiastic and constant in their legislative agitation. The State educational convention considered the child-welfare program and endorsed it by resolutions which were forwarded to the legislature. One or two other conventions did likewise. The Civic and Commerce Association of Minneapolis was of constant help and assistance. Not a great deal was done in the way of public speaking. The executive secretary made perhaps fifteen addresses in the course of six months before various interested groups.

RESULTS ATTAINED

The commission set out to revise and codify the laws of the State relating to children. The result of its labor was extensive revision but only incidental codification in the technical sense of that word. The thirty-five measures enacted into law repealed one hundred fourteen sections of previously existing law and amended sixty sections. Only three of the thirty-five laws contained no repealing or amending clauses. Time did not permit the assembling of these measures in such a way as to make possible their passage as a code rather than as individual laws, but the existing statutes are now for the most part coherent, consistent, and inter-dependent. They seek to express the State's responsibility for its handicapped children as far as it seems possible to go at this time. The administration of the new child-welfare laws was centralized in the State board of control. That board was given unusually broad powers and was authorized to create a new division for this work and to organize county child-welfare boards in order that with centralization of responsibility might go, so far as possible, decentralization of administration. The board of control, which had previously managed all State institutions, was given more complete control by the abolition of local advisory boards in the few instances where those advisory boards still existed.

Under the new laws, private homes for children, hospitals doing maternity work, child-helping and child-placing organizations are subjected to the supervisory power of the board of control. All placements of children in private families must be reported to that board for its investigation and approval. Restrictions of like nature are placed on the importation and exportation of children. Petitions for adoption are referred by the district court for report and recommendation after inspection of the homes of the petitioners. The board is made particularly responsible for the illegitimate child. In the language of the statute, the board "shall take care that the interests of the child are safeguarded, that appropriate steps are taken to establish his paternity, and that there is secured for him the nearest possible approximation to the care, support, and education that he would be entitled to if born of lawful marriage."

Feeble-minded persons under the new laws may be committed to the care and custody of the State board of control, and the board has full powers of guardianship and may make whatever disposition of the case seems best under the circumstances. Commitments are now possible even against the will of the patient, or of his parents, or guardians, whenever public policy makes such commitment necessary.

The so-called mothers' pension law has been entirely rewritten, with special reference to the requirement of careful preliminary and frequent subsequent investigation, and is made of more generous application. The board of control is given certain advisory functions in promoting efficiency, and the law is administered as before by the various Juvenile Courts of the State. The general purposes of the act are stated to be as follows:

"This act shall be liberally construed with a view to accomplishing its purpose, which is hereby declared to be to enable the State and its several counties to cooperate with responsible mothers in rearing future citizens, when such cooperation is necessary on account of relatively permanent conditions, in order to keep the mother and children together in the same household, reasonably safeguard the health of the mother and secure to the children during their tender years her personal care and training."

The law governing illegitimacy proceedings has been changed, and the responsibility of the adjudged father is declared to be the same as that of the father of a legitimate child. The board of control is authorized to accept and administer money settlements in behalf of illegitimate children. The abandonment of issue of fornication is made a felony and extradition is thus made possible without a previous adjudication of paternity.

The law relating to desertion and non-support has been quite radically changed by raising the age of the child to be protected, making the provisions apply to fathers of illegitimate children, increasing the penalty, and making three months' failure to support presumptive evidence of intent to abandon.

On the side of health, the existing laws were amended to give the State board of health specific control over venereal disease and power to prescribe a prophylactic for the eyes of the newly born. The laws relating to vital statistics have been changed in order to protect illegitimate children in the matter of a public record of parentage.

There were other measures of less importance which need not be detailed here. It is worth recording that thirty-three of the above outlined measures passed the upper house of our legislature unanimously; the other two had but a single dissenting vote. In the lower house thirty-one passed unanimously and the largest vote against any of the other measures was four. Seven minor and relatively unimportant amendments to the whole program were adopted. This rather unusual result may be accounted for in a variety of ways. Of course the legislation was not of a commercial character; it did not therefore incur the opposition of private business or industrial interests. The subjects covered were quite outside the experience of the average legislator, and he took the program partly on faith, especially because of his trust in the standing and character of the commission and the thoroughness with which its work was done, and also because the legislation was largely centralized for administration in the hands of the board of control, which in our State has won the confidence of people and legislature. The joint-committee method of dealing with the subject and the adroit work of the members of that committee on the floor, backed by the considerable propaganda carried on by the commission, were also factors in the result.

I have discussed what was gained; let me conclude briefly with what was lost. A child-labor bill which strengthened and amplified our present law without making any far-reaching changes was withdrawn. The same fate befell our street-trades bill, which incurred the enmity of the large daily papers. A marriage bill providing for a decent period of hesitation between application and granting of license, and adding venereal disease and tuberculosis as disqualification, met the united opposition of the clerks of court, who deal in licenses. Two bills providing for inheritance by illegitimate children from adjudged fathers were sacrificed to the cry of "blackmail." Three other minor bills have since become law.

DISCUSSION

Dr. Hastings H. Hart (Russell Sage Foundation, New York City): This Minnesota commission was to my mind, one of the most significant things of which I have ever known. I have never heard of a finer piece of team work than was done on that job.

I was called in consultation while that commission was sitting; and I told them frankly I thought it would be impossible for them to carry out their program; that the time was too short, and that they would not accomplish it. I advised them to wait until the next legislature, two years later. But they disregarded my advice and went ahead, for which I am very thankful; and they demonstrated the possibility of doing this work within six months, by the combination which they made and the admirable way in which they worked together.

I want to call your attention to one thing: the difference between the method followed in Minnesota and the method followed (at the same time) in Missouri, which also had a code commission. The Missouri code commission divided up into eight subcommittees, and each one of those subcommittees worked independently. The test came when they tried to get together. They could not coordinate their work; and the result was that they had to go before the legislature with a report upon which they could not unanimously agree. That, of course, weakened them considerably. They passed eleven bills out of forty-five, whereas Minnesota passed thirty-five out of forty-three.

Then, too, the character of this Minnesota legislation is very remarkable. They have tried some experiments which are of national significance, especially in this matter of dealing with the child of the unmarried mother, and also in the investigation of adoption applications by the State board of control.

Mr. J. Lawrence Solly (Executive Secretary of the Board of Children's Guardians, District of Columbia): I believe it is the duty of everybody in the District of Columbia at the present time to call the attention of the people from out of town to the fact that we have no vote in the District of Columbia, and that for our legislation we are entirely dependent on the representatives from your States who come here to Washington, and when they can spare the time occasionally pass legislation affecting our city and our district.

We have a board of children's guardians, and I, as the executive secretary, am perfectly willing to accept the responsibility of administering any laws that your representatives pass through Congress and put in our hands.

We have asked for many changes in our laws: For example, we asked for a mothers pension law, to be administered by the board of children's guardians, but we did not get it. We had a commission appointed a few years ago, which drafted one bill which did not pass.

We are now having a survey made by the Russell Sage Foundation, which will probably be finished this summer, and when that survey is finished, we will call on those of you whom we know to help us get through the recommendations made in their report.

Section VI
Standards

COMMITTEES

The following committees were appointed by the Washington conference to formulate minimum standards of child welfare:

1. Committee to submit standards in regard to children entering employment:

Owen R. Lovejoy, Secretary, National Child Labor Committee, New York City.

Dr. Jessica B. Peixotto, Professor of Social Economics, University of California, Berkeley, California.

Miss Tracy Copp, Wisconsin Industrial Commission, Milwaukee, Wisconsin.

Dean S. P. Breckinridge, University of Chicago.

Miss Agnes Nestor, President, Women's Trade Union League, Chicago.

Miss Grace Abbott, Children's Bureau.

2. Committees to submit standards for the protection of the health of children and mothers:

(a) Committee on maternity—

Dr. Mary Sherwood, *Chairman*, Baltimore, Maryland.

Dr. S. Josephine Baker, Director, Division of Child Hygiene, Department of Health, New York City.

Dr. Henry J. Gerstenberger, Babies' Dispensary and Hospital, Cleveland, Ohio.

Dr. Alan Brown, Toronto, Canada.

Dr. Anna E. Rude, Children's Bureau.

(b) Committee on infancy and the preschool child—

Dr. H. L. K. Shaw, *Chairman*, Division of Child Hygiene, State Board of Health, New York.

Dr. Henry F. Helmholz, Attending Physician, Children's Memorial Hospital, Chicago.

Dr. Louis I. Dublin, Metropolitan Life Insurance Company, New York City.

Dr. William R. P. Emerson, Boston, Massachusetts.

Dr. Dorothy Reed Mendenhall, Children's Bureau.

(c) Committee on the school child and the adolescent child—

Dr. Charles V. Chapin, *Chairman*, Superintendent of Health, Providence, Rhode Island.

Dr. Ellen Stone, Superintendent of Child Hygiene, Health Department, Providence, Rhode Island.

Dr. George P. Barth, Director, School Hygiene Bureau, Milwaukee, Wisconsin.

Dr. H. L. K. Shaw, Division of Child Hygiene, State Board of Health, New York.

Dr. William R. P. Emerson, Boston, Massachusetts.

Dr. Dorothy Reed Mendenhall, Children's Bureau.

3. Committee to submit standards for the protection of children in need of special care:

Edmond J. Butler, Executive Secretary, Catholic Home Bureau for Dependent Children, New York City.

Dr. C. Macfie Campbell, Associate Professor of Psychiatry, Phipps Psychiatric Clinic, Johns Hopkins Hospital, Baltimore, Maryland.

C. C. Carstens, Secretary, Massachusetts Society for the Prevention of Cruelty to Children, Boston, Massachusetts.

Judge Victor P. Arnold, Cook County Juvenile Court, Chicago.

J. Prentice Murphy, General Secretary, Children's Aid Society, Boston, Massachusetts.

C. V. Williams, Director, Children's Welfare Department, Ohio Board of State Charities, Columbus, Ohio.

Judge Kathryn Sellers, Juvenile Court of the District of Columbia.

Miss Emma O. Lundberg, Children's Bureau, *Secretary*.

At the close of the sessions, these committees submitted reports which, after discussion and amendment, were accepted by the Washington conference for reference to the consideration of the regional conferences to be held in Boston, New York, Cleveland, Chicago, Minneapolis, Denver, San Francisco, and Seattle, and to the consideration of interested groups and citizens generally. An advisory committee to incorporate the suggestions for amendment thus offered and further to develop standards was appointed. On the following pages will be found the standards as submitted by the Washington conference.

MINIMUM STANDARDS FOR CHILDREN ENTERING EMPLOYMENT

AGE MINIMUM

An age minimum of 16 for employment in any occupation, except that children between 14 and 16 may be employed in agriculture and domestic service during vacation periods.

An age minimum of 18 for employment in and about mines and quarries.

An age minimum of 21 for night messenger service.

An age minimum of 21 for girls employed as messengers for telegraph and messenger companies.

Prohibition of the employment of minors in dangerous or hazardous occupations or at any work which will retard their proper physical development.

EDUCATIONAL MINIMUM

All children shall be required to attend school for at least nine months each year, either full time or part time, between the ages of 7 and 18.

Children between 16 and 18 years of age who have completed the eighth grade and are legally and regularly employed shall be required to attend day continuation schools eight hours a week.

Children between 16 and 18 who have not completed the eighth grade or who are not regularly employed shall attend full-time school.

Vacation schools placing special emphasis on healthful play and leisure time activities, shall be provided for all children.

PHYSICAL MINIMUM

A child shall not be allowed to go to work until he has had a physical examination by a public-health physician or school physician and has been found to be of normal development for a child of his age and physically fit for the work at which he is to be employed.

There shall be periodical medical examination of all working children who are under 18 years of age.

HOURS OF EMPLOYMENT

No minor shall be employed more than 8 hours a day. The maximum working day for children between 16 and 18 shall be shorter than the legal working day for adults.

The hours spent at continuation schools by children under 18 years of age shall be counted as part of the working day.

Night work for minors shall be prohibited between 6 p. m. and 7 a. m.

MINIMUM WAGE

Minors at work shall be paid at a rate of wages which for full-time work shall yield not less than the minimum essential for the "necessary cost of proper living." During a period of learning they may be rated as learners and paid accordingly. The length of the learning period should be fixed on educational principles only.

PLACEMENT AND EMPLOYMENT SUPERVISION

There shall be a central agency which shall deal with all juvenile employment problems. Adequate provision shall be made for advising children when they leave school of the employment opportunities open to them, for assisting them in finding suitable work, and providing for them such supervision as may be needed during the first few years of their employment. All agencies working towards these ends shall be coordinated through the central agency.

ADMINISTRATION

EMPLOYMENT CERTIFICATES

Provision shall be made for issuing employment certificates to all children entering employment who are under 18 years of age.

An employment certificate shall not be issued to the child until the issuing officer has received, approved, and filed the following:

1. Reliable documentary proof of the child's age.
2. Satisfactory evidence that the child has completed the eighth grade.
3. A certificate of physical fitness signed by a public-health physician or school physician. This certificate shall state that the minor has been thoroughly examined by the physician and that he is physically qualified for the employment contemplated.
4. Promise of employment.

The certificate shall be issued to the employer and shall be returned by the employer to the issuing officer when the child leaves his employment.

The school last attended, the compulsory education department, and the continuation schools shall be kept informed by the issuing officers of certificates issued or refused and of unemployed children for whom certificates have been issued.

Minors over 18 years of age shall be required to present evidence of age before being permitted to work in occupations having an age prohibition.

Record forms shall be standardized and the issuing of employment certificates shall be under State supervision.

Reports shall be made to the factory inspection department of all certificates issued and refused.

COMPULSORY SCHOOL ATTENDANCE LAWS

Full-time attendance officers adequately proportioned to the school population shall be provided in cities, towns, and counties to enforce the school attendance law.

The enforcement of school attendance laws by city, town, or county school authorities shall be under State supervision.

FACTORY INSPECTION AND PHYSICAL EXAMINATION OF EMPLOYED MINORS

Inspection for the enforcement of all child-labor laws, including those regulating the employment of children in mines or quarries, shall be under one and the same department. The number of inspectors shall be sufficient to insure the regular observance of the laws.

Provision should be made for a staff of physicians adequate to examine periodically all employed children under 18 years of age.

MINIMUM STANDARDS FOR THE PUBLIC PROTECTION OF THE HEALTH OF CHILDREN AND MOTHERS

MATERNITY

1. Maternity or prenatal centers, sufficient to provide for all cases not receiving prenatal supervision from private physicians. The work of such a center should include:

(a) Complete physical examination by physician as early in pregnancy as possible, including examination of heart, lungs, abdomen and urine, and the taking of blood pressure; internal examination and pelvic measurements before seventh month in primipara; examination of urine every four weeks during early months, at least every two weeks after sixth month, and more frequently if indicated; Wassermann test, when indicated.

(b) Instruction in hygiene of maternity and supervision throughout pregnancy, through at least monthly visits to a maternity center until end of sixth month, and every two weeks thereafter. Literature to be given mother to acquaint her with the principles of infant hygiene.

(c) Employment of sufficient number of public-health nurses to do home visiting and to give instructions to expectant mothers in hygiene of pregnancy and early infancy; to make visits and to care for patient in puerperium; and to see that every infant is referred to an infant-welfare center.

(d) Confinement at home by a physician or a properly trained and qualified attendant, or in a hospital.

(e) Nursing service at home at the time of confinement and during the lying-in period, or hospital care.

(f) Daily visits through fifth day, and at least two other visits during second week by physician or nurse from maternity center.

(g) At least ten days' rest in bed after a normal delivery, with sufficient household service to allow mother to recuperate.

(h) Examination by physician before discharging patient, not later than six weeks after delivery.

2. Clinics, such as dental clinics and venereal clinics, for needed treatment during pregnancy.

3. Maternity hospitals, or maternity wards in general hospitals, sufficient to provide care in all complicated cases and for all women

wishing hospital care; free or part-payment obstetrical care to be provided in every necessitous case at home or in a hospital.

4. All midwives to be required by law to show adequate training, and to be licensed and supervised.

5. Training and registration of household attendants to care, under the supervision of physician or public-health nurse, for sicknesses in the home and for the home during sickness.

6. Education of general public as to problems presented by maternal and infant mortality and their solution.

INFANTS AND PRESCHOOL CHILDREN

1. Complete birth registration by adequate legislation requiring reporting within three days after birth.

2. Prevention of infantile blindness by making and enforcing adequate laws for treatment of eyes of every infant at birth and supervision of all positive cases.

3. Sufficient number of children's health centers to give health instruction under medical supervision for all infants and children not under care of private physician, and to give instruction in care and feeding of children to mothers, at least once a month throughout first year, and at regular intervals throughout preschool age. This center to include a nutrition clinic.

4. Children's health center to provide or to cooperate with sufficient number of public-health nurses to make home visits to all infants and children of preschool age needing care—one public-health nurse for average population of 2,000.

Visits to the home are for the purpose of instructing the mother in:

(a) Value of breast feeding.
(b) Technique of nursing.
(c) Technique of bath, sleep, clothing, ventilation, and general care of the baby, with demonstrations.
(d) Preparation and technique of artificial feeding.
(e) Dietary essentials and selection of food for the infant and for older children.
(f) Prevention of disease in children.

5. Dental clinics; eye, ear, nose, and throat clinics; venereal and other clinics for the treatment of defects and disease.

6. Children's hospitals, or beds in general hospitals, or provision for medical and nursing care at home, sufficient to care for all sick infants and young children.

7. State licensing and supervision of all child-caring institutions or homes in which infants or young children are cared for.

8. General educational work in prevention of communicable dis-

ease and in hygiene and feeding of infants and young children, including compulsory course in child hygiene in the public schools.

SCHOOL CHILDREN

1. Proper location, construction, hygiene and sanitation of schoolhouse; adequate room space—no overcrowding.

2. Adequate playground and recreational facilities, physical training, and supervised recreation.

3. Open-air classes and rest periods for pretubercular and certain tuberculous children, and children with grave malnutrition. Special classes for children needing some form of special instruction due to physical or mental defect.

4. Full-time school nurse for not more than 1,000 children to give instruction in personal hygiene and diet, to make home visits to advise and instruct mothers in principles of hygiene, nutrition, and selection of family diet, and to take children to clinics with permission of parents.

5. Adequate space and equipment for school medical work and available laboratory service.

6. Part-time physician with one full-time nurse for not more than 2,000 children, or full-time physician with two full-time nurses for 4,000 children for:

  (a) Complete standardized basic physical examinations once a year, with determination of weight and height at beginning and end of each school year; monthly weighing wherever possible.

  (b) Continuous health record for each child to be kept on file with other records of the pupil. This should be a continuation of the preschool health record which should accompany the child to school.

  (c) Special examinations to be made of children referred by teacher or nurse.

  (d) Supervision to control communicable disease.

  (e) Recommendation of treatment for all remediable defects, diseases, deformities, and cases of malnutrition.

  (f) Follow-up work by nurse to see that physician's recommendations are carried out.

7. Available clinics for dentistry, nose, throat, eye, ear, skin, and orthopedic work; and for free vaccination for smallpox and typhoid.

8. Nutrition classes for physically subnormal children, and the maintenance of midmorning lunch or hot noonday meal when necessary.

9. Examination by psychiatrist of all atypical or retarded children.

10. Education of school child in health essentials.

11. General educational work in health and hygiene, including education of parent and teacher, to secure full cooperation in health program.

ADOLESCENT CHILDREN

1. Complete standardized basic physical examinations by physician, including weight and height, at least once a year, and recommendation for necessary treatment to be given at children's health center or school.
2. Clinics for treatment of defect and disease.
3. Supervision and instruction to insure:

   (a) Ample diet, with special attention to growth-producing foods.
   (b) Sufficient sleep and rest and fresh air.
   (c) Adequate and suitable clothing.
   (d) Proper exercise for physical development.
   (e) Knowledge of sex hygiene and reproduction.

4. Full-time education compulsory to at least 16 years of age, adapted to meet the needs and interest of the adolescent mind, with vocational guidance and training.
5. Clean, ample recreational opportunities to meet social needs.
6. Legal protection from exploitation, vice, drug habits, etc.

MINIMUM STANDARDS FOR THE PROTECTION OF CHILDREN IN NEED OF SPECIAL CARE

1. GENERAL STATEMENT

Every child should have normal home life, an opportunity for education, recreation, vocational preparation for life, and for moral and spiritual development in harmony with American ideals and the educational and spiritual agencies by which these rights of the child are normally safeguarded. The Conference recognizes the fundamental rôle of home, religion, and education in the development of childhood.

Aside from the general fundamental duty of the State toward children in normal social conditions, ultimate responsibility for children who, on account of improper home conditions, physical handicap, or delinquency, are in need of special care devolves upon the State. Particular legislation is required for children in need of such care, the aim of which should be the nearest approach to normal development. Laws enacted by the several States for these purposes should be coordinated as far as practicable in view of conditions in the several States, and in line with national ideals.

2. HOME CARE

The aim of all provision for children in need of special care necessitating removals from their own homes, should be to secure for each child home life as nearly normal as possible, to safeguard his health, and provide opportunities for education, recreation, vocational preparation, and moral and spiritual development. To a much larger degree than at present, family homes may be used to advantage in the care of special classes of children.

3. ADEQUATE INCOME

Home life, which is, in the words of the Conclusions of the White House Conference, "the highest and finest product of civilization," cannot be provided except upon the basis of an adequate income for each family, and hence private and governmental agencies charged with the responsibility for the welfare of children in need of special care should be urged to supplement the resources of the family wherever the income is insufficient, in such measure that the family budget conforms to the average standard of the community.

4. INCORPORATION, LICENSING, AND SUPERVISION

A State board of charities, or a similar supervisory body, should be held responsible for the regular inspection and licensing of every institution, agency, or association, public or private, incorporated or otherwise, that receives or cares for children who suffer from physical handicaps, or who are delinquent, dependent, or without suitable parental care.

This supervision should be conceived and exercised in harmony with democratic ideals which invite and encourage the service of efficient, altruistic forces of society in the common welfare. The incorporation of such institutions, agencies, and associations should be required, and should be subject to the approval of the State board of charities or similar body.

5. REMOVAL OF CHILDREN FROM THEIR HOMES

Unless unusual conditions exist, the child's welfare is best promoted by keeping him in his own home. No child should be removed from his home unless it is impossible so to reconstruct family conditions or build and supplement family resources as to make the home safe for the child, or so to supervise the child as to make his continued presence safe for the community.

6. PRINCIPLES GOVERNING CHILD PLACING

This Conference reaffirms in all essentials the resolutions of the White House Conference of 1909 on the Care of Dependent Children. We believe they have been guides for communities and States that have sought to reshape their plans for children in need of special care. We commend them for consideration to all communities whose standards do not as yet conform to them, so that such standards may be translated into practice in the various States.

Before a child is placed in other than a temporary foster home adequate consideration should be given to his health, mentality, character, and family history and circumstances. Remediable physical defects should be corrected.

Complete records of every child under care are necessary to a proper understanding of the child's heredity, development, and progress while under the care of the agency.

Careful and wise investigation of foster homes is prerequisite to the placing of children. Adequate standards should be required of the foster families as to character, intelligence, experience, training, ability, income, and environment.

A complete record should be kept of each foster home, giving the information on which approval was based. The records should also show the agency's contacts with the family from time to time for the purpose of indicating the care it gave to the child entrusted to it. In this way special abilities in the families will be developed and conserved for children.

Supervision of children placed in foster homes should include adequate visits by properly qualified and well-trained visitors and constant watchfulness over the child's health, education, and moral and spiritual development. Supervision of children in boarding homes should also involve the careful training of the foster parents in their task. Supervision is not a substitute for the responsibilities which properly rest with the foster family.

7. CARE OF CHILDREN OF ILLEGITIMATE BIRTH

The child of illegitimate birth represents a very serious condition of neglect, and for this reason special safeguards should be provided for these children.

Save for unusual reasons both parents should be responsible for the child during its minority, and especially should the responsibility of the father be emphasized. Care of the child by its mother during the first nursing months is highly desirable, and no parents of a child of illegitimate birth should be permitted to surrender the child outside of its own family, save with the consent of a properly designated State department or a court of proper jurisdiction. More adequate and humane treatment of such cases in court procedure and otherwise will result in greater willingness to have them considered, which is in line with the protection needed. The whole treatment and care of the unmarried mother and her child should include the best medical supervision and the widest opportunity for education under wholesome, normal conditions in the community.

8. RURAL SOCIAL WORK

Social work for children in rural parts of the country has been neglected. The essential principles of child-welfare work should be applied to rural needs, and agencies for rural service encouraged.

9. RECREATION

The desire for recreation and amusement is a normal expression of every child and an important avenue for moral education and for the prevention of delinquency. It should be the concern of the State that wholesome play, recreation, and amusement be provided by cities and towns and that commercialized recreation be supervised and safeguarded.

10. JUVENILE COURT

Every locality should have available a court organization providing for separate hearings of children's cases, a special method of detention for children, adequate investigation for every case, provision for supervision or probation by trained officers, and a system for recording and filing social as well as legal information. In dealing with children the procedure should be under chancery jurisdiction, and juvenile records should not stand as criminal records against the children. Whenever possible such administrative duties as child-placing and relief should not be required of the juvenile court, but should be administered by existing agencies provided for that purpose, or in the absence of such agencies, special provision should be made therefor; nor should cases of dependency or destitution in which no questions of improper guardianship or final and conclusive surrender of guardianship are involved, be instituted in juvenile courts.

The juvenile victims of sex offenses are without adequate protection against unnecessary publicity and further corruption in our courts. To safeguard them, the jurisdiction of the juvenile court should be extended to deal with adult sex offenders against children, and all safeguards of that court be accorded to their victims.

In all cases of adoption of children, the court should make a full inquiry into all the facts through its own visitor or through some other unbiased agency, before awarding the child's custody.

11. MENTAL HYGIENE AND CARE OF MENTALLY DEFECTIVE CHILDREN

The value of the first seven years of childhood from the point of health, education and morals, and formative habits cannot be overestimated. Throughout childhood attention should be given to the mental hygiene of the child—the care of the instincts, emotions, and general personality of the child, and of environmental conditions. Special attention should be given to the need for training teachers and social workers in mental hygiene principles.

Each State should assume the responsibility for thorough study of the school and general population for the purpose of securing data concerning the extent of feeble-mindedness and subnormality, and should make adequate provision for such mentally defective children as require institutional care, and provide special schools or classes with qualified teachers and adequate equipment for such defective children as may be properly cared for outside of institutions. Custodial care in institutions for feeble-minded children should not be resorted to until after due consideration of the possibility of adjustment within the community.

12. SCIENTIFIC INFORMATION

There is urgent need of a more adequate body of scientific literature dealing with principles and practice in the children's field of social work, and the meeting of this need is a responsibility resting on those so engaged. Careful interpretation and analysis of methods and results of care and the publishing of these findings must precede the correcting of many present evils in practice. Boards of directors, trustees, and managers should particularly consider participation in the preparation of such a body of facts and experience as being a vital part of the work of their staff members.

13. CHILD WELFARE LEGISLATION

The child-welfare legislation of every State requires careful reconsideration as a whole at reasonable intervals in order that necessary revision and coordination may be made, and that new provisions may be incorporated in harmony with the best experience of the day. This Conference recommends that in States where children's laws have not had careful revision as a whole within recent years, the governor be requested to take the necessary steps for the creation of a child-welfare committee or commission. It is also urged that the President of the United States be asked to call a conference during the next year in conjunction with the governors of the various States, to consider the whole question of the child-welfare legislation.

INDEX

INDEX

	Page.
Adolescent children, standards for the care of	439
Adoption	353
Probation period for	355
After-care in placing-out work	359
Age minimum:	
For child labor in Japan	337
For dangerous industries	82
For employment	82, 113, 433
For full-time employment	102
For morally dangerous work	82
For part-time employment	102
Agriculture, children in	83
Aid, government:	
For child-welfare work in England	283
To the States	103
For maternity work	146, 165, 284, 436
Antenatal care. (See Maternity care.)	
Anthropological characteristics	293
Appel, Dr. Emma Mackay	86
Apprenticeship	117
Minimum rates for	120
Arnold, Judge Victor P.	345, 352, 432
Association of Sociologic Medicine	25
Atwater, on Food requirements	259, 261
Baby farms. (See Child placing.)	
Baker, Dr. S. Josephine	155, 156, 158, 165, 172, 206, 210, 219, 431
Baldwin, Major Bird T.	381
Barth, Dr. George P.	96, 127, 432
Barton, Mrs. Eleanor	8, 167, 171, 172, 227, 230, 233
Belgium:	
Baby clinics in	289
Child welfare in	71, 289, 291
Compulsory education in	72
Country homes for children in	75
Debility and weakness of children in	76
Maternity care in	290
Medical inspection in schools of	72
Schools of	71
Blake, Miss Mabelle B.	361, 380
Birth rate:	
In France during the war	213
In Japan	327
Births:	
Compulsory notification of	168, 272
Registration of	168, 437
Blindness:	
In children	24
Protection from infantile	437
Boarding-out of children	353
Booth, Charles	38
Bowley, A. L.	38
Breast feeding, importance of	271
Breckinridge, Miss S. P.	34, 431
Brockett, Miss Myrn	225, 233
Bronner, Dr. Augusta	382
Brown, Dr. Alan	431
Brown, Dr. E. V. L.	91
Budgets, family	29, 34*ff*
Budin, Professor, on Infant consultations	271
Burklin, Miss Lydia	232
Butler, Edmond J.	353, 432
Byington, Margaret F., on Cost of living	39
Calories, amount necessary for children	260*ff*
Campbell, Dr. C. Macfie	381, 432
Camps	101
Cardiac lesions in children applying for work permits	88
Carstens, C. C.	319, 351, 352, 416, 432
Carter, Miss L. E.	8, 71
Census of the feeble-minded	400

447

448 INDEX

Page.

Centers: 228, 272, 279, 437
    Child welfare 194*ff*, 197, 437
    Health 179*ff*, 217, 284, 436
    Maternity 60
    Play
Certificates, employment. (*See* Work permits.) 105
Chadsey, Charles E.. 194
Champion, Dr. Merrill E... 369
Chancery, courts of... 369
Chancery powers 379
    Extension of..157, 431
Chapin, Dr. Charles V.. 38, 39
Chapin, Robert C.. 85
Chatfield, George G... 186*ff*
Child care in rural communities... 313, 341
Child-caring agencies 319
    Private 319
    Public 353*ff*
    Responsibility of the state for standardizing.. 313*ff*, 437
    State supervision and licensing of.
Child hygiene. (*See* Hygiene.)
Child labor: 337
    Restrictions on, in Japan... 102
    Rural 433*ff*
    Standards for 338
Child Laborers in Japan, number of...
Child-labor laws: 110
    Administration of 89
    In Illinois 414
    Relaxation of 433*ff*
    Standards for 314, 315, 343, 353*ff*, 360*ff*, 371, 441
Child-placing 23, 71, 389*ff*, 291
Child welfare: 272, 279, 284
    In Belgium...
    Centers 228
    Centers compared with day nurseries... 417*ff*
    Commissions 31
    Economics of 211
    In France 303
    And International Red Cross... 417*ff*, 444
    Legislation 273
    And maternity act.. 391
    And mental hygiene.. 421*ff*
    In Minnesota 173
    In Serbia 283
Child-welfare work: ....
    Government aid in.. 208
    Health visiting in.. 335
Children's act, Japan... 412
Children's code 414
    In New York State... 307
Children in need of special care, responsibility for...................................... 351
Children's protective agencies, work of... 115, 188
Children's year campaign... 137
Choice of employment act, England.. 197
Cincinnati, national social unit organization of.. 380
Cincinnati, vocation bureau in.. 85, 102, 103, 104, 139, 140
Claxton, Hon. P. P..
Clinics:
    For adolescent children.. 439
    For babies in Belgium... 289
    Dental 234*ff*, 436, 437
    Eye, ear, nose, and throat... 148, 183, 185, 289
    Maternity 238*ff*, 244, 437
    Nutrition 163
    Pay 188, 192, 402
    Traveling 436
    Venereal ....
    (*See* also Centers.)
Codes, children's 412, 414
Commission on international labor legislation... 82
Committees:
    On standards for children entering employment....................................... 431
    On standards for children in need of special care.................................... 432
    On standards for the protection of the health of children and mothers............... 431
    To revise standards.. 9
Compensation act, Wisconsin... 126
Compulsory education 106
    For adolescent children.. 439
    In Belgium 71
    Laws 110, 435
    Laws of Tennessee.. 111
Condit, Miss Abbie... 54

	Page.
Continuation schools	84, 101, 103, 104, 125, 128, 434
In England	99
Coöperative enterprise in housing in United States	51
Copp, Miss Tracy	125, 131, 431
Corcoran, Miss Julia C	232
Cost of living	44ff
(See also Family budgets and family incomes.)	
County:	
Administrative unit for rural organization	366
Maternity hospitals	188
Training schools	311
As unit for maternity care	188
Creches. (See Day nurseries.)	
Criminals, juvenile, in Japan	334
Criminals, mental examination of	405
Crippled children applying for work permits	89
Crowder, Dr. Grace Meigs, on Rural obstetrics	188
Curry, Miss H. Ida	318, 363
Curtis, Dr. Henry S., on Recreation	55, 56
Dangerous occupations. (See Occupations.)	
Davies, David, on Cost of living	37
Davison, Ronald C	8, ... 7, 138, 139
Day camps in Belgium	290ff
Day nurseries	219ff, 282ff
In Chicago	225ff
Compared with child-welfare centers	228
Contagious diseases in, in France	216
Control of contagious diseases in	222
In France	216
Hygiene and maintenance of routine in	222
The industrial aspect of	227
In Japan	325
Licensing of	231
Night care in	224
Supervision of	225
Nursing rooms	229
In France	215ff
Deafness. (See Hearing.)	
Death rate:	
Of infants	40, 41, 155, 173, 180, 200, 208, 212, 269, 274
Of mothers	165
Deibler, Professor F. S.	116
Deming, Robert C	104, 138
Diet. (See Food.)	
Donation for juveniles out of work	134, 140
Defective:	
Legal status of	40
(See also Feeble-minded.)	
Defective children	310, 400, 406, 421ff, 443
In nutrition clinics	244
Defective and destitute children, institutions for relief of, Japan	329
Delinquency	318, 368ff
Increase of	414
Medicopsychological study of	382ff
Sources of	309
Delinquent boys	348
Delinquent children	149, 309, 421ff
In nutrition clinics	244
Delinquent girls	348
In Philadelphia	381
Delinquent school children	380
Dental caries	234
Dental clinics	234ff
For children	437
In maternity care	436
Dental defects among school children	250
Dental service:	
Public	237
In schools	236
In securing work permits	88
Dependency	318
Dependent children	308
In nutrition clinics	244
Standards of care for	353ff
Dependent and neglected children	421ff
Desertion of children (France)	212
Desertion and non-support, laws relating to	425ff
Desertions act, uniform	309
Detention homes in Massachusetts	374
Detention of children, special method for	442
Diet:	
Importance of	256ff
(See also Nutrition.)	

INDEX

	Page.
Diseases, communicable:	
Control of, in day nurseries	222
Municipal control of	197*ff*
In nursing rooms (France)	216
Prevention of	437
Dublin, Dr. Louis I.	431
Du Bois, on the Metabolism of children	260
Economics of child welfare	31
Edmondson, Mrs. Edna Hatfield	190
Edsall, Dr. D. L.	93
Education:	
United States Bureau of	267
Compulsory	106
Compulsory in Belgium	71
Of industrial managers	96
Laws for compulsory	110
Religious, in Japan	332
Sex	262*ff*
Standards for	433*ff*
Tennessee laws for compulsory	111
(*See also* Schools.)	
Educational minimum for children in employment	433
Educational propaganda in Minnesota	423*ff*
Educational work of the public-health nurse	199
Educator, health	201
Eight-hour day. (*See* Hours of labor.)	
Eldon, Lord, on Chancery jurisdiction	369
Emerson, Dr. William R. P.	238, 246, 247, 431, 432
Employment:	
Age limits for	82, 102, 113, 337, 433
Committees in England, juvenile	133, 135
Exchange act in England	137
Exchanges, England	132
Manager	117
Service in United States	138
(*See also* Occupations, Hours of labor.)	
Epstein, on Food requirements	257
Examination, physical. (*See* Physical examination.)	
Examinations for malnutrition	238*ff*
Exchange, juvenile	138
Exchanges, employment, in England	132
Exner, Dr. M. J., on Sex instruction	264
Factory act, Japan	337
Factory inspection	130, 435
Fagan, Bernard J.	351, 352, 379, 389
Family budgets	29, 34*ff*
Family endowment. (*See* Mothers' pensions.)	
Family expenditure	32*f*
Farm work for children	83
Farrand, Livingston	303
Fatigue studies in Illinois	114
Father, responsibility of	171
Federal child-labor law	89
Fisk, Dr. Eugene Lyman, on Physical unfitness	56
Feeble-minded:	
Census of	400
Children	399*ff*
Extra-institutional supervision of	400
Registration of	401
Institutional care for	402
Persons	425
Feeble-mindedness, in children applying for work certificates	89
Fernald, Walter E.	399, 407
Fisher act	98
Food:	
Conditions in Germany	256*ff*
Cost of	34*f*
For children in nutrition classes	241
Requirements for adolescent children	256*ff*
Forty-eight-hour week. (*See* Hours of labor.)	
Foster homes	144, 313, 343, 355, 359
Supervision of children in	314, 441
Foundling act in Japan	321
Fox, Miss Elizabeth G.	186, 209
Framingham, health demonstration in	196
France:	
Birth rate in, during the war	213
Child welfare in	211
Maternity centers in	217
Frassetto, Professor Fabio	8, 292, 297, 298
Fuhge, on Food requirements	260

INDEX 451

	Page.
Gephart, on Food requirements	260
Germany, food conditions in	250 ff
Gerstenberger, Dr. H. J.	209, 237, 431
Gibb, Miss Winifred	
Gonorrhea	88
Gorgas, Surgeon General	149
Government aid:	24, 199
For child-welfare work	288
For maternal care	146
For maternity and child-welfare work	284
For maternity homes, in England	
To the States	165
Guests of the conference	103
Guidance, vocational	8
	133, 140
Hall, W. E.	137, 138
Hart, Dr. Hastings H.	9, 320, 339, 352, 374, 427
Haynes, Rowland, on Recreation	
Healy, Dr. William	58
Health:	382, 388
Annual examination	248
Centers	194, 197
Centers, organizations to establish	194 ff
Inspection, daily	248
Demonstration, at Framingham, Mass.	196
Educator	201
Imperial Ministry of, Germany	256
Insurance act, national	280
Needs of children	248
Officers	254
Public. (*See* Public health.)	
Records for school children	251, 438
Visitor	168, 278 ff
Visitor in England	207
Visiting, in child-welfare work	208
Hearing:	
Defects of, in children applying for work permits	87
Routine tests for	250
Helmholz, Dr. Henry F.	176, 431
Hermann, Ernst, on Recreation	59
Hill, Hon. Albert E.	109
Hodson, W. W.	361, 420
Holiday Camps	101
Holidays, for child laborers in Japan	337
Holman, Miss Lydia	190
Holt, Dr., on venereal infection	155
Home care for children in need of special care	440
Home finding:	
Agents	356
Investigation for	356
Home:	
Helps	169, 172, 209, 283, 437
Hygiene of the	178
Loan banks	47
Management	52
"Own-your-own-home" movement	48
Removal of children from	345 ff, 441
The child's	46
Home training, for boys and girls	52
Homes:	
Foster	131, 144, 343, 355, 441
Maternity	169
Hospitals:	
Children's	437
Lying-in	176 f
Lying-in, in France	217
Maternity	436, 162, 176 f
Maternity, county	188
Maternity, in New York City	181
Hours of labor:	
Eight-hour day	83, 113, 433
Eight-hour law for women, in Illinois	114
Forty-eight-hour week	83, 113
National basis of, in England	100
Night work for children	109
Night work for children in Japan	337
Night work for minors, prohibition of	434
Night work, in Illinois	114
Six-hour day	83
Six-hour day for children	115
Standards of	433
Housing	177, 208
Copartnership scheme of	51
Federal aid in	47

INDEX

	Page.
Hoyt, Judge Franklin Chase	413
Hubbard, Henry V., on Playgrounds	57
Hygiene:	
In day nurseries	222
Of the home	178
Mental	391, 396, 443
Preventive work for children	205
(*See* also Sanitation.)	
Illegitimacy:	
In France during the war	212
Unmarried mothers	360
Illegitimate children	308, 360, 435
Care of	442
In Minnesota	361
Illinois:	
Child-labor law	86
Fatigue studies in	114
Night work in	113*f*
Incomes:	
Family	26, 44
Apportionment of family	51
Family, source of	40
Industrial commission, Wisconsin	125*ff*
Industrial nurseries. (*See* Day nurseries.)	
Industrial training school	310
Infant consultations	272
Infant mortality	40, 180, 200, 208
In Belgium	290
Causes of	180
In France	212
In England	269*ff*
In Japan	327
In relation to syphilis	155
In Serbia	173
In the United States among foreign born	41
Infant welfare. (*See* Child welfare.)	
Infants, standards for the care of	436*ff*
Inter-allied scientific food commission	259, 261
International labor legislation, commission on	82
Institutions:	
For defectives, dependents, and delinquents in Japan	329
For the feeble-minded	402
Incorporation of	441
Licensing of	441
Supervision of	441
For temporary care	355
Inter-departmental social hygiene board	267
International child survey	296
International Red Cross	303*ff*
Japan:	
Birth rate in	327
Children's Act	335
Day nurseries in	325
Factory Act	337
Foundling Act	322
Holidays for child laborers in	337
Industrial schools in	331
Institutions for defective and destitute children in	329
Juvenile criminals in	334
Juvenile prisons in	334
Minimum age for child labor in	337
Night work for children in	337
Reform schools in	323
Orphan asylums in	324
Poor Law in	321*ff*
Reformatory Act in	323
Sanitary reform in	328
Religious education in	332
Schools in	328
School physicians in	330
Welfare work in	338
Young Men's Association in	332
Jackson, Sir Cyril	8, 98, 102, 103, 104, 406
Jeans, Dr. Philip C.	146, 155, 156
Johnson, George E., on Recreation	60, 61
Juvenile Advisory Committees	97
Juvenile court	368*ff*, 373*ff*, 442*f*
Act of Illinois	346
And the home	350
Investigation	377
Laws	345
Massachusetts plan	374

INDEX

	Page.
Probation	347*ff*, 371, 376*ff*, 389
Records	371*f*
System, for rural communities	364
And truancy	380
Juvenile court work, public agencies vs. private agencies in	378*ff*
Juvenile criminals in Japan	334
Juvenile delinquency. (*See* Delinquents.)	
Juvenile employment committees	133*ff*
Juvenile exchange	138

Kelso, Robert W.	307, 373
Kerby, Rev. W. J.	411
King, Dr. Truby, on Health centers	195
Kennedy, John C., on Cost of living	39
Kingsley, S. C.	344
Knox, Dr. J. H. Mason, on Public-health nursing	201
Kraus, on Food requirements	257

Labor. (*See* Child labor, Occupations, Hours of labor, etc.)

Labor Legislation, Commission on International	82
Labor permits. (*See* Work permits.)	
Lane, Franklin K., Secretary of Interior, on Illiteracy	84
Lauck, W. Jett, on Cost of living	37, 39

Laws:

Children's	86*ff*, 334*ff*, 411*ff*
Compensation	126
Compulsory school attendance	110, 111, 435
Desertion	425-426
Juvenile court	345
Minimum wage	118, 120, 122
Mothers' pension	110
For the protection of maternity	146
Public health	273
Lazarevitch, Dr. Radmila Milochevitch	8, 173
Leavitt, Frank M.	138
Lee, Professor Frederick S.	23
Lee, Joseph	63
Leigh, Robert D.	262
Levy, Dr. Julius	163, 191, 205
Living Wage, Principle of	116
Lobenstine, Dr. R. W.	179
Lovejoy, Owen R.	9, 81, 431
Lusk, Dr. Graham	256, 261

Lying-in hospitals. (*See* Maternity hospitals.)

MacMurchy, Dr. Helen	166, 171
Malnutrition	238*ff*
Manager, employment	117
Maternal mortality	165, 277
Maternity Act	169
Maternity benefit	170
In France	214
Maternity care	176
In Belgium	290
Dental and venereal clinics in	436
Grants for	146, 165
Legislation for	146
Natal	176, 285
In New York City	181
Prenatal	100, 147, 157, 176, 184, 281
Postnatal	176, 285
For rural mothers	186
Standards of	436*f*
State aid in	146
Maternity cases, zoning system of	181
Maternity centers	169, 183, 217, 284, 436
Maternity center association	182
Maternity clinics	185
In Belgium	289
In England	148
In New York	183
Maternity homes	169
Maternity hospitals	176*f*, 436
County	188
Grants for, in England	165
In France	217
In New York City	181
Service	162
Maternity laws	193, 273
Maternity nursing	147, 187, 281*ff*, 436
Maternity, standards for the protection of	436*ff*
Maus, Isador	8
Medical care of school children	243
Medical inspection in schools	72, 86, 100, 275*ff*, 437

454 INDEX

	Page.
Medical service in rural communities	189, 365
Medical social service	198
Medicine:	
Preventive	180, 396ff
Sociologic	24
Medicopsychological clinic	390
Medicopsychological study of delinquency	382ff
Meeker, Dr. Royal	31
Mental clinic, traveling	402
Mental examination	402
For children suffering from malnutrition	239
Of persons accused of crime	405
Mental hygiene	391, 396, 443
Mentally defective children	443
Midwife problem, solution of	159
Midwifery, decreasing	169
Midwives	147
Control of	157
Control of, in England	164
Control of, in New York	165
Inspection of, in England	277
Licensing of	160, 437
School for	161
Midwives Act, England	169, 277
Mill, J. S., on Productive consumption	38
Miller, Professor Kelly	66
Minimum age. (*See* Age minimum.)	
Minimum standards:	
For children entering employment	433ff
For the protection of children in need of special care	440ff
For the public protection of the health of children and mothers	436ff
Minimum wage	38, 434
Commissions	123
Laws in Canada	119
Laws for minors	122
Laws in various states	120
Legislation	118ff
Rates for apprentices and learners	120
For women	121
Missouri Code Commission	427
Minnesota:	
Child Welfare Commission	420ff
Child welfare in	421
Educational propaganda in	423ff
Mitchell, Dr. David	244, 389
Mortality:	
Causes of infant	180
Infant	40ff, 180, 200, 208, 274ff
Infant, in Belgium	290
Infant, in England	269ff
Infant, in France during the war	212
Infant, in Japan	327
Infant, in Serbia	173
Infant, among foreign-born in United States	41
Maternal	165, 277
Mothers' pensions	419
In California	231
In Minnesota	425
In France	214
Laws	110
Law in Tennessee	111
Mulon, Dr. Clothilde	8, 211, 225, 229, 230, 231, 233
Mumford, Mrs. Joseph P.	380
Munition workers, day nurseries for	228
Murphy, J. Prentice	374, 389, 432
Namaye, Takayuki	8, 321
Natal care. (*See* Maternity care.)	
National basis of hours in England	100
National Social Unit Organization of Cincinnati	197
National (Health) Insurance Act	280
Neglect of children in rural communities	186
Neglected children	309
System for the protection of	315
Negro problem	66
Nesbitt, Miss Florence	34, 37, 42, 44
Nestor, Miss Agnes	113, 431
Newsholme, Sir Arthur	8, 148, 155, 164, 207, 237, 269
New York:	
Maternity work in	179ff
Midwives in	165
New Zealand Industrial and Conciliation Act	119

INDEX 455

Night work: | Page.
- In Illinois ... 114
- For minors in Japan ... 337
- Prohibition of ... 434
- (*See* also Hours of labor.)

North Carolina, public-health work in ... 191
Notification of births ... 168, 272*ff*, 437
Nurses, registered, for schools ... 254
Nurseries, day. (*See* Day nurseries.)
Nursing:
- Maternity ... 147, 187, 281*ff*, 436
- Public-health ... 177, 198*f*, 436*f*
- Public-health, in rural communities ... 187*ff*, 193, 366
- Rooms, in France ... 215, 229
- School ... 254, 438
- Training school for public health ... 204
- Visiting ... 147
- Visiting, for mental cases ... 396

Nutrition:
- Classes ... 239*ff*, 244*ff*, 438
- Clinics ... 238*ff*, 437
- Clinics for dependent, delinquent, and defective children ... 244
- And prevention of dental decay ... 237
- In treatment of syphilitic infants ... 153

Obstetrical care ... 176*ff*
- Standards for ... 145
- (*See* also Maternity care.)

Obstetrical work ... 177
- Out-patient ... 162, 177

Obstetrics as a branch of surgery ... 166
Occupations:
- Age limit for full time ... 102
- Age limit for part time ... 102
- Agricultural, children in ... 83
- Dangerous ... 93*ff*, 109
- Dangerous, minimum age for children in ... 82
- Morally dangerous, minimum age for children in ... 82
- For mothers ... 227
- Street ... 109

Out-of-work donation for juveniles in England ... 134, 140
Out-patient service. (*See* Maternity care.)
Ogburn, William F ... 26
Ohio, child-caring associations in ... 315*ff*
Orphan asylums, in Japan ... 324
Osler, Dr. William, on dental hygiene ... 234, 250

Peace Treaty, 6th article of ... 82
Peace conference ... 82
Peixotto, Dr. Jessica B ... 7, 29, 118, 231, 431
Pensions. (*See* Mothers' pensions.)
Permits, employment. (*See* Work permits.)
Pfaundler, on Food requirements ... 261
Philippines, schools in the ... 103
Physical defects:
- Of Belgian children ... 76
- In children applying for employment certificates in Chicago ... 87
- In school children ... 95, 250, 253
- Visual ... 24, 91*ff*

Physical examination:
- For adolescents ... 439
- Of employed children ... 435
- For malnutrition ... 238*ff*
- In maternity care ... 437
- For school certificates ... 86
- For work permits ... 81, 86, 243
- (*See* also Health examinations.)

Physical fitness, standards ... 86
Physical minimum, for children entering employment ... 433
Physical training ... 55
Physician's, school ... 330, 438
Physiological and pathological characteristics ... 294
Placement, vocational ... 129, 136, 434
Placing-out work:
- For children ... 314*f*, 343, 353*ff*, 360*ff*, 371, 441
- For unmarried mothers ... 360

Play center ... 60
Play:
- Organized ... 56*ff*
- Minimum requirements for children's ... 64

Playgrounds ... 58, 64, 438
- Standards for ... 56*ff*

Postnatal care. (*See* Maternity care.)
Power, Miss Mary ... 189

456 INDEX

	Page.
Pratt, Miss Anna B.	381
Pregnancy:	
Compulsory registration of	146
(*See* also Maternity and Obstetrical care.)	
Prenatal care. (*See* Maternity care.)	
Preschool children, standards for the care of	437
Preventive hygiene	205
Preventive medicine	180, 396*ff*
Prisons, for juveniles in Japan	335
Probation:	
Juvenile	347*ff*, 371, 376, 389
Officer	371, 376, 384
Period for legal adoption	355
System for rural communities	364
Productivity principle	116
Psychological analysis	387
Psychological inquiry	385
Psychiatrist, examination of school children by	438
Psychopathic clinic	389
Public health	24, 199*ff* 303*ff*
Acts	273
Campaign	199
Dental service	237, 436*f*
Municipal control of	197
Nurse, as an educational agent	200
Nurses for children	437
Nurses for maternity work	147, 187, 281*ff*, 436
Nursing	198*ff*, 436*f*
Official	199
Rural nursing	188, 193, 366
Service	266
Public-health work:	
Maternity	140*ff*, 165, 169, 183, 188, 217, 279*ff*, 284, 436
In North Carolina	191
In schools	72, 86, 100, 235, 250*ff*, 275*ff*, 437
Putnam, Mrs. William Lowell	172, 185
Recreation	56, 63*ff*, 442
Camps	101
Center	60
Opportunities for adolescents	439
Organized	56*ff*
Playgrounds	56*ff*, 63
Reform schools in Japan	323
Registration:	
Of births	168, 272*ff*, 437
Of feeble-minded	401
Of pregnancy	146
Of wards of the State	316
Religious education in Japan	332
Red Cross	303
Richards, Dr., on Sex instruction	265
Ricks, Judge James Hoge	350, 351, 368, 380
Robinson, Dr. Louis N	376
Rowntree, B. Seebohm	38
Rubner, M., on Food difficulties in Germany	256
Rural districts:	
Bill for the protection of infancy in	193
Child labor in	102
Child care in	186*ff*
Maternity care in	186, 192, 193
Maternity nursing in	188
Medical service in	189, 365
Public-health nursing in	186*ff*, 193, 366
Social work in	363, 442
Russell Sage Foundation, Survey in Washington, D. C	427
Sand, Dr. René	8, 23, 289
Sanderson, John P	362
Sanitation	200
In England fifty years ago	199
Municipal	208
In Japan	328
(*See* also Hygiene.)	
Scholarships	106
School attendance laws	141
School certificates. (*See* Work permits.)	
School children:	
Exemptions of, in Japan	329
Health examinations of	250*ff*
Health records for	251, 438
Malnutrition of	244
Physical defects of	95, 250, 253
Standards for	438

INDEX

	Page.
School dental work	235ff
School health examinations	250ff
School health work	250ff
School laws	110, 111, 435
School-leaving forms	135
School medical inspection	72, 86, 100, 275, 437
School medical work in Japan	329
School nursing	254
School, open-air classes in	243, 438
School, physical examinations in	238
School physician	438
School physicians, Japan	330
School for public-health nurses	204

Schools:
- All-year-round 141
- In Belgium 71f
- Continuation 84, 99, 101ff, 125ff, 434
- County training 311
- Dental clinics in 236
- For defective children 329, 402
- For the feeble-minded 401
- Half-time system in 104
- Industrial training in 310
- Industrial training for children 372
- Industrial, Japan 331
- In Japan 328ff
- And the juvenile court 380
- For midwives 161
- In the Philippines 103
- Reform 323
- Vocational 101

Serbia, child welfare in	173
Sex education	262ff
Sellers, Judge Kathryn	432
Shaw, Dr. H. L. K.	9, 431, 432
Sheffield, Mrs. Ada E.	319, 360
Sherwood, Dr. Mary	166, 431
Simon, Sir John, on Sanitation	199
Six-hour day. (See Hours of labor.)	
Sobel, Dr. Jacob, on Infant mortality	180
Social examination for children suffering from malnutrition	238ff
Social Hygiene Board, Interdepartmental	267
Social program for rural communities	363, 442
Social service work, medical	198
Sociologic medicine	24
Soldiers' and Sailors' Allowance, Provision	36
Solenberger, Edwin D.	360, 361
Solly, J. Lawrence	427

Standards:
- For the care of adolescent children 439
- For the care of dependent children 360, 440
- For the care of infants and preschool children 437ff
- For child-labor laws 433ff
- For administration of child-labor laws 434ff
- For child placing 441
- For children entering employment 433
- For children in need of special care 440
- For children's play 63
- For foster parents 355
- For maternity care 436
- For playgrounds 56ff
- For prenatal requirements 436
- For school children 438ff
- For the training and protection of children 413
- For wage legislation for minors 124
- Of physical efficiency 55
- Of physical fitness for employment 86

| State licensing of child-caring agencies | 318 |

State responsibility:
- For children in need of special care 307
- For standardizing child-caring agencies 315

State supervision:
- Of child-caring agencies 313ff, 318, 437
- Of children in foster homes 317
- Of school attendance laws 435
- Of social work 366

Stillbirths and syphilis	155
Stone, Dr. Allen	431
Street trades	109

Supervision:
- In home-finding work 357f
- In placing-out work 357
- (See also State supervision.)

	Page.
Surgery, obstetrics as a branch of	166
Syphilis	149
Control of hereditary	154
And infant mortality	155
Treatment for	150
Syphilitic infants	152
Teleky, Dr. L., on Morbidity of working children	94
Tennessee:	
Compulsory School Attendance Law in	111
Mothers' Pension Law in	111
Terman, Major Lewis	234
Thompson, Sir Henry, on Food requirements	260
Tigerstedt, Carl, on Food requirements	261
Tonsils, defects of, in children applying for work permits	88
Towne, Arthur W.	350
Trade Boards Act, England	119
Traveling clinics	192
Traveling children's clinic	188
Traveling mental clinic	402
Truancy	414
Truancy and juvenile court	380
Tuberculosis, in children applying for work certificates	88
Unemployment center, juvenile	140
Unemployment, out-of-work donation for children in England	134, 140
Undernutrition	244*f*, 256
Vaughan, Mrs. Kate Brew	191
Venereal clinics:	
For children	437
In maternity care	436
Venereal diseases:	
And prenatal care	152, 436
Prevention of	262
Prevention and cure of	149*ff*
Vision:	
Correction of defective, in Chicago working children	91*f*
Defects of, in children applying for work certificates	87
Examination for defective	91
Test	250*ff*
Visiting nurses. (*See* Nurses and Health visiting.)	
Visitor, health	168, 278*ff*
Visual defects	24, 91*f*
Vocation Bureau of Cincinnati	380
Vocational guidance	133
Vocational placement:	
After-care, supervision in	136
Of children	129, 136, 434
Vocational schools	101
Wage-earning mothers	40, 227
Wage, minimum:	
Legislation, standards for young persons	124
Principles	116
Principles, advisory committees for	117
Standards, underlying principles of	116
Wages, in war time	43
Wassermann reaction	151*ff*
Wassermann test	145
Negative, in infants	154
Positive, in infants	153
In maternity care	145, 436
In maternity cases	185
In securing work certificates	89
Weighing and measuring of malnourished children	238
Weir, L. H.	54
Welfare. (*See* Child welfare.)	
Welfare work in Japan	338
Whitbread, Samuel, on Minimum wage	37
White, Mrs. Eva Whiting	46
Widows' pensions. (*See* Mothers' pensions.)	
White House Conference	339
Delegates to	339
Summary of conclusions of	342
Williams, C. V.	313, 432
Williams, Frankwood E.	390
Williams, Dr. J. Whitridge	145
Wilson, Dr. Andrew	192
Wilson, Mrs. Andrew	246
Winslow, Dr. C.-E. A.	199
Wisconsin Compensation Act	126
Wisconsin Industrial Commission	125
Women's Coöperative Guild, England	165, 167

INDEX

	Page.
Wood, Dr. Thomas D.	248
Wood, Mrs. Ira Couch	9
Woodbury, Mrs. Helen Sumner	9
Woodward, Dr., on Midwives in the District of Columbia	159
Wooley, Dr. Helen T.	380
Work permits	81ff, 125ff, 434
Educational standards for	98ff, 105ff, 127, 435
Examinations for	243
Legal proofs for	126
Physical defects in children applying for	86ff
Physical examination for	86
School certificates for	86
School-leaving forms for	135
Young Men's Association in Japan	332

CHILDREN AND YOUTH
Social Problems and Social Policy

An Arno Press Collection

Abt, Henry Edward. **The Care, Cure and Education of the Crippled Child.** 1924

Addams, Jane. **My Friend, Julia Lathrop.** 1935

American Academy of Pediatrics. **Child Health Services and Pediatric Education:** Report of the Committee for the Study of Child Health Services. 1949

American Association for the Study and Prevention of Infant Mortality. **Transactions of the First Annual Meeting of the American Association for the Study and Prevention of Infant Mortality.** 1910

Baker, S. Josephine. **Fighting For Life.** 1939

Bell, Howard M. **Youth Tell Their Story:** A Study of the Conditions and Attitudes of Young People in Maryland Between the Ages of 16 and 24. 1938

Bossard, James H. S. and Eleanor S. Boll, editors. **Adolescents in Wartime.** 1944

Bossard, James H. S., editor. **Children in a Depression Decade.** 1940

Brunner, Edmund DeS. **Working With Rural Youth.** 1942

Care of Dependent Children in the Late Nineteenth and Early Twentieth Centuries. Introduction by Robert H. Bremner. 1974

Care of Handicapped Children. Introduction by Robert H. Bremner. 1974

[Chenery, William L. and Ella A. Merritt, editors]. **Standards of Child Welfare:** A Report of the Children's Bureau Conferences, May and June, 1919. 1919

The Child Labor Bulletin, 1912, 1913. 1974

Children In Confinement. Introduction by Robert M. Mennel. 1974

Children's Bureau Studies. Introduction by William M. Schmidt. 1974

Clopper, Edward N. **Child Labor in City Streets.** 1912

David, Paul T. **Barriers To Youth Employment.** 1942

Deutsch, Albert. **Our Rejected Children.** 1950

Drucker, Saul and Maurice Beck Hexter. **Children Astray.** 1923

Duffus, R[obert] L[uther] and L. Emmett Holt, Jr. **L. Emmett Holt: Pioneer of a Children's Century.** 1940

Fuller, Raymond G. **Child Labor and the Constitution.** 1923

Holland, Kenneth and Frank Ernest Hill. **Youth in the CCC.** 1942

Jacoby, George Paul. **Catholic Child Care in Nineteenth Century New York:** With a Correlated Summary of Public and Protestant Child Welfare. 1941

Johnson, Palmer O. and Oswald L. Harvey. **The National Youth Administration.** 1938

The Juvenile Court. Introduction by Robert M. Mennel. 1974

Klein, Earl E. **Work Accidents to Minors in Illinois.** 1938

Lane, Francis E. **American Charities and the Child of the Immigrant:** A Study of Typical Child Caring Institutions in New York and Massachusetts Between the Years 1845 and 1880. 1932

The Legal Rights of Children. Introduction by Sanford N. Katz. 1974

Letchworth, William P[ryor]. **Homes of Homeless Children:** A Report on Orphan Asylums and Other Institutions for the Care of Children. [1903]

Lorwin, Lewis. **Youth Work Programs:** Problems and Policies. 1941

Lundberg, Emma O[ctavia] and Katharine F. Lenroot. **Illegitimacy As A Child-Welfare Problem, Parts 1 and 2.** 1920/1921

New York State Commission on Relief for Widowed Mothers. **Report of the New York State Commission on Relief for Widowed Mothers.** 1914

Otey, Elizabeth Lewis. **The Beginnings of Child Labor Legislation in Certain States;** A Comparative Study. 1910

Phillips, Wilbur C. **Adventuring For Democracy.** 1940

Polier, Justine Wise. **Everyone's Children, Nobody's Child:** A Judge Looks At Underprivileged Children in the United States. 1941

Proceedings of the Annual Meeting of the National Child Labor Committee, 1905, 1906. 1974

Rainey, Homer P. **How Fare American Youth?** 1940

Reeder, Rudolph R. **How Two Hundred Children Live and Learn.** 1910

Security and Services For Children. 1974

Sinai, Nathan and Odin W. Anderson. **EMIC (Emergency Maternity and Infant Care):** A Study of Administrative Experience. 1948

Slingerland, W. H. **Child-Placing in Families:** A Manual For Students and Social Workers. 1919

[Solenberger], Edith Reeves. **Care and Education of Crippled Children in the United States.** 1914

Spencer, Anna Garlin and Charles Wesley Birtwell, editors. **The Care of Dependent, Neglected and Wayward Children:** Being a Report of the Second Section of the International Congress of Charities, Correction and Philanthropy, Chicago, June, 1893. 1894

Theis, Sophie Van Senden. **How Foster Children Turn Out.** 1924

Thurston, Henry W. **The Dependent Child:** A Story of Changing Aims and Methods in the Care of Dependent Children. 1930

U.S. Advisory Committee on Education. **Report of the Committee, February, 1938.** 1938

The United States Children's Bureau, 1912-1972. 1974

White House Conference on Child Health and Protection. **Dependent and Neglected Children:** Report of the Committee on Socially Handicapped — Dependency and Neglect. 1933

White House Conference on Child Health and Protection. **Organization for the Care of Handicapped Children, National, State, Local.** 1932

White House Conference on Children in a Democracy. **Final Report of the White House Conference on Children in A Democracy.** [1942]

Wilson, Otto. **Fifty Years' Work With Girls, 1883-1933:** A Story of the Florence Crittenton Homes. 1933

Wrenn, C. Gilbert and D. L. Harley. **Time On Their Hands:** A Report on Leisure, Recreation, and Young People. 1941